D1525152

THE AMBIGUITY OF TASTE

The Ambiguity of Taste

Freedom and Food in European Romanticism

JOCELYNE KOLB

Ann Arbor

THE UNIVERSITY OF MICHIGAN PRESS

Copyright © by the University of Michigan 1995
All rights reserved
Published in the United States of America by
The University of Michigan Press
Manufactured in the United States of America
Printed on acid-free paper

1998   1997   1996   1995   4   3   2   1

A CIP catalogue record for this book is available from the British Library.

Library of Congress Cataloging-in-Publication Data

Kolb, Jocelyne.
    The ambiguity of taste : freedom and food in European romanticism
/ Jocelyne Kolb.
        p.   cm.
    Includes bibliographical references and index.
    ISBN 0-472-10554-X (alk. paper).
    1. Romanticism. 2. Food in literature. I. Title.
PN603.K65   1995
809'.9145—dc20   94-44309
                                                                          CIP

To
Philip Kolb
(1907–92)

Contents

Acknowledgments

In Proust's *Remembrance of Things Past,* Swann sends a case of Asti to the narrator's great-aunts Flora and Céline, who thank him with phrases so decorously oblique that neither Swann nor anyone else understands them. Like Céline, who expects Swann to know that she is addressing him when she speaks of "nice neighbors," I hope that the people whose help I have appreciated and whom I do not mention explicitly will recognize themselves. But there are instances where I do not want to risk being overheard; my debts, though more abstract than Asti, are actually more substantial, and I am glad that my generation permits a directness that to Flora and Céline would have seemed vulgar.

My particular debt and thanks are to those who read parts or all of the manuscript: to my teacher Jeffrey Sammons, who for years has read what I have written with speed and generosity of spirit; to Hans Vaget, another teacher and now my colleague, whose unfailing encouragement has been all the more valuable because it is not uncritical; to Paul Fry for help with the articulation of my thesis early on, later with the Byron chapter, and, over the years, for his loyalty; to Jonathan Hill for his astute comments on the Fielding and Byron chapters; to David Sices for help with Hugo and, more generally, for his dependable counsel on intellectual and professional matters; and to Sander Gilman, who encouraged me when I began writing the book and made useful comments when it was finished. My father read and discussed with me a draft of the entire manuscript in the summer of 1991, a year before he died, and it is to him that I dedicate the book.

I gratefully acknowledge the support of the Alexander von Humboldt Foundation, the legendary munificence of which is not exaggerated; a fellowship from them allowed me to work on my project at the University of Hamburg during the academic year of 1987–88. My thanks as well to Gunter Martens, who supported my application before I reached Hamburg and my research while I was there.

I am grateful to Patricia Carter and Marianne Hraibi, the gracious and quietly efficient interloan librarians at the Baker Library of Dartmouth College. For help and advice on computer matters, always offered cheerfully, patiently, and in a flash, I thank Otmar Foelsche. To my intelligent editors at the University of Michigan Press, especially Susan Whitlock, my thanks as well.

In chapters 4 and 5, I have incorporated revised versions of two articles that appeared previously; I gratefully acknowledge permission to use "The Sublime, The Ridiculous, and The Apple Tarts in Heine's *Ideen. Das Buch Le Grand*," which appeared in *German Quarterly* 56 (1983): 28–38, and "Presenting the Unpresentable: Goethe's Translation of *Le Neveu de Rameau*," which appeared in the *Goethe Yearbook* 3 (1986): 149–163.

My fond thanks to some of the friends who have, for many years, provided literary and scholarly references, sound advice, and on many occasions the culinary equivalent to a case of Asti: Martine Gantrel-Ford, Nelly Hoyt, Ann Leone, Brigitte Peucker, Katherine Reeve, Denise Rochat, Jacqueline Sices, and Gottfried Willems.

Finally, I wish to thank my parents, who taught me the love of literature and the ways and necessity of decorum. I owe my greatest debt to my husband, Konrad Kenkel, whose wit and clear head, together with his skills at the computer and in the kitchen, have helped me beyond measure and who, along with Kai, has taught me that decorum occasionally deserves to be challenged.

Abbreviations

I have quoted from critical editions when possible but have modernized the spelling of the French and German texts. Abbreviations for translations are listed here following the original, rather than alphabetically. Translations for which no source is given are my own.

B   Heinrich Heine: Sämtliche Werke. Ed. Klaus Briegleb. 6 vols. Munich: Hanser, 1968–76.

  SF   *The Sword and the Flame: Selections from Heine's Prose*. Ed. Alfred Werner, based on the translations of Charles Godfrey Leland. New York: Thomas Yoseloff, 1960.

BLJ   *Byron's Letters and Journals*. Ed. Leslie Marchand. 12 vols. London: John Murray, 1973–82.

BPW   Lord Byron. *The Complete Poetical Works*. Ed. Jerome McGann. 7 vols. Oxford: Clarendon Press, 1980–.

DHA   Heinrich Heine. *Historisch-kritische Gesamtausgabe der Werke*. Ed. Manfred Windfuhr et. al. Düsseldorfer Ausgabe. Hamburg: Hoffmann und Campe, 1973–.

  DR   Heinrich Heine. *Deutschland.: A Not So Sentimental Journey*. Trans. T. J. Reed. London: Angel Books, 1986.

  HCP   *The Complete Poems of Heinrich Heine*. Trans. Hal Draper. Boston: Suhrkamp/Insel, 1982.

  HPP   *Heinrich Heine: Poetry and Prose*. Ed. Jost Hermand and Robert C. Holub. New York: Continuum, 1982.

  SW   *Heinrich Heine: Selected Works*. Trans. and ed. Helen Mustard. New York: Random House, 1973.

DJ/O   Byron. *Don Juan*. Cited by canto and stanza from vol. 5 of BPW (1986).

DJ/P   Byron. *Don Juan*. Notes from the Penguin edition of T. G. Steffan, E. Steffan, and W. W. Pratt. New Haven: Yale University Press, 1982.

EGG   Johann Peter Eckermann. *Gespräche mit Goethe in den letzten Jahren seines Lebens*. Ed. Fritz Bergemann. 2 vols. Frankfurt am Main: Insel, 1955; rpt. Insel Taschenbuch 500, 1981.

GCE   J. W. Goethe. *Conversations with Eckermann (1823–1832)*. Trans. John Oxenford. San Francisco: North Point Press, 1984.

GF   Goethe. *Sämtliche Werke: Briefe, Tagebücher und Gespräche*. Ed. Dieter Borchmeyer. Frankfurter Ausgabe. Vol. 4. Frankfurt: Deutscher Klassiker Verlag, 1985–.

GB   Johann Wolfgang von Goethe. *Goethe's Collected Works*. Ed. Cyrus Hamlin and Frank Ryder. Trans. Cyrus Hamlin. Vol. 7. New York: Suhrkamp, 1988.

GM   Goethe. *Sämtliche Werke nach Epochen seines Schaffens*. Ed. Gerhard Sauder. Münchner Ausgabe. Vol. 1, book 2. Munich: Hanser, 1987–.

GSW   Johann Wolfgang von Goethe. *Goethe's Collected Works*. Ed. David E. Wellbury. Trans. Victor Lange. Vol. 11. New York: Suhrkamp, 1988.

GS   *Der Briefwechsel zwischen Schiller und Goethe*. Ed. Emil Staiger. 2 vols. Frankfurt am Main: Insel, 1966. Rpt. 1977.

GT   Hans Rudolf Vaget. *Goethe. Der Mann von 60 Jahren. Königstein/Ts.: Athenäum, 1982*.

GD   Johann Wolfgang von Goethe. *Roman Elegies and The Diary*. Trans. David Luke. London: Libris, 1988.

HC   Victor Hugo. *Oeuvres complètes*. Ed. Jacques Seebacher. Vol. 12, *Critique*. Paris: R. Laffont, 1985.

HSA   *Heinrich Heine Säkularausgabe*. Weimarer Ausgabe. 27 vols. Berlin: Akademie Verlag; Paris: CNRS, 1970–.

MFS   Molière. *Oeuvres complètes*. Ed. Georges Couton. Vol. 2. Paris: Gallimard (Édition de la Pléiade), 1971.

MLL   Molière. *The Learned Ladies*. Trans. Richard Wilbur. New York: Dramatists Play Service, 1977.

NdR   Denis Diderot. *Le Neveu de Rameau*. Ed. Jean Fabre. 2nd ed. Geneva: Droz, 1977.

DRN *Rameau's Nephew and Other Works.* Trans. Jacques Barzun and Ralph H. Bowen. Garden City, N.Y.: Doubleday and Company, 1956.

PR Marcel Proust. *A la recherche du temps perdu.* 4 vols. Paris: Gallimard (Édition de la Pléiade), 1987.

PK Marcel Proust. *Remembrance of Things Past.* Trans. C. K. Scott Moncrieff and Terence Kilmartin. New York: Random House, 1980.

RB Victor Hugo. *Ruy Blas.* Ed. Anne Ubersfeld. 2 vols. Paris: Annales littéraires de l'Université de Besançon, 1971–72. Cited by verse number.

RN Denis Diderot. *Rameaus Neffe.* Trans. Goethe. Ed. Horst Günther. Frankfurt: Insel, 1984.

TJ Henry Fielding. *The History of Tom Jones, a Foundling.* Ed. Martin C. Battestin and Fredson Bowers. Wesleyan edition. 2 Vols. Oxford: Oxford University Press, 1975. Quoted by book, chapter number, and page.

WI Washington Irving. *History, Tales, and Sketches.* Ed. James W. Tuttleton. New York: Library of America, 1983.

Introduction

My argument in the present study is simple. It is that poetic references to literal taste during the late eighteenth and early nineteenth centuries are ambiguous, that to speak of eating or preparing food is to allude likewise to the figurative taste that represents a neoclassical aesthetic. Because it is not "in good taste" to mention literal taste (at least not in works of the high style), a reference to food in lyric poetry or tragedy can be called an emblem of poetic revolution. During the Romantic age, such references raise the same kinds of questions that Friedrich Schlegel poses in the "Gespräch über die Poesie," questions that Goethe and Schiller address in their correspondence and that Schiller puts more systematically in his essay "Über naive und sentimentalische Dichtung." These are questions concerning the increasing self-consciousness of poetic texts; the nature of genius and its independence from tradition and poetic laws; the relationship, and increasingly the separation, between literature and life; the simultaneity but not the harmony of tragic and comic; or the balance, in a literary work, of content and form.

Several distinctions must be kept in mind throughout. In the first place, I do not contend that the subject of food appears in literature for the first time at the end of the eighteenth century. Such a thesis would be absurd, easily disproven by the works of Rabelais, Shakespeare, Cervantes, Molière, or Fielding. My contention is rather that references to food before the end of the eighteenth century are limited to the novel or to comedy, "low" genres that tolerate allusions to subjects excluded from tragedy or lyric and epic poetry, Shakespeare being the great exception.[1] From Rabelais to Fielding to Flaubert to Günter Grass, most literary references to food—even during the past two centuries—occur in the novel, because the novel is historically the most permissive and consequently the most inclusive genre. Bakhtin even speaks of "novelization" as a synonym for the liberalization of genre. The function of food changes together with the poeticization of the novel, but in and of itself the presence of food and eating in literature is nothing new. References to food are found in comedy as well, a genre that includes so-called low subjects just as it includes lower classes in society. Both forms are free, marked by what Bakhtin calls the "language of the marketplace," which means that they enjoy "a certain extraterritoriality in a world of official order and official ideology."[2] What is striking, therefore, is not the sudden appearance of food in literature at the end of the eighteenth century and the beginning of the nineteenth, but its appearance in works other than comedies or the novel and, within the novel itself, the fact that food is poeticized.

Throughout the nineteenth century, the culinary (along with whatever subjects have been "bracketed" from works of the high style, for instance money) becomes integrated into all literary genres; as this happens, expectations change, and subjects themselves no longer provide an automatic comic effect or a shocking shift from sublime to ridiculous. Some critics attribute the inclusion of the culinary in literature to the rise of the middle class and of the genre associated with it, the novel; this, for example, is the tenet of James Brown and Alois Wierlacher.[3] But the explanation is historically inaccurate, since the novel, like comedy, contains culinary references well before the nineteenth century. Besides, the explanation is too simple and limiting to be entirely satisfactory. The fact of inclusion does not, after all, change the status of the subject, even when—as in the novels of Flaubert or Zola or Thomas Mann—the subject is transfigured. What does change, however, and what concerns me here, is that food (and everything considered banal) no longer requires the support of the comic to justify its existence in a poetic setting. In *Buddenbrooks,* the culinary details reveal as much about the gradual inversion of physical and spiritual concerns as the references to music; there is no trace in *Buddenbrooks* of the narrator's digressive mock apology about the hero's need for food in book 9, chapter 5 of *Tom Jones.* Genre, therefore, or more broadly form, is a major consideration.

In the second place, my aim is not to provide a thematic catalog of references to food. Some books of that nature already exist, mostly as curiosities or fashionable publications in which texts are gathered, excerpted, and not interpreted. Collections of this sort serve the important function of proving that references to food are much more prevalent than literary scholarship has made it seem, at least until very recently, but they do not explain their presence in literature or their absence in scholarship.[4] Nor do I wish to imply that food acquires a figurative function for the first time at the end of the eighteenth century. The Bible proves the opposite, and in a more complicated way than one might naively assume, as the semiotician Louis Marin shows in *La Parole mangée et autres essais théologico-politiques*.[5] Besides, literal readings of literature have always been inadequate. What I propose to show is the change in that figurative function during the Romantic period, when it becomes a sign of poetic revolution. To support this theory I will look first at two works that were written before that period and in which food plays a significant part: Molière's *Les Femmes savantes* and Fielding's *Tom Jones*.

Third, the kind of food is as important as the literary genre or the period. In striking analogy to Romantic literature, the food that emblematizes poetic revolution must draw attention to itself. Natural foods, therefore—the apple of knowledge in the Bible and therefore in *Paradise Lost*—are not capable of shocking, partly because they are in harmony with landscape, partly because of the religious associations they call forth. Like figurative taste, the apple, bread, and wine of the Bible have sacrificed their literal meaning; any remainder of the apple's literal sense has an association with sin, and the doctrine of transubstantiation depends on the negation of food and the body.[6] One can grasp the difference between the effect of natural and prepared foods most readily by imagining an apple charlotte in place of the apple of knowledge or, at the Last Supper, a Château Margaux instead of the wine and Marie-Antoinette's *brioche* instead of the bread. Not the least of Heine's revolutionary poetic gestures is to depict transubstantiation literally in the poems "Disputation" and "Vitzliputzli."

The distinction between natural and prepared foods becomes more obvious if we consider the visual arts. A still-life painting would nullify the contention that food is incompatible with art; a still life would be a blank canvas, or nearly so, if food were absent. But there is a decorum of the still life as there is a decorum of poetry. It is the state of these edible objects that justifies their existence in painting, and the French term is *nature morte*—literally dead, or arrested, nature. Only in its natural condition is food considered worthy of representation. If we imagine paintings of prepared dishes, however, of pheasant in sauce rather than feathers, the lack of decorum is obvious; in art, as in the anthropological studies of Lévi-Strauss, the distinction is at least partly one between the raw and the cooked. Furthermore, as Meyer Schapiro emphasizes in his analysis of Cézanne's apples, the still life has not always been held in high regard; it is a low form, the literary equivalent to which is the pastoral. What Schapiro says of the still life applies to all forms of art: "The still–life painters have had to contend with the prejudice that their art is of a lower order because of the intrinsic inferiority of its objects; noble and idealized themes, like idealistic philosophies, have won more approval even after all kinds of themes were admitted in principle to be equal and value was located in the quality of the painter's art."[7] It should be noted that Schapiro speaks of a continuing, not of a past reception, and that of the artists he credits with having changed the status of still life, only Chardin painted as early as the eighteenth century. The others, Cézanne and the cubists, come later, and *nature morte* as the name of a genre does not enter the French language until the middle of the nineteenth century. It is against the decorum of the still life that Andy Warhol directs his painting of a Campbell's soup can. He alienates the tradition of the still life by taking literally its culinary signification; and he combines one taboo, that of prepared food (which as Campbell's soup is certainly not natural) with another, money (the commercialization of food). The reevaluation of Dutch painting in the nineteenth century is another case in point: when Heine calls Jan Steen a religious painter and puts him into the same category as Raphael, he upsets aesthetic as well as religious hierarchies.

My choice of terminology also requires some explanation, in particular my use of the terms *emblem, culinary, Romantic,* and *Romanticism,* as does my choice of authors. The function of food in Romantic literature easily fits M. H. Abrams's definition of an emblem as "an object whose significance is made determinate by its own qualities and by its role in the narrative [read: poetic] context."[8] The word *paradigm* would work equally well, and I use it upon occasion, since ambiguous taste provides a literary example of the kind of changing paradigm that Thomas Kuhn posits for revolutions in science. But the popularization of the word *paradigm* has weakened its meaning, at least for the time being, and I therefore prefer to avoid it. Food becomes emblematic of poetic revolution once it is understood to contain an allusion to figurative taste, because the association of taste with aesthetics distinguishes it from the other so-called lower senses, smell and touch, thereby extending its meaning. Linguistically, too, the ambiguity of taste is representative, because puns are themselves indecorous, hence subversive; besides, the pun on taste exemplifies an irreconcilable duality and is therefore illustrative of the effect that form has on meaning. What completes the emblematic function is that taste begins as a synechdoche, standing for all senses and consequently for the body as a whole, but that it is transformed metonymically to represent all things indecorous or taboo.

My choice of the term *culinary* (which I sometimes replace with the word *gustatory* in order to emphasize the etymological connection to taste) is based on the crucial distinction between food in a natural state and food that calls attention to itself because it has been cooked.[9] Again the question is one of form and, in analogy to the relationship between literal and figurative meaning, the food itself takes second place to the way it has been transformed; it loses the immediacy of an original, natural state. I define the word *culinary* much as the chevalier de Jaucourt defines the term *cuisine* in the *Encyclopédie,* as an art—the art of "flattering taste" [cet art de flatter le goût]. Jaucourt distinguishes between cooking as a necessity and cooking as something that goes beyond necessity when it is given more elevated names such as "*cuisine par excellence,*" "*science de la gueule,*" and "*Gastrologie*" (the emphasis is his).[10]

A further advantage to the word *culinary*—aside from the poetic association with Brecht, who uses the term *kulinarisch* to develop his theory of drama—is that it refers to food and not to drink. Tragedy offers the best illustration of the difference: what is meant to shock in Hugo's *Ruy Blas* is not that Don Salluste drinks, but that he eats as well as drinks and that he invites a servant to join him. The same thing holds for *Götz von Berlichingen,* where Goethe sets scenes at table and uses drinking to undo social differences. There is, to be sure, a practical reason for excluding eating but not drinking from tragedy—the difficulty of chewing and declaiming. But the difficulty of declaiming and eating is less critical than the association of eating with digestion and corporality. Brecht and Beckett thematize both factors in their plays, alluding to food but with a vivid sense of the literary decorum that forbids such allusions. Again, it is the context rather than the fact of digestion that matters during and before the eighteenth century. Defecation is not screened by allusion in the passage from St. Simon that Auerbach interprets in *Mimesis,* where the duc d'Orléans, seated on his *chaise percée,* evokes pain and decline, not comedy. Auerbach says of this passage: "I suppose that in all known literature, especially in earlier literature, there is hardly a text that treats such a topic dramatically and tragically."[11] But the genre is what makes

5

it possible for St. Simon to write movingly of this topic; these are memoirs, not a tragedy or a work of lyric poetry.

As for the term *Romanticism,* I choose it for practical reasons as well as by persuasion. I use it practically in its broadest sense nationally and chronologically to bring together what traditionally is divided into Preromanticism in France, Storm and Stress in Germany, and Romanticism in England, France, and Germany. Wellek considers this broad application of the term legitimate if we think of "the general rejection of the neoclassical creed as a common denominator."[12] In a similarly sensible vein, Walter Jackson Bate writes of *classicism* and *romanticism* that "[b]oth words are loose and inadequate, especially the term 'romanticism.' But continued use has given them such a number of connotations that they not only prove more convenient than others but even defy replacement."[13] It is neither accidental nor insignificant that the disagreement about labels should be so fierce with respect to the Romantic period, when the literary historian's need for order and for systems has been undermined by the dissolution of generic hierarchies.

My use of the word *Romanticism* has a polemical dimension as well; it is meant to contain the quality of aesthetic revolution that is central to the literature in question and to my argument (what Wellek calls the "general rejection of the neoclassical creed"). Here I follow the early Friedrich Schlegel, who uses the term to denote a poetic spirit rather than a particular period; the authors who for him are *romantisch* and whose works embody his idea of *Poesie* are authors like Shakespeare, Cervantes, Molière, and Sterne, authors who mingle incongruities and styles and whose fusion of serious and humorous, of lyrical and commonplace, forms the basis for what Schlegel calls "romantic irony." As I use it, then, the term *Romantic* contains an echo of Schlegel's idea of what modern literature should be.[14] I have capitalized the term throughout, despite my distinction between a period and an aesthetic, because my focus is on the emergence of that aesthetic during one lengthy moment in literary history. I am critical of those who have studied literature and food without taking that moment into account, and it would therefore be contradictory for me to prefer romanticism as an aesthetic principle over the Romantic period in which that aesthetic evolves. Furthermore, the concept of revolution that is at the center of my study runs parallel to a specific period of history, and I use the political revolutions of 1789 and 1848 as a chronological frame.

Of the four authors I have chosen to test my premise, only Hugo has consistently been called a Romantic. The other three (Goethe, Byron, and Heine) have been occasionally associated with Romanticism but more often excluded from codifications in literary histories where the term is used, precisely because they are particularly resistant to classification.[15] Goethe, who so resembles Hugo in his career and his longevity, in the scope of his talents and the range of his writings, is the epitome of classicism in his own country (or rather of *Klassik*) and of Romanticism outside it. Byron and Heine, enfants terribles who ridicule and sabotage systems that subsist only as systems, genre for the sake of genre, seem to threaten from beyond the grave anyone who would hold them to a particular literary label. There is no hierarchy of revolution or genius that places the four authors I have chosen at the top; despite their distinct status as non conformists, they are representative, not exclusive, just as the revolutionary function of taste is emblematic, not unique. It is a characteristic of genius to deviate from whatever is recognized as typical for any given period; as Benjamin says in speaking of Proust (and he underscores the truth of his claim by stressing that he was not the first to say so), all great works of literature either invent or destroy a genre—they are all exceptions, "Sonderfälle."[16] In saying this, Benjamin seems to be quoting Proust himself, who wrote a short piece on the terms *classicisme* and *romanticisme* in which he argues that every great work is a classic, but that contemporaries seldom recognize it as such: "Je crois que tout art véritable est classique, mais les lois de l'esprit permettent rarement qu'il soit, à son apparition, reconnu pour tel" [I think that all true art is classic; but the laws of the mind rarely allow for it to be recognized as such when it appears]. Proust resembles Schlegel in his emphasis on a common spirit rather than a common chronology, and he concludes by saying that periodic labels ought to be replaced by the term *classic:* "les grands artistes qui furent appelés romantiques, réalistes, décadents, etc. tant qu'ils ne furent pas compris, voilà ceux que j'appellerais classiques" [the great artists who were called Romantics, realists, decadents, etc., for as long as they were misunderstood—those are the ones I would call classics].[17]

Finally, my choice of the word ambiguity in the phrase *ambiguity of taste,* aside from its echoes of a critical method in which close reading plays the major role, has a culinary and literary association. According to Furetière, an *ambigu* is a meal at which meat and dessert are served together, and in the *Robert,* a second meaning is listed as well: an *ambigu-comique,* in the seventeenth century, is the designation for a play that connects the serious and the comic (one of the Parisian theaters to which Heine refers in *Über die französische Bühne* is called the Ambigu-Comique). Molière plays on the word *ambigu* as a food and as genre in act 1, scene 1 of *Les Précieuses ridicules,* when La Grange calls Magdelon and Cathos "un ambigu de précieuse et de coquette."

Though the authors I have chosen are from different generations (Goethe was born in 1749, Byron in 1788, Heine in 1797, and Hugo in 1802), and although my examples span the time from Goethe's "Zum Schäkspears-Tag" in 1771 to Heine's *Romanzero* poems in 1853, the works upon which the greatest focus falls were composed during the 1820s and 1830s. Byron's *Don Juan* was written between 1818 and 1824; the poems of Heine's *Buch der Lieder* were composed between 1815 or 1816 and 1827 and were published as a collection in 1827, the year, too, of Heine's *Ideen. Das Buch Le Grand.* Heine's *Aus den Memoiren des Herren von Schnabelewopski* was probably written between 1831 and 1833 but is considered by some commentators to have been conceived in the early 1820s. The composition of Goethe's *Faust* stretches from his "Romantic" period (the German Sturm und Drang) to his death in 1832, and the *Tagebuch* poem is from 1810; Hugo's "Préface de *Cromwell*" dates from 1827, and *Ruy Blas* was written in 1838. Pushkin's *Eugene Onegin,* which as I have said would further illustrate my thesis, was written between 1831 and 1835.

Another characteristic connects the authors in the present study: their fusion of literary and political concerns. All of them except Goethe lived in exile at some point in their lives (Goethe's dramatic escape to Italy was self-imposed and has a different character), and all but Heine were active in public life. The complicated connection between their politics and their poetry offers another instance of the increasingly complicated relationship between a subject and its aesthetic treatment. It seems to me (and increasingly to others) that the division so often upheld, most vocally in the case of Heine, between a political and an aesthetic reading or "method" is simplistic, even absurd, and that the separation is as untenable as the separation of subject and genre, especially for this period. A division exists only if one reads with attention for nothing but political subjects or remakes all allusions and images into aesthetic or political statements. It is rather the indistinguishability and the reciprocal effect of political and aesthetic (or formal) concerns that is at issue, as Susan Sontag forcefully argues in "Against Interpretation." For this reason, the term *revolution* applies equally well to poetry and to politics, and it is no accident that the figure who shared with Shakespeare a mythical status as the model of liberation was Napoleon, whom Heine and Hugo both cite as the author of the bon mot that captures the spirit of their aesthetic innovations: "Du sublime au ridicule il n'y a qu'un pas." My glances backward to Molière and Fielding and forward to Mann and Proust are meant to illuminate that moment of radical change, not to be exhaustive in their own right.

One source of legitimization for this study can be found in the writings of Elias, Auerbach, and Bakhtin, who treated subjects that did not belong to the canon before them. Their works have themselves acquired the status of classics, and they remain fresh as models of sensitivity, courage, and reason supported by a sovereign control of periods and disciplines. They are intellectual rather than methodological models. My manner of approaching this topic must necessarily be eclectic, for it would be inconsistent to adhere rigidly to one critical school while writing about poetic revolution, which is based on a questioning of all institutions and rejects the rigid application of systems. It would be equally mistaken to proceed anarchically, however, for to do so would implicitly revitalize the outdated notion that works of the Romantic age, no matter how brilliant, are chaotic and lack recognizable form. On the contrary, the main focus of my intertextual study, as I have said, is the changing perception of form when neoclassical categories are consciously undermined and replaced by forms that are not visible at first. This is what in Friedrich Schlegel's famous phrase is "artfully ordered chaos" [künstlich geordnetes Chaos], and it replaces the literary decorum of the eighteenth century. My method is itself an ambiguous one: I proceed with a series of close readings but strive to avoid myopia.

CHAPTER 1

The Poetics of Ambiguous Taste

Ah! la forme, là est le grand crime!
— Zola, preface to *L'Assommoir*

To generalize about the eighteenth century is to be an idiot, as Jonathan Bate says with a mixture of pathos and frustration in *Shakespeare and the English Romantic Imagination*. Nowhere is Bate's rephrasing of Blake more appropriate than with regard to taste, which by the end of the eighteenth century has become, paradoxically, both a guardian of conservative aesthetic doctrine and an emblem of poetic liberation.[1] To mention food in a lyrical context calls into question the doctrine of good taste and becomes an emblem for what Friedrich Schlegel, writing not long after the Revolution of 1789, calls poetic revolution. The ambiguous meaning of taste—its figurative usage as a gauge of artistic value and its literal meaning as a reminder of physical rather than spiritual concerns—is representative of the period's complexities, complexities whose only thinkable consequence is the revolution of which Schlegel speaks. For one word to harbor contradictory meanings is a warning not to take things at face value. Even in its form, therefore, ambiguous taste invites study rather than a snicker. What deserves attention is the poetic context in which the ambiguity of taste occurs and the way in which the paradoxical fusion of spirit and matter, of sublime and ridiculous, exemplifies poetic change. In its combined literal and figurative meanings, the word *taste* undergoes a kind of enharmonic shift: taste contains and displays the duality characteristic of Romantic art, that ambiguous adoption and rejection of tradition.

All definitions and discussions of taste from this period rest on a belief in the virtues of harmony and reason. Figurative taste refers to the proper

11

manner or form of treating a particular subject as measured by a rational application of rules; it therefore functions as a synonym for literary decorum. Gottsched equates good taste with rules and reason in the *Versuch einer critischen Dichtkunst:* "that kind of taste is good which adheres to rules that reason has fixed beforehand, in all manner of things" [derjenige Geschmack ist gut, der mit den Regeln übereinkömmt, die von der Vernunft, in einer Art von Sachen, allbereit fest gesetzt werden].[2] His argument, a one-sided imitation of Boileau, has a typically circular and dogmatic quality that is exemplary of the neoclassical creed against which the Romantics rebel. Sometimes, on the other hand—as in the so-called School of Taste of the late seventeenth and early eighteenth centuries— the term taste refers to the indefinable quality present in all art, the je ne sais quoi that is a blend of intuition and inclination beyond the jurisdiction of rules. By taking over the term taste from their more dogmatic adversaries and giving it a different emphasis, the adherents of the School of Taste anticipate, but more decorously, the polemical use of literal taste by the Romantics.[3] For this kind of taste the rules come rather from within than from without, from instinct rather than dogma, in a manner remarkably analogous to the movement from *Fremdzwang* to *Selbstzwang* that Norbert Elias considers fundamental to the civilizing process in society.[4] Elias argues that an increased permissiveness can only come about in a society whose laws are so soundly engrained by self-control (*Selbstzwang*) that they cannot be threatened. If one applies the theory to literature, one could say that the lifting of taboos in literature necessarily furthers the rift between decorum in literature and decorum in society. Despite differences in definition or emphasis, however, there is unanimity among theorists of taste on the usefulness of adhering to laws of genre and rules of decorum in order to produce excellent works of literature. Taste therefore imposes limitations on an author, whether they are the limitations of neoclassical rules, of *Selbstzwang,* or of a reading public whose predilections affect the author's freedom to choose styles and subjects.

Taste, generally qualified as "good," dominates aesthetic discussions of the eighteenth century. Gottsched devoted a chapter of the *Versuch einer critischen Dichtkunst* (1730) to the term; Voltaire wrote a fanciful treatise in verse and prose called *Le Temple du goût* (1731) and contributed one of the articles on *goût* to the *Encyclopédie;* Edmund Burke prefaced his second edition of *A Philosophical Inquiry into the Origin of our Ideas of the Sublime and Beautiful* with a "Discourse on Taste"

(1759); Herder, like Goethe during the same period, argues for the replacement of the old figurative taste with a new and freer version in "Ursachen des gesunkenen Geschmacks" (1775); and Kant defined taste as the ability to judge beauty ("das Vermögen zur Beurteilung des Schönen") in a note to the first subheading of the *Kritik der Urteilskraft* (1790), which deals with judgment in matters of taste. Every major and minor writer commented or discoursed on the subject of taste. Regardless of the variations, the term is always applied figuratively to aesthetic matters, even when, as in the case of Burke, the literal meaning of taste is the starting point for his argument.

The frequency with which taste is discussed and the invariable association of "good taste" with restricted freedom makes it a visible target for the Romantics. Taste becomes a synonym for what Victor Hugo, in his "Préface de *Cromwell*," calls the literary "ancien régime" or for the conservative and inhibiting aesthetic that Goethe derided some sixty years earlier in his legendary manifesto, "Zum Schäkespears-Tag." For Goethe—not just in the Storm and Stress period but later as well—good taste represents the institutionalization of stodginess, boredom, and lacklustrer imagination. He ends "Zum Schäkespears-Tag" with a call to arms against good taste:

> Auf, meine Herren, und trompeten Sie mir alle edle Seelen *aus dem Elysium des sogenannten guten Geschmacks,* wo sie schlaftrunken in langweiliger Dämmerung halb sind, halb nicht sind. (GM 424; my emphasis)

> [Onto your feet, Gentlemen! Do me the favor of trumpeting all noble souls out of the Elysium of so-called good taste, where they are half present, half absent, drowsily so in a boring twilight.]

Goethe's qualification of good taste as "so-called" [sogenannt] questions the automatic use of the adjective good and the notion of taste as a measure of excellence in art. By calling good taste "sogenannt," Goethe draws attention to the literal meaning of the phrase and ironically reminds his readers that figurative and literal taste are in disaccord.[5] Furthermore, in the paragraph immediately preceding his attack on good taste, Goethe equates literal taste with poetic liberation: he associates Shakespeare with the word *fressen*, which designates the eating of animals and is extended to humans whose table manners are poor. Goethe makes the same con-

13

nection between Shakespeare and ambiguous taste in the play *Götz von Berlichingen* (1773).

Jonathan Bate speaks of the "close correlation between the rise of Shakespeare and the rise of Romanticism in Germany" and says that "it should not be forgotten that Shakespeare was the stick with which the *Sturm und Drang* beat off French cultural hegemony and initiated the Romantic revolution."[6] Authors and critics invoked the name of Shakespeare and the question of taste to articulate their declaration of allegiance either to the new or the old aesthetic regime. For the young Goethe, Shakespeare was a champion and a model for whom the laws represented by "good taste" did not exist and who frequently used culinary metaphors.[7] In the eyes of Voltaire, on the other hand—whose "temple of taste" is parodied by Goethe in the phrase "Elysium des sogenannten guten Geschmacks"—Shakespeare fosters "bad" taste: "he was natural and sublime, but had not so much as a single spark of good Taste, or knew one Rule of the Drama."[8] Frederick the Great echoes Voltaire by equating Shakespeare with bad taste in his notorious essay about German literature, "De la littérature allemande" (1780); for Frederick the Great, Shakespeare and his followers are "savages" because they have "sinned" against the laws of the theater. He associates a lack of taste with the "abominable" plays of Shakespeare:

> Pour vous convaincre du peu de goût qui jusqu'à nos jours règne en Allemagne, vous n'avez qu'à vous rendre aux Spectacles publics. Vous y verrez représenter les abominables pièces de Shakespeare traduites en notre langue, et tout l'Auditoire se pâmer d'aise en entendant ces farces ridicules et dignes des Sauvages du Canada. Je les appelle telles parce qu'elles pèchent contre toutes les règles du Théâtre.[9]

> [To convince yourself of the lack of taste that reigns in Germany to this day, you need only go to one of the public theaters. There you will find performances of the abominable plays of Shakespeare translated into our language, and the entire audience will swoon on hearing these ridiculous farces worthy of the savages in Canada. I call them such because they sin against all rules of the theater.]

Many similar examples exist. And it is only by recalling the influence of figurative taste and the example of Shakespeare that one understands the proliferation of references to food in works of the high style during the late eighteenth and early nineteenth centuries. Up to that point, a work in the high style was expected to provide a purified representation of reality, one from which eating was banned along with all bodily functions. Any allusion to eating in epic and lyric poetry or in a tragedy therefore indicates a deliberate misunderstanding of good taste in the figurative, aesthetic sense. To speak of food in the wrong setting appears flippant and seems to be a gratuitous provocation; but if one looks more closely, one perceives a considered, and a revolutionary, purpose.

Bakhtin emphasizes the connection of revolution with food and laughter in his study of Rabelais, and he cites evidence from the eighteenth century that is related to the question of ambiguous taste. He shows, for example, how Voltaire errs by taking literally the comments of Rabelais in the prologues to *Gargantua* and *Pantagruel,* in particular Rabelais's assertion that he writes only while eating and drinking: "The substantial traditional link of wise and free speech with food and wine, the specific 'truth' of table talk is no longer understood by Voltaire (though this tradition was still alive). The entire aspect of the popular banquet in Rabelais' novel lost its meaning."[10] Bakhtin exposes the distortions of anachronistic thinking to show how Voltaire and others misapplied their norms to the works of Rabelais. But the undeniable failing exposed by Bakhtin is distinct from the creative source of *deliberate* anachronism that Romantic authors exploit when they connect a "carnivalistic" world view—one that includes laughter and what Bakhtin calls the "material lower stratum"—with serious and philosophical questions, thereby breaking the rigid neoclassical laws that separate high from low, tragic from comic. Bakhtin does not address the question of deliberate anachronism, partly because in *Rabelais and His World* he does not concentrate on the effect of form on a subject, which is my principal concern.

One should not assume that the rejection of literary decorum is identical with a rejection of literary forms. On the contrary, the rejection of neoclassical forms—of genres and styles that separate high from low, tragic from comic—demonstrates the importance of form and inspires new ones. Zola was right to call his "crime" in *L'Assommoir* one of form, and the history of literature confirms his claim: the indignation at Goethe's *Das Tagebuch,* Byron's *Don Juan,* Baudelaire's *Les Fleurs du mal,* or Flaubert's *Madame Bovary* has less to do with the subjects of these works than with the literary setting in which they are presented. Questions of form are revitalized in each discussion of obscenity and pornography, and the controversy cannot be resolved without particular attention to formal considerations. What changes as a result of poetic revolution is not that formal questions disappear, but that form is redefined and liberalized so that it comes to resemble irony rather than genre. The dissolution of generic hierarchies necessarily disenfranchizes the vocabulary of genre, but the problem remains: what should or should not be expressed and how?

To speak of food or eating in an elevated context already constitutes a breach of neoclassical decorum. But it is the pun on literal and figurative taste that makes ambiguous taste an emblem of a rejected neoclassical aesthetic, since punning, particularly in the eighteenth century, is considered indecorous. In *Le Temple du goût,* for example, Voltaire calls puns "la pire espèce du faux bel esprit" [the worst sort of false wit], and another eighteenth-century critic, the abbé Deville, explicitly associates the pun with bad taste: "Le calembour, enfant gâté / Du mauvais goût et de l'obscurité" [The pun, spoiled child / Of bad taste and obscurity]. It is obvious, therefore, that puns will provoke.[11] But provocation, as I have said already, is only the first and simplest of its aims. More important is that the verbal ambiguity of the pun—that "obscurité" condemned by the abbé Deville—is a source of poetry. Again, Shakespeare is the measure. Voltaire and Samuel Johnson condemned his puns, and in this century William Empson finds them "effeminate." Samuel Coleridge, on the other hand, planned a defense of Shakespeare's wordplay that was eventually undertaken, in the 1950s, by Molly Mahood.[12]

As soon as one recognizes the pun on literal and figurative taste, one also acknowledges its subversion. This explains why references to food have been ignored or dismissed either as shocking or merely amusing. The pun on taste unites the elevated and the ordinary, because it combines contradictory meanings and conflicting diction. Its fusion of form and significance exemplifies the dualities of Romantic poetry, and indeed of modern literature as a whole. The connection of high and low that Bakhtin analyzes in the literature of the Renaissance is distinct from that of Romanticism. As Bakhtin demonstrates in the case of Rabelais, philosophical truth derives from laughter and is its necessary complement. In Romantic literature, however, the connection between laughter and the serious has been inverted: what were perceived as two complementary parts of a grand whole become instead a cacophany of incongruities. Beginning with the late eighteenth century, the ridiculous does not complement the sublime as something separate but equal. Instead, the ridiculous and the sublime are simultaneous. They clash within one work, sometimes on the same page.

Beginning with the Romantic age, subjects and styles lose their inhibiting alliance to a particular genre; yet this is partly because subjects that offend in the literal sense have been disembodied in an aesthetic process best illustrated by the symbolist poetic method. Figurative meaning does not cancel out literal meaning; on the contrary, the poet counts on the reader's ability to recognize literal meaning as a basis for surprise, questioning, and interpretation. The use of literal taste to mock and reject figurative taste rests on an awareness of both meanings; but the emphasis, in keeping with the subjectivity that is a distinguishing characteristic of Romantic sensibility, is on the poet's ability to choose and manipulate subjects and styles. In part it is the tension between the initial recognition of one meaning and the subsequent questioning of that meaning that makes taste paradigmatic of aesthetic revolution.[13]

The example of food serves to illustrate how it is no longer possible, within and because of Romantic literature, to speak of poetic and non poetic subjects or to categorize styles and genres as high and low without looking behind the facade that such terms are meant to uphold. Goethe, again a good witness, claims that there is no such thing as an unpoetic subject. In the conversation of 5 July 1827 with Eckermann, significantly on the subject of Byron's *Don Juan,* he criticizes the proscriptions of German literary theorists:

"Unsere deutsche Ästhetiker," sagte Goethe, "reden zwar viel von poetischen und unpoetischen Gegenständen, und sie mögen auch in gewisser Hinsicht nicht ganz unrecht haben; allein im Grunde bleibt *kein* realer Gegenstand unpoetisch, sobald der Dichter ihn gehörig zu gebrauchen weiß." (EGG 1: 236)

["Our German aesthetic people," said Goethe, "are always talking about poetical and unpoetical objects; and in one respect they are not quite wrong, yet at bottom no real object is unpoetical if the poet knows how to use it properly."] (GCE 171)

By "gehörig"—properly—Goethe clearly does not have in mind the neo-classical separation of subject and genre. His practice and Byron's poem, which he is defending, demonstrate the contrary. From this conversation it is also clear that Goethe rejects the identification of decorum in the drawing room with decorum in literature. He retains at the end of his life the Promethean drive of the beginning, when all subjects are permissible, regardless of the frame he chooses for them. To charge that *Don Juan* is immoral, Goethe implies, is to betray one's own literal reading, a reading that fails to grasp the transfiguration of subjects and experience into poetry. In the conversation with Eckermann of 29 March 1830, Goethe speaks of the hypocricy of expecting morality from literature when real life offers an excess of "scandalous" scenes:

> "Es müßte schlimm zugehen," sagte Goethe, "wenn ein Buch un-moralischer wirken sollte als das Leben selber, das täglich der skan-dalösen Szenen im Überfluß, wo nicht vor unseren Augen, doch vor unseren Ohren entwickelt." (EGG 2: 690)

> ["It would be a terrible state of affairs," Goethe said, "if a book were considered to have a more immoral effect than life, which produces an excess of scandalous scenes each day, if not before our eyes, then at least before our ears."]

The distinction between a real object and its poetic function concerns Goethe throughout his life. It derives from the distinction between literature and life, which in the vocabulary of neoclasssicism would have been called the relationship between art and nature. For the Romantics, the emphasis is inverted, however, and nature is perceived to imitate art; in Byron's famous lines, "'Tis strange, but true, for truth is always strange, / Stranger than fiction" (DJ/0 14.101). The changing connection between a poetic model and its literary transformation alters the connection between literal and figurative usage and between morality in life and art. At issue is (most broadly stated) the shift from a neoclassical aesthetic of beauty and harmony to one based on the willful disharmony between a subject in and of itself and its significance in an aesthetic setting.

All of the qualities I have listed thus far are common to the literature we call modern, a literature of self-consciousness and ambiguity in which the only remnants of generic hierarchy are found in the most basic of poetic divisions, the division between verse and prose. Even there, the boundaries are fluid, complicated by the "liberation" of prose from the stigma of banality and of verse from restrictions of subject or even meter.

All that remains of generic hierarchies is a vestige of elevated poetic status for verse, calling into question Roland Barthes's piquant phrase in *Degré zéro de l'écriture* that verse is "prose amputée de libertés."

If the ambiguity of taste plays as important and obvious a role as I claim, then one would expect it to have been the object of much and frequent study. I realize that one can extend to topics of literary criticism what Paul Fry observes of its ideologies, that "[f]or every faction, all the pathos of current critical debate depends on suppressing one's comfortable mainstream status. Everyone's view should be dominant but has been unjustly suppressed."[14] Yet I have found that what to the Romantics was a breach of literary decorum persists as a breach of scholarly decorum, if more faintly than ten years ago, when I first published something on ambiguous taste. Why else would there be so little scholarship on a subject that poets have treated with increasing frequency during the last two hundred years? How else can one interpret the silence on the literary treatment of food except as an amusing confirmation of scholarly habits that Heine satirizes in *Ideen. Das Buch Le Grand,* where he uses culinary images to do so? Literary critics, with the notable exception of Bakhtin, Barthes, and their followers, seem to foster and impose a sense of hierarchy and a separation of genres that rivals the rigidity of neoclassical doctrines.

In the systematization of scholarly genres, lectures belong to the low style and therefore, like comedy and Bakhtin's "extraterritoriality" of the marketplace, allow the speaker a carnivalistic freedom. At lectures I have given on the ambiguity of taste, almost everyone has had something to say about the subject—aloud. The best books on the subject are conference proceedings,[15] and there is an occasional lecture on literature and food at the yearly meetings of the Modern Language Association. But except for the occasional éminence grise who does not fear for his reputation (and I use the male pronoun deliberately), very few American scholars have ventured to commit to paper thoughts about taste in the literal sense. When they publish on the subject, as Susan J. Leonardi did recently in an article for *PMLA* that opens with a recipe, the effect, as one friend put it, was more shocking than pornography.[16] The analogy of high and low genres extends to the lengthy scholarly tome—the "novel" of literary criticism, hence a permissive genre. In the past few years, some literary studies have concentrated on culinary questions. One of their principal characteristics, however, has been a defensive tone or an exaggeratedly scientific vocabulary, which seems to derive from a fear that the topic will not be taken seriously. Barthes notes this phenomenon in his preface to *Physiologie du goût,* where he analyzes Brillat-Savarin's style:

> Brillat-Savarin s'essaie à la science, ou au moins au discours scientifique. [...] Son audace est de style: user d'un ton docte pour parler d'un sens réputé futile (parce que platement sensuel), le goût.[17]

> [Brillat-Savarin tries his hand at science, or at least at scientific discourse. [...] His audacity is one of style: to use a learned tone in speaking of a sense that is reputed to be ephemeral (because it is flatly sensual), the sense of taste.]

Surely the fear of not being considered "scholarly" accounts for the pseudoscientific vocabulary in the book of Alois Wierlacher, *Vom Essen in der deutschen Literatur. Mahlzeiten in Erzähltexten von Goethe bis Grass* (1987); the opaque style and interminable footnotes are his armor against the charge that his subject is trivial. In similar fashion, James Brown overuses dense terms in the book *Fictional Meals and Their Function in the French Novel 1789–1848* (1984). At the other extreme is the book by Stefan Hardt, *Tod und Eros beim Essen* (1987), which is completely antischolarly.[18] One explanation for the extremes is obvious: scholarship, despite Schlegel and recent critical trends with a hubristic quality, still remains closer to the norms of society than to those of art; the fact that indecorum is tolerated, even admired, in literature (for example in *Le Neveu de Rameau*) does not mean that the same holds for indecorum in society.

Several other factors explain the avoidance of the subject of food, first in literature of the high style and then in scholarship. The most obvious, which I mentioned earlier, is that eating initiates digestion. Whereas a reference to sexuality can be redeemed as a reminder or an expression of love, any but biblical food commonly lacks spiritual associations. The regenerative power of the body that Bakhtin notes in Rabelais has been lost or suppressed, and the etymological (and Biblical) connection of knowledge with eating (in Latin, *sapere*) has faded into oblivion. In criticism if not in literature, remnants can still be found of the division between "higher" and "lower" senses that the chevalier de Jaucourt makes in his article on *sens externes* for the *Encyclopédie:* the higher senses are those of sight and hearing because, as Jaucourt circuitously argues, they allow us to perceive aesthetic objects.[19] Food is therefore perceived as nonaesthetic, and if poets do mention food, it is assumed to be an amusing or mimetic detail. From the critic's point of view, there is the danger that by calling attention to so banal a subject, one will be dismissed as frivolous, despite the wise axiom that no detail in literature is accidental or unimportant. Frivolity, however, like triviality and flippancy, is often a misnomer, a term used defensively to attack those who, like Heine, question received ideas. As everyone knows from Shakespeare's fools or from Freud's study of *Witz* (in English playfully called the *Joke Book*), the appearance of frivolity can deceive as much as other sorts of appearance, reflecting more on the accuser than the accused.[20] Against a neoclassical background, the presence of food in a work of the high style initially and intentionally prompts laughter, but it is not the legitimate, institutionalized laughter of comedy; it is the laughter that causes insecurity, undermines authority, and threatens systems. The assumption that culinary references are frivolous is therefore as predictable as it is mistaken. To assume that food is a trivial subject not deserving of attention is to misconstrue the very nature of Romantic aesthetics, where any subject can become a poetic, political, or even revolutionary vehicle, regardless of the setting. Subjects may be trivial outside of literature, but to assume the same for their function within a poetic work betokens literal-mindedness.

In *Englische Fragmente*, Heine expresses his belief in the power of wit to express serious concerns, a belief that applies equally to his poetry and to his politics. For him the words *frivolity* and *flippancy* are connected to freedom and revolution. He writes in conscious continuation of an English literary tradition represented by Shakespeare, Fielding, Sterne, and Byron, and he illustrates his thesis by evoking their works and contrasting them with the political present he finds in England. His theory of serious wit is given a political illustration when he cites the discrepancy between the fervor of the French as revolutionaries and the charge that they are frivolous. He repeats the charge in order to refute it and to demonstrate that the vocabulary of liberation has been misappropriated; he extends the example of the French (and implicitly of English literature) to an entire age and shows that he speaks of mentalities, not of nations:

> Aber nicht bloß die Helden der Revolution und die Revolution selbst, sondern sogar unser ganzes Zeitalter hat man verleumdet, die ganze Liturgie unserer heiligsten Ideen hat man parodiert, mit unerhörtem Frevel, und wenn man sie hört oder liest, unsere schnöden Verächter,

so heißt das Volk die Canaille, die Freiheit heißt Frechheit, und mit himmelnden Augen und frommen Seufzern wird geklagt und bedauert, wir wären frivol und hätten leider keine Religion. (DHA 7:1.268)

[Not only the heroes of the revolution and the revolution itself have been maligned, however, but the entire age; the entire liturgy of our most sacred ideas has been parodied with outrageous sacrilege, and when one hears or reads our base deprecators, one finds that the people are called rabble, freedom is called impertinence, and that with eyes raised towards heaven and pious sighs they bemoan and regret that we are frivolous and have no religion.]

In *Englische Fragmente,* wit is associated with revolution and expressive of it.

Especially in the field of social history, and particularly in France, the subject of food has gradually acquired its cachet during the past two decades, thanks mostly to the work of Lucien Febvre and the Annales school. Generally it has been connected to semiotics or Freud; lately it is associated with cannibalism, which can be a figurative and decorative way of denoting intertextuality, since one text "eats up" another. But even in France—which to many, as Heine says, is a "frivolous" country—it has only recently become acceptable to speak of food in a scholarly context. In an article of 1961, "Pour une psycho-sociologie de l'alimentation contemporaine," Barthes regrets that the subject of food is considered trivial by scholars (it should be noted that he speaks of social historians, not of literary critics). But he himself coyly apologizes for speaking of "a veritable grammar of foods," despite his claim in the same article that "it is obvious that if the subject of food had not been so trivialized and invested with guilt, it could easily be subjected to the kind of 'poetic' analysis that G. Bachelard applied to language."[21] Barthes avoids criticism by keeping his language highly metaphorical, much as it was in the discussions of taste during the eighteenth century; some of his followers outdo him, sounding at times like the *précieuses* of Molière. Jean-François Revel's fascinating and erudite study, *Un Festin en paroles* (1979), does not fall into the latter category, but Revel pays homage to scholarly hierarchies when he emphasizes that he worked on his book only during his vacations (the French are luckily entitled to long ones). Writing it, he says, "fut ma récréation," and he adds: "je souhaite que le lecteur y trouve la sienne" [Writing it was my recreation; I hope the reader will get his from reading it].[22]

Though Barthes and Revel do not say so, the stigma of triviality is related to the fact that food has ordinarily been the domain of women. Two literary examples will suffice. In Molière's *Les Femmes savantes*, a major source of the satire derives from the belief that it is absurd to associate women with the intellect and men with food. In *Jenseits von Gut und Böse*, Nietzsche twists the identification of women and food by saying that women are not "worthy" of cooking and that the lack of "reason" [Vernunft] in their kitchens has retarded human development more than any other factor. Nietzsche fulminates against the "horrifying thoughtlessness" [schauerliche Gedankenlosigkeit] with which the family and the male head of house [Hausherr] have been nourished. Woman— disdainfully designated as "das Weib"—does not understand what food means and consequently cannot (or should not) cook.[23]

It is tempting to speculate about the cultural reasons for including or excluding food from scholarship. The results might resemble Heine's famous comparison of women's national characteristics with the foods from their countries in *Aus den Memoiren des Herren von Schnabelewopski*, a passage that opens with a pun on the word taste (Geschmack): "Jedes Land hat seine besondere Küche und seine besondere Weiblichkeiten, und hier ist alles Geschmackssache" [Every country has its particular cuisine and its particular womanlinesses, and here everything is a matter of taste]. The practicality of the British and Americans, the verve of the French, the thoroughness of the German—all are reflected in their scholarly treatment of literary references to food. In works of literature and their translations, cultural stereotypes are likewise evident from the allusions to food. Sterne opens *A Sentimental Journey* with an admiring reference to French cooking that gives him his geographical and cultural orientation and anticipates his criticism of French decorum later on. Yorick knows from the fricasseed chicken set in front of him that he is "incontestibly in France." In *Madame Bovary*, culinary references reproduce the French eating habits of different social classes and geographic regions; in glaring contrast, the misrepresentation of Flaubert's "gigot saignant" as "undercooked leg of mutton" in the Marx-Averling translation of the novel betrays a British perspective and sacrifices a detail that in the original contributes significantly to the portrayal of Emma's father and of her background.

When social historians like Norbert Elias, Pierre Bourdieu, Jean-François Revel, Peter Gay, Stephen Mennell, Alain Corbin, or Margaret Visser consider subjects that traditionally have been excluded from scholarship, they often use literary texts as "evidence" to be read with an eye for its literal rather than its poetic function, as confirmation of their findings in nonliterary documents. Social historians look for a correlation between literature and society and are concerned more with real models than with the transfigurations of those models. But cultural history is not my topic. The culinary details in Flaubert's novel are taken from a recognizable Norman model, to be sure; but they are important to the texture of the novel because Flaubert chooses them and because of the way he uses them, not because they are Norman. They do not reveal something about France and French culture that could not be found in a book about history or geography. If they did, we would not recognize them as Norman, French, bourgeois, or aristocratic—whatever these details signify. But they do reveal much about Flaubert's aesthetic and about its connection to the poetic revolution that is my subject.[24] Flaubert uses culinary references much as he uses zeugma to portray Léon's thoughts about Emma: "Il admirait l'exhaltation de son âme et la dentelle de son jupon" [He admired the exultation of her soul and the lace of her petticoat]. The same aesthetic is apparent when Flaubert juxtaposes Rodolphe's seduction of Emma with a speech at the agricultural fair. For Flaubert the question of culture is subordinated to the question of aesthetics. That the two are distinct is obvious from the fact that the French, who as Heine says are known for their "frivolity" and good living, are the ones to have developed exceedingly rigid exclusionary laws for the theater and for literature generally. Sterne emphasizes the contrast in *A Sentimental Journey,* and Flaubert writes in conscious opposition of such laws. His writing, like that of Mann and Proust, is unthinkable without the poetic revolution of which I speak.

Real Taste or True Taste: Molière's *Les Femmes savantes* and Fielding's *Tom Jones*

MERCURE: Les Dieux sont-ils de fer?
LA NUIT: Non, mais il faut sans cesse
Garder le *decorum* de la divinité.
Il est de certains mots dont l'usage rabaisse
Cette sublime qualité,
Et que, pour leur indignité,
Il est bon qu'aux hommes on laisse.

—Molière, *Amphitryon*

Appetite and Self-Delusion in *Les Femmes savantes*

Every French schoolchild knows that eating never occurs or is even mentioned in a tragedy by Corneille or Racine. The unalterability of that law makes the impudence of kitchen maids and the scenes at table in Molière's comedies extremely appealing: since eating is forbidden in a tragedy, its presence in a comedy is all the more exhilarating. For Bakhtin in *Rabelais and His World* this psychological reaction is connected to the "carnival spirit" that he analyzes in Rabelais and finds, too, in Molière. Molière's writings are among those that "liberate from the prevailing point of view of the world, from conventions and established truths." Out of this "carnival spirit," Bakhtin argues, there arises "a completely new order of things."[1]

Yet the "completely new order" exists only temporarily and more in fantasy than fact. At the end of the carnival season, and at the end of comedies, the old order has been reestablished. In Molière's *Le Bourgeois gentilhomme* (1670), for example, the nobility that Monsieur Jourdain longs for and that is bestowed upon him in the end proves more conclusively than ever that he is a dupe. He may proudly call himself a "Mamamouchi" and exult in his daughter's marriage to the "grand turque," but his ennoblement is part of a masquerade that has been staged for his benefit, precisely in order to uphold the existing social order. Monsieur Jourdain is as much of a bourgeois as ever, despite his new title, and Lucile marries the bourgeois she wants, not the marquess her father had dreamt of for her.

In *Les Femmes savantes* (1672), too, the existing order is restored, albeit with some questions. Trissotin is evicted from the household, the kitchen maid is reinstated, and the play concludes with a command by Chrysale that will actually be followed rather than ignored, if only because everyone already agrees with him. The reestablished social order is underscored by the reconfirmation of an aesthetic order: Molière's repeated references to literal taste in the play ultimately reaffirm rather than undermine the aesthetic ideal of good taste. When he plays with ambiguous taste in *Les Femmes savantes,* Molière questions the division of body and spirit implicit when tragic heroes neither eat nor sleep (and that has a subversive application to Christian doctrine). But Molière's questions, although they touch on grave social and aesthetic issues, occur within the framework that Bakhtin calls "carnivalistic" and that tolerates, even invites, subversion. Molière's questioning may be said to contain the germ of the Romantic revolution against neoclassicism, and in the case of ambiguous taste he anticipates an effective tool for revolt; but one must not confuse his teasing, despite its serious undertones, with the undoing of genre and decorum that begins a century later. For Molière, high and low styles in poetry, like class structure and gender roles, remain fixed. What complicates his acceptance of divisions is that he objects to the unthinking application of divisions. Molière considers divisions necessary, in society and in poetry, but not if they are mindlessly upheld. He believes in the spirit of the law, not in its letter.[2]

In *Les Femmes savantes,* we notice very quickly which qualities transcend the fixed divisions of gender and class. Good sense and intelligence are not distributed according to either. Besides, classes and genders are shown to be dependent upon one another, not separate entities. The division that Molière ridicules in this play, as I have said already, is the one between body and spirit. Philaminte and Trissotin uphold the division in the name of philosophy and decorum, and Chrysale upholds it in the name of his stomach. Since characters reveal their weaknesses through their language more than their actions, Molière uses literal and figurative usage to approximate the relationship between body and spirit. Ambiguous taste is exemplary of the relationship, and a character's use of literal or figurative taste becomes a measure of the ridiculous. At one extreme, then, are the pseudointellectual ladies and the would-be poet Trissotin, whose professions of spirituality conflict with their petty jealousies and their vanity, but most of all with their vocabulary. At the other extreme is the pedestrian Chrysale, a "bon bourgeois" or philistine who leads a life of the antispirit. In between are the characters who represent common sense: Henriette, who is the daughter of Chrysale and Philaminte and the moderation of their extremes; Ariste, the brother of Chrysale and Bélise who like Henriette stands between the extremes; Clitandre, the suitor of Henriette and a figure who can be considered to represent the ideas of Molière; and to an extent Martine, whose association with food is appropriate in the kitchen just as Clitandre's association with figurative taste is appropriate at court.

Chrysale uses a big edition of Plutarch to press his collars, but otherwise he considers books useless. In act 2, scene 7, the great comic scene where he bravely begins by criticizing his wife and quickly turns to address his sister Bélise instead, Chrysale thinks of books as useless furniture that ought to be burned:

> Vos livres éternels ne me contentent pas,
> Et hors un gros Plutarque à mettre mes rabats,
> Vous devriez brûler tout ce meuble inutile,
> Et laisser la science aux docteurs de la ville.
> M'ôter, pour faire bien, du grenier de céans
> Cette longue lunette à faire peur aux gens.
>
> (MFS 561–66)

> [In my opinion, you should burn the lot,
> Save for that Plutarch where I press my collars,
> And leave the studious life to clerks and scholars,
> And do throw out, if I may be emphatic,
> That great long frightful spyglass in the attic.
> And all these other gadgets, and do it soon.]
>
> (MLL 28)

27

Chrysale's materialism is amusing, but it could be dangerous; he is the ancestor of Max Frisch's Biedermann in *Biedermann und die Brandstifter*. His foibles are less important in and of themselves, however, than as a counterpart to the posturing in Philaminte's circle. Philaminte and her followers are figurative-minded people who ignore the source of the figures they use, fanatical believers in the preeminence of spirit over matter and in the importance of decorum. They are the upholders of the false good taste that Goethe condemns exactly a century later as a misunderstood adherence to rules and divisions. Because they believe in good taste and pretend to have no bodily needs, Molière has them take their figures from the realm of the senses, thereby undermining their dogmatism. The plan of these very silly people to purify their life and language is rendered all the more ridiculous through their unconscious choice of a vocabulary that refers to the things they condemn.

Molière does not begin the play by opposing the figurative limitations of Philaminte's circle to the literal limitations of Chrysale. Rather, he counters the fallacy of Armande's extreme "philosophical" position with the common sense of her sister Henriette. The opening dialogue of the play concerns marriage, both the word and the thing. For Armande, the word *marriage* evokes images that are "dégoûtant" [disgusting], itself a significant word, as we later realize. She asks her sister whether she is unable to "conceive" of the "disgusting" qualities of the word, which for her directs the gaze to low and dirty things:

> Ne concevez-vous point ce que, dès qu'on l'entend,
> Un tel mot à l'esprit offre de dégoûtant?
> Sur quelle étrange image on est par lui blessée?
> Sur quelle sale vue il traîne la pensée?
>
> (MFS 9–12)

> [Can you deny what sordid scenes are brought
> To the mind's eye by that distasteful thought,
> What coarse, degrading images arise,
> What shocking things it makes one visualize?]
>
> (MLL 5)

Armande's hypocrisy—or more charitably, her self-deception—is revealed through her choice of images, which betray her suppressed sensuality. Aside from "goût" and "dégoût," she speaks of "désirs" and "plaisirs," words emphasized through rhyme, and she suggests that Henriette "give herself" to the mind:

> À de plus hauts objets élevez vos désirs,
> Songez à prendre un goût des plus nobles plaisirs.
> Et traitant de mépris les sens et la matière,
> À l'esprit comme nous donnez-vous toute entière.
>
> (MLS 33–36)

> [Aspire to nobler objects, seek to attain
> To keener joys upon a higher plane,
> And, scorning gross material things as naught,
> Devote yourself, as we have done, to thought.]
>
> (MLL 6)

Finally, she tries to persuade her sister to "marry" philosophy and submit her animalistic side and her coarse appetites to the laws of reason:

> Mariez-vous, ma sœur, à la philosophie,
> Qui nous monte au-dessus de tout le genre humain,
> Et donne à la raison l'empire souverain,
> Soumettant à ses lois la partie animale,
> Dont l'appétit grossier aux bêtes nous ravale.
>
> (MFS 44–48)

> [Be married to philosophy instead,
> Which lifts us up above mankind, and gives
> All power to reason's pure imperatives,
> Thus rendering our bestial natures tame
> And mastering those lusts which lead to shame.]
>
> (MLL 6)

She is neither philosophical, nor decorous; on the contrary, she pays more attention to the "coarse appetites" she claims to have subdued than does her unconverted sister. She truly resembles their philosophical mother, whose campaign against "dirty syllables" [les syllabes sales] (913) merely brings to light obscene associations that would otherwise have been ignored—"équivoques infâmes" [infamous ambiguities] (917) that insult the delicacy of women.[3]

Armande's thoughts of marriage are much more graphic than those of her sister Henriette, the least learned and most intelligent of the ladies. Henriette is actually more of a philosopher than Armande, because marriage makes her think of abstract qualities like love and "les douceurs d'une innocente vie" [the pleasures of an innocent life] (24), despite her concrete thoughts of a husband and children. Henriette also has a more logical mind than her sister and a capacity for irony that her sister lacks. When Armande encourages her to imitate their mother, for example, Henriette begins by suggesting that each one of them imitate one side, she the material and Armande the spiritual. Armande finds the suggestion preposterous. She rejects their mother's "material" side, which she equates with her coughing and spitting (another detail that is more revelatory than decorous):

> Et ce n'est point du tout la prendre pour modèle,
> Ma sœur, que de tousser et de cracher comme elle.
>
> (MFS 75–76)

> [If someone's worthy to be copied, it's
> Not for the way in which she coughs and spits.]
>
> (MLL 7)

Henriette responds by pointing out the inconsistencies in her sister's thinking. She reminds Armande that neither one of them would exist if their mother had only an idealistic side ("ces beaux côtés"):

> Mais vous ne seriez pas ce dont vous vous vantez,
> Si ma mère n'eût eu que de ces beaux côtés.
>
> (MFS 77–79)

> [You and your intellect would not be here
> If Mother's traits had all been fine, my dear.
>
> (MLL 7)

Armande should be tolerant of the "lowness" ("bassesses") to which she owes her existence:

> De grâce, souffrez-moi, par un peu de bonté,
> Des bassesses à qui vous devez la clarté.
>
> (MFS 81–82)

[Relent, and tolerate in me, I pray,
That urge through which you saw the light of day.]

(MLL 7)

Henriette's strongest argument is also her wittiest. She implores her sister not to suppress the life of some little scholar who wants to come into the world:

Et ne supprimez point, voulant qu'on vous seconde,
Quelque petit savant qui veut venir au monde.

(MFS 83–84)

[And do not bid me be like you, and scorn
The hopes of some small scholar to be born.]

(MLL 7)

Armande's language betrays more than her sensuality. We quickly learn that her objections to Henriette's marriage are inspired by jealously, not philosophy. She wants Clitandre, who originally was her suitor, to be her everlasting platonic lover, though later on she discards her scruples and offers to sacrifice herself to Clitandre's animal appetites.

Only after Molière has shown the delusions of Armande and the solid reasoning of Henriette and Clitandre does he introduce the more extreme contrast between Chrysale's literalism and Bélise's exaggerated figures of speech. Chrysale is, as the dramatis personae tells us, a "bon bourgeois." He is a good-natured fellow of limited intellect who would not object to his wife Philaminte's tyranny or to her fanaticism if they had not had disastrous culinary consequences. Yet because his stomach is at stake, he summons up the courage to oppose Philaminte's decision to dismiss the kitchen maid Martine, who has broken not porcelain but rules of grammar. Chrysale's defense entails a confusion of categories, the apex of which is reached in the line "Je vis de bonne soupe, et non de beau langage" [I live from good soup, and not from beautiful language]. His defense of Martine consists of the opposition between words and food, which is emphasized through rhyme: *herbes* with *verbes, mot* with *pot, langage* with *potage;* and, finally, words are identified with fools (as they will be later on in the case of Trissotin) when *mots* rhymes with *sots:*

J'aime bien mieux, pour moi, qu'en épluchant ses herbes,
Elle accommode mal les noms avec les verbes,
Et redise cent fois un bas ou méchant mot,
Que de brûler ma viande, ou saler trop mon pot.
Je vis de bonne soupe, et non de beau langage.
Vaugelas n'apprend point à bien faire un potage;
Et Malherbe et Balzac, si savants en beaux mots,
En cuisine peut-être auraient été des sots.

(MFS 525–34)

[If she makes a tasty salad, it seems to me
Her subjects and her verbs need not agree.
Let her talk be barbarous, if she'll not
Burn up my beef or over-salt the pot.
It's food, not language, that I'm nourished by.
Vaugelas can't teach you how to bake a pie;
Malherbe, Balzac, for all their learnèd rules,
Might, in a kitchen, have been utter fools.]

(MLL 27)

In Chrysale's language everything is out of place, which underscores the comic inversion of stereotypical roles, he being a weak husband with an interest in the kitchen and Philaminte a dominant wife who philosophizes and ignores household chores. Philaminte is offended by the banality of Chrysale's language and the incongruity of his rhymes. But her own language betrays her, like that of Armande in the first scene of Act 1. She is offended by her husband's choice of a word because it "reeks" [put] of an outdated past:

Ah! *sollicitude* à mon oreille est rude:
Il put étrangement son ancienneté.

(MFS 552–53)

[CHRYSALE: You show no womanly solicitude
For—
PHILAMINTE: "Womanly!" That word is old and crude.
It reeks, in fact, of its antiquity.]

(MLL 27)

When Bélise tries to enlighten Chrysale, she, too, emphasizes the superiority of mind over matter. Like the other "learned ladies," she chooses an image that undermines her argument. She says that one must "nourish" the body with the "juice" [suc] of science:

> L'esprit doit sur le corps prendre le pas devant;
> Et notre plus grand soin, notre première instance,
> Doit être à le nourrir du suc de la science.
>
> (MFS 544–46)

> [The claims of the flesh must be subordinated,
> And it must be our chief delight and care
> To feast the soul on philosophic fare.]
>
> (MLL 27)

When Chrysale answers by taking up the word "nourrir," which Wilbur renders as "to feast," it is in character with his literal-minded understanding; but his response is mainly effective because it alerts the audience to the discrepancy between Bélise's metaphors and her precepts. Through Chrysale, Molière revives her dead metaphors:

> Ma foi! si vous songez à nourrir votre esprit,
> C'est de viande bien creuse, à ce que chacun dit.
>
> (MFS 549–50)

> [I don't know what your soul's been eating of late,
> But it's not a balanced diet, at any rate.]
>
> (MLL 27)

By reviving the dead metaphor in this scene, Molière prepares the audience for the images in the first two scenes of act 3, where Bélise uses culinary imagery to describe Trissotin's poetry. She surpasses herself by mixing metaphors and saying that "Ce sont repas friands qu'on donne à mon oreille" (MFS 716) [Their music is a banquet to my ear] (MLL 34), thereby proving her incompetency to judge poetry. Philaminte takes up the culinary image when she asks Trissotin to "serve us your poetic feast" (MLL 35) [Servez-nous promptement votre aimable repas] (MFS 746). When Philaminte modifies the word *repas* with the adjective *aimable*, which applies only to people's actions and never to meals, she shows that, like Bélise, she lacks a sensitivity to language and thinks only

33

,sotin stays with the culinary metaphor and speaks of his (*grande faim*) and of "a single dish of eight verses" [un huit vers]. But since he, like the ladies, pays no attention to eaning of his image, he is unconscious of double entendre speaks of "délicatesse," "sel attique," or most revealingly of "ragu ' which is made to rhyme with "bon goût." His inattention to language and therefore his incompetence as a poet have been exposed even before he begins to read:

> Pour cette grande faim qu'à mes yeux on expose,
> Un plat seul de huit vers me semble peu de chose,
> Et je pense qu'ici je ne ferai pas mal
> De joindre à l'épigramme, ou bien au madrigal,
> Le ragoût d'un sonnet, qui chez une princesse
> A passé pour avoir quelque délicatesse.
> Il est de sel attique assaisonné partout,
> Et vous le trouverez, je crois, d'assez bon goût.
>
> (MFS 747–54)

> [For such great hunger as confronts me here,
> An eight-line dish would not suffice, I fear.
> My epigram's too slight. It would be wiser,
> I think, to give you first, as appetizer,
> A sonnet which a certain princess found
> Subtle in sense, delectable in sound.
> I've seasoned it with Attic salt throughout,
> And you will find it tasty, I have no doubt.]
>
> (MLL 36)

Tobin has shown the extent to which Molière recasts and ridicules the writings of the principal model for Trissotin, the abbé Cotin, and turns his own images against him. Tobin also shows how Molière underscores his caricature by having Trissotin betray an ignorance of culinary as well as literary conventions: he has the *ragoût* precede the *entrée,* for example, and his affection for salt, which is out of style, is therefore "in bad taste."[4]

For the audience, Trissotin's culinary image is not associated with good taste, as he would like, but with the fate of bad writing, which is used by vendors at the market to wrap up food. Clitandre prepares us for the association of Trissotin and taste in act 1, scene 3 when he describes

Trissotin as a pedant who writes so much that his pages supply the entire market place: "Un pédant dont on voit la plume libérale, / D'officieux papiers fournir toute la halle" (MFS 235–36) [A bore whose dreadful books end, one and all, / As wrapping-paper in some market-stall?] (MLL 12). The connection of bad poetry and the marketplace is a topos that Fielding, Sterne, and Byron use; literal taste, when it is out of place the way it is in the case of Trissotin, becomes the sign of bad taste. Molière's own allusions to food are not out of place, because, as we see here and as Tobin shows to be the case elsewhere, he makes them consciously.

Trissotin's culinary imagery has the effect of dramatic irony. Molière achieves the same effect in another way when he has Trissotin's admirers anticipate and appreciate his poetry with language that is even more erotically suggestive than Armande's in the first scene of the play. Bélise is out of breath:

> Ah! tout doux, laissez-moi, de grâce, respirer.
>
> (MFS 776)
>
> [Oh! Pause a moment, I beg you; one is breathless.]
>
> (MLL 37)

And Philaminte's raptures sound more sensual than philosophical. Her choice of the verbs *couler* and *se pâmer* makes her guilty of the same "équivoques infâmes" that she condemned with such vehemence in act 2, scene 7:

> On se sent à ces vers, jusques au fond de l'âme,
> Couler je ne sais quoi qui fait que l'on se pâme.
>
> (MFS 778–79)
>
> [There's a rare something in those lines which captures
> One's inmost heart, and stirs the soul to raptures.
>
> (MLL 37)]

After Trissotin has finished reading, the delight of the *précieuses* is even more suggestive, and Molière divides one line among the three to show their orgasmic breathlessness. He has Bélise repeat the verb *pâmer* and Armande use the euphemistic verb *to die* ("on se meurt de plaisir"):

PHILAMINTE: On n'en peut plus.
BÉLISE: On pâme.
ARMANDE: On se meurt de plaisir.

(MFS 810)

[PHILAMINTE: I'm overcome
BÉLISE: I'm faint.
ARMANDE: I'm ravished, quite.]

(MLL 39–40)

They applaud the allusion to Laïs as erudite ("Ah! *ma Laïs*! voilà de l'érudition" [MFS 833]), unaware that they are praising a courtesan. Philaminte adds that "On n'a que lui qui puisse écrire de ce goût" [Only he can write in this style] (MFS 838), but the word "goût" has a different meaning for the audience than it does for her.

Trissotin's reputation for bad taste and bad poetry precedes him through Clitandre's description. Clitandre is the standard of excellence in poetry and of manners, partly, as we are given to understand, because he is familiar with life at court. But it is his language rather than his experience that persuade us to trust his judgment: he is direct without being literal-minded, and he is sensitive to figurative usage without using metaphors to hide something from others or himself. He does not divide literal and figurative meanings, just as he does not divide body and soul when he speaks to Armande:

> Pour moi, par un malheur, je m'aperçois, Madame,
> Que j'ai, ne vous déplaise, un corps tout comme une âme.

(MFS 1213–14)

[Well, *I'm* aware, though you may blush to hear it,
That I have both a body and a spirit.]

(MLL 57)

When Clitandre says to Armande that he feels ("Je sens"), for example, he is conscious of an ambiguity that Armande fails to understand:

> Je sens qu'il y tient trop, pour le laisser à part;
> De ces détachements je ne connais point l'art:
> Le Ciel m'a dénié cette philosophie,
> Et mon âme et mon corps marchent de compagnie.

36

(MFS 1215–18)

[Nor can I part with them to my satisfaction;
I fear I lack the power of abstraction
Whereby such philosophic feats are done,
And so my body and soul must live as one.]

(MLL 57)

Clitandre is so sensitive to language that he claims to have known what Trissotin looks like from having read his works:

Jusques à sa figure encor la chose alla,
Et je vis par les vers qu'à la tête il nous jette,
De quel air il fallait que fût fait le poète;
Et j'en avais si bien deviné tous les traits,
Que rencontrant un homme un jour dans le Palais,
Je gageai que c'était Trissotin en personne,
Et je vis qu'en effet la gageure était bonne.

(MFS 262–67)

[I saw still more; for I could visualize,
By studying his dreadful poetry,
Just what the poet's lineaments must be;
I pictured him so truly that one day,
Seeing a foppish man in the *Palais,*
I said, "That's Trissotin, by God!"—and found,
Upon enquiry, that my hunch was sound.]

(MLL 13)

Henriette in her sensible way is skeptical about so much stylistic clairvoyance and remarks that Clitandre must have very good eyes; but we nevertheless obtain from Clitandre a clear portrait of Trissotin and are reminded of how language—written or spoken—reveals character.

After we hear for ourselves how Trissotin speaks and writes, Molière confronts him with Clitandre in act 4, scene 3. The two men are rivals for the hand of Henriette, and they do verbal "combat" (the word used by Philaminte and Trissotin for the exchange, lines 1319 and 1325). Their dialogue is full of puns and ambiguities, willed by Clitandre and unwilled by Trissotin. Trissotin thinks on one level, if at all. In the following passage, for example, he uses the word *voir* (to see) figuratively but does not notice how Clitandre makes the word function both literally and figuratively within the same line (Wilbur renders the wordplay by using the word "stare"):

TRISSOTIN: Pour moi, je ne vois pas ces examples fameux.
CLITANDRE: Moi, je les vois si bien qu'ils me crèvent les yeux.

(MFS 1291–92)

[TRISSOTIN: I cannot think, myself, of such a case.
CLITANDRE: I can; indeed, it stares me in the face.]

(MLL 59)

Their combat proceeds to the ultimate insult, where Clitandre takes over the word *sot* (fool) from Trissotin and uses it to play on his opponent's name: Trissotin's name means thrice the fool ("trois fois sot"), and Clitandre repeats the word *sot* three times in the same line:

TRISSOTIN: J'ai cru jusques ici que c'était l'ignorance
  Qui faisait les grands sots, et non pas la science.
CLITANDRE: Vous avez cru fort mal, et je vous suis garant
  Qu'un sot savant est sot plus qu'un sot ignorant.

(MFS 1293–96)

[TRISSOTIN: I thought it was by ignorance, and not
  By learning, Sir, that great fools were begot.
CLITANDRE: Well, you thought wrongly. It's a well-known rule
  That no fool's greater than a learnèd fool.]

(MLL 59)

Because he cannot take in two meanings at once, Trissotin misunderstands; he lacks the self-awareness and the imagination to grasp Clitandre's paradoxical phrase "sot savant," and he therefore accuses Clitandre of being tautological:

Le sentiment commun est contre vos maximes,
Puisque ignorant et sot sont termes synonymes.

(MFS 1297–98)

[Our common usage contradicts that claim,
Since "fool" and "ignoramus" mean the same.]

(MLL 59)

There is a resemblance between Clitandre's method here and Molière's reworking of the abbé Cotin's texts; such parallels confirm the impression that Clitandre is Molière's mouthpiece.

The scene culminates in an argument about taste. Clitandre is accused of partisanship because he is a courtier, and the court is accused of failing to appreciate the products of the mind ("esprit"). We know that in this play the reverse is true. Trissotin is partisan, since his works are not in favor at court, and the word *esprit*—like the word *taste*—has been corrupted; we remember, too, Armande's famous exclusionary dictum when she separates the intellect and wit ("esprit") of her circle from those outside it: "Nul n'aura de l'esprit hors nous et nos amis" (MFS 924) [We'll show that only we and our friends have wit] (MLL 44). In his defense of the court, Clitandre associates taste with honesty and common sense, qualities that Trissotin and his admirers lack. Against the charge that bad taste rules at court, Clitandre responds that

> Qu'elle a du sens commun pour se connaître à tout;
> Que chez elle on se peut former quelque bon goût;
> Et que l'esprit du monde y vaut, sans flatterie,
> Tout le savoir obscur de la pédanterie.
>
> (MFS 1343–46)

> [That all things, there, are viewed with common sense,
> That good taste, too, is much in evidence,
> And that its knowledge of the world surpasses
> The fusty learning of pedantic asses.]
>
> (MLL 61)

Clitandre opposes two kinds of *esprit*—that of Trissotin and his followers, who are "beaux esprits" (1333), and the "esprit du monde." The *beaux esprits* are pedants and obscure, and to them Clitandre prefers the clarity or common sense of the *esprit du monde* that is to be found at court. Trissotin's only proof for the lack of taste at court is that noone there appreciates his works: "De son bon goût, Monsieur, nous voyons les effets" (MFS 1347) [It has good taste, you say? If only it had!] (MLL 61). The audience, having heard him read from his works already, can agree with Clitandre that there is good reason for contesting the "good taste" of Trissotin's works.

Molière's punning on the literal and figurative meanings of the word *goût* occurs within a system of poetic laws where "good taste" is a valid category, the legitimate gauge of poetry and manners at court. Molière addresses serious concerns in the guise of frivolity, but he respects the laws of an aesthetic tradition. He evidently believes, with Corneille, in taming rules rather than rejecting them. In *Les Femmes savantes,* the old order is restored. Chrysale's authority in the last lines of the play is amusing rather than convincing, and he assumes it just as Monsieur Jourdain becomes a "Mamamouchi" at the end of *Le Bourgeois gentilhomme.* Chrysale is only assertive because he knows that everyone agrees with him already. He was not the one to defend Henriette's marriage to Clitandre; Martine the kitchen maid took on the task for him, and her will and determination cast an ironic light on her insistence that husbands always are the masters. Martine's eloquence qualifies her claim that

> Ce n'est point à la femme à prescrire, et je sommes
> Pour céder le dessus en toute chose aux hommes.
>
> (MFS 1641–42)
>
> [It just ain't right for the wife to run the shop.
> The man, I say, should always be on top.]
>
> (MLL 74)

or that "La poule ne doit chanter devant le coq" (MFS 1644) [It's cocks, not hens, should be the ones to crow] (MLL 74), just as Chrysale's orders are qualified by his actions. Nevertheless, there is what Bakhtin would call "a new outlook on the world" at the end of the play. Molière does not invent static figures, and a progression is achieved through the moderation of two extreme positions: Chrysale has become slightly more self-assertive, and Philaminte has for the first time exchanged some of her philosophical tenets for an opinion influenced by common sense. The traditional roles of men and women have not been reestablished without question; gender is shown to be a less determining factor than character. Likewise, from the aesthetic point of view, we sense Molière's questioning of any extreme. Too rigid a division of comedy and tragedy is as indefensible as the division of matter and spirit in *Les Femmes savantes:* the heroes of tragedies are sensual beings, and comedies treat more than material, bodily concerns. Each of Molière's comedies has a serious theme, and his resolutions are often illusory, which leads some critics to speak of "dark comedies"; nagging questions outlive the laughter, and some plays end in sadness, most memorably *Le Misanthrope*.[5] Decorum, too, is a mistaken end when it has not been tempered by common sense. The language of the *précieuses,* their "syllabes sales" and "équivoques infâmes," are absurd; in the effort to conceal, the *précieuses* reveal more than if they had accepted rather than repressed the material side of human nature.

Literal and figurative taste are considered by Molière to be appropriate and desirable in their place. There is nothing indecorous about the language of Martine, because her dialect and mistakes in grammar are acceptable in the kitchen, which is the realm of literal taste; mistakes in grammar do not affect her most important qualities, which are common sense and courage. It is true that her behavior conflicts with her professed opinions when she speaks for Chrysale, who is her master in name only; but she is forthright and honest, and the discrepancy between her manner and her opinions is a comic trait keenly observed and staged by Molière. Analogously, the court, embodied by Clitandre, is a proper setting for good taste. Trissotin, who claims to be an apostle of good taste, is not accepted at court, which reflects the mediocrity of his poetry rather than an injust social or aesthetic hierarchy. Molière's use of ambiguous taste in *Les Femmes savantes* can be said to anticipate the poetic revolution of the Romantic age, because it records the absurdities of a neoclassicism too rigidly applied; but his criticism does not aim to topple the existing literary order.

One final example from *Les Femmes savantes* will serve to illustrate the claim that for Molière order is a desirable thing both in society and literature. In the penultimate scene of the play, Philaminte and Bélise try to persuade the notary to change his text and to put the contract into "beau langage." He answers sensibly that his style is appropriate to his purpose, and he argues his case by using the word *sot,* which once more is made to rhyme with *mot* (Wilbur felicitously rhymes *absurd* with *word*):

> Notre style est très bon, et je serais un sot,
> Madame, de vouloir y changer un seul mot.
>
> (MFS 1601–04)

> [Our style is excellent, Madam; I'd be absurd
> Were I to modify a single word.]
>
> (MLL 72)

The word "sot" resonates. To be a fool is to lack common sense, and that, as we have seen, betokens an absence of taste.

Appetite and Decorum in *Tom Jones*

Anyone who has seen Osborne and Richardson's film of *Tom Jones* will remember the culinary seduction of Tom by Mrs. Waters after they reach the Inn at Upton. In the novel, the association of eating and eros is more pervasive than it is in the film; it is also more far-reaching and less unambiguous. The chapter in which this particular scene occurs (book 9, chapter 5) contains some of Fielding's most elaborate teasing. Its title is "An Apology for all Heroes who have good Stomachs, with a Description of a Battle of the amorous kind," and just at the moment when Tom and Mrs. Waters retire to pursue their amorous adventure, the narrator interrupts with a long digression about the bodily needs of heroes, who "have certainly more of mortal than divine about them" (TJ 9, 5, 509). This statement in turn leads to speculation about how other authors present their heroes, specifically Homer when he portrays Ulysses. Fielding says of Ulysses in an aside that he "by the Way seems to have had the best Stomach of all the Heroes in that eating Poem of the Odyssey" (9, 5, 509). The teasing has a serious literary undercurrent that places Fielding in a direct line between Molière, who as we have seen comments occasionally on the disjunction in literature between heroes and eating, and Byron, whose culinary allusions and digressions in *Don Juan* are more insistently poetological. Fielding admired Molière (he adapted *L'Avare* and *Le Médecin malgré lui* for the British stage) and therefore had a model for the comic effects to be obtained with culinary allusions. In some ways, particularly in the association of eating with aesthetic taste, there is a resemblance between Molière and Fielding and Byron. But ambiguous taste has a wider range in *Tom Jones*. This does not merely reflect Fielding's own qualities as a bon vivant, though they may well have inspired him, but rather the genre in which he writes.[6]

Fielding's comments in book 9, chapter 5, aside from teasing and controlling the reader, are meant to educate. They are another example of how we are taught throughout the work not to be too complacent in our expectations or too quick in our judgment. Allworthy provides the preeminent warning example when he mistakes the character of Tom Jones and Blifil, but the reader is taught and tested by means of subjects as well as characters. In the digression about heroes and eating, for example, Fielding refers to a fundamental characteristic of human nature (human nature being, as we are told in the first chapter, the subject of the novel), in this case the clash between the sublime and the ridiculous. The attempt to hide this clash, which Molière shows in *Les Femmes savantes* to be a misguided one, has an application to neoclassical norms. Fielding is more explicit about the connection in the prefatory chapter to book 11, where he speaks of the literary restrictions imposed on authors in the name of taste (much as Byron does later in *Don Juan*), and we are expected to make the connection between the two passages. The aesthetic implications of the author's comments in Book 9, chapter 5 are, in retrospect, revealed to be as important as the connection of literal and figurative appetites. It is for this reason that the adaptation of the passage to the screen, though brilliant in its rendering of one part, remains incomplete.[7]

The connection between the passages in 9, 5 and 11, 1 is effected through the amatory and aesthetic meanings of taste. In book 9, chapter 5, the narrator says that to "several wise Men" (where context exposes the irony of the word "wise") the "Act of Eating" is "considered as extremely mean and derogatory from the Philosophic Dignity." This perception is shown to be hypocritical (and hypocrisy, as Fielding says in the preface to *Joseph Andrews*, is the most vicious of vices): nature, because she is "frolicksome," does not always assign dainty appetites to "dignified Characters" and gluttony to people "of the lowest Order." It can therefore happen that "the greatest Prince, Heroe, or Philosopher on Earth" disproves the notion that grand figures are sustained by spiritual nourishment alone. This observation by the narrator is a reflection after the fact of the discrepancy between Square's fleshless philosophy and his exposure behind the curtain in Molly Seagrim's bedroom. Indirectly we are asked to contrast the honesty with which Tom Jones eats and the falsehood with which Square tries to hide his sensuality behind a curtain. The critique here of a philosophy contrary to nature is extended to literary rules, implicitly in book 9, chapter 5 and explicitly in book 11, chapter 1. Following his authorial intrusions about the needs of heroes, Fielding concludes the chapter with his narration of a "battle of an amorous kind" in the mock-epic style he also uses for the Barnyard Battle and occasionally for descriptions of landscape or the time of day. When he says that he can only narrate the seduction with "the Assistance of certain Aerial Beings" and invokes Milton by saying that "we are about to attempt a

Description hitherto unessayed either in Prose or Verse" (9, 5, 511), he is not altogether facetious. He has indeed raised a series of questions about the nature of the epic, both in style and in subject. It is another of those instances where, as Empson and others remind us, we should be cautious about taking Fielding's authorial comments too lightly.[8]

The prefatory chapter to book 11 contains one of Fielding's attacks on critics, in this case because they judge—or misjudge—works based on a strict application of the rules of "taste." A detail that does not conform to a critic's notion of taste can lead to a condemnation of the whole work: "a single Expression which doth not coincide with the Taste of the Audience, or with any individual Critic of that Audience, is sure to be hissed" (11, 1, 571). The idea that a detail can distract from the whole and lead to a false perception is one of the novel's recurrent themes. Here it is associated specifically with the flaws of critics (other notable passages where the failure is applied to critics are the prefatory chapters to books 5 and 10). The "taste" here is another name for the hypocrisy Fielding caricatures in the authorial comments of the "eating scene" and in the figure of Square; the narrator says that restrictions based on a small-minded notion of taste are intolerable, adding that "To write within such severe Rules as these, is as impossible, as to live up to some splenetic Opinions." The narrator then extends the pettiness of "some critics" to the little-mindedness of "some Christians," saying that "if we judge according to the Sentiments of some Critics, and of some Christians, no Author will be saved in this World, and no Man in the next" (11, 1, 571). Fielding's use of the word *judge* has begun to ring by this stage of the novel, and we know on the requisite second reading that the word requires scrutiny.[9] Passages like these, in which food is associated with aesthetic taste, add meaning to the topos that bad works end up as paper for pastry cooks, to which Fielding alludes in 4,1 and the French version of which occurs in *Les Femmes savantes;* they also lend significance to the term "nourished" in the prefatory chapter to book 13, where Fielding ponders posterity and names his "Muses," among them genius "nourished by Art." As Battestin has shown with respect to the word *prudence,* the meaning of a word can emblematize the mutability of context and the fallibility of perception; we must learn to judge a word's meaning depending on where it is used and by whom, and such judgment requires time and experience. Jones does not understand or practice "prudence" until the final chapter of the novel, and the reader understands only in retrospect the meaning of the word and the nature of those who use it. The word *prudence* is used in the novel to denote both virtue or vice, and the difficulty with which one distinguishes the two is "deliberately complex, as significant yet elusive as the meaning or wisdom itself."[10]

When critics like Battestin analyze the importance of order and of emblems in the novel, despite their emphasis on judgment, they tend to pass over the role of a subject like food in conveying philosophical, theological, or aesthetic questions. Perhaps this is because the function of the culinary seems obvious, or perhaps critics wish to deflect from examples that appear to support those who, in the tradition of Samuel Johnson, find Fielding's novel trivial or even obscene. But the culinary allusions in *Tom Jones* are the background against which the Romantic ambiguity of taste acquires its role. In *Tom Jones* even more pronouncedly than in *Les Femmes savantes* (and as the passages discussed already have begun to show), ambiguous taste is associated with the Christian division of body and spirit and therefore gives rise to social, philosophical, and aesthetic questions. The meaning of taste can fluctuate like the meaning of prudence. For Bridget the word *prudent* has a negative sense; she is also said to be "a Woman of the greatest Delicacy of Taste," and we understand taste as the negative kind that Fielding associates with the censure of critics in 11, 1.

That taste in *Tom Jones* has an ambiguous function—that it is used both literally and figuratively and that it can be differently weighted and perceived—is immediately apparent from the first of the prefatory chapters, "The Introduction to the Work, or Bill of Fare to the Feast." This is so in a rhetorical sense, given the famous opening metaphor chosen by the narrator to compare himself with the keeper of an ordinary: he presents his customers (or readers) with a bill of fare before they enter (or start reading). The bill of fare he presents is "Human Nature," which like turtle (a food associated with aldermen, hence with politics and satire) has more to offer than a single name would seem to indicate.[11] Against the charge that to some "this Dish is too common and vulgar" because it is so often considered to be the subject of literary works "with which the Stalls abound," the narrator counters that names can be deceiving; it is as hard to find "true Nature" in literary works as it is to find true Bayonne ham or Bologna sausage in the shops that sell them under those names. The implication of fraud, in merchants and in literature, is one that occurs often in the course of the novel. When for example the landlady of the Inn at Upton showers her most generous praise on Tom

45

and Mrs. Waters, shortly after the eating scene mentioned already, she unwittingly admits that she is guilty of fraud: she praises her guests because they allow themselves to be cheated, saying that they have ordered the best supper of the last half year and that they "found no fault with my *Worcestershire* Perry, which I sold them for *Champagne*" (533).[12] Already in the first chapter of the novel, then, Fielding makes it clear that the reader must be wary of deception, and the figure of taste is offered as a model for leaning how.

Through the figure of taste, we are to acquire an aesthetic as well as a moral education.[13] When he pursues the culinary metaphor, the narrator shifts his comparison of the author with a "Master of an Ordinary" to one of the author with a cook. We are told that "true Nature" depends on the "Cookery of the Author." What matters is not so much the subject (a ham may not be from Bayonne and still be a ham) as "the Author's Skill in well dressing it up." To support his claim, the narrator quotes a famous couplet from Pope's *Essay on Criticism* about the relation between art and nature:

> True Wit is Nature to Advantage drest,
> What oft' was thought, but ne'er so well exprest.
>
> (1, 1, 33)

By quoting these lines in particular, Fielding demonstrates his claim that words do not always denote the same thing: the word "drest" does not originally have the exclusively culinary connotation that Fielding wryly gives it here through his context. Finally, the comparison of author and cook ironizes the neoclassical analogy between the author and God.[14] The analogy of author and cook admirably illustrates the relationship between Fielding's playfulness and his neoclassical belief in the artist's godlike power to order a literary universe. As Battestin says: "For all its generous exuberance and cheerful, bumptious energy, *Tom Jones* is the celebration of the rational values of Art, of the controlling intelligence which creates Order out of Chaos and which alone gives meaning to vitality, making it a source of wonder and joy."[15]

The function of this comparison between author, master of an ordinary, and cook, like the function of details and trivialities, is not immediately apparent, which is precisely the point (as will be the case for Byron's culinary allusions in *Don Juan*). For most critics, the opening image of the bill of fare is related exclusively to Fielding's depiction of the "feast

46

of life." Andrew Wright, whose title *Mask and Feast* alludes to the gusta-
tory image, says that Fielding "is asking us to take *Tom Jones* in this festive
spirit" and that "the meaning of the novel depends" on the image.[16]
Battestin notes the connection between the opening image and the con-
cluding marriage dinner for Tom and Sophia, saying that "not unlike the
banquet of Socrates, the wedding dinner of Tom and Sophia celebrates
the power of Beauty and Virtue."[17] And Simon Varey considers the image
and the subsequent culinary references to be a reflection of the narrator's
"good-natured hospitality" toward his readers, "for whose welfare, as
always, he is solicitous."[18] Other readers have been offended or irritated
by the culinary images ever since the novel was published, thereby putting
into practice the error of judgment against which Fielding warns us re-
peatedly. Mostly the censure derives from the assumption that a trivial
subject has a trivial function, the same false assumption that deflects
attention from the culinary allusions of Romantic authors. Patrick Reilly
criticizes the image of the author as the master of an ordinary on the
grounds that the comparison is skewed: the reader does not have the
choice in a novel that the customer does in an ordinary. Yet Reilly appears
to underestimate the importance of an image that confirms his own posi-
tion: that this novel teaches us to judge. One chooses—or "judges"—
when putting together a meal from a bill of fare; besides, a bill of fare
indicates limits as well as choice, bearing out the analogy to the novel.
The analogy holds further in the sense that a bill of fare presents items
that are disparate yet related; seeming arbitrariness is an accepted charac-
teristic of the bill of fare as a "genre," and the "reader" is expected to
choose and order things that will form a coherent culinary whole. The
image therefore has an application not only to the judgment one learns
as the novel progresses, but also to the relationship between the prefatory
chapters (which Empson dismisses as "introductory prattle") and the rest
of the novel: the prefatory chapters, too, may seem disparate (or "prat-
tle"), but, taken together, they represent theoretical statements that help
us to read the novel, as do the authorial intrusions.[19] Reilly also criticizes
Fielding on the grounds that the culinary image is "too casual and 'easy,'
too nonchalantly detached from the gravity of the issues to be debated,"
but an analysis of Fielding's ambiguous taste counters the charge.[20] Field-
ing's culinary metaphor offers another example of what Wright calls
Fielding's "feigned frivolity."[21]

Ambiguous taste has a literary and philosophical dimension in *Tom
Jones*, as it does in *Les Femmes savantes* and later during the Romantic

age. But Fielding extends the figure further than Molière or the Romantics, and the fact that he does so underscores the effect of genre on the representation of food. In his novel, Fielding uses culinary allusions as a short hand for representing (and sometimes "judging") a milieu and for noting the passage of time. Social and narrative order are conveyed through culinary allusions, a technique that becomes even more pronounced in the novel of the nineteenth century. Sometimes Fielding uses eating habits for caricature, much as Hogarth does in a work like the *Gates of Calais* (which has the alternate title *O the Roastbeef of Old England, &c.*). Parson Supple, for example, is "chiefly remarkable for his great Taciturnity at Table, though his Mouth was never shut at it. In short, he had one of the best Appetites in the World" (4, 10, 187–88). When Parson Supple dines at the squire's, he is willing because of his enormous hunger to ignore the coarse conversation there: "To say Truth, the Parson submitted to please his Palate at the Squire's Table, at the expense of suffering now and then this Violence to his Ears" (6, 9, 72). Parson Supple's appetite at table is implicitly connected to sexual appetite when we learn in the final pages of the novel that he has married Mrs. Waters, an ironic sequel to her culinary seduction of Tom in 9, 5. His eagerness to eat is attached to him like a leitmotif, and Fielding connects the culinary caricature of Parson Supple to the contrasting characterization of Allworthy and Squire Western. Allworthy's goodness is evident in the "hearty Welcome at his Table" (1, 3, 38) from which Parson Supple benefits. His generosity is natural rather than forced, and he leaves the guests at his "eleemosynary Abode" the freedom to eat or not, as they choose, so that everyone at his table "might at his Pleasure satisfy all his Appetites within the Restrictions only of Law, Virtue, and Religion" (1, 10, 61). Squire Western's habits at table, which we witness often, reflect his brutish ways, among them his cruel treatment of Sophia's mother (7, 4). It is in character for Squire Western to "persuade" his daughter with repeated threats to lock her up in a garret and feed her only bread and water, and it is equally in character for him to bring food to her himself after having locked her in her room. He even has some of her "most favorite Dainties" brought to her by Black George, who takes advantage of the squire's indulgence and hides Tom's letter to Sophia in the belly of a fowl (16, 3).

When the words *hunger* and *appetite* are applied to Allworthy, the associations are altogether different and demonstrate the variability of words as much as a difference in character. Allworthy's sleep is the kind "which a Heart that hungers after Goodness, is apt to enjoy, when thoroughly satisfied. As these are probably sweeter than what are occasioned by any other hearty Meal, I should take more Pains to display them to the Reader, if I knew any Air to recommend him to the procuring such an Appetite" (1, 3, 41). When Allworthy takes leave of his family on what he thinks is his deathbed, he compares death to leaving a feast: "One of our Roman poets, I remember, likens our leaving Life to our Departure from a Feast" (5, 7, 242). Fielding also uses the image of appetite to distinguish between love and lust in the prefatory chapter to book 6, which he calls "Of Love," and to counter those philosophers who say that love does not exist. Sexual appetite is often mistaken for love, he says, but is actually "the Desire of satisfying a voracious Appetite with a certain Quantity of delicate white human Flesh." This is "more properly Hunger" and can only be called love in the sense meant by the glutton who is not ashamed "to apply the Word Love to his Appetite, and to say he LOVES such and such Dishes." In the case of real love, however—"this Love for which I am an Advocate"—the "hunger" plays a part, because "it heightens all its Delights" (6, 1, 270). At the end of the chapter, the author advises readers who do not understand love as he does to stop reading; love for them is purely material, no more than an appetite to be satisfied, and "probably may, in your Opinion, very greatly resemble a Dish of Soup, or a Sir-loin of Roast-beef" (6, 1, 272). As in the first chapter of the novel, there is a connection between the author, the reader, and cookery. Readers for whom cooking or love are purely material have misunderstood him.

The appetites of Parson Supple are comic and harmless; those of Squire Western show his limitations; and Allworthy's are related to his goodness. There are sexual appetites and appetites for money and power, and there is the physical hunger that can become an expression of love. When the word *appetite* is applied to Blifil, its meaning is rather more complicated. Fielding uses it first for his father (just as false taste is associated with his mother): Captain Blifil is said to have "a very good Appetite," and his absence from the table is what prompts Allworthy to suspect that something has happened to him, "for he was always very punctual at his Meals" (2, 9, 110). Here as in the case of Parson Supple, culinary details are used for caricature. With Blifil *fils,* there is contempt and innuendo when the narrator says that "his Appetites were, by Nature, so moderate, that he was able by Philosophy or by Study, or by some other Method, easily to subdue them" (6, 4, 284). For Blifil, the figures of appetite and taste have an odious quality. His appetite is contrasted to that of Jones ("Mr. Blifil was not of the Complexion of Jones, nor ready to eat every Woman he saw") and is "that Appetite which is said to be the common Property of all Animals." What distinguishes Blifil and Jones further is that Blifil's "taste" is a mental property devoid of feeling, a negative kind like his mother's: "he had likewise that distinguishing Taste, which serves to direct Men in their Choice of the Objects, or Food of their several Appetites." For Blifil, Sophia is scarcely human; she is desirable because his "taste" has "taught him to consider Sophia as a most delicious Morsel, indeed to regard her with the same Desires which an Ortolan inspires into the Soul of an Epicure" (7, 6, 345–46). By the end of the novel, Blifil has no appetites, only the passions of avarice and hatred (16, 6, 858). Consequently we have even more evidence that he is a monster.

We compare Blifil's lack of appetite to the honest hunger of Jones, which, however, is not of the animalistic or comical variety attributed to Squire Western or Partridge. The distinction is of note, as we know from the chapter "On Love." Even though he has appetites, Tom Jones can go without eating. After he and Partridge meet with the gypsies, for example—where excessive eating and drinking get Partridge into trouble—the narrator tells us that Jones has eaten scarcely anything for a long time, because "with the Gypsies, he had feasted only his Understanding" (12, 13, 674). Or again in this chapter, Partridge (who like Chrysale thinks only of his material needs) says to Jones that "It must be certainly Love that you live upon," to which Jones replies, "'And a very rich Diet too, Partridge'" (12, 13, 675). Their dialogue resembles those of Don Quixote and Sancho Panza, except that Jones takes up Partridge's image consciously and shows that something material can possess spiritual attributes. In a similar dialogue, Jones imagines that Sophia has her eyes "fixed on that very Moon which I behold at this Instant," to which Partridge answers that he would prefer to have his eyes "fixed on a good Surloin of Roast Beef" (8, 9, 437). Like Tom, Sophia has enough sensuality to eat (though she does so only in moderation), but she is not dominated by hunger; when she hears the story of her cousin Harriet Fitzpatrick, for example, her mind takes over and "she has no Appetite except for the story." Harriet, on the other hand, eats "heartily" (11, 6, 591), although one would expect her to be more affected by the story than Sophia.

What and when people eat (or do not eat) is as revealing as what they

say. When Allworthy or Squire Western or Mrs. Mille[
table—something that Fielding records each time with g[
we are given a sense of order, though not always of pr[
of the regularity with which people normally eat, and b
eating are taken for granted, the act of eating is easily overlooked or
considered little more than a measure of time or travel, possibly of charac-
ter.[22] This is one of the misperceptions emblematized by taste. Since
meals signify order, their absence indicates disorder. Captain Blifil's death
is foretold by his absence from dinner; Sophia's escape is discovered at
breakfast, which prompts the first of her father's idle threats to keep her
in her room on bread and water "as long as she lived" (10, 5, 555);
Lady Bellaston arranges to meet Tom after dinner and never invites him
to join her, which reproduces the irregularity of their situation. One
symptom of the alienation from which the Man of the Hill suffers is that
he has nothing to eat or drink in his home except for a "Dram of Brandy"
that he forgets to offer after having promised it (8, 10). Partridge is
horrified by the Man of the Hill's diet, which to him offers the ultimate
proof of his strangeness: "'his Diet, as the old Woman told me, is chiefly
upon Herbs, which is a fitter Food for a Horse than a Christian'" (12,
3, 628). Allworthy, who tries to preserve order under any circumstances,
waits until the tea has been poured out before telling Bridget that he has
adopted Tom (1, 5); and as soon as he recovers from the illness that has
caused him to miss an engagement to dine with Squire Western, All-
worthy "thought (as was usual with him on all Occasions, both the
highest and the lowest) of fulfilling his Engagement" (6, 3, 279). Even
when he turns Tom out of Paradise Hall, Allworthy waits until after
dinner: "The poor young man attended at dinner, as usual" (6, 11,
309–10). Throughout the novel, disputes are settled at the table, whether
on the evening of the Battle of Blifil (where it works once but not twice)
or after the Battle at Upton. The difference between life at home and life
on the road is discernible largely through the preparation, serving, and
eating of meals, which happens irregularly and haphazardly. Tom's ex-
treme hunger when he and Mrs. Waters finally sit down together alone
to eat illustrates the disorder in his life now that he has been cast out by
his uncle and gone in search of Sophia.

Eating marks the progress of the narrative because it evokes emotional
states and real settings. Different milieus are instantly manifest through
culinary references; who eats what and when evokes more than the food
present or absent on the table, whether it is Black George who poaches

to get food for his family or Squire Western at the other extreme, who likewise divides his time between hunting and eating. Black George's survival and that of his family depend on his poaching, just as the needs of Enderson's family make him into a highwayman; these are existential questions in the truest sense, and in both cases, what we remember best is the generosity of Jones in helping to feed the families of Black George and Enderson, even at the risk of starving himself. Again we are shown that the appetites of Tom Jones, though healthy, are subordinated to more important things. The wedding dinner of Tom and Sophia at the end of the novel "celebrates the power of Beauty and Virtue," as Battestin says; but it also displays the combination of physical and spiritual attributes that make up the novel's subject, human nature.

I have situated Fielding's use of ambiguous taste between that of Molière and Byron. It resembles Molière's because the neoclassical literary order is retained: the culinary references in *Tom Jones,* like the other examples of indecorum, take place in a novel, not in an epic poem or a tragedy. Although Fielding stresses that his is "a new Province of Writing" (2, 1, 77) and speaks of his "Prosai-comi-epic Writing" (5,1, 209), he nevertheless writes a comic work. That this is a comic genre in no way diminishes its seriousness, however, as Fielding says when he quotes from Horace's *Satires:* "Surely a Man may speak Truth with a smiling Countenance" (11, 1, 569). Molière questions the separation of subjects and styles to an extent, as I have shown, but he does so softly and indirectly. Fielding's questioning is more explicit—as for example in 11, 1—but his statements about genre, which are meant to educate the reader, occur mostly in the opening theoretical chapters. They are separate from the narrative proper and are otherwise hidden behind his teasing tone. The prefatory chapters make us read the rest of each book with a different eye, but they are separated from it. Nevertheless, the poetological commentary of the opening chapters anticipates those essayistic passages in Proust or Thomas Mann that are a mark of their modernity. Fielding's ambiguity of taste differs from that of the Romantics or from the culinary passages in Proust and Mann, yet his education of the reader, like Molière's education of his audience, calls received assumptions into question. Molière and Fielding uphold an order in aesthetics and in society, but their comedy questions that order and heralds the poetic revolution of Romanticism. Ambiguous taste in *Tom Jones* reproduces the "Augustan order" of which critics speak, but it also contains a spark of poetic revolution. Culinary allusions in *Tom Jones,* like those in *Les Femmes savantes,* offer a model for ambiguous taste in the works of Byron, Heine, Goethe, and Hugo.

CHAPTER 3

Byron's *Don Juan,* or Four and Twenty Blackbirds in a Pie

I thought [*Don Juan*] would *not* [succeed] because it's real qualities are not on the *surface*—but still if people will drive a little—I think it will reward them for their trouble.
—Byron to Kinnaird, 4 November 1821

Taste as the Sign of Change

Barring works like *Madame Bovary* and *Les Fleurs du mal,* whose perceived improprieties led to court battles, there is hardly a work more notorious than *Don Juan* for the moral indignation it aroused, always in the name of offended taste. But times change, and the swelling admiration for *Don Juan* over the past decades derives as much from changes in the decorum of society (and consequently of scholarship) as from an increased appreciation of the poem's qualities. Though some passages continue to elicit disapproval, few readers would sympathize with Paul West's censure of Byron as a "raper of decorum" in *Don Juan,* where West's phrase itself, in uncanny correspondence to some of Southey's, acknowledges and then misconstrues one of the most important and innovative characteristics of the poem—the rejection of a neoclassical aesthetic.[1] West's image contains an echo of the passage that has most tenaciously offended readers, the comments on rapes and "continence" at the siege of Ismail in canto 8. What is remarkable in the present context is that the battle over the indecorum of this passage is still fought with the vocabulary of taste: Rutherford criticizes Byron for his "frivolous bad taste" that "cannot be justified," for example,[2] while Cooke counters

55

that "Byron is not indulging a lubricious taste, but an indignant distaste for certain anomalies in human conduct."[3]

Such use of the vocabulary of taste—although it differs from one critic to the other, despite the shared figurative usage—offers a good introduction to the function and meanings of the word in *Don Juan*. Both Rutherford and Cooke have a clear notion of what they mean when they speak of taste, as does Ridenour when he remarks that in *Don Juan* Byron is rarely guilty of bad taste.[4] But their assurance obscures for them Byron's own usage and the fact that taste works as a model both for uncertainty and for the permanence of change. It is as if they had forgotten that a major impetus for the poem and one of its most important themes is Byron's rejection of the current taste in poetry and that the impetus is linguistic as well as thematic, since the word *taste* plays a prominent role in the theories of Wordsworth and Coleridge.[5] And finally, the word is a focus for the criticism of Byron's "freedoms" in *Don Juan,* which he both anticipates and answers in the poem. A pertinent example is the seemingly innocent reference to taste in the offending passage about rape, where its position as a rhyming word is meant to catch our attention: "Some odd mistakes, too, happened in the dark, / Which showed a want of lanterns, or of taste" (DJ/O 8.130).

It is only logical that so self-reflexive and punning a poet as Byron would find a source of inspiration in a word that holds so many changeable and loaded meanings. Taste incorporates the quality of mobility that the poet applies to Lady Adeline, himself, and to his poem in the fragmentary last canto, where he says that he is "Changeable too—yet somehow '*Idem semper*'" (17.11). Mark Storey rightly comments that Byron wants to have it both ways, that "although taste can form part of his essential vocabulary, he is not persuaded by the terms of taste that are, in fact, little more than convenience and convention."[6] Byron knows what he is about, and he expects his readers to be alert to his self-consciousness as well. That is a good part of what he means when he says, in the letter from which the motto for this chapter is taken, that the poem's real qualities are "not on the surface." His manipulation of literal and figurative taste exemplifies perhaps better than any other theme or wordplay in the poem the need to "drive a little" in order to achieve a reward.[7]

The taste to which Rutherford and Cooke refer is not the same taste as that of Byron's time; but the fact that taste remains a criterion for judging a work, even as the meaning of taste changes, is something Byron observes in the past and projects into the future. Byron uses ambiguous taste to show what Heine puts more generally in speaking of Goethe in *Die Nordsee. Dritte Abteilung:* that criticism—except when it has the artistic quality of Schlegel's—is changeable and transient. Unlike literature, criticism is dependent entirely on the opinions (or taste) of the time in which it was written: "Die Werke des Geistes sind ewig feststehend, aber die Kritik ist etwas Wandelbares, sie geht hervor aus den Ansichten der Zeit, hat nur für diese ihre Bedeutung, und wenn sie nicht selbst kunstwertlicher Art ist, wie z.B. die Schlegelsche, so geht sie mit ihrer Zeit zu Grabe" [Works of the imagination are fixed forever, but criticism is something transient, it grows out of the ideas of its time and only has meaning for that time; if it does not possess artistic merit, like Schlegel's, for example, then it does not outlive its time] (DHA 6:148).[8] For Byron taste becomes a synonym for posterity as well as decorum; the changing and admiring tastes of later generations redeem the errors of an earlier audience, whose rejection often was grounded on taste in the sense of decorum. Byron introduces the connection as early as the "Dedication" in connection with Milton; he carries it through to the end of the poem, where it is recapitulated in canto 17 in the witty couplet "What *was* a paradox becomes a truth or / A something like it—as bear witness Luther!" (17.6) and more extensively a few stanzas further:

> Pythagoras, Locke, Socrates—but pages
>   Might be filled up, as vainly as before,
> With the sad usage of all sorts of sages,
>   Who in his life-time, each, was deemed a Bore!
> The loftiest minds outrun their tardy ages:
>   This they must bear with and, perhaps, much more;
> The wise man's sure when he no more can share it, he
> Will have a firm Post Obit on posterity.
>
> (17.9)

For poets it is not a simple matter of redemption by posterity, hence of a "progress" in matters of taste; it can also happen that an author is out of favor, as Byron reminds us repeatedly in speaking of Pope.

Were there such a thing for poetry, taste would be the "point *d'appui*" for the whole poem. As it is, I reserve the hypothetical quality of the Archimedean "point *d'appui*" in 14. 84, aware that it would be as deadly to explain away everything in a poem as it would be to move the world:

> Shut up the world at large, let Bedlam out;
>   And you will be perhaps surprised to find
> All things pursue exactly the same route,
>   As now with those of *soi-disant* sound mind.
> This I could prove beyond a single doubt,
>   Were there a jot of sense among mankind;
> But till that point *d'appui* is found, alas!
>   Like Archimedes, I leave earth as 'twas.
>
>   (14.84)

What Byron wants to "prove" in the lines that lead up to the "point *d'appui*," and what he suggests, is that oppositions are not as opposed as they seem. His prize example is the similarity between people in Bedlam and those "of *soi-disant* sound mind," who are present within the same stanza and who demonstrate that institutional separations are ineffectual. But similarities do not resolve conflict; the image suggests that the chaos of Bedlam is more the rule than the supposed order of sound minds. In the case of taste, the idea is particularly striking because the opposition is visible not in the word, but only through its context. Besides revealing unsuspected similarities, the different meanings of taste suggest the "ordered chaos" of Friedrich Schlegel, which is essential to revolutions in thought and art. There is a variation here on Byron's playful paradox "I doubt if doubt itself be doubting," which is meant to echo the motto of Montaigne, "Que sçais-je?," that he has quoted in 9. 17.

The way literal taste includes figurative taste and combines with it to criticize systems is effectively expressed in the striking example from canto 14, where "One system eats another up, and this / Much as old Saturn ate his progeny" (14.1).[9] "System" here illustrates the fluctuating taste of past, present, and future readers, especially once Byron elaborates to "reverse" his first example with a reference to digestion, the "antipode" to eating:

> But System doth reverse the Titan's breakfast,
>   And eats her parents, albeit the digestion
> Is difficult.
>
>   (14.2)

Ambiguous taste exemplifies what Cooke calls Byron's "imagery of contradiction," because the contradictions already present in the literal sense (eating brings about digestion or indigestion) are multiplied by the incompatibility of the word's literal and figurative meanings. Byron works with taste much as he works with the ottava rima stanza, the fixedness of which sets off his liberties better, as he himself remarks, than would the lack of rhyme and the proselike rhythm of blank verse, or even prose itself. Ambiguous taste is not merely one of what Ridenour calls the poem's "organizing themes"; it embraces the others. Everything touched on in the poem can be related to taste, not merely the inconsistencies of the human condition, but also the "epic" subjects of glory, war, and love as well as questions of freedom, religion, truth, and poetry.

That literal taste is significant is most obvious structurally, in the way it frames the poem.[10] The opening octave of the suppressed "Dedication" contains the punning line about "four and twenty blackbirds in a pie," and the penultimate octave of the fragmentary seventeenth canto opens with the lines:

> I leave the thing a problem, like all things:—
> > The morning came—and breakfast, tea and toast,
> Of which most men partake, but no one sings.
>
> > > > (18.13)

Both references make clear the connection of food to poetry and therefore of literal to figurative taste. Taste in its literal sense is further associated with physical love: despite the Don Juan theme, there are more direct references to food in the poem than there are to erotic love, though the connection between the two is regularly made explicit. One example is the significant—and significantly irreverent—association in canto 2 of Venus with vermicelli:

> While Venus fills the heart (without heart really
> > Love, though good always, is not quite so good)
> Ceres presents a plate of vermicelli,—
> > (For love must be sustained like flesh and blood),—
> While Bacchus pours out wine or hands a jelly:
> > Eggs, oysters too, are amatory food,

> But who is their purveyor from above
> Heaven knows,—it may be Neptune, Pan, or Jove.
>
> (2.170)

A reference to oysters as "amatory food" probably contains a punning adversion to the myth of Venus's birth (in 12.51 the poet refers to "Cytherea's shell"), where art predictably becomes the *tertium comparationes:* if oysters are meant to make us think of Venus in poetry and Botticelli in painting, then food has at least as much of an association with art as it does with love. At the very end of the poem, we again find an explicit connection between food and art, this time through what in McGann's edition is identified as a reference to Terence:

> A slight repast makes people love much more,
>   Bacchus and Ceres being, as we know,
> Even from our grammar upwards, friends of yore
>   With vivifying Venus, who doth owe
> To these the invention of champagne and truffles:
> Temperance delights her, but long fasting ruffles.
>
> (16.86)

Nowhere is the connection of the stomach and love more effectively made than when Juan retches while declaring his love for Julia: "He felt that chilling heaviness of heart, / Or rather stomach" (2.21). This passage, with its mocking imitation of the waves, displays the simultaneity of opposites even more vividly than the parallel passage on Shooter's Hill, when Juan is held up by a highwayman, because the clash comes after a certain point rather than continuously. Food and love are further related to figurative taste through their shared transience; the lines about love in canto 14 that are extended to "nature's whole analogies" apply equally well to figurative taste:

> Love bears within its breast the very germ
> Of change; and how should this be otherwise?
> That violent things more quickly find a term
> Is shown through nature's whole analogies;
> And how should the most fierce of all be firm?
> Would you have endless lightning in the skies?
>
> (14.94)

60

My aim is not to slight the thematic significance of food in the poem, but to put it into perspective and to show how the thematic association yields its original status to a more important function. Byron's references to food always occur in the midst of or close to self-reflexive references about the nature of poetry and "tastes" in poetry that are as changeable as all human behavior. In a poem noted for its self-consciousness, the references to food are among the most self-conscious, and by the end of the poem it is nearly by reflex that we can make the connection between a "problem" and the practice of eating breakfast every day (but omitting the activity from poetry). Byron rarely uses food as an image for the creative process, unlike Proust when he describes the cooking of Françoise. Occasionally Byron uses a culinary metaphor for his poem, as when he refers both to the *satura lanx* topos—the correct etymology of satire—and to his poem, saying that "The whole together is what I could wish / To serve in this conundrum of a dish" (15.21). For the most part, however, the culinary references demonstrate rather than describe his poetic manner; they are meant to set his poetry apart from that of his precursors and contemporaries. One striking example is the stanza from canto 16 in which he uses gustatory metaphors to describe his daring treatment of all subjects; the designation here of his poem as "this epic" is meant to clash with his treatment in the same stanza of subjects excluded from any but a mock epic. Equally typical of his irony is the use of the future to evoke the manner that he has practiced for fifteen cantos already ("this Epic will contain"):

> And as she treats all things, and ne'er retreats
>   From any thing, this Epic will contain
> A wilderness of the most rare conceits,
>   Which you might elsewhere hope to find in vain.
>
> (16.3)

His irony is likewise apparent when he acknowledges in passing ("'Tis true") that he combines "some bitters with the sweets" but justifies himself by saying that he has "mixed" them "so slightly that you can't complain." By this stage of the poem we know that such "unepic" subjects are the rule rather than the exception:

> 'Tis true there be some bitters with the sweets,
>   Yet mixed so slightly that you can't complain,

But wonder they so few are, since my tale is
"De rebus cunctis et quibûsdam aliis."

(16.3)

One final example of the connection between cooking and poetry will suffice for the time being, the aside in canto 2 about the soup that Zoë and Haidée make for Juan:

They made a most superior mess of broth,
    A thing which poesy but seldom mentions,
But the best dish that e'er was cooked since Homer's
Achilles order'd dinner for new comers.

(2.123)

Like the octave from canto 16, which ends with a quotation from Horace, the allusion to Homer shows Byron's awareness of what he is doing and of what others have done, and it shows his direct and irreverent rapport with his audience.

Both the judgment of the public ("mixed so slightly *that you can't complain*"; my emphasis) and the prescriptions of literary decorum (food as "a thing which poesy but seldom mentions") are variations of figurative taste. In each case, taste represents an inhibited freedom. But the poet asserts the liberty he claims to lack when he calls breakfast something of which "no one sings," much as he "reverses" the image of Saturn eating his children. Furthermore, he ridicules the tastes that impinge on his freedom by citing Homer in the second example. Taste ordinarily represents restrictions, but in *Don Juan* it comes to represent the freedom that is the poem's raison d'être: freedom of form, political and religious freedom, freedom from "cant" (which in the Bowles controversy is explicitly equated with "verbal decorum"), freedom from the taste of a reading public and from the neoclassical laws of taste. The enharmonic technique—the connection of incompatible figurative and literal meanings in the word *taste*—suits Byron because of its playfulness, which as always is deceptive, for to "jest in earnest is the object of Don Juanism," as Boyd astutely comments.[11] By using the literal meaning of taste to undermine what the figurative stands for, Byron can retain both meanings at once. His use of the culinary emblematizes a flippancy that is apparent but not actual—the need to go beyond the surface of things that he speaks of in his letter to Kinnaird. In its double sense, taste exposes the

62

problems of deception as vividly as Shakespeare's twins in *Twelfth Night* or the gods with human forms in Molière's *Amphitryon*. The deluded attempt to deny incongruities, manifest in literature by the separation of subjects and styles, is an example of such deception.

Byron's "Transfiguration of the Commonplace"

If they associate Byron with gustatory matters, most readers probably think first of his famous quip to Lady Melbourne about his future wife, Annabella:

> I only wish she did not swallow so much supper, chicken wings— sweetbreads,—custards—peaches & *Port* wine—a woman should never be seen eating or drinking, unless it be *lobster sallad & Champagne,* the only truly feminine & becoming viands.—I recollect imploring one Lady not to eat more than a fowl at a sitting without effect, & have never yet made a single proselyte to Pythagoras. (BLJ 2:208)

To some readers it will seem impossible for Byron to have granted poetic significance to a subject that, if we judge from his correspondence, does not inspire much interest or thought, even though it occasionally prompts amusingly exaggerated images like those about the eating habits of Annabella. He says of Lady Caroline that "certainly truth is an Artichoke to her" (BLJ 2: 233), and just after Annabella had rejected his first proposal of marriage, he wrote to Lady Melbourne that "I congratulate A[nnabella] and myself on our mutual escape.—That would have been but a *cold collation,* and I prefer hot suppers" (BLJ 2:246). In another letter to Lady Melbourne, written in between the break with Caroline Lamb and the proposal to Annabella Milbanke, he says of his skills at "wooing" that "I am sadly out of practice lately, except for a few sighs to a Gentlewoman at supper who was too much occupied with ye. *fourth* wing of her *second* chicken to mind anything that was not material" (BLJ 2:219). These are the remarks one would expect from a man who adopted regimens of various kinds throughout his life, including a diet of boiled potatoes and vinegar. His eating habits were strange enough to prompt one student of medicine to diagnose him as an anorexic, though bulimia would seem more probable, given the bouts of eating and purging of which he speaks openly in his letters.[12]

A comparison between the culinary references in *Don Juan* and those in the letters (and those in works written before *Don Juan*) brings into focus Byron's aesthetic manipulation of taste. M. K. Joseph speculates that "Byron is perhaps unusually sensitive to [the subject] because of his own abstemious habits" and interprets the references to eating and digestion in *Don Juan* as "a stock illustration of man's material condition."[13] Surely it is noteworthy that the poem contains more references to food than the letters, but frequency is only one factor. There is also a literary quality to the gustatory references in Byron's letters that suggests a connection to *Don Juan*. In the injunction that women eat only "lobster sallad & Champagne," for instance, the same mixed feelings and mocking spirit prevail as in *Don Juan,* and the portrait of women eating fowl is too frequent and stylized to reflect experience alone. Both in the letters and the poem Byron associates eating with eros to achieve a comic effect; and because the effect is reminiscent of Fielding, one can consider it literary. Another common trait between the letters and the poem is the association of victuals and wordplay. In one letter Byron says that "If I was born, as the nurses say, 'with a silver spoon in my mouth', it has stuck in my throat, and spoiled my palate, so that nothing put into it is swallowed with much relish;—unless it be cayenne" (BLJ 4:153). His pun on the word *relish* is a warning not to take the passage literally: Byron refers here more generally to sensual experience and to the danger of ennui, and cayenne—like women eating fowl—works as an image. Even when he speaks of his regimens or of binging and purging, his tone is ironic rather than factual, for example when he says to Lady Melbourne in the letter of 12 January 1814: "alternate extremes have utterly destroyed—oh! unsentimental word!—my *stomach*—and as Lady Oxford used *seriously* to say a *broken heart* means nothing but a *bad digestion*" (BLJ 4:26). What distinguishes the culinary allusions in Byron's letters from those in *Don Juan* follows logically from the difference of genre: the poetological dimension of culinary references in the poem—the self-reflexive aesthetic function that Byron affixes to ambiguous taste—is necessarily absent from the letters.

Byron's indifference in his letters to the subject of food provides an inversion of the argument that Barthes makes in *Mythologies,* the argument that in accomplishing ordinary tasks an author does not strike us as ordinary, but as more miraculous. Byron the man avoids the ordinary, whereas Byron the poet does not. The distinction in *Mythologies* between daily existence and writing is related to the one I am drawing here, to be sure. But Barthes comes to the opposite conclusion: that art excludes the ordinary. Even though Barthes is right about the incongruity between banal habits and artistic genius, one can counter that such incongruity had itself become integral to art long before Barthes began writing. Banality has not become less banal, but it has become a literary subject. As Peter Graham says of *Don Juan,* one of the poem's "distinctive excellences is its ability to make thematic use of the most prosaic-seeming particulars."[14]

All of Barthes's illustrations emphasize the purification of writing from living, of spirit from body, not the ability to transfigure the physical by making it into poetry: "Pourvoir publiquement l'écrivain d'un corps bien charnel, révéler qu'il aime le blanc sec et le bifteck bleu, c'est me rendre encore plus miraculeux, d'essence plus divine, les produits de son art."[15] Barthes reiterates one myth—the neoclassical myth that separates body and spirit—even as he exposes another, the fascination with an author's habits, eating principal among them. In the process he shows his allegiance to the hierarchies and vocabulary of neoclassicism, much like Victor Hugo before him. He speaks for instance of "[l]'alliance spectaculaire de tant de *noblesse* et de tant de futilité" [the spectacular alliance of so much nobility and so much futility] or of "sa *noble* parole" [his *noble* speech; my emphasis], or he compares the writer to Louis XIV, whose "nobility" is manifest even when he is seated on the chamber pot: "on est écrivain comme Louis XIV était roi, même sur la chaise percée" [one is a writer as Louis XIV was a king, even on the commode]. Equally telling is Barthes's use of a gustatory image to describe writing: "l'ambrosie est [...] une substance miraculeuse, éternelle, qui condescend à la forme sociale pour se faire mieux saisir dans sa prestigieuse différence" [ambrosia is (...) a miraculous, eternal substance, which condescends to take a social form so that its prestigious difference is better grasped]. Ambrosia represents art and mystery in the equation, while bread is a lowly physical object without "prestige." Yet in dividing the two so clearly Barthes avoids altogether the problem of simultaneous opposites (in Hugo's terms the mixture of grotesque and sublime) that characterizes the liberation from neoclassical divisions. Such examples ignore the "transfiguration of the commonplace" that Arthur Danto rightly considers essential to modern art.[16] How does Barthes deal, one wonders, with Proust's connection between the hues of asparagus and their scent in the narrator's chamber pot? Or with the comparison in Flaubert's correspondence—which graphically illustrates a major tenet of his aesthetic—of life to a bowl of soup that has hair floating in it: "Quelle mauvaise chose que la vie, n'est-ce pas? C'est un potage sur lequel il y a beaucoup de cheveux, et qu'il faut manger pourtant."[17]

Nowhere does Byron more explicitly challenge the traditional division upheld by Barthes than in *Don Juan*. Byron's poem effects a liberation from the limitations of literary propriety and public opinion, from the "tastes" that, in the figurative sense, restrict creativity. It is the restrictive sort of taste that he has in mind when he says in a letter to Murray of 1 August 1819 that "I never will flatter the Million's canting in any shape— circumstances may or may not have placed me at times in a place to lead the public opinion—but the public opinion—never led or ever shall lead me" (BLJ 6:192) or again, in a letter to Murray of 22 July 1821, that "I have carefully consulted anything but the *taste* of the day" (8:156). Byron does not condemn figurative taste in and of itself; as in all things, he is careful to distinguish. His exasperated "I wish you all better taste" in a letter to Hobhouse of the same period (20 August 1819, 6:212) shows how important taste is to him, as does the similar complaint to Hoppner a few months later, on 29 October 1819: "of course I am in a damned passion at the bad taste of the times—and swear that there is nothing like posterity" (6:237), where he connects taste and posterity just as he does in *Don Juan*. What he disparages is a critical posture that misjudges works of poetry in the name of a taste that changes definition to suit the purpose and prejudice of the speaker. In this he resembles Goethe and Hugo.

There are many references in the letters of the *Don Juan* period to what Byron considers *bad* taste—the poetry of Southey or the "Lakers," for example (6:31 to Murray) and, since he considers the works of Pope to be the "touchstone of taste," the failure to appreciate Pope's writings (8:200). One thinks, too, of his letter to Shelley of 20 May 1822: "As long as I wrote the exaggerated nonsense which has corrupted the public taste—they applauded to the very echo" or "no man has contributed more than me in my earlier compositions to produce that exaggerated & false taste" (9:161). There is also the comment from the "Detached Thoughts" of 1821–22: "One of my notions different from those of my contemporaries, is that the present is not a high age of English Poetry— there are *more* poets (soi-disant) than ever there were and proportionally *less* poetry" (9:35). Such references to taste confirm something that may seem obvious but that deserves to be emphasized: the fact that taste is always associated with past and present poetry. The equation of taste with a style of poetry for which he holds himself partly responsible and for which *Don Juan* is to be the antidote is so obvious, in fact, that it is easy to overlook Byron's artful manipulation of the word taste itself. The failure to understand taste as anything but a synonym for contemporary poetry or the laws of neoclassical decorum confirms one of the poem's main paradoxes: the fact that prejudices and habits may blind us to the obvious.

Byron perceives the laws engendered by and upheld in the name of taste to bear the same relation to poetry that "cant" bears to morality and religion. He rejects the institutionalization or systematization of taste, its thoughtless misapplication, and condemns the gap between the letter and the spirit of the law, between literalism and interpretative understanding. The distinction is an essential one and exemplifies Byron's complicated relationship to tradition, the combination of adopting and rejecting that is related but not identical to the "anxiety of influence" in Harold Bloom's famous formulation (Byron being conspicuously absent from Bloom's monograph, though surely he is a "strong" poet). Byron is less anxious, because he allows the influence to come from a tradition that has gotten far enough removed from its source to be alienated and unrecognizable in a modern setting. As we see from the example of taste, Byron is less hostile to the existence of tradition than to its misuse. He frequently invokes great poets by way of legitimization, Homer or Juvenal or Milton or Dante, whose names are therefore never far from his culinary allusions; but even the greatest similarities have a different effect on a contemporary audience, as he knows and as Schiller theorizes in "Über naive und sentimentalische Dichtung." He uses the example of other poets to defend his poem against the charge of impropriety; he speaks of Ariosto, Voltaire, and Chaucer in one letter; La Fontaine and Shakespeare in another; and of Smollett and Fielding in yet another. But the comparison is willfully false; Byron knows that fame has obscured the indecorum of these authors, and that they limit their indecorum to certain styles rather than mixing genres and subjects the way he does. Even Shakespeare only lets his nobles speak nobly, at least in tragedies: Sir Toby Belch belches only in comedy.

Byron's awareness of models is not slavish but conscious, and his echoes of past and contemporary poets demand to be recognized, not obscured, along with the wealth of references to history and politics. It is because Byron acknowledges rather than hides his predecessors that recognition is both a singular source of irony and one of the greatest difficulties the poem presents. Southey's response to the poem offers an excellent example of the irony and inadequacy of reading *Don Juan* as mere imitation:

> [*Don Juan*] is of Italian growth,—an adaptation of the manner of Pulci, Berni, and Ariosto in his sportive mood. Frere began it. What he produced was too good in itself and too inoffensive to become popular; for it attacked nothing and nobody; and it had the fault of his Italian models, that the transition from what is serious to what is burlesque was capricious. Lord Byron immediately followed; first with his *Beppo*, which implied the profligacy of the writer, and, lastly, with his *Don Juan*,which is a foul blot on the literature of his country, an act of high treason on English poetry.[18]

In a negative and unintended sense, Southey's comparison points to a source of Byron's innovations—the "attacks" and "offensive" qualities of the poem. If Byron has, in Southey's memorable phrase, committed "an act of high treason on English poetry," then he has successfully fulfilled his aim, for treason is proof of his conscious deviation from tradition. As Shelley says, *Don Juan* "carries with it at once the stamp of originality and a defiance of imitation."[19]

Even critics favorable to Byron equate his awareness of predecessors with imitation, the notable exception besides Shelley being John Gibson Lockhart, alias John Bull, who concentrates on what he calls Byron's "spirit":

> in truth I think the great charm of [*Don Juan's*] style is, that it is not much like the style of any other poem in the world. It is utter humbug to say, that it is borrowed from the style of the Italian weavers of merry *rima ottava;* their merriment is nothing, because they have nothing but their merriment; yours is every thing, because it is delightfully intermingled with and contrasted by all manner of serious things— murder and lust included.[20]

One dramatic instance of Byron's awareness of and independence from what others have done is the passage at the conclusion of the first canto that he lifts, slyly, from Southey. Although the words are quoted directly (as critics have often remarked with amazement), their setting transforms them in a perfect example of the primacy of form and of the indivisibility of form and content:

"Go, little book, from this my solitude!
    I cast thee on the waters, go thy ways!
And if, as I believe, thy vein be good,
    The world will find thee after many days."
When Southey's read, and Wordsworth understood,
    I can't help putting in my claim to praise.
The four first rhymes are Southey's every line;
For God's sake, reader, take them not for mine.

                          (DJ/0, 222)

This passage shows what Jonathan Bate means when he says that "the original is acknowledged and turned to commodity."[21]

The ability to cite a source and make it his own is on the grand scale what Byron does on the small scale with the pun—in *Don Juan* mostly the etymological pun—or what he does by reviving dead metaphors. Goethe, in his introduction to the octaves he translated from *Don Juan*, refers to the plays on words as an essential characteristic of the poem and a major hindrance to its translation. By reflecting Byron's manner and themes, the pun helps gives the poem its structure, illustrating the claim that "great things spring from little" (14.100).[22] Byron unequivocally expresses the connection between poetry and wordplay in one of his impassioned letters to Murray when he writes "you shan't make *Canticles* of my Cantos" (BLJ 6:105). The injunction to Murray, aside from revealing something about Byron's public and his publisher, says a good deal about his poetic style as well; the play on words, which contains the word cant as well as the common root of singing, allows him to show the distance between the freedom of his cantos and the dogmatism of religion (or of any institution).[23] In a letter to Kinnaird of 26 October 1819, Byron adds a scurrilous dimension to the same play on words: "I had such projects for the Don—but the *Cant* is so much stronger than *Cunt*—now a days,—that the benefit of experience in a man who had well weighted the worth of both monosyllables—must be lost to despairing posterity" (BLJ 6:232). *Don Juan* is permeated by the awareness of a past estranged in the present through etymology and in a larger sense by the estrangement that comes from imitating a transformed poetic tradition; wordplay thus becomes emblematic of impermanence, uncertainty, and, paradoxically, of poetry's ability to overcome intransience through posterity.[24]

Taste as the "point *d'appui*" of *Don Juan*

In concentrating on Byron's gustatory references in *Don Juan,* it is not my aim to try and change our understanding of the poem, but, as Ridenour says of his interpretation, to "make sure we understand something of what we already know" and to give more proof that, as Joseph says, "In the end, nothing is irrevelant."[25] My aim is to show that the theme of ambiguous taste cannot be divorced from our understanding of the poem. Few would deny the role of figurative taste in the poem. A glance at the concordance must convince even a skeptic that the word taste is frequently mentioned; more important are the explicit and implicit references to taste throughout the poem. As early as the prose preface there is a reference to Wordsworth as "[t]his rustic Gongora and vulgar Marini of his country's taste" (DJ/O, 82). That reference is followed by examples of the taste Byron deplores, a mention of "olla podrida" (DJ/O, 83), and by the topos he likes as much as Molière and Fielding: of how bad poetry is used by pastry cooks or to cover portmanteaus.[26] More than once *portmanteau* is made to rhyme with *canto,* and the practice of pastry cooks offers material evidence for the whims of figurative taste as well as an ironic identification of cooks and poets in the manner of Fielding:

> What, must I go to the oblivious cooks,
> Those Cornish plunderers of Parnassian wrecks?
>
> (4.108)[27]

Such fusions of literal and figurative taste demonstrate how a reference to the culinary contains an allusion to figurative taste, to what is or is not allowed in poetry, and ultimately touches on the essence of poetry. Once alert to the conscious association of figurative and literal taste, one discovers an embarrassing wealth of allusions and associations that reveal much about the poem's structure and complexities. I say embarrassing not because Byron lacks subtlety (as Ridenour, McGann, and others have occasionally charged), but because the failure to acknowledge the function of food or of the pun confirms the attack in *Don Juan* on the human tendency to judge by categories and systems that are inherited rather than rethought, in poetry as well as in religion or politics.[28]

Although the subject of food in *Don Juan* has not gone unnoticed, it has mostly been treated, and treated cursorily, as a sublimated reference to the erotic; as more evidence of Byron's flippancy; or occasionally as his tribute to the satiric tradition. Most readers agree that food plays a note-worthy thematic role in the poem. The remark of M. K. Joseph cited earlier is representative, but to call food and digestion "a recurrent theme in the poem, a stock illustration of man's material condition," though true, does not go far enough.[29] Alvin Kernan notes how the allusions to food reflect the "endless shifts of perspective on more complicated mat-ters such as women, love, glory, society, or pleasure," but he does not speak of how food can reflect those "more complicated matters" them-selves as well as the poet's changing perspective of them.[30] In his "Memo-rials of Gormandising," Thackeray links his contempt for Byron's poem with what he considers an inappropriate and unjustified excess of gastro-nomic details: "Ah, what a poet Byron would have been had he taken his meals properly, and allowed himself to grow fat—if nature intended him to grow fat—and not have physicked his intellect with wretched opium pills and acrid vinegar, that sent his principle to sleep, and turned his feelings sour! If that man had respected his dinner, he never would have written *Don Juan*."[31] Thackeray's own piece is written in the satiric style that permits references to food and is meant to contrast with Byron; but his culinary examples are so close to Byron's that they show how attentive he was to the culinary details in *Don Juan*.

There are times when the confusion of cookery (Byron's word) and poesy (the word Byron uses, like Heine, for the Schlegelian transcendence or fusion of genres) may rightly be perceived as flippant, and when flip-pancy itself is the desired effect. There is no need to look for anything more than a casual witticism in Byron's connection of *Don Juan* and "The Art of Cookery" by Mrs. Rundell in one of his letters to Murray, for example, partly because of the epistolary context:

> Along thy sprucest bookshelves shine
> The works thou deemest most divine—
> The "Art of Cookery" and Mine
> My Murray.—

> (BLJ 6:29)

In *Don Juan,* however, the danger exists that we will consider seriously whatever suits our own understanding of the poem and discard as flippant whatever does not. My contention that the references to food in *Don Juan* cannot be summarily dismissed as flippant is based on several factors: (1) the importance in the poem of poetic taste; (2) the creative exploitation of punning in *Don Juan;* (3) the fact that the context of Byron's culinary allusions is always self-reflexive and nearly always touches on the nature of poetry and of poetic creation; and (4) the predictability, hence the danger, of assuming that references to the culinary are invariably frivolous. The famous final couplet of an octave in canto 15 that harkens back to Dryden—

> But if a writer should be quite consistent,
> How could he possibly show things existent?—

is only the summary of Byron's hints about reading the poem that come just before:

> Also observe, that like the great Lord Coke,
>   (See Littleton) whene'er I have expressed
> Opinions two, which at first sight may look
>   Twin opposites, the second is the best.
> Perhaps I have a third too in a nook,
>   Or none at all—which seems a sorry jest.
>
> (15.87)

Given Byron's sense of sounds and the centrality of ambiguous taste in canto 15, it is significant that Lord Coke's name—as the rhyme informs us—must be pronounced "cook."

Taste and Truth: The Dedication, Motto, and Title of *Don Juan*

In the dedication, where Byron introduces the relationship of poetry to creativity, tyranny, and freedom, he does so through ambiguous taste. Even the theme of the Fall, which Ridenour chooses as the focus for his interpretation, receives its initial statement through ambiguous taste. Southey's flight and fall (or rather his inability to fly and the fact that he

has fallen before he even tries to fly, in part because he and his wings
have been baked) are expressed through the image of blackbirds in a pie:

> BOB SOUTHEY! You're a poet—poet Laureate,
>   And representative of all the race;
> Although 'tis true that you turned out a Tory at
>   Last,—yours has lately been a common case:—
> And now, my epic renegade! what are ye at,
>   With all the Lakers in and out of place?
> A nest of tuneful persons, to my eye
> Like "four and twenty blackbirds in a pie;
>
> "Which pie being open'd, they began to sing"—
>   (This old song and new simile holds good)
> "A dainty dish to set before the King,"
>   Or Regent, who admires such kind of food.
>
>   (Dedication, 1–2)

In most editions what McGann calls the "unauthorized" spelling of *pie*
as *Pye* makes explicit the reference to Southey's predecessor as poet laure-
ate; the pun is important as a pun, and the blackbird is the first and most
trivial in a series of winged creatures associated with creativity throughout
the dedication: Coleridge is "a hawk encumbered with his hood" (2);
Southey is "like the flying fish / Gasping on deck" (3), in imitation of
the equally grotesque and impotent baked blackbird; and finally, there is
Pegasus (8).[32]

Other aspects of the pun on *pie* and *Pye* require attention, but for the
moment it is sufficient to note that food, rather than being associated
with the ordinary, is associated with poetry, and that the first gustatory
image of the poem conveys the idea of things hidden: "which being
opened they began to sing." The poetry with which Pye and the pie are
first associated is condemned (it is in *bad* taste); it is a poetry to which
Byron's own presents the alternative (the "antidote" mentioned earlier),
one from which the trivial is not excluded. Every reference to food refers
to and simultaneously undoes the poetic tradition that excludes common-
place subjects, in this case the epic (as Ridenour rightly emphasizes, the
word "epic" is present already in the first stanza). Though the subject of
food, like many others in the poem, lacks the abstraction required of
neoclassical or metaphysical poetry and is therefore at odds with past and

present tastes, Byron shows that it can be incorporated into his poem. He anticipates here the dramatic exemplification of his theory in canto 10, where a prescription for purging and emetic is put into verse.

Byron demonstrates his independence from the tyranny of poetical and political taste before he introduces "unpoetic" subjects and shows, as Rutherford puts it, his rejection of the "false principle of selection which makes literature falsify life."[33] It is through ambiguous taste that the question of poetic subjects and forms is posed in these opening stanzas: the poet laureate ("my epic renegade") sacrifices poetic and political individuality to an institution, the regent's *taste* having determined what Southey will write; the Lakers have gone too far in the opposite direction by secluding themselves from political reality; Wordsworth, who is Byron's "fall guy," speaks of creating the *taste* by which his readers will learn to appreciate his work; and Coleridge has sacrificed the physical, represented here by literal taste, for the metaphysical. Food further links poetry and politics when the king of the nursery rhyme is replaced by the regent and pie becomes a "dainty dish" and "such kind of food." Willed double meanings revive the dead metaphors.

The problem of what contemporary poetry should or should not be—the problem of the poet's, the critic's, and the public's *taste* in poetry—is underscored by what later reveals itself to be an impertinent allusion to the opening of *Paradise Lost*. Only after the octave on Milton more than half-way through the dedication can one connect the manipulation of taste in the opening pun on pie and Pye to Milton's opening: "Of man's first disobedience, and the fruit / Of that forbidden tree, whose mortal taste / Brought death into the world." The "mortal taste" in Milton's poem is unambiguously literal, but the apple in *Paradise Lost* is disembodied. In Byron's opening, the opposite is true: the culinary images are meant to seem disembodied as dead metaphors, for example in the phrase "such kind of food," but they are brought back to life. There is no similarity between the tone of the two openings, yet the connection between the taste in Milton's opening and Byron's opening pun on *pie* and *Pye* is assured because of Milton's status as the poetic and political hero of the dedication. Byron had already worked with similar associations in *English Bards and Scotch Reviewers* when he paraphrased Horace and remade a line of Milton's to criticize Pye and praise Pope: "Better to err with POPE, than shine with PYE" (line 102).

The metonymic reference to Milton is not parodistic; it is rather an affectionate allusion that proves the legitimacy and originality of Byron's own poem (it should not be forgotten that Shelley considered the Byron of *Don Juan* to be Milton's successor). The opening gustatory image calls Milton's poem to mind, but the taste is more than literal: Byron thinks of Milton as a poet whose poetry and politics did not suit the taste of his contemporaries but who stood firm and has been vindicated by the taste of an admiring posterity:

> If fallen in evil days on evil tongues,
>   Milton appeal'd to the Avenger, Time,
> If Time, the avenger, execrates his wrongs,
>   And makes the word "*Miltonic*" mean "*sublime*,"
> *He* deign'd not to belie his soul in songs,
>   Nor turn his very talent to a crime.
> *He* did not loathe the sire to laud the son,
> But closed the tyrant-hater he begun.
>
> (Dedication, 10)

Byron speaks as much of himself as of Milton, clearly, though less with regard to posterity than in the implication that he does "not loathe the sire to laud the son" and in the connection of canto and cant ("*He* deign'd not to belie his soul in songs"). He associates himself with Milton to distance himself even more from poets like Pye and Southey.[34]

Just as noteworthy as the semantic relation of literal to figurative taste is the pun by which the connection is made, because the pun, as I have said, functions formally and semantically as a microcosm of the poem. Aside from its challenge to the tyranny of neoclassicism, the pun forces a rethinking of meanings just as Byron forces a rethinking of institutions; it frees words from their fixedness and yokes the incongruous, thereby subverting intellectually and poetically. With the pun, Byron maintains similarities he then discards, a process he describes in the final couplet of the octave where the poet calls himself "changeable too, yet somehow *idem semper*":

> So that I almost think that the same skin
> For one without—has two or three within.
>
> (17.11)

Puns offer an example of what Cooke calls Byron's Socratic agnosticism, since the variable meaning of every word reflects his "gospel of uncertainty." Byron further associates the pun with politics, for example in the figure of the "Orator, the latest of the session," whose talents (like Byron's, as many have remarked) include "wit to hatch a pun or tell a story" (13.90–91). Earlier, in a note to his *Hints from Horace,* Byron had likewise connected politics and punning: "With all the vulgar applause and critical abhorrence of *puns,* they [the authors of comedy] have Aristotle on their side; who permits them to orators, and gives them consequences by a grave disquisition" (BPW 1:433). For Byron, punning assumes a breadth of knowledge that he counts on elsewhere, an awareness of historical and literary and even linguistic traditions that require different kinds of thinking simultaneously. He again reverses expected hierarchies by using the "low" form of the pun to make a "high" poetic statement, just as he uses the "high" forms of epic and verse to discuss food or digestion. The pun is therefore paradigmatic of Byron's poetical method and of the political and moral beliefs he displays in *Don Juan;* and taste is the paradigm of the paradigm.

In the opening octave of the dedication, a pun establishes the connection of poetry, taste, and politics. The first word, "Bob," challenges taste in two ways, as an insolent nickname for Robert Southey and in anticipation of Byron's supreme sin against "good taste" two octaves later, where the phrase "dry Bob" is Regency slang for coition without emission.[35] Southey's name is made to stand for the creative, poetical, and political impotence with which the poem deals:

> You, Bob! are rather insolent, you know,
>   At being disappointed in your wish
> To supersede all warblers here below,
>   And be the only Blackbird in the dish;
> And then you overstrain yourself, or so,
>   And tumble downward like the flying fish
> Gasping on deck, because you soar too high, Bob,
> And fall, for lack of moisture, quite adry, Bob!
>
> (Dedication, 3)

Structurally and through its meaning, the pun on "dry Bob" in the third stanza of the dedication is in the same position as the pun on Pye in the first. The references to the submissive and impotent poetry of Southey, and by implication to that of Pye, frame the reference to Coleridge in the second stanza; the word "food" concludes the line preceding the reference to Coleridge ("such kind of food. /And Coleridge, too, has lately taken wing"), and the ironic juxtaposition of the physical with the metaphysical is analogous to the shift from literal to figurative taste.

It is plausible, even likely, that Byron has yet another association in mind here and that he is thinking of Coleridge's contemptuous connection of literal and figurative taste in the essays "On the Principles of Genial Criticism," which first appeared in 1814.[36] In such a self-reflexive setting, especially on the subject of taste, and given the naming of Coleridge and Milton in the dedication, Byron may be thinking of the near-pun on *Milton* and *mutton* in the following passage from Coleridge's essay:

> If a man, upon questioning his own experience, can detect no difference in *kind* between the enjoyment derived from the eating of turtle, and that from the perception of a new truth; if in *his* feelings a taste *for* Milton is essentially the same as the taste *of* mutton, he may still be a sensible and a valuable member of society; but it would be desecration to argue with him about the Fine Arts.

Coleridge also speaks in the essay of a "taste-meter to the fashionable world," a phrase resembling the narrator's comment later in the poem that "we are touching upon taste, / Which now-a-days is the thermometer / By whose degrees all characters are classed" (16.48).

Byron deliberately misrepresents Coleridge's position as a denial of physical concerns, and he makes the word *truth* function in the same way as taste: the "truth" of coarse reality is repeatedly contrasted with philosophical truth. In *Don Juan,* the word *true,* like the word *taste,* provides another example of the poet's "mobility." On the one hand truth, like figurative taste, is the universally acknowledged and desirable truth, the object of philosophy, politics, or aesthetics—"truth, the grand desideratum" (7.81). But truth, like taste, has more than a philosophical meaning; truth also denotes physical details, the "matter" in the puns on Berkeley at the opening of canto 11 or the "true truth" and facts that follow his definition of a lie later in the same canto:

> And after all, what is a lie? 'Tis but
>   The truth in masquerade; and I defy
> Historians, heroes, lawyers, priests to put
>   A fact without some leaven of a lie.

> The very shadow of true Truth would shut
> Up annals, revelations, poesy,
> And prophecy.
>
> (11. 37)

Like the word taste, the word truth is frequently used, sometimes over-used, by Byron's contemporaries. Wordsworth speaks in the preface to *Lyrical Ballads* of truth as the object of poetry, a truth that is directed inward and "not standing upon external testimony, but carried alive into the heart by passion; truth which is its own testimony, which gives competence and confidence to the tribunal to which it appeals, and receives them from the same tribunal." Shelley speaks of a similar and grand truth in the *Defense of Poetry:* "A poem is the very image of life expressed in its eternal truth" and exists "in the mind of the Creator."[37]

Byron uses the vocabulary of his contemporaries to parody their philosophy of poetry and display his own; we are doubtless expected to associate his comments on truth in *Don Juan* with passages like the ones by Wordsworth and Coleridge and perhaps even with the "Ode on a Grecian Urn," which appeared in 1820. Byron speaks in *Don Juan* of "Southey, that incarnate lie" (10.13), and in the long description of Haidée's court poet, who "praised the present and abused the past" (3.79), there is an explicit connection between truth and taste in the variant for the second line: "But now he sung the sultan and the pasha / With truth and taste like Southey and like Crashaw" (DJ/0, 186).[38] It is with both kinds of truth in mind that one comes to read a line like the following, "For too much truth, at first sight, ne'er attracts" (14:13), where what seems to refer to the reaction of Byron's audience can also refer to Byron's thoughts on contemporary poetry. No one meaning is fixed, and Byron even drains the word *truth* of sense altogether in idiomatic phrases like "Truth to say" (1.161) or the phrase "in truth." Even when the phrases lose their tendentious nature, however, Byron has us trained to consider the inconstancy and complexities of meaning.

A passage like the one in the first octave of canto 11 illustrates the connection between truth, taste, poetry, and tradition through a play on the word *matter:*

> When Bishop Berkeley said "there was no matter,"
> And proved it—'twas no matter what he said:
> They say his system 'tis in vain to batter,

> Too subtle for the airiest human head;
>   And yet who can believe it! I would shatter
>   Gladly all matters down to stone or lead
>   Or adamant, to find the World a spirit
>   And wear my head, denying that I wear it.
>
> (11.1)

In the octaves that follow this one, Byron assembles an arsenal of lofty words ("sublime," "ideal," "universal," "truth," "schism," and the "spirit" from the first octave) and mixes them with "doubt," which he apostrophizes as "thou sole prism / Of the Truth's rays":

> What a sublime discovery 'twas to make the
>   Universe universal Egotism!
> That all's ideal—*all ourselves:* I'll stake the
>   World (be it what you will) that *that's* no Schism.
> Oh, Doubt!—if thou be'st Doubt, for which some take thee,
>   But which I doubt extremely—thou sole prism
> Of the Truth's rays, spoil not my draught of spirit!
> Heaven's brandy,—though our brain can hardly bear it.
>
> (11.2)

The mixture induces indigestion ("Heaven's brandy" is strong):

> For ever and anon comes Indigestion,
>   (Not the most "dainty Ariel") and perplexes
>   Our soarings with another sort of question.
>
> (11.3)

The shift from philosophical to bodily questions is not a gratuitous shock; the indigestion here sends us back to the the end of the previous canto and the ironic advice for curing social ills: "Teach them the decencies of good threescore" (10.86). At the end of canto 10, Byron intertwines physiology and truth—and consequently poetry—in preparation for the comments on truth at the beginning of canto 11. His description of London at the end of canto 10 contains the kind of realism he calls truth and contains a self-description of the poem in the elaborate image that begins "Each wreath of smoke / Appeared to him but as the magic vapour / Of some alchymic furnace" (10.83). Byron's comments on

79

philosophy have often been criticized as superficial, but if so it is su-
perficiality of a taxing kind. To sort out all the different associations here
is not easy, especially when they seem to be undone by the "meaningless"
use of the word "truth" a few lines later: "The truth is, I've grown lately
rather phthisical" ("phthisical" being the rhyme first for "metaphysical"
and then for "this I call"). What "hovers" over all references to truth is
the comment from canto 4 that often serves as a summary of Byron's
themes and of his stance in *Don Juan:*

> And the sad truth which hovers o'er my desk
> Turns what was once romantic to burlesque.
>
> (4.3)

Another passage that merges truth with taste and poetry occurs in
canto 8, where a Turk bites and holds onto the foot of a Russian officer
at the siege of Ismail. The scene is narrated with a touch of the burlesque
that Byron mixes with "sad truth" and "romantic" in the lines just
quoted, after which the poet comments:

> But then the fact's a fact—and 'tis the part
>   Of a true poet to escape from fiction
> Whene'er he can; for there is little art
>   In leaving verse more free from the restriction
> Of truth than prose, unless to suit the mart
>   For what is sometimes called poetic diction,
> And that outrageous appetite for lies,
> Which Satan angles with, for souls, like flies.
>
> (8.86)

Byron again turns the principles of his opponents against them and
equates "poetic diction" with hypocrisy. Figurative taste ("the mart") and
literal taste ("appetite for lies") are major considerations for poets who
exclude the subjects of money or food from their works. We think by
contrast of the question "Why call a miser miserable?" or of the apos-
trophic "ambrosial cash" in Byron's own poem. The octave here follows
his graphic account of war's terrors, which are more evidence of his kind
of "truth" and of his acknowledgment and reversal of tradition: Byron
deliberately abides by the letter rather than the spirit of epic law, since
war is a subject that belongs to poetry in the high style. In this way he

can ridicule divisions like "truth" for prose and "fiction" for verse, and he can imitate the absurdity of writing or living by the letter rather than the spirit of the law. He mimics the cant that he condemns, and he also questions the expected and received meanings of the words *truth, art, verse,* and *poetic diction.* In a similar passage from canto 14 he takes up the vocabulary of truth and fiction to describe the paradox of his poetry, which does not hide subjects but whose qualities do not lie on the surface:

> Besides, my Muse by no means deals in fiction:
> She gathers a repertory of facts,
> Of course with some reserve and slight restriction,
> But mostly sings of human things and acts—
> And that's one cause she meets with contradiction;
> For too much truth, at first sight, ne'er attracts.

In the closing couplet of this octave, he says that if he were writing only to please the taste of his audience (for "what's call'd glory"), his poetry would be easier to write:

> And were her object only what's call'd glory,
> With more ease too she'd tell a different story.
>
> (14.13)

What Byron shows by remaking the words *taste* and *truth* is that he can infuse "common things," whether words or themes or representations of a coarse reality, with a distinction unique to him. This power and the significance of punning are heralded by the Horatian motto "Difficile est proprie communia dicere." The dispute over the meaning of *communia* for Horace has a long and notorious history that amused Byron, as he shows in *Hints from Horace* with a lengthy gloss of this line and the two that follow it. Byron himself was not clear what meaning to choose, whether "common things" or "vulgar life" or, in the final version, "a twice-told tale," and we have in his variants an example of the kind of layers of meaning he presents simultaneously in his poem. Some things are clear about his choice of the motto, however: one is the allusive nature of the line, which he associates with Pope and with the neoclassical rigor of Boileau (Pope, in Byron's gloss, is called "a better poet than Boileau"). Another is that *communia* has a series of meanings, a fact of

81

more significance than the meanings themselves. Byron's awareness of double meanings (at least double) in the motto is clear from the variants cited above and when he chides Leigh Hunt for rendering the phrase "as if to avoid saying common things in the common way—'difficile est proprié communia dicere' seems at times to have met with in you a literal translator" (BLJ 4:319–21). The importance of double meaning is further evident in the use of the word *common* in the poem: there is the "common case" in the first stanza of the dedication, or the "not uncommon want" of 1:1, where the narrator "need[s] a hero." There is also the use of the word *commonplace,* which vacillates but always contains a reminder of Bostetter's comment that "Byron's apotheosis of the commonplace is one of his great contributions to the language of poetry."[39] Regardless of how the word is used, its significance lies in its mobility and its Horatian source.

Horace is a good figurehead for the poem, not because his name is synonymous with literary tradition, but because his *Ars poetica* epitomizes the alienating effects of history on meaning. On the grand scale, the alienation is apparent in the way lines from *Ars poetica* have been taken out of context and made into prescriptions that bear no resemblance to the original, for example in the phrase "ut pictura poesis." On a smaller scale, as we have seen, the effect is present in the etymology of a word, taste being the dominant example. Seen in this way, the contradictory and punning layers of meaning in *communia* exemplify Byron's understanding of tradition and his independence from it. As early as the motto there is reason to agree with Auden's remark that he "can think of no other poet in the world whose work demonstrates so clearly the creative role played by form."[40]

Even the title of the poem is connected to the emblematic function of taste, if not directly to its meaning: it is only at the end of the first octave of canto 1 that we become aware of the Anglicized pronunciation of *Juan,* which rhymes, significantly, with "true one" and "new one."[41] Not until well into canto 1 is it apparent that the figure of Don Juan, like Byron's pronunciation, resembles his ancestors in name but not in manner.[42] We need to know the "straight" pronunciation and similarly the tradition on which he plays if we are to understand. Already in the title, motto, dedication, and first canto of the poem we sense an analogous and self-reflexive control. Byron's comment that the poem lacks a "plan" must therefore be understood as a joke or as another paradox that forces the rethinking of received meanings. Graham is right to call these opening parts of the poem "signals" that "alert the reader to what the subjects, themes, and methods of proceeding will be" and that, taken together, make up a kind of "map."[43]

A Culinary "Center of Meaning" in
Don Juan: Goût and the Gout

One gets the best sense of Byron's self-awareness and control in those passages Ridenour calls "centers of meaning," passages of sometimes as little as an octave in which "a number of central issues dealt with throughout the poem are brought together and given a firmer and more authoritative statement than is possible in the more diffuse, discursive mode of the poem as a whole."[44] It is not sufficient to nod in satisfied recognition of such passages and continue reading; these "centers of meaning" prompt an active reevaluation of passages that came before and force us to read backward as well as forward, in accordance with the Sternean advice to the reader from canto 13:

> Oh reader! If that thou canst read,—and know,
>   'Tis not enough to spell, or even to read,
> To constitute a reader; there must go
>   Virtues of which both you and I have need.
> Firstly, begin with the beginning—(though
>   That clause is hard); and secondly, proceed;
> Thirdly, commence not with the end—or, sinning
> In this sort, end at least with the beginning.
>
> (13.73)

Though the injunction to "begin with the beginning" is facetious, coming as it does so far into the poem, it is a lie only as lies are "the truth in masquerade" or in the coy sense that Byron uses in canto 12: "But now I will begin my poem." Given the associative nature of the poem, it is indeed crucial to "end at least with the beginning." In a figurative sense, Byron's "beginning" is accurate, because what comes after the opening alters the understanding of what came before or makes explicit what was only hinted at earlier. The rethinking of a word's usage, as we have seen, is a detail that imitates the rethinking of greater issues throughout the poem—of the grand subjects of love and war, for ex-

83

ample, and of how these subjects are treated in the epic tradition that brings them together. It is not because *Don Juan* is a fragment or because it was written in spurts over a number of years that one must develop a special way of reading the poem; rather it is because *Don Juan* questions, in form and in theme, all institutions. Foremost among these institutions is the traditional poetic hierarchy of genres and the neoclassical demand for a harmony of subject and style. At the risk of reducing the progression of Juan's adventures to an allegorical statement, it is tempting to take seriously Byron's "plan" to have Juan end on the guillotine and to inter- pret it as analogous to what happens stylistically in *Don Juan:* though they are not actually "guillotined" in the poem, the aristocratic genres of lyric poetry and tragedy and the likewise aristocratic division of subjects lose their privileged status.

One center of meaning is the octave on *goût* and gout in canto 15 that brings together the questions raised thus far: the manipulation of accepted meanings as a way of questioning assumptions; the simultaneous recognition and rejection of tradition through a fusion of literal and figurative meanings; the retrospective and associative manner of reading; and the paradox that the obvious can be a veil just as absences can be conspicuous. The octave provides the conclusion for the bill of fare at Norman Abbey in the banquet from canto 15; it refers to the passage that precedes it and, in the manner of what one critic calls "ever widening concentric circles,"[45] illuminates passages in the poem both before and after. The "and" with which the octave opens is larger than it seems to be:

> And fruits, and ice, and all that art refines
>   From nature for the service of the goût,—
> *Taste* or the *gout,*—pronounce it as inclines
>   Your stomach! Ere you dine, the French will do;
> But *after,* there are sometimes certain signs
>   Which prove plain English truer of the two.
> Hast ever *had* the *gout?* I have not had it,
> But I may have, and you too, Reader, dread it.
>
>   (15.72)

What Byron says and shows here should dispel any doubts about the danger of "overinterpreting" the presence and function of ambiguous taste in the poem. Even without studying the context of this octave, some things are immediately apparent. The first is that the wordplay on *goût* and *gout* contains an aesthetic statement. This is evident from the introduction of art and nature in the first two lines of the octave, since art and nature, along with taste, are constants in any discussion of eighteenth-century aesthetics. In *Don Juan*, Byron gives more attention to taste than to art and nature, but the question of art's relationship to nature, particularly as Rousseau conceives of it in his critique of civilization, pervades a passage like the island idyll. Byron manipulates the meaning of art and nature as he does the meaning of taste and truth.[46] Examples of his ironic treatment of art and nature elsewhere in the poem include the description of Juan's uniform at the court of Catherine the Great:

> Suppose him sword by side, and hat in hand,
>   Made up by Youth, Fame, and an Army tailor—
> That great Enchanter, at whose rod's command
>   Beauty springs forth, and Nature's self turns paler,
> Seeing how Art can make her work more grand,
>   (When she don't pin men's limbs in like a jailor).
>
> (9.44)

There is also the ironic commentary on warfare in canto 8, where the narrator observes that "Here War forgot his own destructive Art / In more destroying Nature" (8.82) and takes up the observation a few stanzas later after describing "two villainous Cossacques":

> And whom for this at last must we condemn?
> Their natures? or their sovereigns, who employ
> All arts to teach their subjects to destroy?
>
> (8.92)

In the octave on gout and *goût*, Byron is ironical, but not as one might expect, which is a manifestation of that irony. Although the association of dessert with artistic "refinement" may seem at worst inappropriate and at best silly, the impression deceives; Byron forces us to reconsider the assumption that a connection between food and art is inappropriate. We are invited instead to ask the question: can one justify the exclusion of food and by extension of any commonplace subject from art? In this case it is the word *refined* that shifts: Byron's poem treats of common things without being any less a poem. He rejects and disproves the equation of art with refinement just as he did in the octave on facts, art, and poetic diction. He further demonstrates the absurdity of the equation when he depicts art as subordinated to taste instead of the reverse. Art sacrifices liberty—here synonymous with creativity—when it refines things "for the service of the *goût.*" Any service, in this poem, is suspect, whether aesthetic or political; here it is proven to be nonsensical.

But art in this canto—and consequently in this octave—has more than aesthetic associations. In the English cantos it has come to be a synonym for hypocrisy: the connection between art and refinement sends us back to the opening of canto 15 and the series of images that expose the discrepancy between what lies on the surface and what lies beneath it, in society as in poetry. Nature (or truth) is clearly preferred to art, for example in the following octave:

> But all are better than the sigh supprest,
>   Corroding in the cavern of the heart,
> Making the countenance a masque of rest,
>   And turning human nature to an art.
> Few men dare show their thoughts of worst or best;
>   Dissimulation always sets apart
> A corner for herself; and therefore Fiction
> Is that which passes with least contradiction.
>
> (15.3)

The vocabulary here (fiction, contradiction) is familiar from the previous canto, as is the argument in defense of the poet's muse: since there is no defense for covering things up in society, there is no reason to cover them up in poetry. It is in canto 15 that the final couplet of the first octave rhymes "pooh!" with "true," where "pooh!" is not a commentary on truth but rather an example of the kind of truth that Byron includes in his poem along with prescriptions, flash language, or references to eating and digesting. This is also the canto in which we read one of Byron's most explicit statements about the relation of poetry to truth and the commonplace:

> There's music in all things, if men had ears:
> Their Earth is but an echo of the spheres.
>
> (15.5)

86

And it is the canto in which the second octave contains the image of the ocean as

> That Watery Outline of Eternity
>   Or miniature at least, as is my notion,
> Which ministers unto the soul's delight,
>   In seeing matters which are out of sight,
>
> (15.2)

which is another statement about the power and poetic necessity of details (something "miniature") to convey a sense of hidden and larger things.

From the opening of the octave on gout and *goût*, then, Byron introduces a considered ambiguity and a wealth of seemingly incompatible subjects in order to express the complexities and contradictions that help make up what Michael Cooke calls the "universe of the unpredictable" in the poem. One can appreciate in this octave Jerome McGann's remark that it is difficult to exhaust meanings in the poem because they are "multiple," though I disagree with McGann's hierarchical distinction between multiplicity and complexity.[47] What is valuable about this octave is that it helps reveal how that multiplicity is achieved, in form as well as meaning. The visual impression misleads as deliberately as the meaning: with the exception of the circumflex, there is an indistinguishability between the words *goût* and *gout* that is belied by their sense and by their pronunciation. The fact that the joke depends on the difference between French and English is only a basic, or literal, characteristic; the reader quickly notices that the wordplay represents more than the exploitation of a deceptive similarity on the order of words like *demand* in English and *demander* in French (whereby the kinship between the words—as in the case of taste as well—adds to their interest). The point of such deception in this poem is clear. The same letters, spoken in different languages, denote both the sublime and the ridiculous. What is equally important about this linguistic example is that the sublime and the ridiculous are not separated by the famous Napoleonic step; they are simultaneous, just as the lyric and the satiric are joined throughout the poem, for example in the shipwreck, the island idyll, or the description of Norman Abbey and the people in it. Byron's bilingual pun illustrates that selfsameness can be the frame for opposites; the play on words is emblematic, in a formal and substantive sense, of the poet's reiterated claim that in *Don Juan* he represents contradictions of the human condition, the coincidence of high and low, of tragedy and comedy.[48]

When he translates the word *goût,* Byron shows that the fusion of opposite meanings in one word does not require two different languages. As he has done since the Dedication, he makes the word *taste,* in English, function in the same way as gout and *goût:* the same letters refer either to the stomach or to aesthetics, here to both at once. It is here, for the first time, that Byron is explicit about how literal taste becomes the vehicle by which conservative aesthetic laws are called into question, laws that are likened to a disease. When he writes, "Hast ever had the gout?" Byron leaves off the circumflex, but he retains the French pronunciation through internal rhyme; the word retains both meanings and even both pronunciations through the merger of a visual response combined with the repeated sounds of "truer" and "two" in the preceding line and the reiteration in the last line of the final couplet, "you too." The use of the definite article—*the* gout/*goût*—can be read both as the English idiom for speaking of a disease and as an imitation of French usage. The point is underscored by the internal rhyme and by the rhyming word, "truer," and by the association of bad art with disease.[49] Byron's aesthetic emphasis culminates in the final couplet, as is usual for the ottava rima stanza. His question to the reader, "Hast ever had the gout?" is answered with the warning that "I have not had it, / But I may have, and you too, reader, dread it." No example of ambiguous taste could be more direct: the reader is told to be grateful that he does not write according to the laws of "taste," but that instead he writes about literal taste and of the indecorous things it stands for.[50]

Through the pairs of *goût* and gout and of taste and taste there emerges a conflict between eye, ear, and sense that provides a formal variation on the repeated claim that things of importance lie beneath the surface. Aside from the conflict of eye and ear in Juan's name, there is the pronunciation of Haidée's name, the acute accent of which makes the eye expect a pronunciation later contradicted by rhyme, just as the accentuation of her name, like Juan's, varies with the prosody (the *ai* in Haidée's name is also pronounced differently depending on the context).[51] Throughout the poem, Byron's pronunciation trips us up, sometimes through meaning—as in the rhyme of Juan's name with true and new—sometimes only through sound, as a reminder not to succumb to complacent habits of reading (or of anything else) that keep us from noticing more than the things we expect. The initial expectation is not necessarily wrong; but it is generally too simple. Similarly, there are many examples of the expectation fostered by rhythm and sense that is thwarted when one line seems to require a full stop but the next line completes the meaning, effecting an enharmonic shift in the word that came before. In Juan's search for a person to bring up Leila, for example, what seems to be a "society for vice" becomes instead a "society for vice / Suppression," and the hesitation rather strengthens than weakens the first meaning:

> So when he saw each ancient dame a suitor
>   To make his little wild Asiatic tame,
> Consulting "the Society for Vice
>   Suppression," Lady Pinchbeck was his choice.
>
>   (12.42)

The first meaning is not canceled out by the second, merely modified. Another example is the passage on Shooter's Hill, where Juan's raptures about England, grand sounding because of the anaphoric (and affected) series launched by the word "here," is interrupted by a holdup just when he says that "none lay / Traps for the traveller; every highway's clear." The ploy would seem too obvious if it were not for the narrator's voice repeating and changing the *here* that we come to expect; he locates it in the poem rather than on English soil, making his irony more clear and his poem more "true" than Juan's sentimental vision:

> "And here," he cried, "is Freedom's chosen station;
>   Here peals the people's voice, nor can entomb it
> Racks, prisons, inquisitions; resurrection
>   Awaits it, each new meeting or election.
>
> "Here are chaste wives, pure lives; here people pay
>   But what they please; and if that things be dear,
> 'Tis only that they love to throw away
>   Their cash, to show how much they have a-year.
> Here laws are all inviolate; none lay
>   Traps for the traveller; every highway's clear.

Here"—he was interrupted by a knife,
With "Damn your eyes! your money or your life!"

(9.9–10)

The enharmonic technique resembles zeugma, of which the following
example best fits the present discussion:

There was Dick Dubious the metaphysician,
Who loved philosophy and a good dinner.

(13.87)

As in the dedication, metaphysics are confronted with the needs of the
body, and the surprise and amusement with which we discover that din-
ner can be in the same syntactic position as philosophy achieves the same
effect Byron gets more succinctly when one word expresses opposites.

In isolation, the octave about gout/*goût* reveals a good deal; but the
association of art, nature, and hypocrisy together with the confrontation
of foods in French with "plain English" and "our rough John Bull way"
gain from their context. Read against the whole canto and the whole
poem, the octave on gout/*goût* shows again how taste is emblematic of
poetic and thematic questions. Ridenour speaks of the "laws of physiol-
ogy and assonance" that connect this octave to the description of heavy
foods; but there are other connections as well. Ten octaves about French
dishes are sickening not so much in the physical sense, as a source of
satiety, but because they reflect the reliance in poetry and society on a
vocabulary that obscures truth (both kinds) in the name of decorum. As
Lovell remarks, echoing Byron's comment that the foods are "all in mas-
querade" (15.74): "In Juan's England, even the food masquerades in
foreign dress, fit nourishment for a hypocritical people."[52]

When Byron describes the banquet in such detail, he seems to be
following a satiric model or teasing the reader as he does at the end of
canto 14, when he leaves Juan and Adeline "hovering, as the effect is fine
/ And keeps the atrocious reader in *suspense*" (14.97). But the teasing
has an edge; it is calculated to trick the reader into reading over the
passage either because the subject of food is out of place in a poem, a
trivial subject that cannot convey serious issues, or out of curiosity to
learn about Juan's fate. A digression, neoclassically, is bad enough, and a
digression about food is a double breach of decorum. Yet food has an
eloquent if silent function in the society at the Amundevilles, where Lady

Amundeville expresses allegiance to her husband by composing dinners for his constituents and where literal and figurative taste are pointedly at odds in the figure of Lord Henry. Theirs is the society Brecht meant when he said that the wealthy consider it lowly to speak of eating because they have already eaten:

> Bei den Hochgestellten
> Gilt das Reden vom Essen als niedrig.
> Das kommt: sie haben
> Schon gegessen.[53]

The reader is put into the position of a member of the society Byron is describing, having most probably been tempted to dismiss as trivial an extended menu in a poetic setting. Byron's description is a radical departure from the expectations—the taste—of his public. It exemplifies the difference between literature and life, since the Frenchified references to food embellish a "low" subject that cannot be included in poetry.

The description of the bill of fare is introduced with a reference to poetic tradition, implicitly and explicitly. Byron is explicit when he speaks of Muses, Homer, and the epic tradition. He is implicit when he speaks of "a single day-bill / Of modern dinners," surely a reference to Fielding's image of the bill of fare at the beginning of *Tom Jones:*

> Great things were now to be achieved at table,
>   With massy plate for armour, knives and forks
> For weapons; but what Muse since Homer's able
>   (His feasts are not the worst part of his works)
> To draw up in array a single day-bill
>   Of modern dinners, where more mystery lurks
> In soups or sauces or a sole ragoût
> Than witches, b—ches, or physicians brew?
>
> (15.62)

Furthermore, the rhyming word "ragoût" in the final couplet anticipates the wordplay on *goût* and gout ten octaves later: here the word "ragoût" must be pronounced in the French manner, but even here there is the association with illness (the gout) because of the "physicians brew" in the second line of the final couplet.

Related to the enormous number of literary allusions in the passage are the self-allusions. Byron's transformation of epic weapons into massy plate, knives, and forks is a self-caricature of his poetics in *Don Juan*. Ridenour understates when he says that "Perhaps the lines on the great things to be achieved at table were not merely facetious," and his own analysis of the passage shows what some of the "great things" are.[54] Ridenour concentrates on the thematic importance of what he calls this "brilliant episode"; for him cookery is an art that comes from the Fall but "is one of man's means of dealing with the conditions brought about by the Fall."[55] He shows how the passage is based on the satiric tradition of Juvenal, Horace, and Pope, though he takes it further ("It is satire, of course, but it is not merely satire") and stresses the poet's detached "amusement" from the cooking, eating, and indigestion of others. Ridenour's emphasis on cooking as the "positive pole of the paradox" misrepresents Byron's ability to present both poles at once, however, and to combine opposites. In the bill of fare passage Byron even succeeds in suspending time and space: past, present, and future are fused here through etymology, wordplay, and allusions to poetry, history, and geography.

Interpreted in combination with what we know already, weapons, the Muse, Homer, feasts, modernity, mystery, and the language of the last line (where the word "bitches" was originally not printed out) give a telegraphic account of the poet's preoccupations.[56] Since Homer stands for literary tradition—just as literal taste stands for all that is indecorous—and since the feasts of Homer are compared to "modern dinners," it is to poetry in general that Byron refers here. Through Homer, and specifically through the feasts of Homer, Byron distances himself from two kinds of figurative taste: the taste inherited from the eighteenth century that criticizes parts of Homer as indecorous, and the more recent metaphysical taste represented by Coleridge. Semantically he demonstrates his own kind of taste by concentrating on food; technically he demonstrates his flamboyant poetics by incorporating into his poem a list from a book that has been identified as a book by Louis Eustache Ude, *The French Cook*. At the beginning of canto 1, Byron does something similar with his rhymed and rhythmic list of names; there they are "borrowed" from the French Revolution and make a revolutionary statement in the same double sense Byron conveys elsewhere through ambiguous taste. Everything is a source for his poetry, whether Homer or lists of names or cookbooks.

Byron's signposts are clear enough. It is a mistake to pass over the elaborate description of dinner as the joke of an iconoclastic poet, or to interpret the passage as an exaggerated and literal understanding of satire as *satura lanx.* Byron's iconoclasm is not gratuitous. In the rhetorical question already quoted, he brings together past and present through an enharmonic shift in the word "able," where a part of speech changes along with the meaning:

> but what Muse since Homer's able
> (His feasts are not the worst part of his works)
> To draw up in array a single day-bill
> Of modern dinners, where more mystery lurks
> In soups or sauces or a sole ragoût
> Than witches, b—ches, or physicians brew.—

The technique is all the more dramatic (or "mysterious") because the change is withheld in the parenthetical aside that takes up an entire line. What starts out as an adjective (Homer's muse is an "able" one) changes its function in the course of the stanza so that it applies to modern muses—or at least to muses after Homer—and refers to permission instead of ability ("able / [. . .] / To draw up"). Permission means decorum, which means taste. And taste is the overarching example of double entendre that is imitated throughout the passage in details like the muse whose "stomach's not her peccant part" (64), the young partridge fillets (66) that are turned into the "fillets on the victor's brow" (67), the "petits puits d'amour" that are both culinary and erotic (68), the allusion to Adam and the "commonest demands of nature" (69), the "spare rib" (70), and, finally, in the bilingual pun on *goût* and gout (72), which contains and repeats all the examples of ambiguous taste that came before.

In granting so much space and significance to a bill of fare, Byron not only alludes to Fielding, he also anticipates the symbolist method of putting the stress on the poet's subjective associations rather than on the intrinsic qualities of an object. This passage offers a more elaborate example of what we find in the famous comparison of Lady Adeline to a bottle of champagne, an image that McGann calls a "good example of the kind of stylistic renovation Byron was trying to bring about with *Beppo* and *Don Juan*" (DJ/O, 756). The champagne image precedes the description of the banquet in canto 15, but it should be present to the reader throughout in the same way that champagne accompanies the meal at Norman Abbey: "And then there was champagne with foaming whirls, / As white as Cleopatra's melted pearls." (15.65). Byron begins with a conventional poetic tool, the metaphor, taken from a conventional realm, nature; but he interrupts himself because he finds the image boring—"a common place" (where the word "common" should put us on guard):

> But Adeline was not indifferent: for
>   (*Now* for a common place!) beneath the snow,
> As a Volcano holds the lava more
>   Within—*et cetera*. Shall I go on?—No!
> I hate to hunt down a tired metaphor:
>   So let the often used volcano go.
> Poor thing! How frequently, by me and others,
> It hath been stirred up till its smoke quite smothers.
>
>   (13.36)

He retains a conventional form, the metaphor, just as he retains the ottava rima stanza; but he alters its content. By feigning to ask his reader about the choice ("What say you to a bottle of champagne?"), he further emphasizes the discrepancy between the "taste" of his reader and his use of literal taste in the poem:

> I'll have another figure in a trice.
>   What say you to a bottle of champagne?
> Frozen into a very vinous ice,
>   Which leaves few drops of that immortal rain,
> Yet in the very centre, past all price,
>   About a liquid glassful will remain;
> And this is stronger than the strongest grape
> Could e'er express in its expanded shape.
>
>   (13.37)

He concludes his commentary with a description that applies as much to his poem as to the Lady Adeline:

> 'Tis the whole spirit brought to a quintessence,
>   And thus the chilliest aspects may concentre
> A hidden nectar under a cold presence.

> And such are many—though I only meant her,
> From whom I now deduce these moral lessons.
>
> (13.38)

These lines summarize the development of the three stanzas, which in turn summarize the development of the whole poem: the Horatian motto is echoed in the "common place" of stanza 36 and is followed by the words "express" and "spirit," puns that are the "quintessence" of his poetic revolutionary style. Above all, there is the idea of a center that condenses the whole, "the very centre, past all price," from which Ridenour perhaps derives his own apt phrase, "centers of meaning."[57] Byron more than once associates Adeline with his poem and his poetics. Although the taste of Adeline's audience is ridiculed, her own poem is not; it contains nonparodistic examples of Byron's vocabulary ("clay," "pall") and reproduces his kind of enjambment. Unlike her husband, for whom taste is the same as fashion, Adeline has the independence to admire Pope; her "mobility" is defended at the end of canto 16 and transferred to the poet in the "idem semper" lines of canto 17.

Dense associations of this sort, both to other authors and to other parts of the poem, are seemingly endless and even bewildering. The banquet at Norman Abbey does not actually begin with the reference to Homer and the "great things" at table, for example, but is preceded by a digression in which the poet comments on his portraits of Haidée and Aurora and alludes to Scott, Shakespeare, and Voltaire (15.59). Yet the variety is extraordinarily constant in its return to the fixed point of ambiguous taste.

The Literary Politics of Taste

So far I have concentrated on the function of ambiguous taste as an emblem of poetic liberation. As such, it is analogous to the theme of political liberation. Institutions of society—religion and war and marriage foremost among them—are questioned and reevaluated, as are the institutions of poetry and the fixed definitions of words. References to food are a kind of anticant: the connection of eating and oppression is made in poetry through the exclusion of eating from "aristocratic" genres, and in politics through hunger, as for example in the line from canto 8, "Though Ireland starve, great George weighs twenty stone" (8.126). The gustatory connection of poetry and politics is implicitly present as early as the pun on Pye, which comes in the octave where "laureate" rhymes with "Tory at." In another example, the association of politics, poetry, and food is made through a reworking of Shakespeare's phrase from *Macbeth*, "supp'd full of horrors," which Byron uses in the fiercest part of the attack on Wellington in canto 9:

> I am no flatterer—you've supped full of flattery:
>> They say you like it too—'tis no great wonder:
> He whose whole life has been assault and battery,
>> At last may get a little tired of thunder;
> And swallowing eulogy much more than satire, he
>> May like being praised for every lucky blunder;
> Called "Saviour of the Nations"—not yet saved;
> And Europe's Liberator—still enslaved.
>
> (9.5)

Byron stays with the gustatory image and uses its contradictions as the link between his commentary on politics and poetry; taste, which exemplifies the inadequacy of representing things in oppositional pairs, is transferred to Napoleon, whom it suits even better than Wellington. At the end of the next octave, oppression and famine are again connected as they were in the line about "great George" from canto 8:

> Never had mortal Man such opportunity,
>> Except Napoleon, or abused it more:
> You might have freed fall'n Europe from the Unity
>> Of Tyrants, and been blest from shore to shore:
> And *now*—what *is* your fame? Shall the Muse tune it ye?
>> *Now*—that the rabble's first vain shouts are o'er?
> Go, hear it in your famished Country's cries!
> Behold the World! and curse your victories!
>
> (9.9)

The passage about Napoleon is full of modulations that reflect his conflicting reputation and that are all related in some way to poetry. Conflict is expressed in the Shakespearean alternation of "famish" in this stanza with "fatten" in the next; the stanzas about death culminate in another quotation from Shakespeare, "To be or not to be," which is

96

introduced with a reference to figurative taste: "Shakespeare, who just now is much in fashion." By way of literal taste, Byron moves to Napoleon's cancer: "Without a stomach—what were a good name?" Finally, the combined literal and figurative meanings of taste lead to literal and figurative indigestion, and like taste, indigestion is a detail that reveals complexities of the human condition usually given grander names.

We are meant to think of these themes when the poet calls himself "The grand Napoleon of the realms of rhyme" (11.55) and elaborates on the comparison:

> But Juan was my Moscow, and Faliero
>   My Leipsic, and my Mont Saint Jean seems Cain:
> "La Belle Alliance" of dunces down at zero,
>   Now that the Lion's fall'n, may rise again:
> But I will fall at least as fell my hero;
>   Nor reign at all, or as a *monarch* reign;
> Or to some lonely isle of Jailors go,
> With turncoat Southey for my turnkey Lowe.
>
> (11.56)

McGann says of this octave that "The passage illustrates one of the most important and recurrent aspects of all Byron's poetry: i.e. its insistence that the reader understand Byron's life and literary career in world-historical terms. Byron's poetry forces its readers to take the deeds and experiences of his life as a coherent objective correlative for the entire European experience between 1789 and 1824" (DJ/O, 749–50).[58] To an extent this is so, but not so directly and simply. As the examples from canto 9 demonstrate, the balance does not tip towards the "world-historical" as plainly as McGann would have it, because in this poem poetry and politics cannot be severed. Furthermore, even the "world-historical" themes occur within a poetic frame and must therefore be interpreted.

In canto 15, which contains so many demonstrations of poetic liberation, images of poetry and politics merge when images for poetry are taken from the realm of politics, as in the comment

> Of this I'm sure at least, there's no servility
>   In mine irregularity of chime
>
> (15.20)

or in the famous lines two octaves later that are often taken out of context as evidence of Byron's political sentiments, but that refer in the first place to his poetry:

> No doubt, if I had wished to pay my court
>   To critics or to hail the *setting* sun
> Of tyranny of all kinds, my concision
>   Were more;—but I was born for opposition.
>
> (15.22)

To "pay court to critics" is to give in to the "tyranny" of public taste; *his* taste, however, since he is "born for opposition," is literal as much as figurative, producing "this conundrum of a dish," as he calls it in the octave that precedes this one. When he speaks of concision, the reference is to a quotation from an epigram of Martial that contains the advice to mix the beautiful with the good and the middling. There may be another reason, in the vicinity of ambiguous taste, for the reference to Martial and his epigrams. Byron could be thinking of an anecdote about epigrams from the eighteenth century in which the ignorant confusion of literal and figurative meanings resembles some of the comic misunderstandings in Molière. A society lady hears someone speak of having "savored" some "excellent epigrams" and orders her cook to prepare a "dish of epigrams" for the next day.[59] Lord Henry would be capable of the same sort of misunderstanding.

Like the "femme du monde" in the anecdote, Lord Henry wants to impress others with his sophistication and his cuisine, but instead he exposes himself to ridicule. The joke is a joke only for the people who can think on more than one level, the "initiated" whom Byron describes in one of the two octaves of which Cecil Lang writes that Byron "gaily warns us that he writes in code."[60] In the second of the two, Byron calls his poetry an idealized version of reality that should not be taken literally (a warning that applies equally to the historical and biographical details of the poem):

> And therefore what I throw off is ideal—
>   Lower'd, leaven'd, like a history of Freemasons;
> Which bears the same relation to the real,
>   As Captain Parry's voyage may do to Jason's.
> The grand Arcanum's not for men to see all;

> My music has some mystic diapasons;
> And there is much which could not be appreciated
> In any manner by the uninitiated.
>
> (14.22)

The images here anticipate the series of images at the beginning of canto 15, where the poet speaks of "seeing matters which are out of sight." In particular the line "My music has some mystic diapasons" anticipates those from canto 15 quoted earlier, the lines "There's music in all things, if men had ears: / Their Earth is but an echo of the spheres" (15.5). Since the bill of fare in canto 15 is a good example of code, it is surely not by accident that the octave about the "uninitiated" contains the gustatory metaphor "leaven'd": the French names mean one thing to Lord Henry and his guests but another to the "initiated" reader, who recognizes in them the affectations of Lord Henry on the one hand and a series of literary, historical, and geographical allusions by the poet-narrator on the other.

Lord Henry is repeatedly associated with literal and figurative taste; in this he resembles Chrysale of *Les Femmes savantes,* though he is a hypocrite and therefore less lovable than Chrysale.[61] Whereas Chrysale's attachment to material things crowds out any interest in spiritual ones, Lord Henry pretends to a refinement associated with figurative taste. Lord Henry is an aristocrat, but he is servile, and his servility is manifest in his near-obsession with taste. He has no profile as a placeman (13.21) and gives in to public pressures, as we know from the narrator's ironical advice (an inversion of Addison's *Cato*) to "watch the time and always serve it; / Give gently way, when there's too great a press" (13.18). The grand dinner that Lord Henry serves to his constituents is the physical manifestation of his subserviance to their literal and figurative tastes:

> But Adeline was occupied by fame
>   This day; and watching, witching, condescending
> To the consumers of fish, fowl and game,
>   And dignity with courtesy so blending,
> As all must blend whose part it is to aim
>   (Especially as the sixth year is ending)
> At their lord's, son's, or similar connection's
> Safe conduct through the rocks of re-elections.
>
> (16.95)

Adeline's independence with regard to Pope's poetry does not extend to her role as a politician's wife. In this she contrasts with Juan, whose lack of attention to the turbot costs Lord Henry some votes and provides a comic detail while also putting him at a reassuring distance from his materialist hosts.[62]

Lord Henry and his guests embody the absurdity and the delusion of making clear divisions of all kinds, usually in the name of taste. As Byron says in 14.90 (and there are many similar comments in the poem): "I leave it to your people of sagacity / To draw the line between the false and true. / If such can e'er be drawn by man's capacity." This is not a bad thing: it is as important in life as it is in poetry. When he concludes his loving evocation of Norman Abbey, Byron modulates from the lyrical tone to a satirical portrayal of the guests with a "center of meaning" that admirably expresses the inadequacy of uniformity and the intolerance it breeds, in poetry and politics. He uses an architectural image to describe the complexities and contraries of the human condition that are displayed through the form and themes of *Don Juan*. One easily transfers the description of the abbey to Byron's poem, which as a whole leaves "a grand impression on the mind" even though it is "irregular in parts":

> Huge halls, long galleries, spacious chambers, join'd
>   By no quite lawful marriage of the Arts,
> Might shock a connoisseur; but when combined,
>   Form'd a whole which, irregular in parts,
> Yet left a grand impression on the mind,
>   At least of those whose eyes are in their hearts.
> We gaze upon a Giant for his stature,
> Nor judge at first if all be true to Nature.
>
> (13.67)

This is the building that Lord Henry, later called "a connoisseur,—/ The friend of artists, if not arts" (16.57), wants to remake into a regular, "tasteful" whole. In other words, his taste is one of pretense; he is not someone "whose eyes are in their hearts."

Having opened this canto with an architectural image, Byron invites the comparison between the building and his poem, then. In the first octave of canto 13, he compares his poetic method to "an old temple dwindled to a column," a simile that aptly suggests the incomplete yet recognizable presence of tradition in his work. But Byron's use of the Romantic topos of the ruin is itself alienated: the simile "limps" and is meant to, because the column is a crucial but an isolated example of the sublime, surrounded by the spirit of laughter that puts the sublime into relief. The column stands alone at the end of an octave that does not resemble a temple, even though it talks of templelike things:

> I now mean to be serious;—it is time,
>   Since laughter now-a-days is deemed too serious.
> A jest at Vice by Virtue's called a crime,
>   And critically held as deleterious;
> Besides, the sad's a source of the sublime,
>   Although when long a little apt to weary us;
> And therefore shall my lay soar high and solemn
> As an old temple dwindled to a column.
>
> (13.1)

McGann comments that "The image of the ruin aptly sums up this stanza's comment on contemporary taste in poetry (and in particular on the dominance of Romantic 'seriousness')" (DJ/O, 755), and his remark is confirmed by the association of taste with architecture throughout the canto. But as so often, Byron uses something we recognize in order to subvert and then appropriate it: the octave mocks the "seriousness" of his contemporaries, as McGann says, but he himself is serious here. The image of the column, introduced as it is here, graphically illustrates the contrast that is demonstrated linguistically by the word taste.

Byron contrasts his moving description of the abbey with the architectural fashion of building something new that is "of correctest conformation":

> There was a modern Goth, I mean a Gothic
>   Bricklayer of Babel, called an architect,
> Brought to survey these grey walls, which though so thick,
>   Might have from time acquired some slight defect,
> Who after rummaging the Abbey through thick
>   And thin, produced a play whereby to erect
> New buildings of correctest conformation
> And throw down old, which he called *restoration.*
>
> (16.58)

The result is to be a "sublime" monument to Lord Henry's "good taste":

> The price would speedily repay its worth in
> An edifice no less sublime than strong,
>   By which *Lord Henry's good taste* would go forth in
> Its glory, through all ages shining sunny,
> For Gothic daring shown in English money.
>
> (16.59 [my emphasis])

Lord Henry is incapable of noticing the inconsistency between the architect's "restoration" and the claim that such changes will "go forth in /Its glory, through all ages shining sunny." His is the typical ahistorical fallacy that Byron has criticized all along with regard to poetry, where current taste scorns what came before and considers its own judgment and works to be immortal. Lord Henry expects permanence from the "good taste" that he brings literally to his banquets and figuratively to his restorations, whereas in fact his expensive projects resemble the "triumph" of the *femme du monde*.

What we learn about Lord Henry's interest in art and architecture clashes with his interest in literal taste. Before we learn of his figurative taste, we see him at the breakfast table, where he notices only the food in front of him and is impervious to Juan's palor: "Lord Henry said, his muffin was ill buttered" (16.31). Not until three octaves later, once his material needs have been satisfied and discussed, does he notice Juan's looks: "Lord Henry, who had now discussed his chocolate, / Also the muffin whereof he complained, / Said, Juan had not got his usual look elate" (16.34). His subsequent comments on the Black Friar provide comic confirmation of his insensitivity, which in a social context is a lack of taste. Such details must be reread in light of the narrator's comment later on that taste "now-a-days is the thermometer / By whose degrees all characters are classed" (16.48).

Both dinners at Norman Abbey are preceded by the lengthy and lyrical description of the abbey itself and by a wittily malicious satire of the guests, people inferred to be oracles of "good taste." The guest list and the description conclude with a summary in which the seemingly trivial reference to "ragoûts or roasts" gives rise to more existential questions:

> I will not dwell upon ragoûts or roasts,
>   Albeit all human history attests

That happiness for Man—the hungry sinner!—
Since Eve ate apples, much depends on dinner.

(13.99)

It is true that the narrator does not "dwell upon ragoûts and roasts" in their literal sense; but his comment here has otherwise been disproven since the opening of the poem. Once more we are reminded of the complicated relationship between things: a lie is "but the truth in masquerade," and we need to unmask the truth of his statement that "I will not dwell upon ragoûts or roasts." The lyrical description of Norman Abbey as a building cannot be separated from the humor and satire that Byron uses to present the people who inhabit it; like literal and figurative taste, they are inseparable. The philosophical implications in this octave are related to those in another reference to "a roast and a ragout [*sic*]" in canto 5:

I think with Alexander, that the act
    Of eating, with another act or two,
Makes us feel our mortality in fact
    Redoubled; when a roast and a ragout,
And fish, and soup, by some side dishes back'd,
    Can give us either pain or pleasure, who
Would pique himself on intellects, whose use
Depends so much upon the gastric juice?

(5.32)

Food often is used in this poem as a reminder of mortality. But it is basic to the paradoxical nature of *Don Juan* that by bringing the subject of food into his poem, Byron weakens the association: at the same time that he complains of transience, his poem guarantees permanence.

Cannibalism and Beefsteak: Canto 2 and the Island Idyll

One cluster of gustatory references in *Don Juan* has been conspicuously absent from my discussion thus far: the series in canto 2 that begins with Juan's love and retching, moves to starvation and cannibalism, and ends with the island idyll. The presence and absence of food structures the

103

second canto; taste provides "the whole spirit brought to a quintessence," as Byron says of his image of frozen champagne. The second canto contains some of Byron's most memorable attacks on the "cant of Christendom," and the survivors of the shipwreck, like the diners at Norman Abbey, are a microcosm of a society whose cant contrasts with the cantless society on Haidée's island. When the canto opens, Juan's conflict between heart and stomach has a decidedly Christian cast: it irreverently reproduces the Christian battle between spirit and matter. Ridenour has been rightly criticized (for example by Cooke and Mellor) for paying too little attention to the difference between Byron's context and that of the Bible or Milton; here as elsewhere, Byron distorts his biblical source just enough to cite and change it.[63]

Byron prepares for the identification of cannibalism and Christianity by depicting the chasm between cant and true belief in the preceding canto. At the end of canto 1 there is the ironical list of ten "poetic" commandments, for example. Julia is firm in her belief that "Christians have burnt each other, quite persuaded / That all the apostles would have done as they did" (2.83). Donna Inez's materialistic understanding of the Christian faith is demonstrated when she vows "several pounds of candles" to the Virgin Mary in order to atone for Juan's "sin"; she further confuses hypocrisy with pedagogy at the Sunday school she opens, and in one variant, Byron ridicules both her precepts and the absurdity of dividing spirit and body: "She taught them to suppress their vice and urine."

In connection with the shipwreck, where the focus is on death and fear, Byron's references to religion become more insistent. One of the famous lines in a poem known for famous lines is the comment that "There's nought, no doubt, so much the spirit calms / As rum and true religion" (2.34). Pedrillo, who will shortly provide real sustenance for the others when they sacrifice and eat him, refuses to offer the spiritual comfort someone requests. His refusal contains an example of double entendre that underscores the Christian contradictions exposed by Byron in this passage: "there was one / That begg'd Pedrillo for an absolution, /Who told him to be damn'd—in his confusion" (2.44). A glaring contrast is made between spiritual need and Catholic monetary interest in the passage that Rutherford finds offensive:

> All the rest perish'd; near two hundred souls
> Had left their bodies; and, what's worse, alas!

When over Catholics the ocean rolls,
  They must wait several weeks before a mass
Takes off one peck of purgatorial coals,
  Because, till people know what's come to pass,
They won't lay out their money on the dead—
  It costs three francs for every mass that's said.

(2.55)

Without the doctrine of transubstantiation, Byron's account of cannibalism is unthinkable. His literal representation of the doctrine exemplifies his disrespectful acknowledgment of traditions in order to reject them; for him biblical images are dead metaphors whose distance from literal meaning is as suspect as the exclusive materialism of Lord Henry.

When he depicts Pedrillo's "sacrifice," Byron brings the association of cannibalism and Christianity out into the open. Pedrillo dies with a crucifix in his hand, holding out his arm:

He died as born, a Catholic in faith,
  Like most in the belief in which they're bred,
And first a little crucifix he kissed,
  And then held out his jugular and wrist.

(2.76)

The Christian connection is underscored when the surgeon drinks Pedrillo's blood and in the use of the word "pastor" when Juan refuses to "dine on his pastor and his master" (2.78). Concurrent with the biblical assocations is an allusion to cannibalism in Dante, which provides the literary "legitimization" for Byron's subject:

And if Pedrillo's fate should shocking be,
  Remember Ugolino condescends
To eat the head of his arch-enemy,
  The moment after he politely ends
His tale; if foes be food in hell, at sea
  'Tis surely fair to dine upon our friends,
When shipwreck's short allowance grows too scanty,
Without being much more horrible than Dante.

(2.83)

105

The death of the two sons in the boat and the dissimilar reactions of their fathers further confront the illusions fostered by belief with the hardships of reality. There is something profoundly unsettling about the acquiescence of one of the fathers, who accepts his son's death as the will of God. As important as the pathos in this passage is the comic element that accompanies it, for example when a dove is thought by some to be an omen and by others to be a source of food:

> But in this case I also must remark,
>   'Twas well this bird of promise did not perch,
> Because the tackle of our shatter'd bark
>   Was not so safe for roosting as a church;
> And had it been the dove from Noah's ark,
>   Returning there from her successful search,
> Which in their way that moment chanced to fall,
> They would have eat her, olive-branch and all.
>
> (2.95)[64]

Christian associations with eating occur again in the island idyll. When Zoe and Haidée cook for Juan, they seem to have used the Bible as their cookbook, but Byron again distorts his source and adds a comic note by including coffee among the biblical foods: "But there were eggs, fruit, coffee, bread, fish, honey." He also specifies that the wine comes from Scio (perhaps so that it will not be confused with the blood of Christ) and speaks of money: "With Scio wine, and all for love, not money" (2.145). Added to the narrator's irreverence is the irony that Juan ignores the paradisical connotations of the food before him and longs instead for a beefsteak. That longing prompts a digression on beef (2.154–56) in which different kinds of taste are merged: thoughts about the kinds of meat on "these oxless isles" (2.154) turn to thoughts of the Minotaur and the "royal lady's taste who wore / A cow's shape for a mask" (2.155), and the digression concludes with a characterization of the English as beefeaters (2.156). Juan's hunger for a beefsteak further contains an echo of the seasickness at the beginning of canto 2, where the narrator says that "The best of remedies is a beef-steak / Against sea-sickness" (2.13); along with the other topics it raises, therefore, the beefsteak recalls Julia and the emotional as well as physical distance that separates her from Juan, always with a reminder of the body's claims over mind and emotion. The beefsteak in canto 2 further introduces the series of connections between cannibalism, Christianity, and war: in canto 5, for example, Byron associates beefsteak and war when the mercenary John Johnson adds his hunger for beefsteak to the arguments against Juan's plan for escape: " 'Besides, I'm hungry, and just now would take, / Like Esau, for my birthright a beef-steak' " (5.44). At the beginning of canto 8, the connection of Christianity with brutality is less culinary but more explicit:

> "Carnage" (so Wordsworth tells you) "is God's daughter":
> If *he* speaks truth, she is Christ's sister, and
> Just now behaved as in the Holy Land.
>
> (8.9)

Byron's literal reading of Christian dogma has the same effect in canto 8 that it does in the case of transubstantiation: there is a grim undertone that immediately counteracts the humor. And yet the humor is present, not least because of the way Byron strikes two targets at once, Wordsworth and the brutality that masquerades as Christianity.[65]

The canto ends with a seemingly motley assortment of philosophical, literary, and religious allusions that actually reiterate one of its main themes—the inconsistencies and absurdities of the human condition. Here as elsewhere in the poem the theme is represented by ambiguous taste: love and beauty, manifest in the figures of Juan and Haidée, coexist with coarse and comical necessities such as hunger, which can engender cannibalism. The opening opposition of the heart and the stomach, where Juan's declaration of love was interrupted by his retching, is replaced at the end of the canto by a fanciful consideration of what McGann calls "the ancient debate between Platonists and Aristotelians as to whether the heart or the liver is the central human organ" (DJ/O, 692):

> The heart is like the sky, a part of heaven,
>   But changes night and day too, like the sky;
> Now o'er it clouds and thunder must be driven,
>   And darkness and destruction as on high:
> But when it hath been scorch'd, and pierced, and riven,
>   Its storms expire in water-drops; the eye
> Pours forth at last the heart's-blood turn'd to tears,
> Which make the English climate of our years.

> The liver is the lazaret of bile,
>   But very rarely executes its function,
> For the first passion stays there such a while,
>   That all the rest creep in and form a junction,
> Like knots of vipers on a dunghill's soil,
>   Rage, fear, hate, jealousy, revenge, compunction,
> So that all mischiefs spring up from this entrail,
> Like earthquakes from the hidden fire call'd "central."
>
> (2.214–15)

The change from a connection of heart and stomach to heart and liver marks Juan's shift from Julia to Haidée ("But Juan! had he quite forgotten Julia?" [2. 208]); it is one more illustration of human inconsistency. Furthermore, the connection of heart and liver at the end reformulates in a wider philosophical context the opposition that otherwise is associated with Christianity. And finally, the move from heart to liver marks a poetic change: the imagery for emotion shifts from storms and climate in one octave ("the English climate of our years") to the sordid ("knots of vipers on a dunghill's soil"). The first image is representative of an old, the second of a new kind of taste.

Taste as a Sign of Genre

The question of taste can be reformulated as one of conspicuous presences and absences. The exclusion of literal taste—and of all the bodily things it elicits—from a work "in good taste" makes the forbidden loom larger instead of disappear, much as the absence of Aurora Raby's name from Adeline's list makes her more rather than less prominent. Byron evokes this psychological reaction already in canto 1, where he describes the expurgations imposed on Juan's tutors by his mother. McGann comments of the stanzas that they "amount to an ironic defence of *DJ*, which was attacked for its supposed indecency and coarseness, as well as its candid social and political satire."[66] It is a memorable passage of five octaves that allows the poet to bring together a number of subjects; he can ridicule Donna Inez and illustrate his argument at the same time that he makes the literary allusions that always demand particular scrutiny. Since the passage refers to a lengthy poetic tradition, and since Donna

Inez is a caricature of "good taste," it is almost predictable when Byron uses gustatory images in the third of the five octaves, exactly at the center of the passage:

> Lucretius' irreligion is too strong
>   For early stomachs, to prove wholesome food;
> I can't help thinking Juvenal was wrong,
>   Although no doubt his real intent was good,
> For speaking out so plainly in his song,
>   So much indeed as to be downright rude;
> And then what proper person can be partial
> To all those nauseous epigrams of Martial.

(1.43)

Byron does not expurgate merely in order to make the forbidden more vivid or those who suppress it more ridiculous, as Fielding would or as Goethe does in his notes to Diderot's *Le Neveu de Rameau*. He goes a step further and includes the forbidden or the commonplace in order to weaken its power. In a sense Byron puts into practice the argument of Norbert Elias that a civilized society is no longer threatened by the "uncivilized" things it needed to repress at an earlier stage. The effect in poetry is different from the effect in a social context, however; what is true for society is in this case revolutionary for poetry. The tenacious aesthetic resistance to indecorum is clear from the scandals over Baudelaire's poems and Zola's *L'Assommoir,* the "crime" of which, as Zola puts it, is its form.

Elsewhere in *Don Juan,* Byron achieves a similar effect with his image of the petticoat. Again he begins by drawing attention to his poetry, first with an allusion to *Joseph Andrews*—"as from hungry pikes a roach," which is one in a series of similes applied to Mrs. Slipslop's unveiled declaration of love to Joseph—and then with the phrase "mystical sublimity":

> I for one venerate a petticoat—
> A garment of a mystical sublimity,
> No matter whether russet, silk, or dimity.
>
> Much I respect, and much I have adored,
>   In my young days, that chaste and goodly veil,

> Which holds a treasure, like a Miser's hoard,
> And more attracts by all it doth conceal.
>
> (14.26–27)

Veiling and unveiling are the source of literary decorum, which depends not only on subjects, but also on context and euphemisms. Again the problem is emblematized by taste, which denotes both decorum and indecorum. But the issue is not exclusive to taste. It is present in the discrepancy between Don Juan's name and the way he acts, or in the feats of Lambro (3.14), Napoleon (14.90), and Caesar (14.102), which are given different names depending on the setting or the speaker. In canto 3, Byron playfully expresses the theme:

> The same things change their names at such a rate;
> For instance, passion in a lover's glorious,
> But in a husband is pronounced uxorious.
>
> (3.6)

Yet the application here, which is to Juan and Haidée, tempers the playfulness in a further illustration of how context affects meaning.

The question of presence and absence is no less paradoxical than the conflicting meanings of taste or the freedom within the constraints of the ottava rima stanza. Byron does not censor himself, yet too much clarity would be antithetical to poetry. He says that it is absurd to hide things, but he remarks that the qualities of his poem are not on the surface. Although he shows that the only way to weaken the power of the forbidden is to bring it out into the open (one thinks of Juan's reaching out in terror for the ghost of the Black Friar and finding sensual comfort in the duchess of Fitz-Fulke instead), it does not follow that all things should be made obvious. On the contrary, he distinguishes between things that are taboo because of a false morality or for purposes of oppression and those that need to be hidden so that they maintain their "mysterious diapasons." It is a basic paradox of *Don Juan* that poetry can use one for the other: subjects that usually are hidden can be made to convey ideas that are both elusive and complex, ideas hidden to all but the "initiated" because their literal meaning eclipses their figurative function. What this proves is ultimately the poet's power to mold any subject, a power that Byron does not attempt to master until he writes *Don Juan*.

This we know from a letter he wrote several years before he started the poem:

> the true voluptuary will never abandon his mind to the grossness of reality. It is by exalting [...] the *physique* of our pleasures, by veiling these ideas, by forgetting them altogether, or at least, never naming them hardly to one's self, that we alone can prevent them from disgusting. (BLJ 2:377)[67]

By the time he writes *Don Juan,* Byron has learned to "exalt the physique" without forgetting it. The ability to combine physical subjects and poetic ideas, body and spirit, literal and figurative, has become indistinguishable from his poetry. Even in *Beppo,* he has not quite reached this point; *Beppo* bears the relation to *Don Juan* that Proust's early novella *L'Indifférent* does to *A la Recherche du temps perdu:* the earlier works adumbrate but do not accomplish the poetic assurance and style of the later ones. One can gauge the difference between *Don Juan* and *Beppo* by concentrating on the gustatory details, which in *Beppo* cause humorous surprise or evoke details of local color. In *Beppo* culinary referents underscore the carnivalistic frame and the Pulci subjects; they are "deliberately shy," as Cooke says of the allusion to King Arthur's table at the beginning of Frere's *The Monks and the Giants,*[68] and they do not go beyond the comic or the real as they do in *Don Juan.* The change is evident if we imagine how an important line from the beginning of *Childe Harold* would work in *Don Juan,* the line "He felt the fullness of satiety." Childe Harold's departure from England is analogous to Juan's departure from Spain; but it is inconceivable that Childe Harold's "fullness of satiety" would be juxtaposed with seasickness. Part of the difference is due to the context, but mainly there is a difference in the way Byron uses language.

When Byron cites the works of his predecessors to legitimize his own, he conveniently forgets to mention the difference in genre, which is also a difference in name, though he knows that freedoms are not the same for the high as for the low style. There is an understandable tendency, in speaking of *Don Juan,* to adopt the vocabulary of genre even while acknowledging the difficulty of classifying the poem. It may be simply that we are faced with a dilemma not unlike Byron's own toward literary tradition: that in order to make ourselves understood, we must use a vocabulary rooted in tradition. But it is absurd to argue that the forbidden subjects and mixture of tones in *Don Juan* become understandable once the poem is called a satire or a burlesque. Such arguments illustrate the effect of naming that Byron thematizes, but they do not help us to read the poem. If one calls the poem a satire or a burlesque, then one mutes the essence of the poem—its relentless questioning of all institutions, poetical and political. In *Don Juan,* Byron consciously does not resort to the trick he used years before with *English Bards and Scotch Reviewers,* when he said that "if we call it a *Satire,* that will obviate the objection."[69]

To call the poem an epic is to grant it the stature it deserves, which is crucial and constitutes, I believe, Byron's main reason for insisting on the term, another being the pleasure he got from challenging his readers' expectations when they compare *Don Juan* with *Paradise Lost.* One can make the term epic fit by adopting Thomas Greene's theory that "norms for epic" change with each generation, which is what McGann does. One can also stress the metaphorical nature of the word, like Ridenour and Cooke. Another solution, adopted by Boyd, Kroeber, and Bakhtin, has been to call the poem a "novel in verse" because of its inclusive nature and because novels are associated with the epic. But the qualification "in verse" seems an afterthought that wrongly shifts the emphasis from the poetic to the prosaic. It is crucial to note the use of the adjective "poetical" when Byron refers to the poem as "a poetical T[ristram] Shandy" (BLJ 10:150). The distinction between prose and verse is central to *Don Juan,* where it functions like a leitmotif, and to the topic of poetic revolution in general. The choice of verse and the narrator's designation of the poem as epic are both serious and ironic, because Byron treats subjects in verse that would traditionally have been better suited to prose. In this case as in others, what shocks is not that he breaks with tradition, but that he uses it.[70] Any label, though it may dispel confusion, stifles or skirts the poem's daring, its unsettling simultaneity of lyrical and satirical tones. The best designation is Byron's own, "poesy," which includes all forms and subjects.

Nevertheless, one must acknowledge that despite the inclusivity of poesy, Byron holds on to the distinction of verse as high and prose as low. He is not unlike Frere, who says in the proem 2 of *The Monks and the Giants* that "I submissively propose / To erect one Board for Verse and one for Prose." The terms *prosaic* and *poetic* are dead metaphors that Byron revives to good effect, much as Molière does in *Le Bourgeois gentil-homme* or *Les Femmes savantes.* By the beginning of the nineteenth century, however, the literal distinction reasserts itself, because the elaborate systemization of verse forms has faded out. When Byron writes "of common things"—this time meaning coarse—and does so in verse, that alone is a breach of decorum. It is no longer sufficient, as it was for Pope or for Byron himself in *English Bards and Scotch Reviewers,* to cite labels as a dispensation from impropriety. The effect of verse, even visually—as the Russian formalists argue—is a sufficient indication of high style.

The form of *Don Juan* is thus at odds with the subjects Byron includes. What is "revolutionary" is the reassessment of high and low as well as the mixture of the two. One can no longer separate high and low, good and bad, true and false, tragedy and comedy, body and spirit, or even literal and figurative. People and poetry are as mobile as Adeline; they, too, derive their meaning from context and are "strongly acted on by what is nearest" (16.97). The logical consequence of so much mobility would seem to be nihilism, and many readers have understood the poem as a dark one despite its humor. But for all the skepticism, for all the questioning, for all the different layers of meaning and despite what Hermione de Almeida calls "the impossibility of true representation" in the poem,[71] there is a "point d'*appui*": the sense that uncertainty is itself a desirable, not a dreaded quality. Uncertainty is essential to poetry or to any art, which cannot have a finite number of meanings. Uncertainty possesses the quality that Byron describes at the beginning of canto 14 as the "secret prepossession / To plunge with all your fears," something of the frisson in witty form. To the admirer of *Don Juan,* it is both a frustration and a comfort to want to uncover associations and allusions in the poem and yet be unable to do so completely, for "Contented, when translated, means but cloyed." We get a sense in this poem that, as Friedrich Schlegel says in one of the *Athenäums-Fragmente,* it is equally deadening to the spirit to have a system and to have none; one must combine the two: "Es ist gleich tödlich für den Geist, ein System zu haben, und keins zu haben. Er wird sich also wohl entschließen müssen, beides zu verbinden."[72]

This is also the sense we get emblematically from ambiguous taste, which as I have argued mirrors Byron's equally emblematic manipulation of the ottava rima stanza. Taste and ottava rima are examples of freedom as Byron understands and displays it in *Don Juan,* and Boyd aptly calls the work his "declaration of independence." But freedom is clearly not the same as anarchy any more than the suspicion of systems is identical with chaos. Byron makes the distinction in a letter that is often cited and in which he claims the right to poetic liberties. He compares his poetic rights with the writ of habeas corpus in another example of the analogy between poetry and politics:

> Why Man the Soul of such writing is it's license?—at least the *liberty* of that *licence* if one likes—*not* that one should abuse it—it is like trial by Jury and Peerage—and the Habeas Corpus—a very fine thing—but chiefly in the *reversion*—because no one wishes to be tried for the mere pleasure of proving his possession of the privilege. (BLJ 6:208)

When he speaks of "such writing," Byron is disingenuous, since the nature of his poem, as I have argued, differs from those with which he compares it. Still, the comparison is important because of the insistence that liberty must not be abused and that it is ultimately exempt from his skepticism. Byron's indecorum in *Don Juan* is the emblem of a poetical revolution in which works of the high style are guillotined, or at least lose their privileges.[73] Through ambiguous taste and the things it stands for, *Don Juan* does indeed commit an "act of high treason on English poetry," as Southey says. In the process, something new takes shape that is more prominent still in the works of Heine.

CHAPTER 4

Heine and the Aesthetics
of the Tea Table

Laßt uns die Franzosen preisen! Sie sorgten für die zwei größten Bedürfnisse der
menschlichen Gesellschaft, für gutes Essen und bürgerliche Gleichheit; in der
Kochkunst und in der Freiheit haben sie die größten Fortschritte gemacht.
—Heine, *Die Reise von München nach Genua*

Das junge Mädchen sagte: "Der Herr muß sehr reich sein, denn er ist sehr
häßlich." Das Publikum urteilt in derselben Weise: Der Mann muß sehr gelehrt
sein, denn er ist sehr langweilig.
—Heine, "Aufzeichnungen"

It takes no great effort to remember references to food in Heine's works.
They are present in early works and late ones, in works of verse and of
prose, and are one of the constants of his writings. The best critics of
Heine naturally note the prevalence of his culinary allusions, however
briefly, and the *Chiffrenindex* to the Briegleb edition of his works in-
cludes an entry for "Essen und Trinken" [eating and drinking] (while
revealingly and decorously omitting an entry for digestion). Indeed, the
gustatory is so noticeable a part of Heine's world that scattered studies
deal with it. Barker Fairley published an essay called "Heine and the
Festive Board" in 1967, one that should by rights have been a chapter
in his influential book of 1954 on Heine's images; he himself says so and
credits Laura Hofrichter with pointing out to him the frequency and
importance of the topic. Since Fairley was an alert reader with a legendary
memory, the acknowledgment of his oversight seems to confirm the claim
that culinary questions often go unnoticed because they seem unimpor-
tant. In the essay of 1967, Fairley corrects his error and calls the image
of food "the one with the widest range, extending [...] from the lowest

115

in life to the highest, or from the least serious use of it to the most serious, even to the most urgent." But because he is working on new territory, Fairley is more concerned with presenting his evidence than interpreting it. Another critic who draws attention to Heine's culinary emphasis is Werner Vordtriede, who speaks of Heine's *Eßgedichte* ("eating" or "food" poems) in the introduction to his *Heine-Kommentar*. Vordtriede has also been credited with inspiring a dissertation by Bernd Wetzel that deals carefully with the subject of Heine and food, "Das Motiv des Essens im Werk Heinrich Heines" (1972).[1]

What has saved the topic from being avoided altogether is that Heine's references to food are often associated with his political themes. Again, many examples come to mind. There is the famous veiling of political statements in *Deutschland. Ein Wintermärchen*, where a vision of "Zukkererbsen für Jedermann" [peas for everyone] introduces a series of culinary references that are carried through to the end of the poem. When the narrator's mother asks her "Gretchenfrage" about his political loyalties ("Zu welcher Partei / Gehörst du mit Überzeugung?"), for example, the narrator answers obliquely with appreciative remarks about roast goose and peeled oranges, in Fairley's words "entrench[ing] himself behind the victuals."[2] The narrator's voice is audible nonetheless, and it is inadequate to dismiss his answer as a witty avoidance of her question; his answer is eloquent when one reads it against the other culinary references in the poem, especially when one juxtaposes it with the *absence* of culinary references in the Barbarossa chapter. Other combinations of the culinary and the political include the "Wanderratten" poem with its unforgettable opening, "Es gibt zwei Sorten Ratten, / Die hungrigen und satten" [There are two kinds of rat: / One hungry and one fat] (HCP 783), a Shakespearean categorization that Heine used earlier and less whimsically when he had the innkeeper in *William Ratcliff* divide the world into "full and famished" [die Satten und Hungerleidenden]. In the late preface to *William Ratcliff*, Heine designates poverty and social injustice as "the great soup quesiton" [die große Suppenfrage], and the culinary depiction of poverty and social class recurs poignantly in poems like "Der Philantrop" and "Jammerthal."

When they analyze these and other culinary examples, critics usually identify them with politics and satire only, even when they note the inseparability of aesthetic and political questions. Even the best of such interpretations tend toward a uniform interpretation of culinary images. In his article "Heines Appetit," for example, T. J. Reed calls food a "key for unlocking political meaning," but he does not try the key on anything else.[3] One article that deals with Heine's culinary allusions in a nonpolitical sense is the one by Peter Rühmkorf, a poet who has himself been compared to Heine (and whose poetry contains many culinary details). Rühmkorf objects to the equation of food and politics in his essay "Suppentopf und Guillotine: Zu Heines Frauengestalten" and stresses instead another common association with food: the erotic. Rühmkorf views the culinary references from the wider perspective related to my own, the perspective of aesthetic revolution.[4] Whether politics or erotics is his subtext, however, Heine is as always hard to pin down.

Mostly Heine's emphasis on food is explained as a sometimes amusing, sometimes embarrassing, and usually frivolous means toward a worthy political end. That the subject of politics serves to legitimize the indecorous is obvious from the vastly differing reception of three works that are dense with culinary allusions: *Ideen. Das Buch Le Grand, Aus den Memoiren des Herren von Schnabelewopski,* and *Deutschland. Ein Wintermärchen.* Of the three, only *Ideen. Das Buch Le Grand* is unanimously admired. But the culinary passages in it are generally abridged or overlooked. All but a few critics ignore the narrator's culinary description of his craft in chapter 14, for example, a central passage that makes sense only in connection with the other culinary references throughout the text.[5] As for *Deutschland. Ein Wintermärchen,* there are two distinct positions. Commentators either consider the eating and excrement a political necessity, or they condemn it as a poetic mistake. Jeffrey Sammons has little patience with the details from what Bakhtin would call the "material lower stratum" and calls the chamber pot episode at the end of the poem "the most stupendously disgusting posture of the poet-persona to be found anywhere in Heine's writing." His conclusion is witty but disputable: "One is tempted to say that only a psychiatrist could offer a satisfactory interpretation of the poet, who from beginning to end wrestles with images of his own dignity, with his head in a chamber pot. How even a doctrinaire Marxist can live easily with this scene is hard to understand."[6] Others defend the passage on the grounds that it is written in the tradition of Aristophanic satire. All of these interpretations underestimate the function of the indecorous in the rest of the work (which includes *Atta Troll*).

Only *Schnabelewopski* lacks overt references to politics, though it does contain a sharp critique of materialist society, and it is also the only one of the three works that lacks a secure place in the Heine canon. This raises

117

some questions. Either *Schnabelewopski* has more to do with politics than is generally assumed, since food is a dominant motif, or else culinary allusions do not have the automatic correlation to political subjects that critics have supposed. Yet to put the question this way, as an either/or, is a mistake. There is no work of Heine's in which politics is his exclusive theme, and I can think of no example where food is associated exclusively with politics. *Schnabelewopski* offers a test of this assumption, and one can counter criticism of the work by showing how and why Heine includes so many allusions to eating.[7]

For Heine to thematize food makes obvious sense, as it does for Byron, because of the subject's symbolic range from Christianity to the French Revolution, from the apple of knowledge to the brioche of Marie-Antoinette. Since it can be associated equally with the spirituality of love or the inevitability of excrement, food is a good vehicle for the aesthetic of ambiguity that Heine already begins to articulate in the letter to Immermann of 10 June 1823, where he says that we grasp things through their opposites and that there would be no poetry if there were nothing coarse or trivial: "Alle Dinge sind uns ja nur durch ihren Gegensatz erkennbar, es gäbe für uns gar keine Poesie, wenn wir nicht überall auch das Gemeine und Triviale sehen könnten" [Everything is manifest to us only through its opposite; there would be no poetry for us if we could not see coarse and trivial things everywhere] (HSA 23:91).[8] Gerhard Höhn, in imitation of the famous term applied to Brecht, *Verfremdungseffekt* (alienation effect) or *V-Effekt,* refers to this aesthetic tenet as "Kontrast-Effekt" or "K-Effekt."[9] For Heine as for Byron, indecorum serves a function that is willfully out of proportion with its literal significance. By overlooking their indecorum—mostly culinary and sometimes olfactory or fecal—we confirm one of the things they observe and expose: the tendency to be misled by appearances and habit. This has an advantage, however, because the presence of food or feces in a lyrical setting continues to elicit a shock that has faded with regard to other taboos. And shock is a measure of poetic revolution.[10] An analysis of Heine's references to literal taste confirms what Luciano Zagari says of the need to scrutinize and reassess precisely those passages or works of Heine's that have been considered flawed or embarrassing.[11]

One understands easily enough how the culinary conveys for Heine a connection between religion, politics, and sensuality. But just as those

118

issues and Heine's attitude toward them are complicated, so, too, are the culinary allusions that regularly represent them. Food never "means" politics or religion or eroticism, nor does it simply signal satire. Whenever Heine refers to food, it is in order to show two sides that seem mutually exclusive and yet can be represented by the same thing, as happens in the *Doppelgänger* or the "Apollogott" poems. His culinary allusions can represent rich *and* poor, as they do in "Der Philantrop"; sensuality *and* spirituality, as they do in *Ludwig Börne* or *Schnabelewopski*; poetry *and* politics, as they do in *Ideen. Das Buch Le Grand*; good *and* bad poetry, as they do in *Atta Troll*. They epitomize ambiguity, allowing him to structure while appearing to contradict or digress. By studying his culinary allusions in context, therefore, it is possible to show how Heine sets up his ambiguities and means them to remain dissonant; it is possible, in other words, to show much about his style. There are three questions of style that come into focus, remarkably so, when culinary subjects are present, and all are central to Heine's unresolvable (though not nihilistic) tensions: (1) the ability of a detail to represent the whole; (2) the revival of dead metaphors; and (3) his choice of prose or verse. These questions are not so separate as my listing of them makes them appear, but it is well to consider each briefly in turn before proceeding to their interdependence in two of Heine's poems and in *Buch Le Grand, Schnabelewopski,* the *Wintermärchen,* and *Atta Troll.*

From a Detail to the Whole

Culinary allusions exemplify what for Heine is axiomatic: that his details—among which I include his flourishes and apparent flippancy—demand special scrutiny. For Heine as for any author with his concerns, the relationship of a detail to the whole tests the reader's attention. He himself supplies the image for the relationship in *Shakespeares Mädchen und Frauen,* where he compares the mathematician and the poet, each of whom can reproduce a whole and a center from a fragment. The mathematician reproduces a whole circle, the poet an entire universe:

> Und wie der Mathematiker, wenn man ihm nur das kleinste Fragment
> eines Kreises gibt, unverzüglich den ganzen Kreis und den Mittelpunkt
> desselben angeben kann: so auch der Dichter, wenn seiner An-

schauung nur das kleinste Bruchstück der Erscheinungswelt von außen geboten wird, offenbart sich ihm gleich der ganze universelle Zusammenhang dieses Bruchstücks; er kennt gleichsam Zirkulatur und Zentrum aller Dinge; er begreift die Dinge in ihrem weitesten Umfang und tiefsten Mittelpunkt. (DHA 10:16)

[And like the mathematician who unhesitatingly reconstructs the whole circle and its center from the smallest fragment of a circle, the poet, if presented with the smallest fraction of the phenomenological world, instantly beholds the entire, universal connection to this fraction; he knows, so to speak, the circumference and the center of all things; he grasps things in their widest perimeter and at their innermost center.]

Heine's culinary details, too, must be considered as fragments from which to reconstruct a whole.

Heine works with culinary allusions much as he does with comparisons when he repeats only the second term and expects the reader to remember the first. One such example, not culinary but indecorous, is the comparison of Signora Lätitia's bosom to a red sea in *Die Bäder von Lucca.* A few paragraphs after the two are compared, Gumpelino bends his forehead so that Signora Lätitia can kiss it, and his face is said to reach ever deeper until his nose, the "helm" of his face, "rows around" in the Red Sea: "so daß sein Gesicht tiefer hinabreichte, und das Steuer desselben, die Nase, im roten Meere herumruderte" [so that his face reached down deeper and its helm, the nose, rowed around in the Red Sea] (DHA 7:1.98). Multiple associations are meant to jostle each other in the reader's mind, principal among them the Shandyan function of the nose, which in turn recalls the Sternean use of allusion and digression throughout *Die Bäder von Lucca.* The task of the reader, here and elsewhere, is to make these associations despite the appearance of a loose and haphazard order. In *Die Bäder von Lucca,* the mixture of motif and extended metaphor is connected to questions of poetry and anti-Semitism; it is a mixture that occurs within a literary frame including Sterne and Shakespeare as well as Platen. Alone, the extended metaphor of the Red Sea would be an example of bawdiness, no more. What makes it characteristic of Heine is its connection to the rest of the work.[12] Like the details of *Die Bäder von Lucca,* culinary allusions cannot be fully understood if they are separated from the works in which they occur. To collect them (or

120

any other theme or image) and to study them without their setting, as
Fairley, Wetzel, and Reed do to varying degrees, is useful but in-
sufficient.[13]

The treatment of ambiguous taste in "Sie saßen und tranken am Tee-
tisch" from *Buch der Lieder* ("Lyrisches Intermezzo" 50) exemplifies the
manner in which a detail is expressive of a whole and influences it, first
within the poem and then as a poem within the cycle. The poem is a love
poem, but like so many in *Buch der Lieder,* it is also a poetological poem
that speaks of and shows Heine's break with an aesthetic tradition, a
tradition represented here by figurative taste:

> Sie saßen und tranken am Teetisch,
> Und sprachen von Liebe viel.
> Die Herren, die waren ästhetisch,
> Die Damen von zartem Gefühl.
>
> Die Liebe muß sein platonisch,
> Der dürre Hofrat sprach.
> Die Hofrätin lächelt ironisch,
> Und dennoch seufzet sie: Ach!
>
> Der Domherr öffnet den Mund weit:
> Die Liebe sei nicht zu roh,
> Sie schadet sonst der Gesundheit.
> Das Fräulein lispelt: wie so?
>
> Die Gräfin spricht wehmütig:
> Die Liebe ist eine Passion!
> Und präsentieret gütig
> Die Tasse dem Herren Baron.
>
> Am Tische war noch ein Plätzchen;
> Mein Liebchen, da hast du gefehlt.
> Du hättest so hübsch, mein Schätzchen,
> Von deiner Liebe erzählt.
>
> (DHA 1:1.183–85)

> [They talked of love and devotion
> Over the tea and the sweets—
> The ladies, of tender emotion;
> The men talked like aesthetes.

121

"True love must be platonic,"
A wizened old councillor cried.
His wife, with a smile ironic,
Bent down her head and sighed.

The canon opened his fat face:
"Love must not be coarse, you know,
It's bad for the health in that case."
A young girl lisped, "Why so?"

The countess sadly dissented:
"Oh, love must be wild and free!"
And graciously presented
The baron a cup of tea.

You should have been there, my treasure;
An empty chair stood near.
You'd talk of love and its pleasure
So charmingly, my dear.

(HCP 68–69)]

Like Byron in the octave on *goût* and the gout, who alerts the reader to poetological questions by alluding in the first line to art and nature, Heine lets the word "ästhetisch" fall in the first stanza. By rhyming the word "ästhetisch" with "Teetisch" (a union that is visually all the more striking with the nineteenth-century spelling "Theetisch"), he demonstrates an aesthetic program that is distinct from the one implicated and to which the people at this table are shown to adhere. The rhyme often is cited as one of Heine's most amusing and impertinent, as a good example of his *Stimmungsbrechung*, which it is. His introduction of the comic into a lyric setting is as indecorous as his evocation of people taking tea. In and of itself, however, the act of eating and drinking (especially the latter) is not shocking. "Sie saßen und tranken" would be acceptable in a poem modeled after some from *Des Knaben Wunderhorn*—"Der Himmel hängt voll Geigen," for example—or that imitates one of Goethe's versions of the *Volkslied*, something like "Der König in Thule" in *Faust*. However, any connection with the artlessness and naturalness of the *Volkslied* or with the stylization of such qualities in *Faust* (though Goethe is less decorous than his reputation, as I will argue later) is severed by the word "Teetisch"; that unexpected word in turn makes us mistrust the "poetic" word order in the second line, "Und sprachen von Liebe viel," making it seem pseudopoetic. What Heine attacks in his poem are a system and expectation that tolerate a subject in one frame and not in another.[14]

With the word *ästhetisch* at the end of the third line, Heine has succinctly called into question received notions of poetry; he has cited and begins to remake a poetic tradition, formally and semantically, as Perraudin shows him doing in the whole of *Buch der Lieder*. Formally, "Die Herren, sie waren ästhetisch" satirizes the poetry approved by these "Herren"; semantically, the word "ästhetisch" is misapplied by the gentlemen just as Heine misuses the word when he attributes the quality to men rather than to works of art. The difference is that the poet knows what he is doing, whereas the gentlemen speak and think in clichés. The poet's free usage contrasts with the stiff and narrow-minded speech of the gentlemen described as "ästhetisch." What they say has the same prescriptive, disembodied, impotent qualities as a work "in good taste" does to a Romantic poet. The wordplay here has a considered purpose, the kind that Wulf Wülfing demonstrates in all of Heine's writings. It is an aspect of the comic that is fundamental to his style, and the comic rhyme of "Gesundheit" and "den Mund weit" further ironizes the dissociation of aesthetics and eating.[15]

Heine's challenge to poetic convention also contains a challenge to the structure of society, the seating at this *Teetisch* having been composed with as much deliberation as the language. Bourgeoisie, clergy, and aristocracy are represented by each set of guests, and it is possible that the poet's absent sweetheart, like many of the sweethearts in the cycle, is from the fourth estate. She is perhaps excluded from the company just as the rhyme of *Teetisch* and *ästhetisch* has been excluded from "tasteful" poetry. Heine never says why "Mein Liebchen" is absent, however; it could also be that she might say something less *hübsch* (pretty) than the poet imagines. Either way, her absence shows off a series of conflicts on which the poem is structured: the *Domherr*'s wide-open mouth subverts his stilted injunction against vulgarity; the *Gräfin*'s words about passion are at odds with her placidly gracious gesture when she hands the baron his teacup, a gesture described by the poet as "gütig"; the *Hofrat*'s pompous remarks about platonic love are relativized by his wife's ironic smile, which further contrasts with her sigh and her "ach!" All conflicts in the poem can be summarized as the conflict between a poetry of appearances (or good taste) and one of truth (truth in the range of meanings we know from

Byron); it is the conflict between presence and exclusion both at table and in poetry, or between what is said and what is suppressed. But ultimately the existence of conflicts rather than the naming of them is what matters. More important still is the poet's role as the one who sets them up (Giese aptly calls him a "metteur en scène").[16]

The poet is the main character, the one to thwart poetic expectations and the expectations of language generally, whether in the use of *ästhetisch* to mean something unusual and as a rhyme for *Teetisch*, or in the words he lets his characters speak. Whether the beloved speaks sweetly is less important than the change in tone that is introduced when the poet invokes her, a tone that contrasts with the satirical description of those present. To mention the beloved is a kind of *Stimmungsbrechung* in reverse, and the seamlessness with which the poet moves from one register to another mirrors his ability to evoke different subjects at once and to present, at the same time, a microcosm of society and a summary of old and new poetic forms. Equally important is the placement of this poem in the segment entitled "Lyrisches Intermezzo," a heading that seems to imply a redefinition of what is lyrical. In that sense his poem is a "detail" that affects the whole of "Lyrisches Intermezzo" first and the whole of *Buch der Lieder* second, demonstrating Höhn's claim that Heine's cycle is ordered so that the meaning of individual poems is complicated and augmented by context. Höhn compares the process to concentric circles, each of which is capable of providing a new layer of meaning.[17]

Dead Metaphors Revived

Implicit but not stated in the poem "Sie saßen und tranken am Teetisch" is a play on the word *taste*, which is a signature of Heine as it is of Byron, and to much the same end. The wordplay on taste revives dead metaphors and forces us to rethink habits of usage that stand for other habits, as we have seen already in the case of Byron. For both poets, as many critics have demonstrated and as I have argued for *Don Juan*, the traditions of linguistic usage and poetic form are questioned in a way that approximates our questioning of other institutions. Punning and the revival of dead metaphors accomplish in miniature what Michael Perraudin has brilliantly demonstrated for the whole of *Buch der Lieder*: that Heine makes specific use of poetic traditions and quotations to produce a style that is distinct and original. Heine describes the method when he speaks of Cervantes (and himself) in his introduction to a translation of *Don Quixote:* "So pflegen immer große Poeten zu verfahren: sie begründen zugleich etwas Neues, indem sie das Alte zerstören; sie negieren nie, ohne etwas zu bejahen" [This is how great poets always proceed: they establish something new while destroying something old; they never negate without affirming] (DHA 10:257). By playing on both literal and figurative meanings at once, Heine accomplishes with his style the stance of the doppelgänger; he achieves all at once what the *Stimmungsbruch* does in succession. The result is a sense of tension for which Heine and his contemporaries use the word *Zerrissenheit* (the state of being torn). One can also call the method a symbolist one, because any object, whether it is trivial, ugly, or grand, is capable of acquiring an immaterial, poetic quality.[18]

Any dead metaphor or received tradition that Heine revives will serve to illustrate his manner, but culinary metaphors are deader than most because of the distance between food and spirit. Deadest of all is the Eucharist, as we saw already in the case of Byron and as one knows from Diderot's *Encyclopédie,* where the article *anthropophages* contains cross-references to the Eucharist, communion, and altar ("Voyez Eucharistie, Communion, Autel, etc."). Louis Marin analyzes the Eucharist as an example of the relationship between literal and figurative usage; he speaks of how the figure hides something literal in order to reveal connections on the figurative level. Diderot, Byron, and Heine invert the relation of object and figure: they revive the dead metaphor and hide nothing.[19] Heine's literal treatment of the Eucharist in the *Romanzero* cycle frames the work in the poems "Vitzliputzli" and "Disputation," which conclude the first and final books in the cycle (another instance of how motivic repetition tests the reader's attention). One can speak of a "progression" in poetic revolution when one compares the blasphemy of Heine to that of Byron in canto 2 of *Don Juan:* whereas Byron exposes the connection between cannibalism and Christianity indirectly, Heine states it loudly and feigns to forget the sacrament, as if cannibalism alone were his casual concern. The effect of the shock is similar, but Byron expects us to *find* the connection, whereas Heine expects us to *remember* it, not just in reading the poem at the end of the first part of *Romanzero,* but throughout the cycle.

In "Vitzliputzli," Heine introduces the Eucharist with a literary vocabulary that empties the ritual of its religious origins and reminds us that his blasphemy applies to poetic rituals as well; he also changes the word *transsubstantiation* to "transsubstitution" [transsubstituiert], a change that Draper does not retain:

> "Menschenopfer" heißt das Stück.
> Uralt ist der Stoff, die Fabel;
> In der christlichen Behandlung
> Ist das Schauspiel nicht so gräßlich.
>
> Denn dem Blute wurde Rotwein,
> Und dem Leichnam, welcher vorkam,
> Wurde eine harmlos dünne
> Mehlbreispeis' transsubstituieret—
>
> Diesmal aber, bei den Wilden,
> War der Spaß sehr roh und ernsthaft
> Aufgefaßt: man speiste Fleisch,
> Und das Blut war Menschenblut.
>
> Diesmal war es gar das Vollblut
> Von Altchristen, das sich nie,
> Nie vermischt hat mit dem Blute
> Der Moresken und der Juden.
>
> Freu dich, Vitzliputzli, freu dich,
> Heute gibt es Spanierblut,
> Und am warmen Dufte wirst du
> Gierig laben deine Nase.
>
> Heute werden dir geschlachtet
> Achtzig Spanier, stolze Braten
> Für die Tafel deiner Priester,
> Die sich an dem Fleisch erquicken.
>
> Denn der Priester ist ein Mensch,
> Und der Mensch, der arme Fresser,
> Kann nicht bloß vom Riechen leben
> Und vom Dufte, wie die Götter.
>
> (DHA 3:1.68–69)

> ["Human Sacrifice" is its title.
> Ancient plot, an ancient fable;
> In its Christian form the drama

Is not such a gruesome version—

For the blood is changed to red wine,
And the body that's presented
Is by transsubstantiation
Just a harmless little wafer.

Now, however, savage Indians
Played this jest out in raw earnest:
It was real flesh that they fed on
And the blood was human blood.

Now indeed it was a question
Of the purebred blood of Christians,
Old-time Christians, never mingled
With the blood of Moors and Jews.

Oh, rejoice then, Vitzliputzli,
For today it's Spanish blood that
Will regale your greedy nostrils
With its warm and fragrant vapors.

Yes, today there will be slaughtered
Eighty Spaniards—splendid roastmeat
For the table of your priesthood,
Who need meat to stroke their fires.

For the priests are men and mortals,
And we men must fill our stomachs—
We can't simply live on odors
And aromas, as the gods do.]

(HCP 609)

The literary images—"'Menschenopfer' heißt das Stück," "Stoff," "Fabel"—and the insouciant tone with which sombre and gruesome matters are described show that Heine proceeds with great self-awareness. A third dimension of his wordplay on the Eucharist broadens the scope: blood is used metonymically to designate racial prejudice ("das Vollblut / Der Altchristen, das sich nie / Nie vermischt hat mit dem Blute / Der Moresken und der Juden"). The procedure in these examples challenges Prawer's assumption that in the *Romanzero* poems, Heine "exhibits an occasional obtuseness in things of the spirit which is astonishing in so

127

sensitive and intelligent a poet—one need only recall the wilful misunderstanding of the symbolism of bread and wine in *Vitzliputzli*."[20]

Heine repeats the same "wilful misunderstanding" in "Disputation," where literalism replaces philosophy (or philosophical pretense) in the fight between the rabbi and the priest. Each antagonist exercises culinary persuasion, and Heine dwells on the ridiculous but amusing literalism of each contender in part to show, as he often does, that it is not the culinary in and of itself that is absurd, but the exclusive materialism of those who, like the rabbi and the priest, lack critical distance. In "Disputation," the rabbi first introduces culinary arguments when he describes the Leviathan:

> Doch sein Fleisch ist delikat,
> Delikater als Schildkröten,
> Und am Tag der Auferstehung
> Wird der Herr zu Tische beten
>
> Alle frommen Auserwählten,
> Die Gerechten und die Weisen—
> Unsres Herrgotts Lieblingsfisch
> Werden sie alsdann verspeisen,
>
> Teils mit weißer Knoblauchbrühe
> Teils auch braun in Wein gesotten,
> Mit Gewürzen und Rosinen,
> Ungefähr wie Matelotten.
>
> In der weißen Knoblauchbrühe
> Schwimmen kleine Schäbchen Rettich—
> So bereitet, Frater Jose,
> Mundet dir das Fischlein, wett ich!
>
> Auch die braune ist so lecker,
> Nämlich die Rosinensauce,
> Sie wird himmlisch wohl behagen
> Deinem Bäuchlein, Frater Jose.
>
> Was Gott kocht, ist gut gekocht!
>
> (DHA 3:1.168)

["But his flesh is tasty, more so
Than a turtle's fresh from shore;
On the day of resurrection
God will spread a table for

"All the pious, wise, and upright
Chosen souls from everywhere—
And the Lord God's favorite fish will
Furnish out the bill of fare.

"Partly with white garlic gravy
Partly in a well-browned roux
Made with spicy wine and raisins—
Something like a seafood stew.

"Sizzling in the garlic gravy,
Bits of radish fizz and hiss—
I would wager, friar, you would
Relish fish prepared like this!

"Or the brown one—it's delicious
Raisin sauce right off the fire;
It would make a little Heaven
In your belly, dearest friar.

"God's cuisine is haute cuisine."]

(HCP 685)

The rabbi's lack of self-awareness is further apparent when he uses the word "himmlisch" (heavenly) as a dead metaphor.

The priest's arguments are free of double entendre until he recites a part of the liturgy and says that he has "enjoyed" the body of Christ, unwittingly punning when he calls it his "Leibgericht," *Leib* meaning body as well as favorite, hence "body dish" as well as "favorite dish." His choice of words discredits his arguments and is symptomatic of a lack of perception elsewhere. It is the reader who revives the connection ignored by the priest, as was likewise the case when the rabbi argued before him:

Trotzen kann ich deinen Geistern,
Deinen dunkeln Höllenpossen,

129

Denn in mir ist Jesus Christus,
Habe seinen Leib genossen.

Christus ist mein Leibgericht,
Schmeckt viel besser als Leviathan
Mit der weißen Knoblauchsauce,
Die vielleicht gekocht der Satan.

(DHA 3:1.171)

["I defy your hellish spirits,
All their tricks are cheap and shoddy,
For within me is Christ Jesus,
I've partaken of his body.

"Christ's my favorite dish, much better
Than Leviathan-in-a-pot,
Even with white garlic gravy
Made by Satan, like as not."]

(HCP 687–88)

More revealing still is the use of culinary imagery that follows the priest's
mention of Satan and that betrays his unchristian thoughts:

Ach! anstatt zu disputieren,
Lieber möcht ich schmoren, braten
Auf dem wärmsten Scheiterhaufen
Dich und deine Kameraden. (DHA 3:1.171)

["Oh! instead of wrangling, I would
Rather roast you on a fire,
Stew you and your comrades with you
On the hottest funeral pyre."]

(HCP 688)

Heine exploits the kind of comic convention we find in Molière's *Les
Femmes savantes,* where Trissotin betrays his true feelings through his
images, or in Fielding's *Joseph Andrews,* where Mrs. Slipslop reveals her
subconscious desires through her malapropisms. What is different here is
the lyrical context, which gives both the punning and the blasphemy a
sharper edge and revitalizes a convention, making it appear new. Equally

new is that despite the dark humor of Heine's blasphemous wordplays there is a lyrical dimension to this passage: it comes from the frequent association of food and memory for Heine. For the child food, not dogma and spirit, is the center of religious ritual, and the rabbi and the priest therefore identify food and faith because of childhood associations. But neither recognizes the source of the association, which they confuse instead with spiritual issues. The culinary argumentation exposes yet again the literal-mindedness and intellectual limits of both rabbi and priest; but for the poet and the reader, who know the source of the connection between food and faith, the allusions to food contain a dimension that surpasses the comic.

Prose and Poetry versus Prosaic and Poetic

Heine's use of prose and verse subsumes the first two issues. What with Byron and Goethe is an emerging mistrust of the distinction between prose as low style and poetry as high style is more definite in the case of Heine, whose confusion of the two forms is a source of his originality. Schlegel's theory, when he speaks of a *Poesie* without generic boundaries, has become Heine's practice.[21] This is a question of such centrality that it must be discussed before it is illustrated with culinary examples. It makes little sense to speak of how Heine uses culinary allusions as an emblem of literary revolution without having spoken more specifically about his role in that revolution.

Few question the existence of literary revolution at the end of the eighteenth and the beginning of the nineteenth centuries, as I have said before. Nor is there any doubt about the dissolution of boundaries between prose and verse as a result of that revolution. And yet it is still common to speak of and study separately Heine's writings in verse and in prose. One finds the division in Höhn's ordering of the *Heine-Handbuch*, for example, where there is a practical justification for it but where it jars nevertheless, especially given Höhn's sensitivity to questions of form.[22] Part of the blame can surely be laid on Adorno, who upholds a neoclassical ideal of poetry in "Die Wunde Heine" (1956), the short essay that continues to exert too great an influence on Heine studies. Only at the end of the piece, where Adorno astutely compares Heine and Mahler, is there a grudging acknowledgment that the dissonances in Heine's lyric mode can be considered a sign of modernity. One senses nonetheless that Adorno mourns an earlier, more decorous kind of lyric poetry.[23] To criticize Heine's dissonances or to separate his prose and poetry is to misconstrue the gist of his aesthetic, which combines rather than separates opposites of style, genre, metaphor, or philosophy without neutralizing a sense of the tension among them. Preisendanz appropriately speaks of a "prose-making" [Prosaierung] of the lyric and of Heine's "lyric realism," but he limits these qualities to the late poems. The issue is broader than one of subject or chronology, however. The comic effect achieved when so-called prosaic subjects are mentioned in verse (typically food, as we saw in "Vitzliputzli" and "Disputation") has its counterpart when a traditionally nonpoetic subject transcends its literal meaning, regardless of prose or prosody, as we have begun to see. Heine's method does indeed resemble the transubstantiation of which he makes fun in poems like "Vitzliputzli" and "Disputation," with the difference mentioned earlier that his material referent subsists alongside the figurative, much as the comic is a foil for serious concerns.

As I have said, there is a practical reason for the distinction between prose and verse. But there is a danger as well: the tendency to associate the form, prose or verse, with a metaphorical use of the terms *prosaic* and *poetic*. Here as in the case of taste, inattention to literal and nonliteral meanings obscures something that ought to be obvious: the fact that one cannot assume anything for Heine's verse without asking whether it applies equally to his prose, and vice versa. Heine refuses to put the subjects of his writing into their place, generically speaking, because no fixed place exists; he no more takes a generic party line than he does a political one. This does not mean that he fails to see a difference between prose and verse; on the contrary, he uses that difference to undermine the expectations of his readers and to forge new forms. Hosfeld aptly says that "Heines eigene Innovation liegt [. . .] auf einer formalen Ebene, allerdings auf einer Ebene der Form, die selbst Bedeutung trägt."[24] That Heine is not an either/or poet has rightly become a commonplace of Heine criticism; the formal reflection of that fact, however—the way the prosaic (figuratively) enters his verse and the poetic (again figuratively) enters his prose—still strikes me as underrated. In the past several years, much attention has been paid to the conscious confusion between fact and fiction in Heine's prose; and while that confusion is related to the conflation of prose and verse, it too often has been studied by avoiding questions of form in favor of discussions of historical accuracy or political allegiance.

132

Preisendanz's influential study of Heine's *Schreibart* (style or form), first published in 1973, did not cast the net wide enough, and for good reason. Preisendanz was addressing an audience for whom discussions of Heine's aesthetics were suspect. The division he draws between the early and the late poetry is related to the division he draws between prose and lyric, even though a central part of his thesis is that for Heine there is no such thing as a nonpoetic text. His failure to state and stress the inadequacy of generic distinctions comes from the climate against which he wrote and for which he makes Jost Hermand the spokesman: the belief that Heine was not a poet, that in his prose he had only political thoughts and that he disparaged aesthetic questions. Preisendanz rightly questions Hermand's definition of *Dichtung* and argues instead that a source of Heine's originality lies in his redefinition of *Dichtung*. This is definitely the case, but not only for the prose works. Preisendanz would surely write differently now, some twenty years later; critics who at one time insisted on the division between Heine's prose and verse, like S. S. Prawer, have indeed changed their opinion.[25]

The term *Schreibart* that Preisendanz uses is Heine's own; when Heine remarks that his style, not his thought, was considered a "crime" ("Mein Verbrechen war nicht der Gedanke, sondern die Schreibart, der Stil"), the comment applies to literary decorum more than to political content.[26] Heine's pronouncement is related to Byron's manipulation of the word *crime* and Zola's nearly identical statement that form is "the great crime." It is precisely because these authors reject formal divisions that they are branded as literary criminals. They have transgressed against an order in which "prosaic" is identical with prose and "poetic" with certain types of the lyric. Ritchie Robertson is right to speak of the need "to discard the prejudice (enshrined in the Dewey cataloguing system) which places lyric poetry and satire in separate categories and marks the latter as inferior."[27]

From the visual mixture of forms in the *Reisebilder* it should be clear that the meaning of the word *lyrical* has shifted, a shift already apparent in Heine's title "Lyrisches Intermezzo."[28] No longer is it possible to judge or separate on the basis of a superficial impression like the division between prose and verse. Heine's visual undoing of genre at the beginning of his career announces and epitomizes the subversion one finds in everything he wrote. His mixture of prose and verse in *Die Harzreise* or *Aus den Memoiren des Herren von Schnabelewopski* and of *Nordsee* poems with the prose of *Nordsee III* are only more obvious, visual, examples of a larger aesthetic phenomenon, one typical of the Romantic age and its poetic revolution. Jost Hermand considers the verses in *Die Harzreise* unremarkable, because he associates them with the conventions of travel literature. But Heine's *Reisebilder* are travel literature in name only. Heine, like Sterne and Diderot before him, pretends to choose the genre because of the freedoms it allows; but his practice shows that he questions the raison d'être of genre. In *Die Harzreise* the issue is less crucial than it is in *Die Nordsee*, where free verse and essayistic prose are joined under one title. In *Ideen. Das Buch Le Grand*, the problem is inverted because the work's lyrical strain subverts our expectations of prose.[29] Briegleb's Heine edition makes an important statement about Heine's generic iconoclasm, since it orders the works chronologically and rejects the facile and false generic division adopted by most editors. For Würffel, the impossibility of dividing Heine's works according to prose and verse is of such consequence that he considers it a matter of principle to quote Heine's texts from the Briegleb edition.[30]

Schlegel's characterization of *Poesie* in *Athenäums-Fragment* 116 is based on the dissolution of boundaries between prose and verse. But Schlegel's ideal is frustrated by the difficulty of thinking against expectations that are visually reenforced, expectations that account in part for the differing reception of Byron and Heine. From *Don Juan* we know that Byron rejects a system of genres, not just in his conception of epic but also in his perception of how verse is related to prose. As I discussed earlier, Byron chooses subjects that his contemporaries do not expect to see treated in verse, and he manipulates the ottava rima stanza so that it sounds at times like prose. Yet despite his poetic daring and certain biographical details (his career in the House of Lords and his participation in the Greek fight for liberation), Byron has been spared the ideological appropriation imposed on Heine, who never held political office or physically climbed a barricade, but who wrote in prose and published in newspapers.

Heine did not completely disown the traditional function of prose and verse, and at times he seems to adopt a conventional attitude toward their status. But his vocabulary and usage generally reflect the Schlegelian philosophy in which *Poesie* designates great literature, whether it is in verse or prose, and *prosaisch* denotes a kind of antiliterature. Both words are meant figuratively. Sometimes in Heine's usage, the distinction between the literal and figurative meaning or between conventional and Schlegelian *Poesie* is blurred, but one can usually grasp his meaning by keeping in mind several things that any reader of Heine knows to be necessary in any case. First is the difference I have been stressing between literal and figurative meaning, which to the reader of literature seems hopelessly obvious but which can be frustratingly difficult to maintain, because so often they overlap. Second is the equally obvious factor of context. The caution to heed Heine's context will likewise sound simpleminded; but context works in wondrous ways and is often forgotten, as any careful reader of "Du bist wie eine Blume" and the surrounding poems will testify. The cycle *Buch der Lieder* is the paradigmatic example of how meanings and moods shift depending on their setting. Those meanings and moods are contradictory only in the complementary sense that Heine attributes to the "Doppelfigur" of Don Quixote and Sancho Panza, "[die] sich beständig parodieren und doch so wunderbar ergänzen, daß sie den eigentlichen Helden des Romans bilden" [who parody each other constantly and yet complement each other in such a wondrous way that together they constitute the novel's hero] (DHA 10:261). Heine naturally speaks of himself as much as of Cervantes; his own doppelgänger is the "hero" of *Buch der Lieder* and ought to be the interpreter's muse.[31] Finally, one must remember Heine's questioning, like Byron's, of institutions. The *Signatur* of such questioning is language and within language, inherited poetic forms. Whenever the words *Prosa, prosaisch, Verse,* or *Poesie* occur in Heine's writings, we need to be wary of their inherited meanings, which are mostly of neoclassical origin, and to observe Heine's usage, which is rarely if ever literal and can only be gauged in context. If one keeps in mind these issues—of literal and figurative meanings; of context; and of Heine's calling things into question—some things become understandable that otherwise seem odd.

Two texts of 1837 help to illustrate Heine's usage, the "Einleitung zu *Don Quixote*" and the preface to a new edition of *Buch der Lieder*. In the "Einleitung zu *Don Quixote*" Heine speaks of a "Dichtertriumvirat" [triumvirate of poets] consisting of Cervantes, Shakespeare, and Goethe, each of whom is associated with one of the three genres: "Cervantes, Shakespeare und Goethe bilden das Dichtertriumvirat, das in den drei Gattungen poetischer Darstellung, im Epischen, Dramatischen und Lyrischen, das Höchste hervorgebracht" [Cervantes, Shakespeare, and Goethe constitute the triumvirate of poets that has brought forth the greatest things in the three genres of poetic representation—epic, dramatic, and lyric] (DHA 10:260). But the division is tenuous, and Heine sets it up in order to undo it: having associated Goethe with the lyric genre, Heine praises his prose style and compares it to that of Cervantes. His use of the word *prosaisch* has little to do with prose in the literal sense but becomes the literary counterpart to the mentality of the petit bourgeois, the *Spießbürger*. At one point Heine merges the two and speaks of "prosaische Spießbürgerlichkeit," which he opposes to the "democratic" element in the writings of Cervantes and the "aristocratic" element in the writings of Scott.

In the "Einleitung zu *Don Quixote*," Heine's usage is clearly figurative. In the preface to the 1837 edition of *Buch der Lieder*, on the other hand, he seems to speak literally and to repudiate verse. Many critics read the preface as proof that Heine mistrusts and even rejects verse. Often the preface is quoted together with the passage from *Die Reise von München nach Genua* in which the narrator says that a sword, not a laurel wreath, should be laid on his grave to honor him as "ein braver Soldat im Befreiungskrieg der Menschheit" [a valiant soldier in the war of human literation], a comment likewise complicated by its context. Both passages are moving and remarkable, but they are no more one-sided than anything else Heine wrote. They are as misrepresentative, in isolation, as "Die Lorelei" or "Du bist wie eine Blume" isolated from the rest of *Buch der Lieder*. What makes these passages moving is that they reflect Heine's struggle between an idealized and harmonious world, traditionally represented by verse, and the reality of the commonplace—or to him of oppression—that requires practical, or "prosaic," resistance. This is the struggle that structures *Ideen. Das Buch Le Grand*, and it needs to be met by our own struggle to catch Heine's meaning, for example in the preface of 1837:

> Seit einiger Zeit sträubt sich etwas in mir gegen alle gebundene Rede, und wie ich höre, regt sich bei manchen Zeitgenossen eine ähnliche Abneigung. Es will mich bedünken, als sei in schönen Versen allzuviel gelogen worden, und die Wahrheit scheue sich in metrischen Gewänden zu erscheinen. (DHA 1:1.564)

> [For a while now something in me has resisted verse, and I understand that a similar dislike has been stirring among many of my contemporaries. To me it seems as if there has been too much lying in verse, as if truth shies away from cloaking itself in meter.]

The first thing to consider is the position of this text as a preface to a collection of poems. That apparent contradiction ironizes the statement, but the irony does not come from the fact that Heine is "lying" in prose while seeming to criticize "lies" in verse. Rather, it is an irony of the kind one finds in *Buch der Lieder* between different moods and dictions. At issue is not so much a distinction between prose and verse—at least not where Heine's own works are concerned—as a criticism of a particular kind of verse. Heine's expressed antipathy toward verse makes an exception for his own poems, which he defends further on and, more to the point, which he is in the process of republishing.

There are two different kinds of verse, the "pretty" and the political, and Heine distances himself from both by showing, as so often in his attacks, that he excepts his own writings from the generalizations he makes. He begins by saying that truth is incompatible with verse: "Es will mich dünken, als sei in schönen Versen allzuviel gelogen worden, und die Wahrheit scheue sich, in metrischen Gewänden zu zeigen." The poems of *Buch der Lieder* are in verse ("gebundener Rede"), which he has just called a repository for lies, but Heine implies that he himself does not lie in his poems. On the contrary, he appears to respond to the criticism that his poems contain too much rather than too little truth in Byron's non-idealistic sense.[32] Heine distances himself from a kind of verse that does not resemble his own, not from verse altogether. His comments here have much the same function as his ridicule elsewhere of Platen, Freiligrath, or the poets of his own imagining: Atta Troll's culinary and olfactory images resemble those of the poet-narrator, but the shared referent makes the poet's skill stand out all the more clearly. The culinary images of Heine's ridiculed poets (which he repeats in the article "Der Schwabenspiegel" of the same period) are not inferior because they are culinary, but because they are entirely materialistic despite a pretense to poetic form; whatever refers only to itself is disqualified as poetry. One can poeticize the culinary, and one can write verse without lies, but to do so requires a control that Heine finds lacking in the works he criticizes.

That Heine's own verse is not implicated—that we cannot take him at his literal word—is again evident near the end of the preface, where he applies the word *poetisch* to only a part of his works. At first he seems to uphold the hierarchy of verse and prose when he begs the reader's indulgence and hopes that his political, theological, and philosophical writings will make up for the weaknesses of his poems:

> Bescheidenen Sinnes und um Nachsicht bittend, übergebe ich dem Publikum das Buch der Lieder; für die Schwäche dieser Gedichte mögen vielleicht meine politischen, theologischen und philosophischen Schriften einigen Ersatz bieten. (DHA 1:1.565–66)

> [I offer the *Buch der Lieder* to the public, modestly requesting the reader's indulgence; may my political, theological, and philosophical writings offer some compensation for the weaknesses of these poems.]

Even in a concrete sense it is not possible to apply to Heine's writings the separation that he seems to make here. His mixture of verse and prose in *Die Nordsee* blatantly contradicts him. Heine does not leave it to the reader to note the inconsistency; in the "jedoch" [however] of the sentence that follows, he undermines the division he seemed to uphold at first:

> *Bemerken muß ich jedoch,* daß meine poetischen, eben so gut wie meine politischen, theologischen und philosophischen Schriften, einem und demselben Gedanken entsprossen sind, und daß man die einen nicht verdammen darf, ohne den andern allen Beifall zu entziehen. (DHA 1:1.566; my emphasis)

> [*Nevertheless I must note* that my poetical writings, like my political, theological, and philosophical ones, spring from one and the same idea and that one cannot condemn the one without withdrawing approval for the other.]

He stresses the common source of his works, regardless of their formal characteristics or even, he implies, of their subject. An allegiance to *littérature engagée* need not require the sacrifice of aesthetic interests.

A few sentences later, Heine undercuts his claim even further by quoting and interpreting two lines of verse. The visual effect of verse in the midst of prose embodies his ultimate conviction, which is that boundaries between them are not desirable and cannot be maintained:

Die Melodie dieser Verse summt mir schon den ganzen Morgen im Kopfe und klingt vielleicht wieder aus allem was ich so eben geschrieben. (DHA 1:1.566)

[All morning the melody of these verses has been humming in my head and may possibly ring out from what I have just written.]

The phrase "was ich so eben geschrieben" [what I have just written] refers to the prose preface; but the spirit of what he has written, he says, is akin to verse ("Die Melodie dieser Verse"). Likewise, many of the poems from *Buch der Lieder* contain the "truth" that is absent from the "pretty lies" he condemns. "Sie saßen und tranken am Teetisch" does, as I have shown. Heine's lessons in reading "esoteric" as well as "exoteric" signs are singularly appropriate here; and it should be remembered that he teaches one such lesson in *Die Reise von München nach Genua,* where the pair "prosaisch" and "poetisch" offer a motivic accompaniment to the narrator's thoughts on literature and politics. The playful description of Berlin, which is contrasted with Munich in chapter 2, is based on the poet's metaphorical usage of the terms prose and poetry and is embellished with occasional references to tastelessness (*Geschmacklosigkeit* and *Abgeschmacktheit*) that sound loudly in the present context. In the 1839 edition of *Buch der Lieder,* the third, Heine inverts the tactic of the 1837 edition by making the preface into a poem and concluding with an ironic line of prose: "Das hätte ich alles in guter Prosa schreiben können" [I could have written that all down in good solid prose] (DHA 1:1.15).

The existential and aesthetic dilemma of the age, designated as *Zerrissenheit,* is manifest formally in the impossibility of separating prose and verse. In *Die Bäder von Lucca,* Heine takes his habitual double stance and acknowledges the dilemma while parodying it. He associates the phenomenon of *Zerrissenheit* with Byron, as one would expect, but he has Gumpelino, not the narrator, make the connection: "Sie sind ein zerrissener Mensch, ein zerrissenes Gemüt, so zu sagen, ein Byron" [You are a torn man, a torn soul, a Byron, so to speak] (DHA 7:1.95). That it is Gumpelino rather than the poet-narrator who identifies *Zerrissenheit* with Byron does not discredit the notion. We are merely alerted to the fact that the word *Zerrissenheit* and the image of Byron have become clichés.

Instead of rejecting the cliché, Heine revitalizes it: by having Gumpelino speak as he does, Heine demonstrates his own variation of *Zerrissenheit,* one in keeping with the dictum from *Englische Fragmente* that wit gives clearer contours to what is serious: "der Ernst tritt umso deutlicher hervor, wenn der Scherz ihn angekündigt" (DHA 7:1.269). The narrator uses Gumpelino's pretense and ignorance as a comic mask for serious ideas. The shift from Gumpelino to the narrator demonstrates Heine's aesthetic of contrast, for which he remakes the word *Zerrissenheit* and to which he opposes the word *prosaisch.* The shift takes place in the justly famous passage where the narrator calls the poet's (his) heart the focal point of a world that is torn ("zerrissen"). Anyone claiming to have a whole heart has a "prosaic, remote, provincial heart" instead [ein prosaisches weitabgelegenes Winkelherz]:

> Ach, teurer Leser, wenn du über jene Zerrissenheit klagen willst, so beklage lieber, daß die Welt selbst mitten entzwei gerissen ist. Denn da das Herz des Dichters der Mittelpunkt der Welt ist, so mußte es wohl in jetziger Zeit jämmerlich zerrissen werden. Wer von seinem Herzen rühmt, es sei ganz geblieben, der gesteht nur, daß er *ein prosaisches weitabgelegenes Winkelherz hat.* Durch das meinige ging aber der große Weltriß, und eben deswegen weiß ich, daß die großen Götter mich vor vielen anderen hochbegnadigt und des Dichtermärtyrtums würdig geachtet haben. (DHA 7:1.95; my emphasis)

> [Ah, dear reader, if you want to complain about that state of being torn, then complain instead that the world itself is torn in two, right down the middle. And since the heart of the poet is the center of the universe, it must be desperately torn at the present time. Whoever boasts that his heart has remained whole merely admits that he has *a prosaic, provincial, remote-cornered heart.* But the great world-rip went through mine, and precisely because of that I know how the great gods have blessed me above many others, considering me worthy of poetic martyrdom.]

The built-in *Zerrissenheit* in this passage derives not only from the contrast of the poet-narrator with Gumpelino, but also from the derisive use of the word *prosaisch* in a work of prose. As in the preface to *Buch der Lieder,* Heine appears to denounce exactly what he is doing. But in fact he shows that it is not the thing itself—here prose and in the preface verse—that he attacks but its misuse, as with his reappropriation of the word *Zerrissenheit*. When the narrator cries out: "Armer Byron! solches ruhige Genießen war dir versagt!" [Poor Byron! You were denied such quiet enjoyment!] his emphasis is on the "solches" and his tone is therefore ironic: the "solches" refers to Gumpelino's admiring outburst, to which the word *ruhig* (quiet) scarcely applies: "Gott! Gott! Alles wie gemalt!" ["God! God! Everything like a painting!"] (DHA, 7:1.96). The narrator distances himself from Gumpelino, not from Byron.

The visual distinction between prose and verse is the simplest literary division; and because the associations that accompany the division get jumbled up along with all other divisions and hierarchies that are called into question by poetic revolution, the issue is representative much as culinary allusions are. One of the most marked characteristics of Romantic or modern literature is the hidden nature of form or significance, which brings with it the need to judge independently rather than by inherited categories. For the period and the authors in question, the shock provided by a culinary allusion in the "wrong" place exemplifies the thwarting of literary expectations, expectations that are most directly and frequently raised by the formal distinction between poetry and prose. Heine's culinary allusions seem political in a one-dimensional sense or flippant unless they are analyzed in relation to larger issues like the changing perception of genre.

"Der liebe Gott" as Cook

In "Disputation," when the rabbi tries to convince with culinary arguments, he concludes his description of Leviathan in garlic sauce with the comment that God is a good cook: "Was Gott kocht, ist gut gekocht." The comment summarizes his case, though not as he envisioned, and picks up the image of God as a cook in the poem "Prinzessin Sabbat," the first of the three poems in the same section of *Romanzero*, "Hebräische Melodien." In "Prinzessin Sabbat," Heine evokes the Jewish dish *Schalet*, the "kosher ambrosia" that will be served at the sabbath meal, by parodying Schiller's ode "An die Freude":

> Schalet, schöner Götterfunken,
> Tochter aus Elysium!
> Also klänge Schillers Hochlied,
> Hätt er Schalet je gekostet.

Schalet ist die Himmelspeise,
Die der liebe Herrgott selber
Einst den Moses kochen lehrte
Auf dem Berge Sinai.

(DHA 3:1.128)

[*Schalet, shining gleam from Heaven,*
Daughter of Elysium!—
Schiller's ode would sound like this if
He had ever tasted schalet.

Schalet is the food of Heaven,
And the recipe was given
By the Lord himself to Moses
One fine day upon Mount Sinai.]

(HCP 653)

Here the connection between food and aesthetics is made through the blasphemous depiction of the Creator ("der liebe Herrgott") as a cook. As the quotation from Schiller demonstrates, Heine associates the comic and the culinary with creativity, specifically with poetic creativity. His culinary rendering of one of Schiller's most idealistic hymns varies the connection between food and poetic innovation more succinctly evident in examples of ambiguous taste. The culinary rendition of Schiller also reiterates the connection of food and memory that Heine evokes in "Disputation," where the memory is of religious scenes from childhood; here the memory of childhood foods is associated with memories of a literary "childhood"—to the poetic impressions of the poet's creative beginnings. The Jewish dimension further underscores the connection between food and creation: Heine frequently associates the figure of the Jew and the figure of the poet.[33]

Heine's identification of the poet and the cook in "Prinzessin Sabbat" is reminiscent of Fielding's association of cooking and authorship at the beginning of *Tom Jones*. Heine makes the connection frequently; the early poem of 1822, "Mir träumt': ich bin der liebe Gott" (*Heimkehr* 66), resembles "Sie saßen und tranken am Teetisch" because of the mingling of culinary and aesthetic issues and because of the wordplay and satire. The poet's powers are more explicitly shown in "Mir träumt': ich bin der

142

liebe Gott," because the persona dreams that he is God and that God is a poet ("Und Englein sitzen um mich her, / Die meine Verse loben" [The angels sit around my throne / And praise my poetry (HCP 102)]. The miracles performed by this God are culinary:

Mir träumt': ich bin der liebe Gott,
Und sitz' im Himmel droben,
Und Englein sitzen um mich her,
Die meine Verse loben.

Und Kuchen ess' ich und Confekt
Für manchen lieben Gulden,
Und Kardinal trink' ich dabei,
Und habe keine Schulden.

Doch Langeweile plagt mich sehr,
Ich wollt', ich wär' auf Erden,
Und wär' ich nicht der liebe Gott,
Ich könnt' des Teufels werden.

Du langer Engel Gabriel,
Geh', mach dich auf die Sohlen,
Und meinen teuren Freund Eugen
Sollst du herauf mir holen.

Such' ihn nicht im Kollegium,
Such' ihn beim Glas Tokaier;
Such' ihn nicht in der Hedwigskirch,
Such' ihn bei Mamsell Meyer.

Da breitet aus sein Flügelpaar
Und fliegt herab der Engel,
Und packt ihn auf, und bringt herauf
Den Freund, den lieben Bengel.

Ja, Jung', ich bin der liebe Gott,
Und ich regier' die Erde!
Ich hab's ja immer dir gesagt,
Daß ich was Rechts noch werde.

143

Und Wunder tu' ich alle Tag,
Die sollen dich entzücken,
Und dir zum Spaße will ich heut
Die Stadt Berlin beglücken.

Die Pflastersteine auf der Straß',
Die sollen jetzt sich spalten,
Und eine Auster, frisch und klar,
Soll jeder Stein enthalten.

Ein Regen von Zitronensaft
Soll tauig sie begießen,
Und in den Straßengössen soll
Der beste Rheinwein fließen.

Wie freuen die Berliner sich,
Sie gehen schon an's Fressen;
Die Herren von dem Landgericht,
Die saufen aus den Gössen.

Wie freuen die Poeten sich
Bei solchem Götterfraße!
Die Leutnants und die Fähnderichs,
Die lecken ab die Straße.

Die Leutnants und die Fähnderichs,
Das sind die klügsten Leute,
Sie denken, alle Tag geschieht
Kein Wunder so wie heute.

(DHA 1:1.278–81)

[I dreamed a dream: I'm God himself,
All Heaven kneels to me,
The angels sit around my throne
And praise my poetry.

I eat the finest cakes and sweets
That golden coin can get,
And drink expensive wines to boot
And never run up a debt.

144

Sometimes I wish me down on earth
For boredom makes me sick,
And were I not the Lord himself
I might have been Old Nick.

"You lanky angel, Gabriel,
Go stretch your legs a bit,
Go find my good old friend Eugene
And bring him where I sit.

"Look for him not in college halls
But near a Tokay case;
Look for him not in Hedwig's Church
But M'mselle Meyer's place."

The angel spreads his wings and soars
Down to the lower sphere.
And finds my friend and picks him up
And brings the scamp up here.

"Yes, lad, I am Lord God himself,
Earth trembles 'neath my sway!
I always told you, didn't I,
I'd make the top some day.

"I pass a miracle every hour
That you would revel in,
And just for fun, today I'll beam
A blessing on Berlin.

"The paving stones in every street
Will split and open wide,
And every stone will have a fresh
And tasty oyster inside.

"The oysters will be sprinkled by
A shower of lemon juice,
And down the street the best Rhine wine
Will flow as through a sluice."

145

> The joyful Berliners rush out
> To gulp a bite to eat;
> The judges of the District Court
> Are swilling from the street.
>
> How glad the poets are to see
> This heaven-sent food supply!
> The ensigns and lieutenants too
> Are lapping the gutters dry.
>
> The ensigns and lieutenants are
> The smartest in their way:
> They know that miracles like this
> Don't come along every day.]

(HCP 102–3)

If it is mentioned by critics at all, this poem is usually dismissed as a charming but sophomoric remodeling of Cocaigne or *Schlaraffenland* in the manner of *Des Knaben Wunderhorn*, for example in the poem "Der Himmel hängt voll Geigen." Perraudin takes the poem seriously, however, calling it "a full-scale *Schlaraffenland* fantasy" and showing how Heine innovates "by elaborating on and developing away from *Wunderhorn* models." He speaks of a "comprehensive genre-imitation and even genre-pastiche" and makes it clear that in this poem—as I have tried to show for the poem "Sie saßen und tranken am Teetisch"—Heine alludes to a tradition and consciously alienates it, thereby demonstrating the creativity of which his poem speaks.[34]

The urbanization of Cocaigne has the same effect as replacing the apple of knowledge in the Bible with an apple charlotte; here the fantastic culinary landscape is stylized rather than childlike, and the student jargon in the poem makes the *lieb* in "der liebe Gott" sound more like the casual phrase "mein Lieber" (dear fellow) than a reference to a deity. But the blasphemy is practically incidental: when Heine fuses the poet and God by means of culinary images, he demonstrates the poet's control to wield forms and subjects in a way that is indeed miraculous. In this case, the miracle is that he mixes levels of language and breaks taboos by speaking of money, drinking, and politics as well as food. The poet-God revitalizes dead metaphors like "ich könnt' des Teufels werden" or takes a phrase from a bourgeois context—"was Rechtes werden"—and reworks it into a poetic and mock-religious setting. One of the most striking images in

146

the poem is of groveling officers kneeling in the gutters to lap up oysters, Rhine wine, and lemon juice, again a revived dead metaphor. As in "Sie saßen und tranken am Teetisch," it is what remains after the laughter that counts: Heine remakes a folk tradition in the form of his poem and remakes popular expressions by showing what they actually mean; he therefore contrasts language that is worn or official with the words of the god-poet-cook. Heine's Cocaigne is not the Cocaigne of "Der Himmel hängt voll Geigen." But his allusions to poems like it (as Perraudin shows to be the case for the *Buch der Lieder* as a whole) allow us to gauge his distance from inherited models, which is as great as the distance between the god-poet-cook in heaven and the officers groveling in the gutter.

Ideen. Das Buch Le Grand: Brot, Kuß, Ehre

In *Ideen. Das Buch Le Grand,* God is again a poet. First in chapter 3, as a drunken dreamer whose dreams resemble the poet's works; then in chapter 7, where the poet identifies himself with Christ and cries out in mock seriousness: "O du armer, ebenfalls gequälter Gott" [Oh you poor, likewise tormented God] (DHA 6:188); and finally in the central passage of the work, where God is described as "der Aristophanes des Himmels" [the Aristophanes of heaven]. In *Buch Le Grand,* God is not a cook, but the association of creativity with food and more generally with sensuality plays an important part and is supplemented by the humorous quality of Heine's culinary allusions. Taken together, the culinary images reflect the poet's changing perception of his personal past and of a larger past that consists of poetic works and historical events. *Buch Le Grand* traces the poet's liberation from spiritualism, oppression, and conventions of all kinds—political, religious, poetic, even scholarly. The liberation is completed through wit and wordplay and through the incongruous combinations that are present in all of Heine's culinary allusions; food thus becomes a signifier for liberation and for the resulting complications and contradictions that accompany the poet's creative independence.

If it seems questionable to accord so much importance to the culinary allusions of *Buch Le Grand,* it is not because food is too trivial; on the contrary, in this work, the poet comes to realize that he can mold any subject. One might argue that the culinary allusions in this work are heterogeneous and occur in contexts too varied to warrant a sustained analysis. But it is their heterogeneity that makes them so representative:

like *Don Juan, Buch Le Grand* is a work in which systems are suspect and heterogeneity is desirable. Taken together, the culinary allusions display the ambiguity that is a major source of the poet's creativity. They are associated equally with a poetry of love (or illusion) and a poetry of politics (or reality); with high and low; with comic and tragic; with poetic tradition and poetic liberation. They are much like Napoleon, an ambiguous figure about whom Heine has ambiguous feelings and who is supposed to have been the author of the bon mot that Heine affixes to his central chapter: "Du sublime au ridicule il n'y a qu'un pas" [Only a step separates the sublime from the ridiculous]. It is scarcely accidental that Heine's illustration of this motto is an olfactory one with culinary connotations, the image of a Republican wanting like a Brutus to commit suicide, but smelling the knife first to see whether it has been used to cut herring.

Jeffrey Sammons defines the poet's struggle in *Buch Le Grand* as one between "the Romantic sensibility, which is bound up with poetry and the tribulations of eros, and the alertness to the present, particularly political, reality." Sammons summarizes the work as one in which the "content is not a sequence of events, but a state of being; events are absorbed into this state through various levels of memory. The poet is whole, but not completely steady; the synthesis is fragile. This fragility is the source of aesthetic excitement in Heine's prose masterpiece."[35] It is in *Buch Le Grand* that Heine charts the history of his poetic revolution, a revolution of which the effects are clear in *Buch der Lieder* and the other *Reisebilder*, but that has not become the main and conscious subject that it does here. As with any revolution, his is anchored in the past, a past larger than the "Romantic sensibility" of which Sammons speaks; "das Alte Stück" [the old play] that is cited as a motto refers not only to the poet's own past, but also to a poetic tradition that includes literary models such as Aristophanes, Shakespeare, Sterne, Goethe, and Washington Irving. For Heine as for the other authors in this study, the revolution attempts to incorporate rather than to negate that past, but that very attempt occasions mixed feelings toward tradition. The poet's solution in *Buch Le Grand*—which is hardly automatic and which he reaches and rejects repeatedly all the way through—is to exploit his dichotomous perception poetically.[36]

At the opening of the work, it is the status of dichotomy as such that is important, much as it was in "Sie saßen und tranken am Teetisch." The poetic persona introduces his dualistic perception with a description

148

of opposites, heaven and hell, which he portrays with countering culinary examples. At this point he still considers opposites to be mutually exclusive and is not aware of their union in his mind. To the reader the common image makes the clash more clear even than the common Christian frame. Heaven is presented as a sensual paradise in which appetites are never threatened with satiety; in heaven, one eats all day without getting indigestion. Since the narrator equates heaven with marriage, he implies that in heaven the erotic pleasure is unending. Hell, on the other hand, is imagined as "a big bourgeois kitchen" [eine große bürgerliche Küche] where people are roasted instead of geese, which in heaven fly around with sauceboats in their beaks and are flattered to be eaten ("die gebratenen Gänse fliegen herum mit den Saucenschüsselchen im Schnabel, und fühlen sich geschmeichelt, wenn man sie verzehrt" [DHA 6:171]). In hell, religious prejudice dominates along with all forms of social injustice. Love and politics, the two subjects that most concern the poet-persona, are therefore introduced at the outset: love in heaven and politics in hell. The persona's ambivalence toward love and politics, when he thinks of giving them poetic form, is expressed in his choice of the same culinary image to convey opposites. How much this is so, and how directly we are meant to make a connection between the opening and a new aesthetic, does not become explicit until chapter 14, where the narrator repeats parts of the opening almost verbatim (Sammons calls this method his "familiar delayed-action technique," and Grubačić speaks of "associative retrospection").[37] What one observes at the beginning is that opposites are expressed with the same referent, a technique that resembles the wordplay of Byron; wordplay itself will assume a role in *Buch Le Grand,* but not until the poet has acquired the self-awareness he lacks at first.

At the opening of *Buch Le Grand,* the function of the culinary is no more apparent to the reader than the nature of his new poetry is to the poet; only gradually is the significance of culinary details revealed. Some readers overlook their function altogether. Sammons analyzes the importance of the passage about apple tarts in chapter 5, but not with respect to the culinary referent. In discussing the oysters and Rhine wine from chapter 2, Sammons notes that "Any reader of Heine knows that there are few thoughts that can touch off in him such fireworks of hyperbole as that of food," but he calls this specific instance a "capriccio" that is "not meant seriously, of course."[38] Dierk Möller likewise emphasizes the centrality of the passage about apple tarts without mentioning the role of culinary details; in what is otherwise a fine interpretation of the work, Möller omits one culinary reference and disparages another when he quotes the sentence in which the poet composes his list of present and past passions:

> Im VI. Kapitel erklärt Heine, seine "Passion" (und das ist hier durchaus doppeldeutig gemeint) sei "Liebe, Wahrheit, Freiheit und Krebssuppe." Sieht man einmal von dem humoristischen Anhängsel "Krebssuppe" ab, so enthält diese Aufzählung exakt die für das *Buch Le Grand* maßgeblichen Ideale. Jedem der drei Themenkomplexe ist jeweils einer dieser Begriffe zugeordnet.[39]

> [In chapter 6 Heine explains that his "passion" (and the word is clearly meant ambiguously here) is "love, truth, freedom, and crab soup." If one eliminates the humorously appended "crab soup," then the list contains exactly those ideals that are decisive for *Buch Le Grand*. Each of these concepts is assigned to one of the work's three thematic units.]

What seems to disturb Möller here is the mixture of serious concerns with culinary irrelevancies, since he dismisses the crab soup as a humorous "appendage." Furthermore, he paraphrases the sentence he is quoting so that he can omit the reference to apple tarts. The complete sentence reads: "Apfeltörtchen waren nämlich damals meine Passion—jetzt ist es Liebe, Wahrheit, Freiheit und Krebssuppe" ["Apple tarts were then my passion—now it is love, truth, freedom, and crab soup"] (HPP 187).[40]

All three of the "thematic units" to which Möller refers—love, politics, and the role of the writer—are contained in the culinary reference to crab soup. Heine binds "Liebe, Wahrheit, Freiheit und Krebssuppe" by having culinary allusions express opposites, as I have said, and he reinforces the connection of contraries stylistically by using a singular verb ("ist") and a singular antecedent ("meine Passion") for the plural series that follows. There is an intentional awkwardness to the construction that opens up under scrutiny. Furthermore, the list of "Liebe, Wahrheit, Freiheit und Krebssuppe" is an exact and anticipatory depiction of Le Grand, whose drumming tells of liberty and who knows only three words, each of which represents one of Möller's themes—"Brot, Kuß, Ehre" [bread, kiss, honor]—and who himself represents the sensuality that Sammons associates with the crab soup:

150

Monsieur Le Grand wußte nur wenig gebrochenes Deutsch, nur die Hauptausdrücke—Brot, Kuß, Ehre—doch konnte er sich auf der Trommel sehr gut verständlich machen, z.B. wenn ich nicht wußte, was das Wort *"liberté"* bedeute, so trommelte er den Marseiller Marsch—und ich verstand ihn. (DHA 6:190–91)

[Monsieur Le Grand knew only a little broken German, only the main expressions—bread, kiss, honor—but he could make himself understood very well with his drum. For example, if I did not know what the word *liberté* meant, he drummed the "Marseillaise"—and I understood him.] (HPP 194–95)

How carefully Heine proceeds is further evident from the final sentence of this same passage, where the poet recalls what started his "digression" and refers again to the statue of the Prince Elector mentioned before:

und die Schürzen sind es, welche—doch sie bringen mich ganz aus dem Kontext, ich sprach ja von der Reuterstatue, die so viel silberne Löffel im Leibe hat, und keine Suppe, und den Kurfürsten Jan Wilhelm darstellt. (DHA 6:183)[41]

[and it is aprons, you know, which . . . but I am wandering from the subject. I was speaking of the equestrian statue that has so many silver spoons in its body and no soup and that represents the Prince Elector, Jan Wilhelm. (HPP 187)

This fuses in a striking manner the child's perception with the adult's restructuring of it, and the narrator's list of past and present passions, which he links gastronomically, is similarly related to the subject of past and present poetry. The literal association of silver spoons with money that can buy apple tarts has been exchanged for one of silver spoons and soup, where soup can be understood to represent both a *littérature engagée* and the connection of sensuality and politics that Heine finds embodied in the figure of Le Grand. He will make the connection of soup and poetry explicit in chapter 13, at the center of what Möller calls the "poetological" part; there the poet says that people have the right to eat *Krebssuppe* rather than the "schlechte schwarze Suppe" [poor black soup] of the Spartans (DHA 6:202).

Past and future merge literally when the narrator envisions "die grünverschleierten, vornehmen Engländerinnen" [green-veiled, distinguished Englishwomen] (DHA 6:282) who come to Düsseldorf because it is his birthplace but bypass his house and go straight to the marketplace, where they admire the same statue of the Prince Elector that he saw as a child. It is only logical that they should bypass his house, which is a relic of his historical self, and go to the statue of the Prince Elector, which is an artistic transfiguration of a historical figure. It is equally logical that the admirers should be Englishwomen, because they anticipate in real form the poeticized version of the English traveler in *A Sentimental Journey,* which is cited a few lines later. Heine transfigures Sterne just as he transfigures historical reality, the important thing being the process of transfiguration. For that reason the poet concentrates very little on the figure of the Prince Elector and much more on the artist who made him. According to local yore, the artist ran out of metal when he was casting the statue and had to use the citizens' silver spoons to finish the job, prompting the narrator to wonder as a child how many apple tarts he could buy from the silver spoons. I quote in full to reestablish the context of the climactic sentence in which the narrator lists his present and past passions:

> Als Knabe hörte ich die Sage, der Künstler, der diese Statue gegossen, habe während des Gießens mit Schrecken bemerkt, daß sein Metall nicht dazu ausreiche, und da wären die Bürger der Stadt herbeigelaufen, und hätten ihm ihre silbernen Löffel gebracht, um den Guß zu vollenden—und nun stand ich stundenlang vor dem Reuterbilde, und zerbrach mir den Kopf: wie viel silberne Löffel wohl darin stecken mögen, und wieviel Apfeltörtchen man wohl für all das Silber bekommen könnte? Apfeltörtchen waren nämlich damals meine Passion— jetzt ist es Liebe, Wahrheit, Freiheit und Krebssuppe. (DHA 6:172)

> [As a boy I was told that the artist who made this statue noticed with horror while it was being cast that he did not have enough metal to fill the mold, so all the citizens of the town came running with their silver spoons and threw them in to make up the deficiency—and I often stood before the statue for hours, wondering how many spoons were concealed in it and how many apple tarts the silver would buy. Apple tarts were then my passion—now it is love, truth, freedom, and crab soup.] (HPP 186–87)

The artist's fear of running out of metal is a whimsical rendition of the poet's own dilemma. In order to complete his work, the artist must accept contributions from others, in this case the contributions of literary models, which he incorporates and remakes. Though his reminiscence is a witty rendering of the child's perspective, in this work it is more: the silver spoons he accepts are transformed into apple tarts, which bring to mind two conflicting sorts of poetry. To the poet as a child, the silver spoons represent the ability to buy real apple tarts, which later on come to be associated with a poetry of love; to the poet at this stage, the silver spoons make him think of soup—or the absence of soup ("die soviele Silberlöffel im Leibe hat und keine Suppe")—which is associated with a poetry of politics.

Even when the poet speaks of the historical Prince Elector, as he does when he completes the apparent digression on silver spoons and apple tarts, it is with an emphasis, however mocking, on the Prince Elector's artistic rather than political talents:

> Er soll ein braver Herr gewesen sein, und sehr kunstliebend, und selbst sehr geschickt. Er stiftete die Gemäldegallerie in Düsseldorf, und auf dem dortigen Observatorium zeigt man noch einen überaus künstlichen Einschachtelungsbecher von Holz, den er selbst in seinen Freistunden—er hatte deren täglich vier und zwanzig—geschnitzelt hat. (DHA 6:183)

> [He is alleged to have been a brave gentleman, a lover of art and very talented himself. He founded the picture gallery in Düsseldorf; and in the observatory there they show a very artistic piece of work consisting of one box within another that he himself had carved in his leisure hours—he had twenty-four of them every day.] (HPP 187)

The satirical note does not discredit artistic pursuits, it merely clarifies the distinction between kinds: the ridiculous nature of the Elector's art says more about him than about art; his whittling reflects his ineffectual political role, the implication being that there is another kind of art, just as there is another kind of politics. By the same token, culinary allusions, whether to good or bad food, have no artistic merit in and of themselves and can as easily be the sign of nonpoetry as of poetry. They can be transformed, like the fools in chapter 14, of whom the narrator says that they represent his income in hard cash: "all diese Narren, die ich hier sehe, kann ich in meinen Schriften gebrauchen, sie sind bares Honorar, bares Geld" (DHA 6:208) [all these fools I see here can be used in my writing. They constitute a cash honorarium, ready money (HPP 213)] .

Heine's poetological theme in the apple tart passage is underscored by references to Sterne and possibly to Washington Irving. When Heine describes "der krumme Hermann" [the crooked Hermann] with his "süßen, duftenden Apfeltörtchenton" [sweet, scented apple-tart tone] and his white apron (DHA 6:183), he cites the chapter from *A Sentimental Journey* called "Le Patisser [*sic*], Versailles." In that chapter a dignified but penniless Chevalier de St. Louis is forced to earn a living by selling savory pastries:

He was begirt with a clean linen apron which fell below his knees, and with a sort of a bib that went half way up his breast; upon the top of this, but a little below the hem, hung his croix. His basket of little *patès* was cover'd over with a white damask napkin; another of the same kind was spread at the bottom; and there was a look of *propreté* and neatness throughout; that one might have bought his *patès* of him, as much from appetite as sentiment.[42]

Heine modifies the scene, clearly, and remakes it much as he modulates from one subject to the other with the wordplay on skirts and aprons, *Schürze* and *Schürzen*. One important change is that Heine draws attention to the apron that covers the apple tarts and to the fact that it makes the tarts all the more alluring: "Und wahrlich, nie würden Apfeltörtchen mich so sehr angereizt haben, hätte der krumme Hermann sie nicht so geheimnisvoll mit seiner weißen Schürze bedeckt" (DHA 6:183) [And, in fact, apple tarts would never have tempted me so if crooked Hermann had not covered them up so mysteriously with his white apron (HPP 187)]. Sterne himself is a master of indirection, of speaking out while seeming to obscure, especially in the sexual innuendo that masquerades as innocence each time Yorick meets a woman. Heine's is also an aesthetic of indirection, and the covering up of the apple tarts is an image for using culinary images to cover up erotic and aesthetic concerns. In the preface "To the Reader" from *Tales of a Traveller*, Washington Irving's persona Geoffrey Crayon describes this kind of indirect aesthetic, and there is surely design in his choice of a culinary image:

154

I am not, therefore, for those barefaced tales which carry their moral on the surface, staring one in the face; they are enough to deter the squeamish reader. On the contrary, I have often hid my moral from sight, and disguised it as much as possible by sweets and spices, so that while the simple reader is listening with open mouth to a ghost or a love story, he may have a bolus of sound morality popped down his throat, and be never the wiser for the fraud.

Irving's irony carries over to the last paragraph of the preface, where he repeats the culinary metaphor: "These matters being premised, fall to, worthy reader, with good appetite, and above all, with good humor, to what is here set before thee."[43]

Another critic who omits a culinary referent of importance is Wolfgang Preisendanz in his discussion of Heine and the idyll. In a lengthy quotation from the opening of chapter 5, the passage in which the narrator casts off his fraudulent identity as the "Graf vom Ganges" [count of the Ganges], Preisendanz brackets the sentence that occurs exactly in the middle, the sentence in which Heine moves from sublime to ridiculous by comparing the city of Calcutta with a roast called "Kalkuttenbraten": "Ich war eben so wenig jemals in Kalkutten wie der Kalkuttenbraten, den ich gestern Mittag gegessen" [I myself was no more in Calcutta than the Calcutta roast that I ate yesterday at noon] (DHA 6:178).[44] Possibly Preisendanz is influenced here by Freud, who disapproves of this pun in *Der Witz und seine Beziehung zum Unbewußten,* which Preisendanz quotes earlier in his book.[45] In this abridged form, however, the paragraph loses one of its main objectives. Although Preisendanz says that one must consider the idyllic in conjunction with sentiment and irony, he omits a sentence that exemplifies his claim: when Heine plays with the word *Kalkuttenbraten,* he acknowledges yet breaks with a tradition that one can call Romantic or idyllic. It is important that *Kalkuttenbraten* be mentioned at a moment where the question of identity is at issue, because the comedy signals self-awareness and a distance occasioned through the culinary allusion. The persona's distance from an earlier identity, and therefore from tradition, is expressed by association as well as by proclamation, verbally and in substance. Heine shows here an example of what Sammons calls "that process of association, particularly verbal association, that characterizes Heine's style," which is a broader (and more decorous) way of describing wordplay.[46]

Hosfeld is a critic who takes Heine's culinary allusions seriously. He reads chapter 14 of *Buch Le Grand* in the tradition of Sterne and Menippean satire, and he proposes a Bakhtinian model to explain the shifting identities of Madame and to connect her metamorphoses with the narrator's artistic transformation. Hosfeld also considers the apparently haphazard association of ideas in chapter 13 against the background of book 5 of *Tristram Shandy,* the passage where Susannah's association of ideas from death to dresses seems to lack coherence and takes place in the kitchen. Hosfeld focuses on passages that have been slighted before, specifically on culinary references, and lends support to the claim that each allusion to the culinary marks a stage in the poet's emotional, philosophical, and aesthetic journey. It is a jerky journey, intentionally so, and a consideration of each culinary reference in turn will show how Heine proceeds.

Between the culinary images of the opening and the wordplay on *Kalkuttenbraten* in chapter 5, the poet recovers from his contemplated suicide in chapter 2, where he is in a Hamburg with Italianate names. When suicide is still on his mind, he goes to a *Weinkeller* for his "Henkersmahlzeit," a final supper of oysters and Rhine wine. He comments that he cannot eat, much less drink, which Sammons rightly calls a sign of "really serious emotional disturbance."[47] But when he looks at the wine, his associative manner takes over. The wine reminds him visually of the Ganges and of his "Heimat" [homeland], which from his description is purely literary and evokes a Romantic literary past. Finally he drinks: "und ich trank hastig den Wein, den hellen, freudigen Wein, und doch wurde es in meiner Seele immer dunkler und trauriger—Ich war zum Tode verurteilt" (DHA 6:174) [and I quickly drank up the wine, the clear, joyous wine, and nonetheless my soul grew darker and sadder. I was condemned to death . . . (HPP 177)]. What seemed to be an insignificant detail, the drinking of the wine, turns out to be pivotal, not in any real sense (Heine was no drinker, which makes the literary function of the reference all the more striking), but because of its connection to imaginative powers. After he climbs the steps from the *Weinkeller,* which in itself repeats the opening juxtaposition of heaven to hell in chapter 1 and may be a playful allusion to Dante as well, he recites his soliloquy. He follows his evocation of Romantic exoticism with references to other literary models whose presence serves throughout the work as a background to

156

the poet's quest for an individual style. Principal among them are Shakespeare and Goethe. He tries to free himself from such models, an attempt that is manifest in his rejection of Hamlet's monologue in favor of one from his own play, *Almansor,* after which he comments on his choice and by doing so illustrates the curative properties of ironic distance:

> Es ist allgemein rezipiert, Madame, daß man einen Monolog hält, ehe man sich tot schießt. Die meisten Menschen benutzen bei solcher Gelegenheit das hamletische "Sein oder Nichtsein." Es ist eine gute Stelle, und ich hätte sie hier auch gern zitiert—aber, jeder ist sich selbst der Nächste, und hat man, wie ich, ebenfalls Tragödien geschrieben, worin solche Lebensabiturienten-Reden enthalten sind, z.B. den unsterblichen "Almansor," so ist es sehr natürlich, daß man seinen eigenen Worten, sogar vor den Shakespearschen, den Vorzug gibt. (DHA 6:174–75).

> [It is generally agreed, Madame, that everyone should deliver a soliloquy before committing suicide. Most people on such occasions use Hamlet's "To be or not to be." It is an excellent passage, and I would gladly have quoted it here, but charity begins at home, and if someone has, as I have, likewise written tragedies in which such farewell-to-life speeches occur—as, for instance, the immortal "Almansor"—it is very natural that one should prefer one's own words even to Shakespeare's.] (HPP 178)

The poet-persona could not have spoken with such sovereign wit before his recitation, and the strength comes from the restorative powers, in a literary and figurative sense, of the oysters and Rhine wine. Implicitly the narrator also cites Faust's attempted suicide, but he inverts and perhaps parodies it, thus indicating his emerging independence: Faust does not drink from the vial, and the "Armesünderglöckchen" [little bells tolling for a condemned man] mentioned in *Buch Le Grand* are scarcely the same as the Easter bells in Goethe's *Faust*. There may also be an allusion to Hoffmann, specifically to *Der goldene Topf,* a suspicion that is strengthened by Heine's treatment of Hoffmann in *Die romantische Schule,* where he links inebriation and creativity in an embellished version of biographical criticism. Ultimately it is not the look from the beloved that saves the persona but literature, in particular his own. The importance of comedy to his aesthetic is fully evident here, because his recitation gives him occasion to remark—much as Woody Allen might—that monologues allow the candidate for suicide to buy time.[48]

Michael Perraudin's careful interpretation of the poem "Im Hafen" from *Nordsee III*, which as Perraudin notes is the versified equivalent to chapter 2 of *Buch Le Grand*, complements my emphasis on the aesthetic significance of oysters and Rhine wine. Perraudin calls the poem "both a review and a conscious culmination of [Heine's] poetic progress to date" and shows how the connection of inebriation and poetic inspiration is made by Goethe in the *Divan*. What attracts Heine there, Perraudin argues, is "above all his interest in the idea of the poet's intoxication representing a heightened consciousness and inspiration," where the connection is also one of wine and poetry with love.[49] Perraudin considers "Im Hafen" to be one of only two poems in *Buch der Lieder* that "take on a kind of twentieth-century arcaneness," and he persuasively elucidates the allusions. He concludes that "Im Hafen" "offers a summary account of the early love poetry itself" as well as a "philosophical and cultural confession."[50]

Within *Buch Le Grand*, the association of sensuality and creativity only becomes explicit afterward, in keeping with the process of induction, of hiding the apple tarts under the apron. Images or events can be reflected only later, just as the narrator's childhood memories can be understood only from the distance of adulthood. The oysters and Rhine wine of chapter 2 anticipate the opening image of chapter 3, where the world is portrayed as the dreams of a drunken god who unknowingly creates what he dreams and whose world will dissolve when he awakens. That this is a self-projection would be obvious even without the restorative powers of the wine and oysters in chapter 2. The god's dreams are reminiscent of "Mir träumt': ich bin der liebe Gott" and, more generally, of Heine's practice throughout *Buch der Lieder*. It is not by coincidence that the god produces "Traumgebilde," a variation of the title "Traumbilder" in *Buch der Lieder* or even of the "Bild" in *Reisebilder*, and that the narrator's adjectives for the dreamed creations of a drunken god apply equally to Heine's poems: "die Traumgebilde gestalten sich oft buntscheckig toll und oft auch harmonisch vernünftig" (DHA 6:175) [and the dream images often form so motley and wildly, often so harmoniously and reasonably (HPP 179)]. Furthermore, when the narrator lists good ideas in this dream ("einzelne gute Gedanken in diesem schaffenden Gottestraum"), we can match each one with a theme of Heine's:

die Traumgebilde gestalten sich oft buntscheckig toll, oft auch har-
monisch vernünftig—die Ilias, Plato, die Schlacht bei Marathon,
Moses, die medizäische Venus, der Straßburger Münster, die fran-
zösische Revolution, Hegel, die Dampfschiffe u.s.w. sind einzelne gute
Gedanken in diesem schaffenden Gottestraum—aber es wird nicht
lange dauern, und der Gott erwacht, und reibt sich die verschlafenen
Augen, und lächelt—und unsre Welt ist zerronnen in Nichts, ja, sie
hat nie existiert. (DHA 6:175)

[and the dream images often form so motley and wildly, often so
harmoniously and reasonably—the *Iliad*, Plato, the battle of Mara-
thon, Moses, the Medician Venus, the Cathedral of Strasbourg, the
French Revolution, Hegel, steamboats, etc., are single good thoughts
in this divine dream of creation—but it will not last long before the
god will awake and rub his sleepy eyes and smile, and our world melts
into nothingness; in fact, it never existed.] (HPP 179)

If there were any doubt about the application of this description to
Heine's own works, it would be dispelled by the final example in the
series, the steamboats. Instead of negating the importance of art, philoso-
phy, revolution, and religion, all of which are represented by the other
examples, the steamboats add Heine's signature and once again illustrate
his poetic manner. His final example sounds a modern note, referentially
and stylistically, and juxtaposes progress and modernity with a past that
is literary and political. Heine uses the same technique in a poetological
passage from *Aus den Memoiren des Herren von Schnabelewopski*, where
the equation of sailing and writing poetry (a theme of the earlier *Nordsee*
poems) is mimicked and modernized in his comparison of some people
with sailboats and others with steamboats:

Aber es gibt auch Menschen, die nicht mit gewöhnlichen Schiffen
verglichen werden dürfen, sondern mit Dampfschiffen. Diese tragen
ein dunkles Feuer in der Brust und sie fahren gegen Wind und Wet-
ter—Ihre Rauchflagge flattert wie der schwarze Federbusch des nächt-
lichen Reuters, ihre Zackenräder sind wie kolossale Pfundsporen,
womit sie das Meer in die Wellenrippen stacheln, und das widerspen-
stisch schäumende Element muß ihrem Willen gehorchen, wie ein
Roß—aber sehr oft platzt der Kessel, und der innere Brand verzehrt
uns.

Doch ich will mich aus der Metapher wieder herausziehn und auf ein wirkliches Schiff setzen, welches von Hamburg nach Amsterdam fährt. (B 1:526)

[But there are men who cannot be compared to common ships, because they are like steamboats. They carry a gloomy fire within, and sail against wind and weather; their smoky banner streams behind, like the black plume of the wild Huntsman; their zig-zagged wheels remind one of weighty spurs with which they pick the ribs of the waves, and the obstinate, resistant element must obey their will like a steed; but sometimes the boiler bursts, and the internal fire burns up!

But now I will escape from metaphor, and get on board a real ship bound from Hamburg to Amsterdam.] (SF 172)

The context here is remarkably similar to that in *Buch Le Grand,* not only geographically; in *Schnabelewopski,* the image of sailing recalls the persona's dilemma in *Buch Le Grand* when the exhilaration of setting sail turns quickly to shipwreck. Both sailing and shipwreck are clearly identified as metaphors for writing, at the very latest when Heine opposes the terms prosaic and Romantic: "das arme Schiff zerschellt an romantischen Klippen oder strandet auf seicht-prosaischem Sand" (B 1:525).

Such indirect hints that the god's dream is self-reflexive recur when the narrator returns to his own voice. When he says "Gleichviel! ich lebe" (DHA 6:175) [and I live, that is the main point] (HPP 179) in an apparently offhand way, the emphasis should be on the "ich" [I] rather than on the "lebe" [live], and we observe the persona fusing his identity with that of the dreaming drunken god. The oysters and the Rhine wine that seemed trivial in chapter 2 are revealed as initimately connected to the poet's creative development. His addition of oysters to the wine is a good example, in miniature, of the distinction between his evocation of creativity here and Goethe's in the *Divan.* But the poet himself has not yet realized precisely how this is so. At this stage, these connections are still somewhat "drunken," and the persona is preoccupied by the traditions, personal and poetic, from which he wishes to liberate himself. This preoccupation is visible in the remainder of chapter 3, which consists of a catalog of literary suicides from Homer to Immermann. Although the examples underscore the theme of poetic creativity and the power that poets have, like gods, to achieve immortality (a power that is particularly

160

striking when the topic is death), they nevertheless seem to obscure his own achievements.

The next culinary allusion is the one in chapter 6 to apple tartlets, where the association of creativity and sensuality is broadened to include eroticism and politics. In chapter 7 the narrator makes the connection between political revolution and eating when the narrator tells of having learned and forgotten the Marseillaise from Le Grand. He is reminded of the lesson when he sits at the dinner table, and the memory is at first unconscious. Here the legacy is both historical and literary: the figure of Le Grand is fictitious, hence literary, and he is associated with Napoleon. The connection between eating and politics in chapter 7 repeats and retrospectively clarifies the inclusion of *Krebssuppe* in the narrator's list of passions:

> und wirklich, trotz allem Stirnreiben konnte ich mich lange Zeit nicht mehr auf jene gewaltige Melodie besinnen. Aber denken Sie sich, Madame! unlängst sitze ich an der Tafel mit einer ganzen Menagerie von Grafen, Prinzen, Prinzessinnen, Kammerherren, Hofmarschallinnen, Hofschenken, Oberhofmeisterinnen, Hofsilberbewahrern, Hofjägermeisterinnen, und wie diese vornehmen Domestiquen noch außerdem heißen mögen, und ihre Unterdomestiquen liefen hinter ihren Stühlen und schoben ihnen die gefüllten Teller vors Maul—ich aber, der übergangen und übersehen wurde, saß müßig, ohne die mindeste Kinnbackenbeschäftigung, und ich knetete Brotkügelchen, und trommelte vor Langerweile mit den Fingern, und zu meinem Entsetzen trommelte ich plötzlich den roten, längstvergessenen Guillotinenmarsch.
>
> "Und was geschah?" Madame, diese Leute lassen sich im Essen nicht stören, und wissen nicht, daß andere Leute, wenn sie nichts zu essen haben, plötzlich anfangen zu trommeln, und zwar gar kuriose Märsche, die man längst vergessen glaubte. (DHA 6:190–91)

[and yet, despite all manner of rubbing my forehead, for a long time I could not recall that powerful melody! And just think, madame, not long ago I was sitting at a table with a whole menagerie of counts, princes, princesses, chamberlains, ladies-in-waiting, court wine pourers, superior court mistresses, court keepers of the royal silverware, court hunting mistresses, and whatever else these elegant domestics are called, and their underdomestics ran about behind their chairs and shoved full plates in front of their traps; but I, who was passed by and overlooked, sat at leisure without the least occupation for my jaws and kneaded little bread balls and drummed my fingers from boredom; and, to my horror, I suddenly found myself drumming the long-forgotten red guillotine march.

"And what happened?" Madame, these people do not permit themselves to be disturbed while eating and do not know that other people, when they have nothing to eat, suddenly start drumming, and what is more, they even drum strange marches believed to have been long forgotten.] (HPP 195–96)

The designation of those present as a "Menagerie" anticipates the poetological description of fools exactly seven chapters later, in chapter 14,[51] and the link between revolution and a lack of food is as obvious here as it is in *Deutschland. Ein Wintermärchen.* But there is a complication: food alone is not enough (the narrator has his "Brotkügelchen" [little bread balls] after all), it must also be good—crab soup rather than the "bad black soup" of the Spartans to which he will refer in chapter 13. That there is a correlation to poetic revolution is equally clear, because Le Grand is associated with literature and sensuality as well as politics; aside from the fact that he is a literary invention, he expresses himself through his drumming—a rhythmic, stylized form of narration. The function of the culinary in implementing poetic revolution is unmistakable; the "weapons" are *Brotkügelchen,* which like any culinary reference can undo the aristocratic poetic order. Without understanding the culinary details elsewhere, however, the *Brotkügelchen* here make little sense. In isolation they would seem flippant, no matter how amusing the image or how fitting as a rendering of social injustice.

In chapter 11, the poet again illustrates his development with a culinary example. It has often been noted that the motto of the chapter, "Du sublime au ridicule il n'y a qu'un pas, Madame," could serve as the motto for Heine's aesthetic because of the simultaneous allusion to a political and a poetic model, Napoleon and Sterne. The double model makes it possible to visualize Heine's poetry of simultaneous opposites in much the way that the figure of the doppelgänger does. The form of the motto is equally significant, because it shows Heine remaking borrowed material: the "Madame" at the end of the phrase, though an imitation of Sterne, alters the context of the Napoleonic remark entirely and puts into practice something of what the phrase describes. The phrase incapsulates what Hosfeld calls the carnivalistic nature of the work, those elements of laughter and metamorphosis that Heine always frames by citing the literary and Napoleonic models to which he is ambiguously inclined.[52]

Chapter 11 suspends the movement of the work by taking stock of what has gone before and anticipating what is to come. Heine provides an explication de texte of the Napoleonic motto by listing a series of vivid examples, first literary and then historical, in which tragedy and comedy are bound:

> Die grauenhaftesten Bilder des menschlichen Wahnsinns zeigt uns Aristophanes nur im lachenden Spiegel des Witzes, den großen Denk-erschmerz, der seine eigne Nichtigkeit begreift, wagt Goethe nur in den Knittelversen eines Puppenspiels auszusprechen, und die tötlichste Klage über den Jammer der Welt legt Shakespeare in den Mund eines Narren, während er dessen Schellenkappe ängstlich schüttelt. (DHA 6:200)

> [The most horrible images of human madness are shown to us by Aristophanes only in the laughing mirror of wit. Only in the doggerel of a puppet show does Goethe dare to utter the great pain of the thinker who comprehends his own nothingness, and Shakespeare puts the gravest indictment about the misery of the world into the mouth of a fool who is anxiously rattling his cap and bells.] (HPP 204)

Heine illustrates the union of grand and trivial things with the culinary example that I cited earlier, where a knife can serve both for cutting herring and committing suicide:

> sogar in das höchste Pathos der Welttragödie pflegen sich komische Züge einzuschleichen, der verzweifelnde Republikaner, der sich wie ein Brutus das Messer ins Herz stieß, hat vielleicht zuvor daran gero-chen, ob auch kein Häring damit geschnitten worden. (DHA 6:200)

> [Comical traits customarily slip into even the highest pathos of the world tragedy. The despairing republican who, like a Brutus, plunged a knife into his heart first smelled it perhaps to make certain it had not also been used for cutting herring.] (HPP 205)

The apparently digressive nature of the leap from poetry to herring would seem gratuitously indecorous if not for the culinary allusions that precede and succeed it. At the end of chapter 14, for example, the connection of food and art recurs in a malicious and roundabout way, when the narrator concludes his creative culinary endeavors with a wordplay on the name of the playwright Willibald Alexis, the pen name for Wilhelm Häring. The indigestion at the end of chapter 14 is to be offset by a cleansing salad, a "Willibald-Alexis-Salat, der reinigt" (DHA 6:212), and the reference to herring is typical in both cases of the tricks Heine plays. Chapter 11 is at the center of *Buch Le Grand* in a literal sense, as the eleventh of twenty chapters, and when it is taken together with the four words and many dashes of chapter 12—a visual rendering of Sterne and a demonstration of political liberation through satire—one can speak of the two chapters as the work's centerpiece. Both chapters demonstrate the narrator's relationship to poetical and historical traditions, one by telling about them and the other by showing how he changes them.

As with Byron or Sterne, it is well to consider what Heine means when he speaks in chapter 13 of "beginning" his work. His manner resembles Byron's in *Don Juan*, who in canto 12 says, "But now I will begin my poem," or Sterne's, whose "Preface in the Désobligeant" is the seventh section of *A Sentimental Journey*. What makes the comment accurate for Heine is that the narrator realizes and therefore draws attention to the issues that have been present but not fully visible up to now; his own realization is to be matched by that of the reader, who at this point should reevaluate what came before. The remark about the beginning comes in connection with a parody of scholarly or philosophical systems, and by analogy of poetic and political ones. To represent all systems Heine chooses scholarly methods; and to represent all scholarly subjects, he chooses food. Whether one cites scholarly works or literary models, it is the notion of a fixed system that is flawed, in particular the artificial (and "tasteful") notion that one must use a specific style to treat certain subjects. His example of a system is visually irreproachable: the outline at the end of the chapter resembles an antique poetic form imitated by Hölderlin or Platen. But the content merely exposes the flaw of relying on appearances, which in a poetic context translates as the flaw of relying on the visual expectations fostered by prose or verse; the outline resembles the list of travelers in Sterne's "Preface in the Désobligeant" rather than a more decorous model. By the same token, the subject of food, though clearly out of place in the scholarly context Heine proposes here, does not necessarily have a trivial connotation. The problem is to learn to differentiate without in the process becoming too orderly oneself.

When the narrator asserts at the beginning of chapter 13 that he avoids "alles Überflüssige," he is right, and again the culinary references demonstrate the care with which he proceeds, the appearance of disorder notwithstanding:

> beklagen Sie sich nicht über meine Abschweifungen. In allen vorhergehenden Kapiteln ist keine Zeile, die nicht zur Sache gehörte, ich schreibe gedrängt, ich vermeide alles Überflüssige, ich übergehe sogar oft das Notwendige, z.B. ich habe noch nicht einmal ordentlich zitiert—ich meine nicht Geister, sondern, im Gegenteil, ich meine Schriftsteller—und doch ist das Zitieren alter und neuer Bücher das Hauptvergnügen eines jungen Autors, und so ein paar grundgelehrte Zitate zieren den ganzen Menschen. Glauben Sie nur nicht, Madame, es fehle mir an Bekanntschaft mit Büchertiteln. Außerdem kenne ich den Kunstgriff großer Geister, die es verstehen, die Korinthen aus den Semmeln und die Zitate aus den Kollegienheften herauszupicken. (DHA 6:201–2)

> [please do not complain about my digressions. In all previous chapters there is not a line that does not belong to the topic. I write concisely, I avoid all superfluity, often I even neglect the necessary. For instance, I have not yet once properly quoted—I do not mean geniuses; on the contrary, I mean authors—and yet quoting from old and new books is the chief pleasure of a young man. Do not believe, madame, that I lack familiarity with book titles. Moreover I am familiar with the knack of those great minds who know how to pick out the currants from the rolls and quotations from their lectures notes.] (HPP 206)

Although we sense immediately that this passage needs to be interpreted, it is hard to know exactly where Heine is teasing. In the first half of the second sentence, for instance ("In allen vorhergehenden Kapiteln [. . .] Notwendige"), he seems to be ironic. Yet when the poet asserts that he has not done a proper job of citing so far, we can only take him at his word if we understand "ordentlich" [properly] in its literal sense ("ich habe noch nicht einmal ordentlich zitiert" [I haven't yet quoted properly]), because he is citing at that very moment. He is quoting from

Book I, chapter 22 of *Tristram Shandy,* where Sterne speaks of his "masterstroke of digressive skill" and his worry that his readers will overlook it (as many did). The important thing about digressions, Sterne explains, is that "all the dexterity is in the good cookery and management of them." As Hosfeld points out, the connection between cookery and art is no more haphazard for Sterne than it is for Heine. Here the connection is underscored by the identification of raisins with quotations and of rolls with lecture notes.[53]

In chapter 13, Heine revives Sterne's metaphor of "good cookery" when he demonstrates his scholarly talents and shows that his apparent digressions are carefully thought out. His quotations, too, are introduced with an apparent digressive quality, an "Übrigens" [By the way] that is doubly ironic because it precedes the loaded word "Idee," which here has been emptied of substantial meaning:

Übrigens, Madame, haben Sie gar keine Idee davon, mit welcher Leichtigkeit ich zitieren kann. Überall finde ich Gelegenheit, meine tiefe Gelehrtheit anzubringen. Spreche ich z.B. vom Essen, so bemerke ich in einer Note, daß die Römer, Griechen und Hebräer ebenfalls gegessen haben, ich zitiere all die köstlichen Gerichte, die von der Köchin des Lucullus bereitet worden—weh mir! daß ich anderthalb Jahrtausend zu spät geboren bin!—ich bemerke auch, daß die gemeinschaftlichen Mahle bei den Griechen so und so hießen, und daß die Spartaner schlechte schwarze Suppen gegessen—Es ist doch gut, daß ich damals noch nicht lebte, ich kann mir nichts Entsetzlicheres denken, als wenn ich armer Mensch ein Spartaner geworden wäre, Suppe ist mein Lieblingsgericht. (DHA 6:202)

[By the way, madame, you can have no idea of the facility with which I quote. Everywhere I discover opportunities to parade my profound learnedness. If I speak of eating, for example, I remark in a note that the Greeks, Romans, Hebrews also ate; I quote all the delightful dishes prepared by Lucullus's cook—woe is me that I was born a millennium and a half too late. I also remark that these communal meals were called thus and thus among the Greeks and that the Spartans ate bad black soups. It is good, after all, that I was not yet alive in those days; I can imagine nothing more terrible than if I, poor soul, had become a Spartan; soup is my favorite dish.] (HPP 207)

The implications are many. On the one hand, Heine mocks a scholarly method that consists of an elaborate system for treating the obvious ("so bemerke ich in einer Note, daß die Römer, Griechen und Hebräer ebenfalls gegessen haben"). He also implicates a neoclassical poetic order that would make it seem as if eating were incompatible with the Good, the True, and the Beautiful. And he further exposes scholarly and poetic systems as protectors of what is obvious and dull, systems that obscure reality instead of revealing it. The latter implication emerges at the end of his digression, where the subject of food, which appears to be irrelevant, leads him to the subject of anti-Semitism; the taboo of food is replaced by other taboos, anti-Semitism and money. The subject of food prompts the obvious statement that ancient peoples ate; the eating habits of ancient Hebrews introduce the subject of modern Jews; and the subject of Jews inspires thoughts of banks and anti-Semitism.

Heine's astutely blasphemous equation of religion and finance (an equation he makes often in his works) comes at the end of his apparently casual list of Jewish "inventions:"

Ich könnte auch anführen, wie human sich viele Berliner Gelehrte über das Essen der Juden geäußert, ich käme dann auf die anderen Vorzüglichkeiten und Vortrefflichkeiten der Juden, auf die Erfindungen, die man ihnen verdankt, z.B. die Wechsel, das Christentum— aber halt! Letzteres wollen wir ihnen nicht allzuhoch anrechnen, da wir eigentlich noch wenig Gebrauch davon gemacht haben. (DHA 6:203)

[I could also cite how humanely many Berlin scholars have expressed themselves about Jewish cuisine. I would then come to the other achievements and superiorities of the Jews, to the inventions to their credit—as, for instance, bills of exchange and Christianity. But wait! We do not want to give them too much credit for the latter, since we actually have not made much use of it.] (HPP 207)

The interruption after the word "Christentum" is calculated to give more sting to the reminder that Christ was a Jew and to the narrator's rebuke that Christian philosophy seldom has been practiced. His pause is also calculated to let the reader dwell on the equation of finance and religion and to recall the same connection in the persona's relation of his French

lesson from chapter 7, where the wordplay on *crédit* and *crédo* was a
source of humiliation during his childhood:

> Da gab es manches saure Wort. Ich erinnere mich noch so gut, als
> wäre es erst gestern geschehen, daß ich durch *la religion* viel Unan-
> nehmlichkeiten erfahren. Wohl sechsmal erging an mich die Frage:
> "Henri, wie heißt der Glaube auf französisch?" Und sechsmal, und
> immer weinerlicher antwortete ich: "Das heißt *le crédit*." Und beim
> siebten Male, kirschbraun im Gesicht, rief der wütende Examinator:
> er heißt *la religion*—und es regnete Prügel und alle Kameraden lach-
> ten. Madame! seit der Zeit kann ich das Wort *Religion* nicht erwähnen
> hören, ohne daß mein Rücken blaß vor Schrecken, und meine Wange
> rot vor Scham wird. (DHA 6: 190)[54]

> [there was many a cross word, and I can remember as though it
> happened only yesterday that I experienced much unpleasantness
> through *la religion*. I was asked at least six times in succession, "Henri,
> what is the French for *faith*?" And six times, ever more weepily, I
> replied, "It is called *le crédit*." And the seventh time, his face brownish
> red with rage, my furious examiner cried, "It is called *la religion*." And
> punishment showered down on me and all my schoolmates laughed.
> Madame, since that time I cannot hear the word "religion" without
> my back turning pale from terror and my cheeks turning red from
> shame. (HPP 194)]

Chapter 14 opens with the series of wordplays on "Ideen," anticipated
by the narrator at the end of chapter 13 in his promise to Madame that
he will explain his title (the word *title* itself being the source of a play
on words). His promise is put forth in the outline that parodies scholarly
logic and imitates Sterne, but it is a promise that he mocks rather than
keeps. He shows once more that a definition is not something fixed, but
depends on context and style. Received meanings of the word *Ideen,* like
other received meanings, are echoed but changed at the will of the poet:

> Madame, haben Sie überhaupt eine Idee von einer Idee? Was ist eine
> Idee? "Es liegen einige gute Ideen in diesem Rock" sagte mein Schnei-
> der, indem er mit ernster Anerkennung den Oberrock betrachtete, der
> sich noch aus meinen berlinisch eleganten Tagen herschreibt, und
> woraus jetzt ein ehrsamer Schlafrock gemacht werden sollte. Meine

Wäscherin klagt: "Der Pastor S. habe ihrer Tochter Ideen in den Kopf gesetzt, und sie sei dadurch unklug geworden und wolle keine Vernunft mehr annehmen." Der Kutscher Pattensen brummt bei jeder Gelegenheit: "das ist eine Idee! das ist eine Idee!" Gestern aber wurde er ordentlich verdrießlich, als ich ihn frug: was er sich unter einer Idee vorstelle? Und verdrießlich brummte er: "Nu, nu, eine Idee ist eine Idee! eine Idee ist alles dumme Zeug, was man sich einbildet." In gleicher Bedeutung wird dieses Wort, also Buchtitel, von dem Hofrat Heeren in Göttingen gebraucht. (DHA 6:205)

[Madame, do you have any idea about an idea? What is an idea? "There are some good ideas in this coat," my tailor said to me as he looked with earnest attention at the overcoat, dating from my elegant Berlin period, that is now to be made into a respectable dressing gown. My washerwoman complains that the Reverend S. has been putting ideas into her daughter's head, as a result of which she has become silly and won't listen to reason. The coachman Pattersen grumbles on every occasion. "That's an idea! That's an idea!" Yesterday, however, he became truly annoyed when I asked him what he imagined an idea to be. And he crossly growled, "Well, well, an idea is an idea! An idea is any stupid thing that is thought up." The word is used in this meaning as the title of a book by Court Councilor Heeren in Göttingen.] (HPP 209–10)

From the first sentence on, there is no doubt about the self-reflexive nature of this passage. Gradually it becomes clear that the word "Ideen" in the title has much the function of the words truth or taste for Byron: it can connote lofty philosophical thoughts (Jost Hermand understands it in a Hegelian sense, for example), and it can refer to material things, as it does when the poet's tailor says: "Es liegen einige gute Ideen in diesem Rock." It can be ambiguous with a touch of sexual innuendo, as it is in the landlady's sentence about her daughter and the pastor, where Heine further plays on the words "Idee" and "Vernunft" [reason]. And it can be completely emptied of meaning, as it is in the narrator's first sentence, "Haben Sie eine Idee von einer Idee?" and in the last, where it is used to describe the contents of a mindless but pretentious philosophical study.[55]

The meaning that is closest to the poet's own work lies in the tailor's usage when he says that there are "einige gute Ideen in diesem Rock" [a few good ideas in this coat]. The sentence contains more than a simple clash of elevated and mundane, because the tailor resembles the poet himself in his grudging acknowledgment that there is merit in something old. The salvaging of an old coat, which lives on as a bathrobe, is an irreverent image for the poet's own use of tradition, and the verb "herschreiben" underscores the connection. Heine may be alluding here to "The Art of Book Making" from Washington Irving's *Sketchbook* (1819–20), which Erich Loewenthal and Hermand list as a model for the dream of the Göttingen library in *Die Harzreise*. Irving's persona describes the reading room in the British Museum and mocks the scholars who use it; he has a daydream in which the readers' intellectual borrowings are transformed into clothes, prompting an angry reaction from the authors whose portraits hang on the walls and who come to life and chase the readers, crying "Thieves! Thieves!" The narrator finds the case of one "learned Theban" so hilarious—that of a scholar who has put a manuscript onto his head as if it were a wig—that he laughs out loud and wakes himself up:

> There was something so ludicrous in the catastrophe of this learned Theban that I burst into an immoderate fit of laughter, which broke the whole illusion. The tumult and the scuffle were at an end. The chamber resumed its usual appearance. The old authors shrunk back into their picture frames and hung in shadowy solemnity along the walls. In short, I found myself wide awake in my corner, with the whole assemblage of bookworms gazing at me with astonishment. Nothing of the dream had been real but my burst of laughter, a sound never before heard in that grave sanctuary, and so abhorrent to the ears of wisdom as to electrify the fraternity. (WI 813–14)

The waking up from a dream and the damning observation that scholarship is incompatible with laughter bear an obvious resemblance to Heine; so, too, does the question of imitation, which adds another layer of irony to the persona's own borrowings in *Buch Le Grand*. Yet it is clear that Heine's use of past reading is the kind observed by Irving's narrator among a few select readers in the room. They do not filch ideas, but incorporate them:

> There were some well dressed gentlemen, it is true, who only helped themselves to a gem or so, which sparkled among their own orna-

ments, without eclipsing them. Some too, seemed to contemplate the costumes of the old writers, merely to imbibe their principles of taste, and catch their air and spirit; but I grieve to say that too many were apt to array themselves from top to toe, in the patch work manner I have mentioned. (WI 812)

Heine belongs to the first group.[56]

When the poet plays on the material and philosophical meanings of his title, he puts into practice his aesthetic as he now conceives it. In the remainder of chapter 14, he sustains the clash of material and spiritual questions with examples that are predominantly culinary. For instance, he equates poetological and culinary matters when he calls one of the laws from the *Ars poetica* (*nonum prematur in annum*) a recipe:

Als Horaz dem Autor die berühmte Regel gab, sein Werk neun Jahre im Pult liegen zu lassen, hätte er ihm auch zu gleicher Zeit das Rezept geben sollen, wie man neun Jahre ohne Essen zubringen kann. Als Horaz diese Regel ersann, saß er vielleicht an der Tafel des Mäcenas und aß Truthähne mit Trüffeln, Fasanenpudding in Wildpretsauce, Lerchenrippchen mit teltower Rübchen, Pfauenzungen, indianische Vogelnester, und Gott weiß! was noch mehr, und alles umsonst. Aber wir, wir unglücklichen Spätgeborenen, wir leben in einer anderen Zeit, unsere Mäcenaten haben ganz andere Prinzipien. (DHA 6:207)

[When Horace provided the author with that famous rule of letting his works lie nine years in his desk, he should also at the same time have provided him with the recipe for going nine years without food. When Horace invented this rule, he was perhaps sitting at the table of Maecenas, eating roast turkey with truffles, pheasant pudding with venison sauce, lark cutlets with teltower turnips, peacock's tongues, Indian bird's nests, and Lord knows what all, and everything for free. But we, we unlucky latecomers, live in a different era. Our art patrons have entirely different principles.] (HPP 211–12)

Horace is cited and changed; the tradition he represents is transformed into the source of Heine's innovation. Heine demonstrates the transformation by comparing a banquet at the table of Maecenas with its modern counterpart. At the Roman banquet, the foods were exotic and reflected the wealth of the host and the detachment of art from social or real issues.

The poets at Maecenas's table were immune from the banal concerns of daily subsistence, because everything they ate was free ("alles umsonst"); they therefore did not mention coarse and commonplace trivia in their works. In exchange they had to avoid political subjects that might offend their patron and cut off the supply of "Truthähne mit Trüffeln" [turkeys with truffles]. Heine suggests that in order to retain his patron's culinary favor, the poet of Horace's time had to submit to rigid aesthetic and political rules; the poet of the nineteenth century enjoys the liberation from such constraints and must, in exchange, be willing to endure poverty, the condemnation of conservative critics, or a life in exile. The dishes at both banquets are fantastic; they are extravagant and recherché at the one and allegorical rather than edible at the other, an opposition consciously reminiscent of that between foods in heaven and hell at the beginning of *Buch Le Grand*. The poet is the cook at the modern banquet, and he describes his satirical method of observing and "cooking" his "food."[57]

The poet of *Buch Le Grand* is liberated from aesthetic constraints but not from material needs, and he shows the change in the writer's position by turning material concerns and other banalities into the subjects of his works. Before he describes the "dexterity" of his "good cookery," he describes his subjects, which are love and fools, hence inexhaustible: "So lange mein Herz voll Liebe und der Kopf meiner Nebenmenschen voll Narrheit ist, wird es mir nie an Stoff zum Schreiben fehlen" (DHA 6:208) [As long as my heart is full of love and the head of my fellow man is full of foolishness, I shall never lack subject matter for writing] (HPP 212). But in chapter 14, his emphasis on material needs makes him concentrate almost entirely on the fools. Just at the point where his style and his revolution seem to have crystallized, he shows that liberation can have its dangers. There is no easy formula for the balance between poetry and history, high and low, or real and ideal; a mixture of extremes may resemble a balance, but the extremity of either position has not actually been overcome. The problem is one to which Heine returns, again with culinary examples, in *Deutschland. Ein Wintermärchen, Aus den Memoiren des Herren von Schnabelewopski*, and the poems "Der Tannhäuser" and "Der Apollogott."

In chapter 14, the poet goes to such an extreme that his satire has as little connection to reality as the opening visions of heaven and hell. Satire is essential to his new mode of poetry, as has often been noted; Laura Hofrichter considers the passage that precedes the banquet—the passage "Diese Leute sind meine Blumen" [These people are my flowers]—to be the turning point in Heine's aesthetic.[58] But she makes the claim too soon and does not consider the end of the chapter, where the poet gets indigestion from his "cookery." He has not yet learned how much he can exaggerate in his satire, and he has sacrificed the first of his subjects, love, to the second, politics. His indigestion at the end of the banquet repeats but changes the opening vision of heaven, where one eats all day without ever getting indigestion. At the beginning, Heine showed how the same subject, food, can convey opposites; here he shows how the same subject is transformed by context:

Man speist von Morgen bis Abend [. . .] , *die gebratenen Gänse fliegen herum mit den Sauceschüsselchen im Schnabel, und fühlen sich geschmeichelt, wenn man sie verzehrt*, butterglänzende Torten wachsen wild wie Sonnenblumen, überall Bäche mit Bouillon und Champagner, überall Bäume, woran Servietten flattern, und *man speist und wischt sich den Mund, und speist wieder, ohne sich den Magen zu verderben.* (DHA 6:171; my emphasis)

und wenn mir auch nicht die Narren gebraten ins Maul fliegen, sondern mir gewöhnlich roh und abgeschmackt entgegenlaufen, so weiß ich sie doch so lange am Spieße herumzudrehen, zu schmoren, zu pfeffern, bis sie mürbe und genießbar werden. [. . .] *Madame, ich hab mir schon in Gedanken den Magen überladen! Der Henker hole solche Schlemmerei! Ich kann nicht viel vertragen. Meine Verdauung ist schlecht.* [. . .] Ruft mir meinen dicken Millionarrn! (DHA 6:211–12; my emphasis)

[There people dine from morning to night (. . .); *roast geese fly around with gravy boats in their bills and feel flattered if anyone eats them;* tarts gleaming with butter grow wild like sunflowers; everywhere there are rivulets of bouillon and champagne, everywhere trees with napkins fluttering from them, *and people dine and wipe their lips and eat again without getting indigestion.*] (HPP 175)

And although fools do not exactly fly roasted into my mouth but run at me rather raw and not even half-baked, still I know how to turn them on a spit, stew them and pepper them until they are tender and tasty. (. . .) *Madame, in my imagination I have already overeaten! The devil*

173

take such gluttony. I cannot stand much; my digestion is poor. (. . .)
Summon me my plump foolionaire!] (HPP 216–17; my emphasis)

The repetitions, some of them almost verbatim, show the demands Heine
makes on his readers' attention. The last sentence of the second passage,
which is also the last sentence of chapter 14, is another example of his
associative manner, but within one chapter, not between the first and the
fourteenth: he checks to see whether the reader remembers the metamor-
phosis of one of his models, the fat millionaire, into a *chaise percée* or
commode. His poetic control is likewise evident in the wordplay on the
name of Willibald Alexis and Häring to which I made reference earlier:
"ich muß einen Willibald Alexis- [read: Häring-] Salat darauf essen, der
reinigt" (DHA 6:212) [I must eat a Willibald Alexis salad, which purges
and purifies] (HPP 217), where again the culinary and the literary are
interchanged.

In chapter 15, the narrator describes the war between the "Narren"
[fools] and the "Vernünftigen" [reasonable people] and ends with the
comment that because his writing is not going well, he will stop for
breakfast: "Ich will unterdessen frühstücken, es will heute morgen mit
dem Schreiben nicht mehr so lustig fortgehn, ich merke, der liebe Gott
läßt mich in Stich" (DHA 6:216) [Meanwhile, I want to have breakfast.
This morning I am not getting ahead very well with my writing; the
good Lord leaves me in the lurch] (HPP 221). This comment appears
to contradict the claim that creativity and sensuality are connected, but
instead the connection is sustained by the context. In describing the war
between folly and reason, the narrator plays with the words *Narr,
Narrheit,* and *Vernunft* in order to show that their meaning—like that
of the word *Ideen*—can shift depending on how the poet uses them. The
fools who were his subjects in the preceding chapter are only nominally
the same as the fools of Shakespeare, who is the poet's model when he
confesses at the end of this chapter that he himself is a fool in disguise.
Once again he illustrates the fallacy of equating things that seem to
resemble each other or even that have the same designation. When we
have ciphered out the connections, the culinary illustration of his
Narrheit makes sense. We have even come to expect it:

[Meine Narrheit] bringt es hoch genug! Ihr schwindelt vor ihrer
eigenen Erhabenheit. Sie macht mich zum Riesen mit Siebenmeilen-
stiefeln. Mir ist des Mittags zu Mute, als könnte ich alle Elephanten

Hindostans aufessen und mir mit dem Straßburger Münster die Zähne stochern; des Abends werde ich so sentimental, daß ich die Milchstraße des Himmels aussaufen möchte, ohne zu bedenken, daß einem die kleinen Fixsterne sehr unverdaulich im Magen liegen bleiben. (DHA 6:216)

[(My foolishness) reaches heights enough. It gets dizzy from its own sublimity. It makes me into a giant with seven-mile boots. At noon I feel as though I could devour all the elephants of Hindustan and then pick my teeth with the spire of the Strasbourg Cathedral; in the evening I become so sentimental that I would like to guzzle down the Milky Way without reflecting how indigestibly the small, fixed stars would remain in my stomach.] (HPP 221)

Heine alludes here to some of his most important models. The seven-league boots are used by Goethe at the beginning of "Zum Schäkespears-Tag" to describe the genius of Shakespeare; the Strasburg cathedral is likewise associated with Goethe and the *Geniezeit* (and is one of the examples of a "good idea" in the god's dream from chapter 2 of *Buch Le Grand*); the elephants of Hindostan recall the *Kalkuttenbraten* and its significance in chapter 5 as well as a Romantic motif; and the use of the word "sentimental" evokes Sterne; there may even be a bilingual pun on the word "Fixsterne," just as there was a pun on the name of Willibald Alexis in the previous chapter. A few lines later, when the persona decides to stop writing and to eat breakfast because he is "not getting ahead," we cannot take his modesty at face value. His comment that "the good Lord" has "left him in the lurch" ("der liebe Gott hat mich in Stich gelassen") loses its sting when we remember that "der liebe Gott" is used by the poet elsewhere as an alias.

In the chapter that follows, Heine again shows that culinary references are not poetic by definition but must be poeticized. The persona tells Madame about sitting at the feet of his "schöne Freundin" [beautiful friend] in Godesberg, and he appears to have gone back to the poetry of love that he abandoned earlier; but his lovemaking is hindered by the presence of the woman's dachshund. Both the poet and the dachshund compete for attention by looking into her eyes, and the eyes are a source of poetic frustration that resembles the poet's search in *Don Juan* for the right image with which to describe Lady Adeline:

O, ich kann jenes Auge nicht beschreiben! Ich will mir einen Poeten, der vor Liebe verrückt worden ist, aus dem Tollhause kommen lassen, damit er aus dem Abgrund des Wahnsinns ein Bild heraufhole, womit ich jenes Auge vergleiche—Unter uns gesagt, ich wäre wohl selber verrückt genug, daß ich zu einem solchen Geschäfte keines Gehülfen bedürfte. (DHA 6:217)

[Oh, those eyes are indescribable! I want to have some poet who went mad from love brought here from a lunatic asylum to fetch from the abyss of his madness an image to be compared with those eyes. Just between you and me, I myself would be mad enough not to require any help in such an undertaking.] (HPP 221–22)

If the poet is crazy, as he claims to be, it is only in the complicated sense he explained in the previous chapter; his self-awareness bespeaks the opposite, as does his ability to put distance between his descriptions and those of others. The "help" he enlists is not that of a poet crazed by love but that of an Englishman, a Frenchman, and a lawyer from Mainz. The first two express their admiration with profanities; one says "*God d—n!*" and the other says "*F—e!*" (both words decorously abridged). Only the lawyer hazards a comparison, the second term of which is culinary and absurd: "ihre Augen sehen aus wie zwei Tassen schwarzen Kaffee" (DHA 6:217) [Her eyes look like two cups of black coffee] (HPP 222). In a patronizing but patient tone, the narrator interprets the lawyer's comparison for the reader: "Er wollte etwas sehr Süßes sagen, denn er warf immer unmenschlich viel Zucker in seinen Kaffee" [He wanted to say something very sweet, for he always put a barbaric amount of sugar into his coffee (HPP 222)]. His summarizing comment is "Schlechte Vergleiche" [Bad comparisons]. But the plural form *Vergleiche* (comparisons) makes no more sense than the lawyer's image: the only comparison was the lawyer's—until we add the poet's own throughout *Buch Le Grand*. By making fun of his own comparisons, Heine does not disavow them, however; on the contrary, he benefits from the parallel between his images and the lawyer's pitiful simile. His affectation of guilt by association functions like rhetorical irony and implies self-praise, not self-reproach.

The reference to food in chapter 17, the last in the work, is structually important because it touches on all of the poet's subjects and shows off his style, indirectly and with confidence in the reader's attention. We are presented with a tableau of the poet in the company of a cake, a dog, and a beautiful woman; the cake can be understood to emblematize his new kind of poetry, which has its source in love (the beautiful woman) but is shared with satire or politics (the dog). Again the poet tells of being at the feet of his "beautiful friend," who slaps him whenever he is irreverent, which he confesses is often, but literally sweetens the blow every time by giving him half of a cake. She gives the other half to her dog, saying that they must have their cake in this world because they lack religion and cannot go to heaven: "'Ihr beide habt keine Religion und werdet nicht selig, und man muß Euch auf dieser Welt mit Kuchen füttern, da für Euch im Himmel kein Tisch gedeckt wird'" (DHA 6:218) ["You two have no religion, and you will never be blessed, so you must be fed cakes in this world, since no place will be set for you at the table in heaven"] (HPP 223).

Both the situation and the woman's comment are reminiscent of chapter 14, where the mock definition of *Ideen* develops into a seemingly desultory discussion of the risks poets run by being nonconformists. Heine gives two principal examples, one the method that "der liebe Gott" [the good Lord] has devised for distributing poetic gifts, and the other, related to the first, the poet's relation to a patron. In both cases success is disproportionate to talent, since genius opposes the norm; and in both cases, as before, an equation is made between creativity and sensuality, first in the statement that poets must enjoy life on earth because they are too subversive to go to heaven, and second in an evocation of the culinary benefits the poet derives from having a patron like Maecenas. According to the parodistic teleological account in chapter 14, mediocre poets (whom Heine calls "Elohasänger und Erbauungspoeten" [Elohist psalmists and edifying poets]) are denied good ideas and fame because they will go to heaven.

The tableau in chapter 17 recalls another apparently digressive passage from chapter 14. Following his interpretation of the Horatian "recipe" for poetry, *nonum prematur in annum,* the poet discusses dogs. He moves back and forth between the literal and the figurative, referring first to real dogs and then calling the writer in the nineteenth century an "armer Hund" [poor dog, meaning poor scoundrel], and finally reviving the metaphor so that he can vary the criticism of mediocre poets on the previous page. Only the patient, obedient, parasitic "dogs" get fed: "der Dachs, der die Hand leckt, oder der winzige Bologneser, der sich in den duftigen Schoß der Hausdame zu schmiegen weiß, oder der geduldige Pudel, der eine Brotwissenschaft gelernt und apportieren, tanzen und trommeln kann" (DHA 6:207) [the dachshund who licks the hands or the tiny Italian toy spaniel who knows how to cuddle up into the lady's perfumed lap or the patient poodle who has learned a practical trade and can fetch and carry, dance and drum] (HPP 212). His pun on *Brotwissen-schaft* (translated here as "practical trade") recalls the *Brotkügelchen* and drumming of chapter 7, where bread evoked poetic revolution rather than pedantry and a lack of imagination. Again, the same image has opposing functions.

With such passages in mind, the tableau in chapter 17 provides a recapitulation, even an allegory of the narrator's development. Next to him is her dog—a dachshund, one of the obedient dog-authors we heard about earlier—and she is feeding both of them cake. The poet's pose becomes emblematic of his poetry of ambiguity, a poetry in which sensuality is connected both to love and to politics, but where love can turn to sentimentality and politics to servility, a position reflected formally in the humorous opposites of wordplay. If he were to go to heaven, he would have to sacrifice his ambiguous stance. To recall the culinary allusions in *Buch Le Grand* is to remember the stages of the poet's development. Each allusion evokes the poet's ambiguous perception and his gradual control over it: the opening images of heaven and hell; the oysters and Rhine wine in chapter 2 and the overcoming of suicidal thoughts; the *Kalkuttenbraten* in chapter 5; the list of the poet's past and present passions and the hiding of apple tarts under an apron in chapter 6; the presence of Napoleon, Aristophanes, Goethe, Shakespeare, and God as aesthetic and political models in chapter 11, combined in the image of a republican who first smells the knife to see if it was used for cutting herring; the culinary examples in chapter 13 that mock systems; the banquet at the table of Maecenas and the poet's own banquet of fools in chapter 14; the exaggerated image of hunger in chapter 15; the lawyer's culinary simile and the poet's criticism of it in chapter 16; and the poet and dachshund who are fed cake by a beautiful woman in chapter 17. Together, the culinary allusions are like a shorthand for the poet's development toward a poetry of tensions in which a whole is represented but not harmonized—except perhaps through the humor of wordplay.

Aus den Memoiren des Herren von Schnabelewopski

The reputation of *Aus den Memoiren des Herren von Schnabelewospki* is strikingly different from that of *Ideen. Das Buch Le Grand*. Whereas *Das Buch Le Grand* is unanimously considered to be a masterpiece, *Schnabelewospki* is generally criticized or abridged. Mostly the latter work is salvaged for the passage about the Flying Dutchman in chapter 7, sometimes, too, for the portrayal of Little Simson (considered by some to be a caricature of Ludwig Börne) and the description of Jan Steen. Since the culinary references in *Schnabelewopski* lack the direct connection to political themes that one finds in works like *Buch Le Grand* or *Deutschland. Ein Wintermärchen,* they are no doubt partly to blame for the skepticism, even hostility, with which *Schnabelewopski* has been received. Fairley says that "if we want to see the image [of food] at its cheapest, we have only to run through *Schnabelewopski,* a work where Heine is notoriously not at his best," and Sammons considers the culinary details a strained and unsuccessful attempt to "bind up the themes that are lying about in such troublesome profusion."[59] Sammons argues further that because "Heine's formal genius was *sui generis,*" he had trouble with "this more conventional kind of narration."[60] Yet the novel is the least conventional or prescriptive of genres, and details like the inclusion of the "Vonved" poem in *Schnabelewopski* would seem to indicate that Heine had a Romantic—or Schlegelian—understanding of the form.

A few attempts to rehabilitate the work have been made over the past twenty-five years. One is by Manfred Windfuhr, who attributes the disparagement of *Schnabelewopski* to neoclassical prejudices and the expectations fostered by neoclassical aesthetic norms ("einer klassizistischen Ästhetik"), which I believe is correct. But it seems to me that Windfuhr is too quick to fit *Schnabelewopski* into another tradition, that of the picaresque novel, thus muting the shocks and putting things back into an order that is contrary to the essence of this work.[61] Grubačić has written a subtle analysis of *Schnabelewopski* in which its perceived flaws—the shift in narrative perspective, the culinary details, and the puns—are convincingly explained as essential to Heine's aesthetic. For Grubačić, Heine's mastery is evident in the way he reverses the expected order of things so that what seems to be ornamental is changed into narrative substance.[62] Grubačić argues that the work is carefully structured, and like Hosfeld for *Buch*

Le Grand, he uses the Bakhtinian model of "carnivalization" to explain
the mixture of styles and the dominance of eating and eros in the work.
He also sees the work as belonging to a genre of sorts—what according
to the aesthetic categories of the period would be called "ein Werk des
'Witzes'" [a work of "wit"], a work in which the formal canon is paro-
died.[63] Grubačić's analysis, which appeared in 1975, has not prompted a
reevaluation of the work or even much interest in it. Almost fifteen years
later, in his *Heine-Handbuch,* Höhn encourages critics to reconsider
Schnabelewopsi, and it remains to be seen whether they will.[64]

In *Schnabelewopski,* Heine again questions institutions. He focuses his
questioning on the Christian religion because of its dominant role in
European society; but religion functions as an archetype for all institu-
tions, including aesthetic ones. In its real or extended sense, religion is
not intrinsically suspect; it becomes so only when belief degenerates into
ritual and symbols are severed from their source, a theme that Heine
treated earlier in *Die Bäder von Lucca* (possibly at the same time as
Schnabelewopski, then, since it is conceivable that parts of the work were
written during the 1820s).[65] In *Schnabelewopski,* ideology breeds a hypoc-
risy that can take either of two extreme forms: that of the materialists in
Hamburg or that of Schnabelewopski's spiritualist landlord and landlady
in Leiden. One can call both extremes literal-minded, the first because it
assumes that rituals have no meaning outside of themselves and the sec-
ond because it assumes that symbols are to be understood as facts. We
find other variants when Schnabelewopski reaches Leiden and records the
theological disputes of the Fichtean, the atheist, and the deist, which
depend on good or bad food; or when we learn that these believers need
mnemonic devices to remember their arguments. Their thinking is with-
out substance, and ultimately Simson is the victim of their literal-minded-
ness and of his own.

What Barry Thomas shows when he unravels the van der Pissen epi-
sode (a name that talks, revealing what its bearer tries to hide) extends
to the rest of the work as well. The description of the theologian's daily
battle is grotesque because of the contrast between van der Pissen in
public and van der Pissen in private. But principally it is grotesque be-
cause Christian symbols have been emptied of their meaning and allegori-
cal figures have become human beings:

the struggle of the laurel wreath [...] represents the need of a doctri-
naire religious view—which has lost touch with its original vital

source—to re-affirm its validity by continually re-enacting the victory of Christianity over hostile forces.[66]

Linguistically the pattern is demonstrated in the metonymic designation of "church" for the Christian religion, which we are meant to remember when Heine speaks of churches and temples. Heine does not criticize the use of concrete images to express abstractions, which is essential to poetry, but an unreflected use of such images. When a Christian thinks of a church as a material object, the relation between a symbol and its source has ceased to exist.

The pun is used in this work as a comic representation of the theme. Puns reveal meanings that are otherwise repressed (the "original vital source" of which Thomas speaks) and that are at odds with the impression a speaker wants to make. It is therefore misleading to say that the dichotomy of body and soul "appears initially on the relatively low level of the pun."[67] High and low, like body and soul, are housed together in a pun as they are in one person, exemplifying the absurdities of the human condition. Only in the conscious combination of material and spiritual, of literal and nonliteral, is it possible to free oneself from this absurdity, at least poetically, which is why the pun becomes a sign of the poet's triumph, here as in *Buch Le Grand* or *Die Bäder von Lucca.*[68] To use puns so that they expose hypocrisy is a traditional technique of satire and a favorite source of dramatic irony, as we know from Molière and Fielding. Simson puns unconsciously when he says "'O Gott! Gott! das ist bei Gott nicht erlaubt, o Gott!'" (B 1:537) ["O God! O God! By God, that is not fair, O God!" (SF 182)], and the landlord swears "aufs heiligste" to renounce his "Umgang mit den alttestamentarischen Weibern" [all contact with the women of the Old Testament] when he dreams. When the landlord promises to have contact only with patriarchs and male prophets ("künftig nur mit Erzvätern und männlichen Propheten zu verkehren" [B 1:544]), the word "verkehren" [to have intercourse] unwittingly betrays his subconscious desires. The pantheist Vanpitter provokes Simson with his puns as well as his blasphemy, this time consciously, when he says that the Egyptian admiration for oxen and onions is justified because both of them are "divine" in certain dishes: "denn erstere, wenn sie gebraten, und letztere, wenn sie gestovt, schmeckten ganz göttlich" [because the former, when they are roasted, and the latter, when they are braised, taste absolutely divine] (B 1:549).

When we are alert to the function of the pun and of the culinary, a passage like the following becomes central rather than supercilious:

Die Hamburger sind gute Leute und essen gut. Über Religion, Politik und Wissenschaft [and one can add *Ästhetik*] sind ihre respektive Meinungen sehr verschieden, aber in Betreff des Essens herrscht das schönste Einverständnis. Mögen die christlichen Theologen dort noch so sehr streiten über die Bedeutung des Abendmahls; über die Bedeutung des Mittagmahls sind sie ganz einig. Mag es unter den Juden dort eine Partei geben, die das Tischgebet auf deutsch spricht, während eine andere es auf hebräisch absingt; beide Parteien essen und essen gut und wissen das Essen gleich richtig zu beurteilen. (B 1:509)

[The Hamburgers are good people who enjoy good eating. They are much divided as regards religion, politics, and science, but they are all beautifully agreed as to cooking. Their theologians may quarrel as much as they like over the Lord's Supper, but there is no difference as to the daily dinner. Though there be among the Jews one division who give grace or the prayer at table in German, while others chant it in Hebrew, they both eat heartily and agree heartily as to what is on the table, and judge its merits with unfailing wisdom.] (SF 156)

For all of these people, despite their professed differences in financial, religious, or aesthetic creed, there is a common material need and culinary pleasure. They are further linked by their absurd pose when, like the theologian van der Pissen later, they hide or ignore the dualities of human existence, of which the pun is the comic and aesthetic measure. In the continuation of this passage, Heine shows his skill at binding everything in the work to the culinary—here most notably the erotic—when he tells of Cupid's arrows, which in Hamburg strike women's stomachs rather than their hearts:

Wenn [die Hamburgerinnen] in der romantischen Liebe sich nicht allzu schwärmerisch zeigen und von der großen Leidenschaft des Herzens wenig ahnen: so ist das nicht ihre Schuld, sondern die Schuld Amors, des kleinen Gottes, der manchmal die schärfsten Liebespfeile auf seinen Bogen legt, aber aus Schalkheit oder Ungeschick viel zu tief schießt, und statt des Herzens der Hamburgerinnen nur ihren Magen zu treffen pflegt. (B 1:510)

[If (the women of Hamburg) do not manifest much wild and dreamy idealism in romantic love, and have little conception of the grand passion of the heart, it is not so much their fault as that of Cupid, who often aims at them his sharpest arrows, but from mischief or unskilfulness shoots too low, and instead of the heart hits them in the stomach.] (SF 157)

Aside from showing here how he remakes legends, Heine uses Cupid to give another example of how spiritual qualities can be materialized through symbols and allegories.[69]

The passage about Cupid is related to the narrator's misogynist but amusing depiction in chapter 8 of how women resemble the dishes of their country. His identification of love with the stomach rather than the heart is enhanced by the connection of both to business interests: love can be bought. In chapter 3, the first Hamburg chapter, we meet the prostitutes Heloise and Minke, and in chapter 4 the procession of Hamburgers includes "die schönen Kaufmannstöchter, mit deren Liebe man auch so viel bares Geld bekommt" (B 1:514) [the beautiful merchants' daughters, with whose love one gets just so much ready money] (SF 161). Heine repeats the connection in chapter 7, where the Flying Dutchman's marriage is described as a business deal (*Handel*): "wie er hört, daß sein Kunde eine schöne Tochter besitzt, verlangt er sie zur Gemahlin. Auch dieser Handel wird abgeschlossen" (B 1:529) [when he hears that his customer has a beautiful daughter, he asks that he may wed her. This bargain also is agreed to] (SF 174).[70]

It is not solely Christianity or Judaism or the spiritualism they represent that come under attack in *Schnabelewopski*, but any unconditional, uncritical belief. Virtually no difference exists between the description of "der heilige Adalbert" [Saint Adalbert] and the great Hamburg bankers, and one easily associates the cathedral where Adalbert lies on his sarcophagous with the city hall and its statues of bankers:

Dort im Dom ist der heilige Adalbert begraben. Dort steht sein silberner Sarkophag, und darauf liegt sein eignes Konterfei, in Lebensgröße, mit Bischofsmütze und Krummstab, die Hände fromm gefaltet, und alles von gegossenem Silber. Wie oft muß ich deiner gedenken, du silberner Heiliger! (B 1:505–6)

Zu den Merkwürdigkeiten der Stadt gehören: 1) Das alte Rathaus, wo die großen Hamburger Bankiers, aus Stein gemeißelt und mit Zepter und Reichsapfel in Händen, abkonterfeit stehen. (B 1:510)

[There, in the cathedral, Saint Adalbert is buried. There is his silver sarcophagus, on which lies his very image, the size of life, with bishop's mitre and crosier, the hands piously folded—and all of molten silver! How often have I thought of thee, thou silver saint! (SF 153–54)

Among the lions of Hamburg we find—
1) The old Council House, or Town Hall, where the great Hamburg bankers are chiseled out of stone, and stand counterfeited with scepters and globes of empire in their hands.] (SF 158)

The interchangeability of saints and bankers and the link between spiritual and material concerns is accentuated further by what follows in each case: a description of Panna Jadviga in the first passage and of the "beautiful Marianne" in the second.

Other buildings are likened to temples in the narrator's sustained satirization of government, finance, and art. Aside from the *Rathaus*, there is the stock market (a connection we know from *Englische Fragmente*), and the *Stadttheater* is a "house of God" whose actors are contemptuously described as bourgeois: "gute Bürger, ehrsame Hausväter, die sich nicht verstellen können und niemanden täuschen, Männer, die das Theater zum Gotteshause machen" [good citizens, honorable family men who can neither dissemble nor deceive and who make the theater into a house of worship] (B 1:510–11). In chapter 3 the temple is an image for poetry when Schnabelewopski describes his plan to "raise a temple of honor for Hamburg" ("Ehrentempel"); he will follow the example of a famous author whom he also identifies as an "entrepreneur" [Unternehmer], a man who collected contributions for his work and then disappeared with the money without getting any further than *Aaron* and *Abendrot*. Every temple in *Schnabelewopski* has a connection to materialism, even when, in the *ubi sunt* passage of chapter 4, the prostitute Minka

184

is compared to "the temple of Solomon after it had been destroyed by Nebuchadnezzar" (B 1:514 / SF 162).

One of the central arguments in *Schnabelewopski* is that philosophy, and by analogy genre, cannot be fixed.[71] Clearly the narrator admires the philosophy of the Saint-Simonists more than the repressions of Christians and Jews; but his skepticism and ambiguous nature do not allow him to adopt either completely. Sensuality or spirituality in isolation is a deformity, as we know from the description of the prostitutes Heloise and Minka next to a description of Madame Pieper and Madame Schnieper, even though Heine's satirical description of the prostitutes is more affectionate than his depiction of the other two. The prostitutes do not repress their sensual nature, but their profession reflects a society in which such repression is the rule and in which love is a commodity. The other "ladies," on the other hand, live from hypocrisy, and each of them in turn is ironically described as "ein Muster von Anstand, Ehrsamkeit, Frömmigkeit und Tugend" [a model of decorum, honorability, piety, and virtue]. What is called into question is the use of words like *Anstand* [decorum] rather than the qualities they mean to denote. In society as in literature, *Anstand* needs to be newly defined to reflect a shift in context and historical period.

Another example of shifts in meaning can be found in the tribute to Jan Steen, where the word *religious* is used in a positive sense. When Schnabelewopski says that he lives in the house of Jan Steen, whom he considers as great as Raphael, he redefines religion and reevaluates genre by calling both Steen and Raphael "religious" painters. One of them depicts the religion of sorrow, while the other portrays the religion of joy:

Auch als religiöser Maler war Jan ebenso groß, und das wird man einst ganz klar einsehn, wenn die Religion des Schmerzes erloschen ist, und die Religion der Freude den trüben Flor von den Rosenbüschen dieser Erde fortreißt, und die Nachtigallen endlich ihre lang verheimlichten Entzückungen hervorjauchzen dürfen.

Aber keine Nachtigall wird je so heiter und jubelnd singen, wie Jan Steen gemalt hat. Keiner hat so tief wie er begriffen, daß auf dieser Erde ewig Kirmes sein sollte; er begriff, daß unser Leben nur ein farbiger Kuß Gottes sei, und er wußte, daß der Heilige Geist sich am herrlichsten offenbart im Licht und Lachen. (B 1:540–41)

[And Jan was his equal as a religious painter as well. That will be clearly seen when the religion of pain and suffering shall have ended, and the religion of joy tear the mournful veil from the rosebushes of this earth, and the nightingales at last dare pour forth in rapture their long-suppressed notes of pleasure.

But really no nightingale will ever sing so gaily and rejoicingly as Jan Steen has painted. No one ever felt so deeply that, on this earth, life ought to be one endless Kermess. He knew that our life is only a colored kiss of God, and that the Holy Ghost reveals Himself most gloriously in light and laughter.] (SF 185)

Heine does not reject Raphael and what Raphael represents. Rather, he places Steen with his material subjects in the same category as Raphael with his spiritual themes. Common, even ugly things are accorded the same value as beautiful and harmonious ones. What the narrator calls the "religion" of Jan Steen reverses the dogma in which spiritual concerns are expressed with material images—the designation of "the church" for Christianity or the symbols of bread and wine—while the material source of such images is forgotten or repressed. Steen can form any subject, and he does so knowingly. He does not try to be what he is not, and when he disguises or remakes the truth by portraying his wife in a manner that probably does not correspond to reality, he is not suppressing the truth but willfully and humorously remodeling it. That is why the description of Steen is immediately preceded by the description of the theologian van der Pissen, who is "ernst und gesetzt" [serious and staid] when he lectures, but not when he is at home. Van der Pissen and Steen set each other off.

Steen's focus on material pleasures has the paradoxical effect of elevating them, of giving them more than material quality. Heine presents him as an artist who is fully aware of his creative powers and delights in using them to rearrange reality. He locates this awareness in the knowing smile of Steen in a self-portrait from the "Bohnenfest," which he interprets as an expression of satisfaction at having tricked his wife by portraying her as she was not:

auf dem Gemälde, welches das Bohnenfest vorstellt, und wo Jan mit seiner ganzen Familie zu Tische sitzt, da sehen wir seine Frau mit einem gar großen Weinkrug in der Hand, und ihre Augen leuchten wie die einer Bacchantin. Ich bin aber überzeugt, die gute Frau hat

186

nie zuviel Wein genossen, und der Schalk hat uns weis machen wollen, nicht er, sondern seine Frau liebe den Trunk. Deshalb lacht er desto vergnügter aus dem Bilde hervor. (B 1:542)

[in his picture of the Bean Feast, where Jan sits with his whole family at table, there we see his wife with a great wine jug in her hand, her eyes gleaming like those of a Bacchante. I am sure, however, that the good woman really drank very little, and the rogue wished to humbug us with the idea that it was his wife and not he who was given to toping. For this cause he himself laughs all the more joyfully from the painting.] (SF 186)

What matters is the artist's choice of subjects, regardless of the material or spiritual associations those subjects possess, and his ability to manipulate them.

Heine expresses the same principle in *Die romantische Schule* when he disapproves of the tendency to praise Schiller by criticizing Goethe: "die Geringschätzung Goethes zu Gunsten des Schiller." It is the famous passage in which he says that blemishes are more difficult to represent than idealized beauties (a passage that he varies in the "Einleitung zu *Don Quixote*"):

Oder wußte man wirklich nicht, daß jene hochgerühmten hochidealischen Gestalten, jene Altarbilder der Tugend und Sittlichkeit, die Schiller aufgestellt, weit leichter zu verfertigen waren als jene sündhaften, kleinweltlichen, befleckten Wesen, die uns Goethe in seinen Werken erblicken läßt? Wissen sie denn nicht, daß mittelmäßige Maler meistens lebensgroße Heiligenbilder auf die Leinwand pinseln, daß aber schon ein großer Meister dazu gehört, um etwa einen spanischen Betteljungen, der sich laust, einen niederländischen Bauern, welcher kotzt, oder dem ein Zahn ausgezogen wird, und häßliche alte Weiber, wie wir sie auf kleinen holländischen Kabinettbildchen sehen, lebenswahr und technisch vollendet zu malen? (DHA 8:1.157)

[Or did people really not know that those altar-pieces of virtue and morality, which Schiller undertook, were far easier to create than the sinful, provincial, imperfect beings which Goethe lets us see in his works? Don't they know that mediocre painters usually daub life-sized saints' pictures on the canvas, but that only a great master can paint a

Spanish beggar lad delousing himself, a Dutch peasant vomiting or having a tooth pulled, and ugly old women as we see them in small Dutch miniatures, true to life and technically perfect?] (SW 173)

The correspondence between this passage and the praise of Jan Steen in *Schnabelewopski* is underscored by the metaphor Heine uses in *Die romantische Schule,* where he describes idealized figures as "Altarbilder." The fusion of religious and aesthetic concerns is repeated at the end of this passage; he identifies Goethe with God and calls it hypocritical to criticize art because of a misunderstood sense of Christian morality. He quotes the biblical phrase "Das ist der Finger Gottes," used by the Egyptian magicians in Exodus 8 when they are unable to imitate the gnats brought forth by Aaron, and punningly transforms it into "der Finger Goethes":

Scheltet immerhin über die Gemeinheiten im Faust, über die Szenen auf dem Brocken, im Auerbachskeller, scheltet auf die Liederlichkeiten im Meister—das könnt Ihr dennoch alles nicht nachmachen; da ist der Finger Goethes! (DHA 8:1.157)

[Go ahead and scold about the vulgarities in *Faust,* about the scenes on the Brocken, in Auerbach's tavern, scold about the dissoluteness in *Meister*—you still can't imitate any of it. This is the finger of Goethe!] (SW 173)

Heine associates creativity with sensuality and punning with poetry here as he did in *Buch Le Grand* and as he does in speaking of Jan Steen.

But sensuality alone, for the persona, is not adequate and at times not especially desirable. Schnabelewopski's admiration for Steen should not be confused with an effort to imitate it.[72] After condemning dreams as a manifestation of the rift between body and spirit and a sign of sickness, the persona shifts his position and qualifies it with "und doch" [and yet]. The "und doch" captures the ambiguity of Heine's nature and could serve as a motto for his works alongside the Napoleonic phrase "Du sublime au ridicule il n'y a qu'un pas":

Und doch, welche süße Träume haben wir träumen können! Unsere gesunden Nachkommen werden es kaum begreifen. Um uns her verschwanden alle Herrlichkeiten der Welt, und wir fanden sie wieder in unserer inneren Seele—in unsere Seele flüchtete sich der Duft der zertretenen Rosen und der lieblichste Gesang der verscheuchten Nachtigallen—(B 1:545–46)

[And yet, what beautiful sweet dreams we have been able to dream! Our healthy descendants will hardly be able to understand them! All the splendors of the world disappeared from around us, and we found them again in our own souls; yes, there the perfume of the trampled roses, and the sweetest songs of the frightened nightingales took refuge.] (SF 189)

Such enthusiasm for the dreams that he has just called a sign of disease recalls the poet's divided allegiance in *Buch Le Grand;* the double perspective exemplifies what Grubačić calls Heine's "Mischungsstil," a style where lyricism is "mixed" with caricature, where elevated diction clashes with linguistic "nonchalance."[73]

What prompts the persona's "und doch" is a passage in which Schnabelewopski muses about his landlord's unhealthy repression of sensuality, which is limited to his dreams, and about dreams generally; in essence if not in tone, the passage resembles the philosophical essays of Schiller and Novalis about historical progressions and lost harmony. The grotesque but comic dilemma of Schnabelewopski's landlord is a cover for thoughts that have the substance but not the shape of philosophy and that can easily be misconstrued as flippant. The repression of sensuality by the narrator's landlord and landlady is essential to the plot of *Schnabelewopski,* since it precipitates jealousy, culinary retribution, and ultimately the death of little Simson. But Heine complicates the connection. The behavior of the landlord and landlady provides a glaring contrast to the setting in which we witness it, the home of Jan Steen. All are put into the same frame, like a pun, and the house of Steen allegorically represents the artist's ability to put anything, especially opposites, into the same frame.

Not until chapter 12 does Heine specifically draw attention to these issues, although they have been present long before then. In his historical scheme of things, from Greeks to Jews to Christians, the dream is made to represent "ein Leben mit allen Schrecknissen der Scheidung, die wir eben zwischen Leib und Geist gestiftet" [a life full of all those terrors of that parting which we have established between life and soul] (SF 188).[74] The more one dreams, the less harmony there is between body and soul, as we see from the schism between the landlord's waking and sleeping selves; the more he tries to repress his dreams, the more daring they become until he is a real "holy roué"—"jetzt erst ganz ein heiliger Roué" (B 1:544). But the narrator's attitude toward dreams is not uniform, as we see from the "und doch" and as we have seen from the contrast between his own dreams and those of his landlord. In Schnabelewopski's dream from chapter 2, Christianity and eroticism are joined in the figure of Panna Jadviga, for example; and in the daydream of chapter 6, Schnabelewopski describes his first voyage at sea and recalls the tales of his *Großmuhme* much as they appear in *Buch der Lieder,* especially in the self-ironizing form of a poem like "Seegespenst." Most revealing for the present discussion is the dream from chapter 8, where Schnabelewopski assumes the form of a harlequin amid an Italian culinary landscape in which willow trees have branches of macaroni, the sunshine is transformed into melted butter, and the rain consists of Parmesan cheese:

Vorgestern träumte mir: ich befände mich in Italien und sei ein bunter Harlekin und läge, recht faulenzerisch unter einer Trauerweide. Die herabhängenden Zweige dieser Trauerweide waren aber lauter Makkaroni, die mir lang und lieblich bis ins Maul hineinfielen; zwischen diesem Laubwerk von Makkaroni flossen, statt Sonnenstrahlen, lauter gelbe Butterströme, und endlich fiel von oben herab ein weißer Regen von geriebenem Parmesankäse. (B 1:533)

[The day before yesterday, I dreamed that I was in Italy—a checquered harlequin, and lay all lazy under a weeping willow. The hanging sprays of the tree were of macaroni, which fell, long and lovely, into my mouth, and in between, instead of sunrays, flowed sweet streams of golden butter, and at last a fair white rain of powdered Parmesan.] (SF 178)

The tradition of commedia dell'arte merges with a completely different Italian literary model through a seemingly flippant allusion to Dante in the sentence that follows this passage: "Ach! von geträumtem Makkaroni wird man nicht satt—Beatrice!" (B 1:533) [But from the macaroni of which one dreams no one grows fat—Beatrice!] (SF 178). What matters here is that dreams, like religion or culinary allusions, are a basis for differentiation, not only in the way the landlord's dreams contrast with Schnabelewopski's, but also in the way Schnabelewopski's contrast with each other. Differentiation, not merely contrast, is the hallmark of

Heine's style. On the surface, dreams or food or religions may seem to be the same, but beneath the surface they are not.

The dual perception and aesthetic represented by the "und doch" of chapter 12 points back to chapter 7, where Schnabelewopski goes to the theater in Amsterdam and watches a play about the Flying Dutchman. This is the formal centerpiece of the work, not merely because it is the seventh of fourteen chapters; and because such an important passage is exactly in the middle of the work, even the designation of the work as a fragment is called into question.[75] Like the other architectural structures in this work, the theater houses oppositions, and the simultaneous actions on stage and in the audience put each other into relief. The Flying Dutchman, like Schnabelewopski, is composed of incongruities. His laughter yields quickly to melancholy, and the rationalist's ridicule of superstition quickly gives way to a Romantic pose reminiscent of the Byronic Byron, for example of Childe Harold bored with life and sickened by it. The Flying Dutchman's sorrow is "as deep as the sea," and his anguish is mocked by the waves after he mocks it himself:

> er lacht über den Aberglauben, er spöttelt selber über den fliegenden Holländer den ewigen Juden des Ozeans; jedoch unwillkürlich in einen wehmütigen Ton übergehend, schildert er, wie Myn Heer auf der unermeßlichen Wasserwüste die unerhörtesten Leiden erdulden müsse, wie sein Leib nichts anders sei als ein Sarg von Fleisch, worin seine Seele sich langweilt, wie das Leben ihn von sich stößt und auch der Tod ihn abweist: gleich einer leeren Tonne, die sich die Wellen einander zuwerfen und sich spottend einander zurückwerfen, so werde der arme Holländer zwischen Tod und Leben hin und hergeschleudert, keins von beiden wolle ihn behalten; sein Schmerz sei tief wie das Meer, worauf er herumschwimmt, sein Schiff sei ohne Anker und sein Herz ohne Hoffnung. (B 1:529–30)

[he with tact and easy conversation turns aside all suspicion, jests at the legend, laughs at the Flying Dutchman, the Wandering Jew of the Ocean, and yet, as if moved by the thought, passed into a pathetic mood, depicting how terrible the life must be of one condemned to endure unheard-of tortures on a wild waste of waters—how his body itself is his living coffin, wherein his soul is truly imprisoned—how life and death alike reject him, like an empty cask scornfully thrown by the sea on the shore, and as contemptuously repulsed again into the sea—

how his agony is as deep as the sea on which he sails—his ship without
anchor, and his heart without hope.] (SF 175)

The instant change of mood from laughter to melancholy ("jedoch un-
willkürlich in einen wehmütigen Ton übergehend"), which contains an
unmistakable description of the poet himself, is repeated in reverse when
the spotlight moves from the stage to the audience. The sombre words
of Katharina on stage, her "Treu bis in den Tod" [faithful unto death]
are interrupted by peals of laughter (and the peels of an orange) from a
"beautiful Eve" [wunderschöne Eva] who draws Schnabelewopski's at-
tention away from the stage and the Flying Dutchman.

But Eva herself resembles the Flying Dutchman and the narrator, in
particular because of a smirk that is both angelic and diabolical:

Nur um die linke Oberlippe zog sich etwas, oder vielmehr ringelte sich
etwas, wie das Schwänzchen einer fortschlüpfenden Eidechse. Es war
ein geheimnisvoller Zug, wie man ihn just nicht bei den reinen
Engeln, aber auch nicht bei häßlichen Teufeln zu finden pflegt. Dieser
Zug bedeutete weder das Gute noch das Böse, sondern bloß ein
schlimmes Wissen; es ist ein Lächeln welches vergiftet worden von
jenem Apfel der Erkenntnis, den der Mund genossen. (B 1:530)

[Only that there was something on the left upper lip which curved or
twined like the tail of a slippery gliding lizard. It was a mysterious trait,
something such as is not found in pure angels, and just as little in
mere devils. This trait comes not from evil, but from the *knowledge*
of good and evil—it is a smile which has been poisoned or flavored
by tasting the Apple of Eden.] (SF 175–76)

The self-reflexive literariness of this description includes a playful allusion
to Goethe. His attraction to Eva, he says, is "Wahlverwandtschaft" [elec-
tive affinity]:

Wenn ich diesen Zug auf weichen vollrosigen Mädchenlippen sehe,
dann fühl ich in den eigenen Lippen ein krampfhaftes Zucken, ein
zuckendes Verlangen jene Lippen zu küssen; es ist Wahlver-
wandtschaft. (B 1:530)

[When I see this expression on soft, full, rosy ladies' lips, then I feel in my own a cramp-like twitching—a convulsive yearning—to kiss those lips: it is our Affinity.] (SF 176)

Aside from the indirect allusion to Goethe, words like *symbolisch* and *metaphorisch* reinforce the poetological nature of the passage, and Eva's kinship to the persona is underscored by the pun with which he introduces her: "in der Hand hielt sie einen Apfel, oder vielmehr eine Apfelsine. Statt mir aber symbolisch die Hälfte anzubieten, warf sie mir bloß metaphorisch die Schalen auf den Kopf" (B 1:530) [in her hand she held an apple, or rather an orange. But instead of symbolically dividing it with me, she only metaphorically cast the peel on my head] (SF 175). The punning clash of "Apfel" with "Apfelsine" revives the source of the biblical image and forces the material to oppose the figurative.

That Heine is presenting an aesthetic as well as a philosophical program here becomes even more obvious in the paragraph that follows, where the narrator claims to suppress an erotic passage but reveals it instead. This is more than a narrative trick, and again Heine uses culinary comparisons to flaunt his aesthetic innovations: "Es ist eine gute Geschichte, köstlich wie eingemachte Ananas, oder wie frischer Kaviar, oder wie Trüffel in Burgunder" (B 1:531) [It is a good story, as delicious as preserved pineapple, or fresh caviar, or truffles in burgundy] (SF 176). He not only exposes what he claims to hide, he also hides meaning under the apparent frivolity of his culinary allusions. By feigning allegiance to prudes, the persona distances himself from them even more dramatically. The prudes (by whom all hypocrites are meant, not just the Christians in *Schnabelewopski*) try to hide material needs but are betrayed by their language or their dreams, as we saw in the name of van der Pissen or in the landlord's progression to a "heiliger Roué." What results is a false morality, in literature as well as society. Heine, on the other hand, pretends to suppress (he twice repeats the word *unterdrücken*), but he knowingly reveals instead:

Aber nein—die ganze Geschichte, die ich hier zu erzählen dachte, und wozu der fliegende Holländer nur als Rahmen dienen sollte, will ich jetzt unterdrücken. Ich räche mich dadurch an die Prüden, die dergleichen Geschichten mit Wonne einschlürfen, und bis an den Nabel, ja noch tiefer, davon entzückt sind, und nachher den Erzähler schelten, und in Gesellschaft über ihn die Nase rümpfen, und ihn als unmoralisch verschreien. Es ist eine gute Geschichte, köstlich wie eingemachte Ananas, oder wie frischer Kaviar, oder wie Trüffel in Burgunder, und wäre eine angenehme Lektüre nach der Betstunde; aber aus Ranküne, zur Strafe für frühere Unbill, will ich sie unterdrücken. (B 1:531)

[But no—the whole story, which I planned to tell here and for which the Flying Dutchman was to serve only as a frame, I will now suppress. Thereby will I revenge myself on the prurient prudes who ecstatically lap up such stories and are enraptured by them all the way down to their navel, even further actually, and then abuse the narrator and turn up their noses at him in society, decrying him as immoral. It is a good story, as delicious as preserved pineapple or fresh caviar or truffles in burgundy, and it would make for pleasant reading after prayers; but out of spite, and to punish old offenses, I will suppress it.] (SF 176)

The narrator's ironical "self-censorship," to borrow Levine's term, resembles Heine's literary models, Sterne or Byron.[76] It is therefore not surprising to find an allusion to Byron a few lines later, as obvious yet veiled as his narration of the erotic encounter. He names neither Byron nor *Don Juan* directly, but speaks rather of "an English poet" and admiringly cites the comparison of Lady Adeline to a bottle of frozen champagne:

Jetzt erst begriff ich, warum ein englischer Dichter solche Damen mit gefrorenem Champagner verglichen hat. In der eisigen Hülle lauert der heißeste Extrakt. Es gibt nichts Pikanteres als der Kontrast jener äußeren Kälte und der inneren Glut, die bacchantisch emporlodert und den glücklichen Zecher unwiderstehlich berauscht. (B 1:531)

[Only now do I understand why an English poet has compared such ladies with frozen champagne. Beneath the icy exterior lurks the hottest extract. There is nothing more piquant than the contrast of that outer coldness and the inner fire, which flames up Bacchante-like and irresistably intoxicates the happy carouser.] (SF 176)

What attracts Heine as much as the image is Byron's ability to characterize both Lady Adeline and his own poetic style through the teasing

194

manner in which he develops the comparison: Lady Adeline's "mobility" resembles the poet's in *Don Juan,* just as Eva resembles the poet in *Schnabelewopksi.*[77]

When Heine mentions food at every stage of the work, then, he is not merely following a picaresque tradition. He challenges the automatic assumption that a subject like food cannot be used for poetic images and trains his reader to think twice before judging on the basis of superficial details. *Aus den Memoiren des Herren von Schnabelewopski* resembles *Tom Jones* in the way it exposes and condemns hypocrisy and the rift between things as they seem and things as they are. Similar, too, is the way Fielding and Heine link hypocrisy to genre and the dictates of good taste. But Heine does not stay within the confines of one genre, as Fielding does; one of the main reasons why *Schnabelewopski* still is controversial is that readers do not have the generic categories with which to judge it. Heine's aim in *Schnabelewopski* is the same as in other works: to use and change existing forms. With his indecorous emphasis on food, regardless of the style he chooses, he shows how the connection of form and theme replaces the requirement of harmony between subject and style. In this work especially, he illustrates the claim cited earlier: "Mein Verbrechen war nicht der Gedanke, sondern die Schreibart, der Stil" [My crime was not the idea, but rather the way I wrote about it, my style]. One can extend his allusion to *Don Juan* in chapter 12 to questions of genre: both figures, Schnabelewopski and Juan, are out of place in an epic poem or a picaresque novel, because—as Kluge says of Schnabelewopski—neither one develops. Yet this strikes me as intentional rather than accidental: Byron uses Juan's passivity to unravel the myth of Don Juan and the formula for epic heroism, and Schnabelewopski, as the poetic persona, needs to have completed his aesthetic development before starting to write.

Deutschland. Ein Wintermärchen / Atta Troll

In the penultimate caput of *Deutschland. Ein Wintermärchen,* Heine commits one of his greatest sins against decorum. The poet-narrator is in Hamburg visiting Hammonia, the daughter of Charlemagne and patron saint of Hamburg who has become a prostitute and an alchoholic. She offers to show him the future of Germany on condition that he not tell about it, and he agrees, whereupon she leads him to her father's "throne" (the familiar and ironic German designation for chamber pot) and tells him to raise the lid and look inside:

Was ich gesehn, verrate ich nicht,
Ich habe zu schweigen versprochen,
Erlaubt ist mir zu sagen kaum,
O Gott! was ich gerochen! - - -

Ich denke mit Widerwillen noch
An jene schnöden, verfluchten
Vorspielgerüche, das schien ein Gemisch
Von altem Kohl und Juchten.

Entsetzlich waren die Düfte, O Gott!
Die sich nachher erhuben;
Es war als fegte man den Mist
Aus sechs und dreißig Gruben. - - -

Ich weiß wohl was Saint-Just gesagt
Weiland im Wohlfahrtsausschuß:
Man heile die große Krankheit nicht
Mit Rosenöl und Moschus -

Doch dieser deutsche Zukunftsduft
Mocht alles überragen
Was meine Nase je geahnt -
Ich konnt es nicht länger ertragen.

(DHA 4:153)

[What I saw, I will not betray,
for I promised never to tell it.
But seeing was only half the tale—
Ye gods! if you could smell it! . . .

It still revolts me when I recall
the smells I smelt to begin with—
the stink of untanned hides, and of old
bad cabbage it was mixed in with.

But the scents that followed this prelude, God!
were anything but respites;

it smelt as if they were sweeping the dung
from six-and-thirty cesspits.

I know that curing a great disease
is harder than one supposes—
as Saint-Just once said, you don't get far
with musk and oil of roses.

But the way the German future smelt
was ghastly, hideous—stronger
than ever my nose had bargained for—
soon I could stand it no longer.]

(DR 92–93)

The clarity with which the poet reveals what he claims to hide is even
greater here than in *Schnabelewopski,* and he defends his indecorum in the
next and final caput by citing his "father" Aristophanes. He does so in
the same disingenuous way that Byron cites Homer in *Don Juan,* know-
ing that his context and the expectations of his readers (their taste) are
not the same as for Aristophanes and his audience. Both Byron and Heine
admire the classical models, but they rightly insist on their distance from
them. Campe unwittingly confirms the success of Heine's strategy when
he writes to "warn" him that modern readers will not tolerate Aristo-
phanean improprieties in contemporary works:

Daß Sie auf Aristophanes hinweisen ist gut; aber die Menschen, welche
Bücher behalten und kaufen, wollen dergleichen in der *modernen* Lit-
eratur nicht gelten lassen: man duldet und verzeihet dergleichen, nach
conventionellen Gesetzen, nicht in der guten Gesellschaft. (HSA
26:104)

[For you to mention Aristophanes is a good thing; but people who
keep and buy books do not want to allow anything of the kind in
modern literature: according to conventional laws, such things are nei-
ther tolerated nor pardoned in polite society.]

Indeed. Heine makes the point himself within the poem when he refers
to "good taste," an allusion that restates the connection between ambigu-
ous taste and literary revolution:

197

Der König liebt das Stück. Das zeugt
Von gutem antiquen Geschmacke;
Den Alten amüsierte weit mehr
Modernes Froschgequacke.

(DHA 4:156)

[The King enjoys the play. That shows
some taste—for an ancient poet.
But when modern frogs begin to croak,
he doesn't want to know it.]

(DR 95)

Heine's qualification of good taste as "antique" is a willed anachronism. As we saw with respect to *Don Juan*, good taste is a modern notion based on a limited and itself anachronistic interpretation of Horace. Heine has taken a past model and alienated it, proving that a past model cannot be imposed upon the present. Other anachronisms in the poem reenforce the effect he achieves in the poem as a whole. Hammonia wears Roman garb that is out of place in contemporary Hamburg and that further clashes with her new occupation as a prostitute. She speaks in quotations that also are out of context. Barbarossa is an anachronism whose adherence to aristocratic forms is absurd, the literary counterpart to which is an anachronistic adherence to aesthetic laws. What Barbarossa calls "Etiquette" is the same as "good taste," and the "Hochverrat" [high treason] and "Majestätsverbrechen" [lèse majesté] of which Barbarossa accuses the poet apply to aristocratic genres of poetry, not just to a political event. This is the same image Southey uses when he condemns *Don Juan* as "an act of high treason on English poetry," and there is a connection.[78]

What Heine rejects is taste or etiquette that has no meaning, the equivalent to automatic ritual in *Schnabelewopski* or to the mindless imitation of Greek and Christian forms in *Die Bäder von Lucca*. When the narrator tells Barbarossa about the French Revolution and the guillotine, Barbarossa is shocked because of the lack of etiquette and says:

"Der König und die Königin!
Geschnallt! an einem Brette!

Das ist ja gegen allen Respekt
Und alle Etiquette!"

(DHA 4:128)

["The Sovereign and his Lady Queen!
Strapped down! It's a disgrace, sir!
Against all the rules of etiquette!
People should know their place, sir!"]

(DR 67)

Barbarossa's indignation on the grounds of form is contrasted with a form that does have meaning—the narrator's use of the familiar *du* a few stanzas earlier when he addresses the emperor, thus claiming the status of an equal. Barbarossa transfers his shock about the guillotine to the poet and chastizes his familiarity; his own use of the familiar *du* is meant to widen the distance between them:

"Und du, wer bist du, daß du es wagst
Mich so vertraulich zu dutzen?
Warte, du Bürschchen, ich werde dir schon
Die kecken Flügel stutzen!

"Es regt mir die innerste Galle auf
Wenn ich dich höre sprechen,
Dein Odem schon ist Hochverrath
Und Majestätsverbrechen!"

(DHA 4:128)

["And who d'you think you are to dare
converse with me like an equal?
Just wait, my lad, I'll take you down
a peg or two in the sequel!

"To hear you talk is quite enough
to goad me beyond reason.
You're guilty, I say, of lèse-majesté,
your very breath is treason!"]

(DR 67)

199

Barbarossa's mythical status as the defender of freedom is dissolved when he displays aristocraticic sympathies and hierarchical views. Similarly, the model of Aristophanes is outdated, his indecorum having been tamed by an adherence to genres that are as hierarchical as the etiquette of Barbarossa. Again Heine differentiates, and it is a distortion to justify his indecorum by citing Aristophanes. The scatalogical passage in caput 26 is not merely an "utopia ex negativo" that derives its legitimacy from an Aristophanic model, as Woesler states, just as his culinary references are not merely an imitation of Homer.[79]

Heine admired Aristophanes and used him as a model, to be sure. But there are a number of reasons to mistrust the poet's invocation of Aristophanes when he defends his own indecorum. Mistrust grows out of a stanza like the following:

> Im letzten Kapitel hab' ich versucht
> Ein bißchen nachzuahmen
> Den Schluß der "Vögel," die sind gewiß
> Das beste von Vaters Dramen.
>
> (DHA 4:156)

> [In chapter twenty-six, I tried
> a modest imitation
> of the final scene of father's *Birds*—
> that's his very finest creation.]
>
> (DR 95)

For one thing, Heine has criticized imitation repeatedly in this poem, in the Armenius caput, for example, and again in the final Barbarossa caput, where he speaks of the "Zwitterwesen" [hybrid] that tries to imitate the Middle Ages and is consequently "weder Fleisch noch Fisch" [neither fish nor fowl] (DHA 4:130). For another, he connects Aristophanes only to the preceding caput ("Im letzten Kapitel") and offers no justification for the culinary and fecal indecorum elsewhere in the poem. He further undermines his invocation of Aristophanes by following it with an invocation of Dante. The move from Aristophanes to Dante shifts the focus away from decorum to the question of poetic power in general, which here means the creative freedom to treat any subject in any form. This is evident from the last two stanzas of the poem, where Heine varies his usual association of poets and gods and places the poet above the god:

Kennst du die Hölle des Dante nicht,
Die schrecklichen Terzetten?
Wen da der Dichter hineingesperrt,
Den kann kein Gott mehr retten -

Kein Gott, kein Heiland, erlöst ihn je
Aus diesen singenden Flammen!
Nimm dich in Acht, daß wir dich nicht
Zu solcher Hölle verdammen.

(DHA 4:157)

[Have you not heard of Dante's Hell,
the terrible *terza rima*?
Whoever has once been shut in there
can hope for no redeemer.

The poet's flames have got him for good,
they scorch and scourge and scorn him.
Take care: we might roast you in just such a hell
as an everlasting warning.]

(DR 97)

The issue is one of freedom, and freedom applies to poetry as well as politics. That explains why Heine chooses literary models with a connection to politics, in the same way as Byron when he alludes to Milton in the "Dedication" of *Don Juan*.

When he concludes his poem by speaking to the king about other poets, Heine applies literary terms to a political issue. From the "neues Lied" [new song] in the opening caput of *Deutschland* to the closing figures of Aristophanes and Dante, Heine sees and depicts the world from a literary point of view. His breaches of decorum take place within poetic limits, even when—as is often the case for his culinary referents—there is a political association. Jürgen Walter expresses the nature of this literary perspective well:

Heine writes neither a programmatic tract nor a political manifesto; nor does he dress up political thought in poetic clothing. Rather he states his express intention of "writing" ("dichten") a "poem" ("Lied"). In other words: a poetical dimension and quality is a basis and constitutive part of his political and social vision of the future. Socio-political requirements and poetics are inseparable here.[80]

Heine's title epitomizes the connection of poetry and politics: every refer-
ence to Germany is at the same time a reference to the poem, and the
Shakespearean subtitle refers both to a literary and a historical moment.

Freedom is the main subject of *Deutschland. Ein Wintermärchen* as it
is of *Don Juan,* and indecorum is a measure of literary freedom just as
censorship is a measure of political freedom. The explanation for the
appearance of a chamber pot at the end must therefore be sought within
the poem. Its presence needs no aesthetic deus ex machina in the form
of Aristophanes, because it follows figuratively and physically from what
preceded it. The poet has taken in food as well as impressions during his
trip, and everything must be digested and excreted. He began his trip
with a sensual vision of utopia, a vision of "Zuckererbsen für jedermann"
[fresh green peas for everyone] and free love. By the end of his journey,
the free love has become prostitution and the foods have been expelled
along with many of the poet's impressions. His idea of freedom has not
been rejected, but it no longer is equated with harmony; freedom is
present in his poetry even if it is threatened by the realities he observed
in his homeland.

At the beginning of the poem, the "Zuckererbsen" of the poet's
"neues Lied" are a deceptive image for freedom (or utopia). From the
literary point of view, which as I have said is the fixed point of his
universe, the opening vision is not daring but folklike, reminiscent of
"Der Himmel hängt voll Geigen" in *Des Knaben Wunderhorn.* The foods
mentioned are the "Zuckererbsen für jedermann" and bread that
"grows": "Es wächst hiernieden Brot genug / Für alle Menschenkinder"
(DHA 4:92) [There's bread enough grows here on earth / to feed man-
kind with ease] (DR 30). These foods have more of a biblical than a
sensual quality and are not offensive in a literary setting. Even if we say,
as Woesler does, that the "neues Lied" contains "a "sketch of the
author's social and aesthetic utopia" (DHA 4:1090), we need to ask
ourselves about the nature of that utopia. That this is an aesthetic as well
as a social statement is clear, but utopia runs counter to Heine's view of
the world and to his aesthetic.[81] As the poet travels, he meets with a
political reality and with details of daily existence that remove him further
and further from the opening vision (it should be remembered that in his
fictionalized journey he moves only in one direction, never returning to
his starting point). This is not to say that the "program" of sensuality and
equality in the first caput lacks his sympathy or that he would not like to
see it fulfilled. But harmony alone is incompatible with the poet's am-

biguous perception. There is no work of Heine's in which the poet's ambiguity is more regularly thematized than *Deutschland,* which makes one wonder how it ever could have been considered programmatic by some readers. Ambiguity is the theme of central passages like the one in caput 6, where the poet's double follows him with an axe and claims to be "Die Tat von deinen Gedanken" [the act from your thoughts] (DHA 4:105); or the controversial passage in caput 12, where the poet's carriage breaks down at midnight in the Teutoberg Forest and he gives a very equivocal speech to his "fellow wolves," the climax of which is "Ja, Mitwölfe, zählt auf mich und helft Euch selbst" [Yes, fellow wolves, count on me and help yourselves] (DHA 4:118); or the poet's dreamed conversations with Barbarossa in capita 16 and 17. Walter again puts it well when he summarizes the parallel between the opening and the end, where the ideal of the beginning—in Schlegelian fashion—is relativized but not rejected:

> Seen in this way, the two visions of the future—the "Zuckererbsen für jedermann" in Caput I and the "Miasmen" in the chamber pot of Charlemagne in Caput XXVI—are ultimately two sides of the same thing: they encompass and reflect the tension between an ideal wish and a realistic possibility of seeing it fulfilled, between a poetical sketch and a concrete fear, between a utopic hope and a skepticism based on reality. And this ambivalence, to which one must be alert, is constitutive of the whole work and a determinent of Heine's political engagement.[82]

When he speaks at the beginning of "Ein neues Lied, ein besseres Lied, / Es klingt wie Flöten und Geigen" [A better song, with fiddles and flutes, / to set the people singing!] (DR 30), the poet has freedom in mind, as he makes explicit in the subsequent stanza:

> Die Jungfer Europa ist verlobt
> Mit dem schönen Geniusse
> Der Freiheit, sie liegen einander im Arm,
> Sie schwelgen im ersten Kusse.
>
> (DHA 4:92)

> [The maiden Europa is betrothed
> to that handsome Genius, Freedom.

203

> They lie in each others' arms embraced,
> it warms my heart to see them.]

(DR 30)

By the end of the poem, that idyllic freedom has been transformed into the freedom to speak of all things, among them chamber pots and their contents. Change has not come to the world, but to the way the poet represents it, and in that sense he does sing "ein neues Lied, ein besseres Lied." What makes it "besser" is not that it is prettier, but that it has gotten rid of the hypocricy in the *Entsagungslied* [song of renunciation] that he describes in the famous stanza from the opening caput:

> Ich kenne die Weise, ich kenne den Text,
> Ich kenn' auch die Herren Verfasser;
> Ich weiß, sie tranken heimlich Wein
> Und predigten öffentlich Wasser.

(DHA 4:92)

> [I know the tune, I know the words,
> I know every single author;
> I know they tippled wine on the quiet
> while publicly preaching water.]

(DR 30)

In the final caput he speaks again of old and new, of hypocrisy (which is dying of a "Lügenkrankeit" [lying disease]). He remembers and echoes the first caput, but his perspective has changed:

> Das alte Geschlecht der Heuchelei
> Verschwindet Gott sei Dank heut,
> Es sinkt allmählig in's Grab, es stirbt
> An seiner Lügenkrankheit.
>
> Es wächst heran ein neues Geschlecht,
> Ganz ohne Schminke und Sünden,
> Mit freien Gedanken, mit freier Lust -
> Dem werde ich Alles verkünden.

(DHA 4:155)

> [The Grundy generation now
> thank Heaven is slowly dying,
> it's ripe for the grave, brought low by its own
> hypocrisy and lying.
>
> A new generation is rising that has
> no hang-ups or pretences;
> it thinks what it likes, enjoys what it likes—
> I will help it keep its senses.]

(DR 94–95)

He has shown that he will not hide anything in the name of literary "etiquette," although he will presumably have to continue to outwit the censors as he did in caput 2. There he smuggled in his "contraband" with wordplay, which as we have seen before is another poetic expression of liberation.

When he arrives in Cologne in caput 4, the persona speaks in an exaggerated lyrical mode that contains echoes of German poetry and evokes the German landscape of poetry and myth. The syntax of the first stanza carries into the second, but with a break:

> Zu Cöllen kam ich spät Abends an,
> Da hörte ich rauschen den Rheinfluß,
> Da fächelte mich schon deutsche Luft,
> Da fühlt' ich ihren Einfluß -
>
> Auf meinen Appetit.

(DHA 4:97)

> [It was getting late when we reached Cologne;
> the Rhine was whispering fondly,
> my cheeks were fanned by German air,
> I felt its influence on me—
>
> on my appetite, that is.]

(DR 35)

This is a famous example of Heine's sudden shift from one register to the other, his *Stimmungsbruch,* here accompanied by a break in the strophic pattern and the introduction of prose rhythm into a metric frame. In

205

what follows, Heine joins incongruities with nominal associations—of Rhine river with Rhine wine or German air with German food—thus making the enharmonic shift for which ambiguous taste is the paradigmatic example:

Auf meinen Appetit. Ich aß
Dort Eierkuchen mit Schinken,
Und da er sehr gesalzen war
Mußt' ich auch Rheinwein trinken.[83]

[on my appetite, that is. I ate
ham omelette, and as my portion
was rather salty, I had to drink
some hock as a precaution.]

In caput 9, eating is neither a necessity of travel literature nor (as Sammons puts it) boring—at least not once one has "decoded" passages like the following:

Sei mir gegrüßt, mein Sauerkraut,
Holdselig sind deine Gerüche.

(DHA 4:111)

[Hail to thee, blithe sauerkraut,
delightful are thy aromas.]

(DR 50)

Heine makes the same implausible connection here between the adjective *holdselig* and the smell of sauerkraut that he makes later when he refers to sweet-smelling urine in the "Armenius" caput. The elevated and anachronistic style is revolutionized by the choice of a banal subject, and the effect anticipates the hymn to *Schalet* and the distancing from a Schillerian aesthetic in the *Romanzero* poem "Prinzessin Sabbat."

The connection between freedom and decorum recurs in caput 11, the "Armenius" caput, where Heine rewrites Tacitus by changing the outcome of the *Hermannsschlacht,* both reversing Kleist's depiction of the battle as a symbol of German independence and remaking history into intellectual history or *Geistesgeschichte.* The insistently literary frame of reference vies with what Sammons calls the "aggressively nonliterary" sounds in the poem (which together with the aggressively *literary* sound of *Atta Troll* characterizes Heine's style).[84] In caput 11, the brilliant satire of intellectual life in Berlin consists of Latinizing figures who enjoy the patronage of Friedrich Wilhelm IV, the contemporary—and phony—personification of "deutsche Freiheit" [German freedom].[85] Heine briefly and sardonically characterizes the theologians Hengstenberg and Neander, the playwrights Birch-Pfeiffer and Raumer, the poet Freiligrath, Turnvater Jahn, the critic Massmann, the philosopher Schelling, and the painter Cornelius, whom he ridicules for believing that monarchy and freedom are compatible, much as Byron ridicules Southey in the dedication to *Don Juan* for his about-face from radical to poet laureate. As usual, Heine procedes indirectly (Friedrich Wilhelm IV is never mentioned explicitly), and the liberties he takes with history, language, and diction contrast with the stance of his subjects, who are represented as passive upholders of decorum. In nearly every stanza there is something coarse: "der klassische Morast" [the classic morass]; "in diesem Drecke" [in this filth]; "Vestalen" as an ironic reference to prostitutes; "in den Gedärmen / Von Ochsen" [in the intestines / Of oxen] and implicitly the reading of bird droppings by augurs; the drinking of turpentine and the urine it produces, where the word *saufen* [to booze] is itself a breach of decorum and is ironized in its elegant subjunctive form ("söffe"); "kein deutscher Lump" [no German rogue]; "Grobianus" [boor]; "Hunden" [dogs]; "Cacatum non est pictum" [Shitting is not drawing]; "Der Esel heißt Esel, nicht *asinus*" [The donkey is called donkey, not *asinus*]; and the repetition of "deutscher Lump" and "Terebentin" (read: "Urin"). On the other hand—and this is most significant—there is no indecorum in the two stanzas where Heine refers directly to "Freiheit" [freedom] and "Knechtschaft" [servitude].

The most blatant examples of indecorum occur in the stanzas about the playwright Birch-Pfeiffer and the painter Cornelius, again with an emphasis on the aesthetic frame:

> Birch-Pfeiffer söffe Terebentin,
> Wie einst die römischen Damen.
> (Man sagt, daß sie danach den Urin
> Besonders wohlriechend bekamen.)
>
> (DHA 4:115)

> [Birch-Pfeiffer'd be swigging turpentine,
> like Rome's ladies aristocratic.
> (It's said that a side effect was to make
> their urine aromatic.)]
>
> (DR 53)

The characterization of urine as "wohlriechend" [aromatic] parodies decorum because of the elevated diction chosen for something unpleasant or improper. As Prawer says, merely to mention bodily functions is a satire on the "pure" universe of Birch-Pfeiffer.[86] The same technique applies when Heine satirizes Cornelius by putting a scatalogical insult into Latin:

> Zu uns'rem Cornelius sagten wir:
> *Cacatum non est pictum.*
>
> (DHA 4:115)

> [We'd look at Cornelius' pictures and say:
> "*Cacatum non est pictum.*"]
>
> (DR 54)

The effect of seeming to hide is carried over in the word *asinus* and has a venerable literary heritage. Diderot uses foreign phrases for some of the scatological insults in *Le Neveu de Rameau,* as does Byron in *Don Juan,* and in the chapter from Sterne's *A Sentimental Journey* called "The Rose," the rose is revealed to be a euphemism for urination in the phrase "to pluck a rose." This is a variation of the kind of "self-censorship" in *Schnabelewopski* discussed earlier, where more is revealed than hidden through what Perraudin calls "the ironic use of *Fremdwort,* civilized society's language of unfeeling."[87]

Once the link is understood between indecorum and freedom, the prolonged *absence* of culinary references from the Barbarossa capita is what strikes the reader as peculiar. Not only is Barbarossa an anachronism, he is disembodied, and the poet, again from his literary perspective, calls him a "Fabelwesen," a fabulous being. There is an otherworldliness to Barbarossa, an unreal quality manifest in his ignorance of the French Revolution and the guillotine, and when he speaks of his concern for "etiquette" and tries to quiet (or censor) the poet by saying "Schweig

208

still" [Be quiet], it is of a piece with his anachronism and impotence. The poet-narrator realizes that the emperor's behavior is incompatible with liberation, and when he returns to the culinary images he has taught us to interpret, we know that he has recovered his critical distance. At the conclusion of the Barbarossa episode, when the present is characterized as "weder Fleisch noch Fisch," the culinary allusion, albeit figurative, provides a welcome contrast to the emperor's abstractions:

> Das Mittelalter, immerhin,
> Das wahre, wie es gewesen,
> Ich will es ertragen—erlöse uns nur
> Von jenem Zwitterwesen.
>
> Von jenem Kamaschenrittertum,
> Das ekelhaft ein Gemisch ist
> Von gotischem Wahn und modernem Lug,
> Das weder Fleisch noch Fisch ist.
>
> (DHA 4:130)

> ["The Middle Ages, well, I suppose
> if you give us the genuine article,
> I'll put up with that. Just rescue us
> from all this hybrid, farcical,
>
> "revolting, pseudo-knightliness
> which, under its Gothic cover,
> is just a lot of modern deceit,
> neither one thing nor the other."]
>
> (DR 69)

The phrase "weder Fleisch noch Fisch" is not as explicitly culinary or indecorous as other references before and after, since the narrator has not yet recovered entirely from his stupefying encounter with the emperor. Nor is the dead metaphor explicitly revived. The poet is still partly dazed, but we watch him wake up slowly and replace the idealized vision of homeland that he had in exile with the realities he has encountered in the course of his journey. The tentative culinary allusion occurs in the negative—he says "weder Fisch noch Fleisch"—and the next caput likewise opens with the poet's lack of appetite:

Im Wirtshaus ward mir noch schlimmer zu Mut,
Das Essen wollt mir nicht schmecken.

(DHA 4:131)

[I felt even worse when we got to the inn,
even the meal was no pleasure.]

(DR 70)

But even references in the negative mark a progression, as does his parody of Luther's "Ein feste Burg" at the opening of caput 18, the song that Heine calls the "Marseillaise of the Reformation" in *Zur Geschichte der Religion und Philosophie in Deutschland*.

The poet's lack of appetite reestablishes a balance after his exuberant enjoyment of German food in caput 4 and caput 9 and his enthusiastic encounter with German featherbeds in caput 7. In caput 18, he combines the motifs of food and featherbeds, but now he is not hungry and the featherbeds are perceived as oppressive rather than incomparably soft ("Mich drückten so schwer die Decken" [The bedclothes oppressed me so]). Earlier, by contrast, his thoughts of featherbeds and dreams had a nostalgic quality, in spite of the implicit criticism of Germans as passive and unrealistic:

Man ruht in deutschen Betten so weich,
Denn das sind Federbetten.

Wie sehnt' ich mich oft nach der Süßigkeit
Des vaterländischen Pfühles,
Wenn ich auf harten Matratzen lag,
In der schlaflosen Nacht des Exiles!

(DHA 4:105)

[You sleep so soft in German beds,
it's the feathers that they're made with.

How often through exile's sleepless night
I yearned for soft German bedding
and the sweetly restful pillow of home
to sink my weary head in.]

(DR 44)

210

But in caput 18, when he is under a soft German featherbed, he has bad dreams of censorship and wishes he were back in exile, which now he calls home ("zu Hause"):

> O, daß ich wäre—seufzte ich—
> Daß ich zu Hause wäre,
> Bei meiner lieben Frau in Paris,
> Im Faubourg Poissonière.

(DHA 4:132)

> ["Oh dear"—I sighed—"I wish I was back
> in the Faubourg Poissonnière
> in Paris, with my dearest wife,
> enjoying her loving care!"]

(DR 71)

From this disillusioned perspective, the foods in caput 9 retrospectively take on a different meaning. Now the annotated catalogue of favorite dishes appears to be a half-affectionate reminder of mistaken perceptions: the *Sauerkraut* was sweet smelling, the *Stockfische* (salt cod) were "smart" [klug], and pigs were decorated with laurel wreaths. By caput 18, when the poet's vision is no longer clouded by the sentimentality and sensuality of homecoming, he has regained his critical eye. The pain of exile that accosted his senses when he lay under a featherbed and ate typical foods has been replaced by the awareness that there was good reason for his exile.

When we have deciphered the culinary allusions and their absence, the poet's conversation with his mother, though it is evasive with respect to political parties, makes a revolutionary statement with respect to poetry. That the persona does not commit himself to one country or one political doctrine is in keeping with his role as a poet, someone who must maintain a critical distance and use the *Witze* and *Spitzen* that he smuggled in when he crossed the border. His deliberately metaphorical manner underscores the literariness of his medium, and the ambiguity of his answers is as much a trademark of his poetic style as his conscious indecorum. Within his medium he is a revolutionary, and the culinary answers to political questions demonstrate the nature of his resistance to an established literary order, a resistance that can be transposed to political themes indirectly but not concretely. The conclusion of his culinary conversation

211

with his mother, where he speaks about political parties, provides a summation of his technique:

> "Mein liebes Kind! wie denkst du jetzt?
> Treibst du noch immer aus Neigung
> Die Politik? Zu welcher Partei
> Gehörst du mit Überzeugung?"
>
> Die Apfelsinen, lieb Mütterlein,
> Sind gut, und mit wahrem Vergnügen
> Verschlucke ich den süßen Saft
> Und ich lasse die Schalen liegen.

(DHA 4:136)

> ["My dear boy! how do you see things now?
> Do you still have your addiction
> to politics? Which party now
> commands your whole-hearted conviction?"
>
> "These oranges, mother dear, are good,
> so rich in tasty juices.
> But I'm not inclined to swallow the peel,
> the wrapping they come in is useless."]

(DR 75)

There is self-irony in this metaphorical description of the uncommitted political practice for which Heine often has been criticized. But the tenor is less important than the culinary vehicle, which in the context of the *Wintermärchen* expresses a radical aesthetic. The answers are politically equivocal but aesthetically precise—and revolutionary.

It is insufficient and even distorting to speak of doubles and ambiguities in *Deutschland. Ein Wintermärchen* when the work itself has a double that complements it, the poem *Atta Troll. Ein Sommernachtstraum*. Although the subject of politics dominates in one poem and the subject of poetry in the other, their respective emphasis is less important than the way the themes mix and clash, ultimately completing each other.[88] How the poems intertwine can be observed in the indecorum of *Atta Troll*. Indecorum provides a measure of the persona's superiority over the poets he ridicules collectively in the figure of the dancing bear Atta Troll, who

212

is not merely an allegory of *Tendenzpoesie,* but of all bad poetry. In order to evoke the awkwardness of Atta Troll within the poem, Heine has him speak more than dance. Through Atta Troll's language, Heine endlessly varies the image of the dancing bear who is grotesque because he pretends to be fine. We have become accustomed to thinking of the dance as one of Heine's emblems of revolution. But dance is also an emblem of propriety. When Atta Troll dances, he combines both revolution and decorum in a mixture that is admirably suited to Heine's criticism of programmatic poetry: a revolutionary subject, when it is put into a flowery frame, becomes ridiculous. This is not a conscious contrast on the part of the dancing bear or the poets he represents, but one that is perceived from the outside as false.[89]

The question is again one of style. Atta Troll's high moral standards are matched by what he considers to be an elevated diction, a diction that actually exposes him to ridicule; furthermore, he never speaks directly, but uses dead metaphors that come alive without his permission or his knowledge. He argues for example that men should not consider themselves superior merely because they cook their food; digestion follows in either case:

> Menschen, seid Ihr etwa besser
> Als wir Andre, weil gesotten
> Und gebraten Eure Speisen?
> Wir verzehren roh die unsern,
>
> Doch das Resultat am Ende
> Ist dasselbe - Nein, es adelt
> Nicht die Atzung; der ist edel,
> Welcher edel fühlt und handelt.

(DHA 4:23)

> ["Men: you think perhaps you're better
> Than we are because your victuals
> Must be boiled or baked or roasted?
> Yes, we eat ours raw, admitted—
>
> "But the end result is always
> Just the same—No, eating doesn't
> Make you noble; one is noble
> If one nobly feels and acts."]

(HCP 430)

213

Atta Troll's sentiments are politically correct, to be sure, but his allusion to digestion has a different effect from those in the *Wintermärchen;* from examples like these we observe that subjects cannot be separated from style and that linguistic hierarchies are inflexible.

The poetry rejected in *Atta Troll* is the kind allegorized in the figure of Atta Troll, not the kind we find in the *Wintermärchen.* Heine sets clear signals so that we understand his rhetorical irony when the bear's criticism or praise is the opposite from the persona's. Atta Troll's detestation of human smiles and laughter offers a dramatic example of the technique; for him, the "decorum" [Anstand] of dancing and love preclude wit and humor. The application to Heine's own indecorous mixture of smiles and serious concerns is unmistakable, and the smile that enrages Atta Troll has the same Heinean "twitch" [Zucken] that characterized the expression of Schnabelewopski and Eva:

"Mich verletzte stets am meisten
Jenes sauersüße Zucken
Um das Maul - ganz unerträglich
Wirkt auf mich dies Menschenlächeln!

Wenn ich in dem weißen Antlitz
Das fatale Zucken schaute
Drehten sich herum entrüstet
Mir im Bauche die Gedärme.

Weit impertinenter noch
Als durch Worte, offenbart sich
Durch das Lächeln eines Menschen
Seiner Seele tiefste Frechheit.

Immer lächeln sie! Sogar
Wo der Anstand einen tiefen
Ernst erfordert, in der Liebe
Feierlichstem Augenblick!

Immer lächeln sie! Sie lächeln
Selbst im Tanzen. Sie entweihen
Solchermaßen diese Kunst
Die ein Kultus bleiben sollte."

(DHA 4:28)

214

["What offends me most is always
That same sweet-sour twitching motion
Round the lips: it's humans smiling
That is worst—I cannot bear it!

"When I see that nasty twitching
In those pale white countenances,
Then I feel my bowels churning
In my guts with furious anger.

"Far more insolent than words are,
Such a smile on human faces
Manifests the deep effrontery
In his spirit, and most clearly.

"And they're always smiling! Even
When sheer decency requires them
To be serious completely,
Even in love's most solemn moment!

"Yes, they're always smiling—smiling
Even when dancing, thus profaning
In this way the art of arts
Which should be a ritual worship."]

(HCP 434)

The final words of this caput are "'Und sie bleiben stets frivol'" ["And they always remain frivolous"], where the word "frivol" summarizes Heine's aesthetic and anticipates his illustration of it in the self-reflexive indecorum of caput 8.

Indecorum in *Atta Troll* generally is shifted from the culinary to the olfactory, because smells are better suited to a bear than taste. In this poem the words *Duft* [scent] and *Geruch* [smell] or *Gestank* [stench] have a function identical to that of ambiguous taste, as for example in the opening of the fourth caput, where *Duft* is associated with Romantic poetry in a variation of synesthesia that itself echoes and gently mocks the tradition evoked:

Ronceval, du edles Tal!
Wenn ich deinen Namen höre,

215

Bebt und duftet mir im Herzen
Die verschollne blaue Blume!

(DHA 4:18)

[Roncevalles, O noble vale!
When I hear your name re-echo,
In my heart the long-forgotten
Old blue flower throbs with fragrance!]

(HCP 427)

Such poetic images are obliterated when the scent changes to a smell or when something stinks—when, for example, the scent of the *blaue Blume* becomes the stench of a chamber pot. The opposition of *Duft* and *Geruch* occurs in the poem "Vitzliputzli" as well, where it serves as the focus for the opening contrast between old and new worlds and, analogously, between the tradition of Goethe and Romanticism and new poetic forms. Heine marks the break with tradition by shifting from "Düfte" to "Geruch" and caricaturing the technique of synesthesia by reviving a dead metaphor, *unerhört* (unheard of):

Neuer Boden, neue Blumen!
Neue Blumen, neue Düfte!
Unerhörte, wilde Düfte,
Die mir in die Nase dringen,

Neckend, prickelnd, leidenschaftlich—
Und mein grübelnder Geruchsinn
Quält sich ab: Wo hab' ich denn
Je dergleichen schon gerochen?

(DHA 3:1.57–58)

[New the soil, and new the flowers!
New the flowers, new the perfumes!
Wild, unheard-of, heady perfumes
That go tingling up my nostrils,

Teasing, tickling, tart with passion—
And my sense of smell is puzzled

216

By a labored thought: Where have I,
Once before this, smelled such odors?]

(HCP 600)

The question of memory applies here to a poetic tradition: it should be "where have I *read* that before?" not "where have I *smelled* that before?" Heine expects his readers to ask the same question again in part 2 of "Vitzliputzli," where the word *Düfte* recurs in connection with cannibalism and Christianity. The last word of *Romanzero* confirms the claim that *Duft* and *Geruch* emblematize old and new styles of poetry; Heine ends with the word *stinken,* spoken by the queen to characterize religious disputes and, presumably, any kind of institutionalized prejudice. Since the word comes from the queen, she is transformed into an allegorical representation of Heine's poetic practice, a practice in which the aristocratic form of verse is filled with words and subjects that traditionally are out of place.[90]

Smells alone do not make poetry modern, however, and there is a vast difference between the smells in the *Wintermärchen,* which are associated with revolution, and the olfactory images used by Atta Troll. When the bear laments the loss of his mate Mumma, for example, he imitates conceits of Romantic poetry and the cliché of a sweet-smelling rose, but his mixture of diction and adoption of human categories are even more ridiculous than they are trite:

"Möchte auch noch einmal schnüffeln
Den Geruch, der eigentümlich
Meiner teuren schwarzen Mumma,
Und wie Rosenduft so lieblich!"

(DHA 4:22)

["And if only I could once more
Sniff the special scent peculiar
To my dearly loved black Mumma,
Lovely as a rose's fragrance!"]

(HCP 430)

Whether he speaks of sentiment or politics, Atta Troll uses olfactory categories:

Grundgesetz sei volle Gleichheit
Aller Gotteskreaturen,
Ohne Unterschied des Glaubens
Und des Fells und des Geruches.

(DHA 4:26)

["Let its law be: all God's creatures
Shall be always fully equal
Irrespective of religion,
Or of hide or kind of odor."]

(HDP 433)

The equal weight given to *Gleichheit, Glauben,* and *Geruch* (equality, creed, and smell) resembles the list in *Buch Le Grand* of "Liebe, Wahrheit, Freiheit und Krebssuppe," except that Atta Troll does not know what he is doing. His faulty logic is underscored by the alliterative association of *Grundgesetz* (constitution)and *Gotteskreaturen* (God's creatures), and Heine presents a stunning parody of political rhetoric as form emptied of meaning. In the rest of this speech, Atta Troll exposes his prejudices and self-interest just when he thinks he is most magnanimous.[91] He concludes his speech with a view of art that is as doctrinaire as his views about politics and social change. Taste is cited as the measure of artistic excellence and is identified with the bear's anti-Semitism, thereby reiterating the equation of decorum and oppression that Heine makes in the *Wintermärchen:*

Ja, sogar die Juden sollen
Volles Bürgerrecht genießen,
Und gesetzlich gleichgestellt sein
Allen andern Säugetieren.

Nur das Tanzen auf den Märkten
Sei den Juden nicht gestattet;
Dies Amendement, ich mach' es
Im Intresse meiner Kunst.

Denn der Sinn für Stil, für strenge
Plastik der Bewegung, fehlt

218

Jener Race, sie verdürben
Den Geschmack des Publikums.

(DHA 4:27)

["Yes, yes, even Jews will likewise
Then enjoy full civic rights, and
Legally be made the equals
Of all mammals whatsoever.

"Only dancing in the plazas
By a Jew shall be forbidden;
I make this amendment solely
In the interests of my art.

"For this race is wholly lacking
In a sense of style, of movement
With a strictly plastic spirit—
It would spoil the public's taste."]

(HCP 433–34)

On the surface, Atta Troll's confusion of politics and art resembles Heine's in the *Wintermärchen;* but deeper down they resemble each other as little as Atta Troll when it is the name of a bear and *Atta Troll* when it is the name of a poem.

Heine follows the speech about taste and Jews with an imitation of the bear's logic that picks up the word *duften,* inappropriately modified as "schlecht." Scent is associated with aristocracy and smell with a virtuous lower class in a variation on the phrase attributed to Saint-Just that Heine quotes at the end of the *Wintermärchen,* "Man heile die große Krankheit nicht / Mit Rosenöl und Moschus" (DHA 4:153) [as Saint-Just once said, you don't get far / with musk of oil or roses] (DR 93):

Mancher tugendhafte Bürger
Duftet schlecht auf Erden, während
Fürstenknechte mit Lavendel
Oder Ambra parfümiert sind.

Jungfräuliche Seelen gibt es,
Die nach grüner Seife riechen,

219

Und das Laster hat zuweilen
Sich mit Rosenöl gewaschen.

Darum rümpfe nicht die Nase,
Teurer Leser, wenn die Höhle
Atta Trolls dich nicht erinnert
An Arabiens Spezerein.

Weile mit mir in dem Dunstkreis,
In dem trüben Mißgeruche

(DHA 4:29)

[Many good and virtuous burghers
On this earth smell bad; however
Princes' lackeys smell of perfume
Or use ambergris to scent them.

There are virgin souls who often
Reek of green soap like a clinic,
While one sometimes finds that vice has
Laved itself in oil of roses.

Therefore don't turn up your noses,
Gentle readers, if the den of
Atta Troll does not remind you
Of Arabia's spicy perfumes.

Tarry with me midst the odors
And the thick miasmic fetor]

(HCP 435)

Elsewhere in the poem, the neologism "Mißduft" [disscent] is applied to the poet-hunter's battle with adversaries, in this case to his "duel" with a bedbug:

Mußt dich ruhig beißen lassen -
Das ist schlimm—Noch schlimmer ist es,
Wenn du sie zerdrückst: der Mißduft
Quält dich dann die ganze Nacht.

Ja, das Schrecklichste auf Erden
Ist der Kampf mit Ungeziefer,

220

Dem Gestank als Waffe dient—
Das Duell mit einer Wanze!

(DHA 4:37–38)

[Helpless, you must let it bite you—
That is bad—But it is worse yet
If you squash it: then the odor
Plagues you through the whole night long.

Yes, the worst thing in the world
Is this fearsome war with vermin
That employ their stench as weapon—
Think, a duel with a bedbug!]

(HCP 442)

The overt target here may be Salomon Strauss, who is generally glossed in this passage. But the choice of unpleasant smells to launch an attack is related to the poetological issues of this work: Heine takes over the weapons of his opponents (or in the case of political poets their themes and vocabulary), which he describes here as smell ("Gestank"), and he ridicules them at the same time that he displays his own superior style. The neologism "Mißduft" is one example.

At issue is again the question of tradition, here exemplified by dead metaphors. It is insufficient to take over old forms and give them a radical content, as the *Tendenzdichter* try to do when they use lyric forms for political utterance or as Heine accuses Platen of doing when he imitates Greek models. In *Atta Troll* Heine addresses the problem directly by calling his poem the "letztes freies Waldlied der Romantik" [the last free forest-song of Romanticism] but noting the "modern trills" that are imposed onto an older form:

Ja, mein Freund, es sind die Klänge
Aus der längst verscholl'nen Traumzeit;
Nur daß oft moderne Triller
Gaukeln durch den alten Grundton.

(DHA 4:86)

[Yes, my friend, these echoes come from
Days of dream now long forgotten,

221

> Though some modern trills and grace notes
> Flicker through the olden music.]

(HCP 480)

This modern version is characterized by enharmonic shifts; the same word or subject acquires a different meaning or a different tone, the title and hero of *Atta Troll* being only the most striking example. Varnhagen von Ense is the spokesman for this aesthetic in the poem:

> "In die Nachtigallenchöre
> Bricht herein der Bärenbrummbaß,
> Dumpf und grollend, dieser wechselt
> Wieder ab mit Geisterlispeln!
>
> Wahnsinn, der sich klug gebährdet!
> Weisheit, welche überschnappt!
> Sterbeseufzer, welche plötzlich
> Sich verwandeln in Gelächter!"

(DHA 4:85–86)

> ["Through the nightingales' sweet carols
> Booms the bears' deep double basses,
> Muffled, rumbling, changing later
> Into secret ghostly whispers!
>
> "Madness that behaves with reason!
> Wisdom that has snapped its moorings!
> Dying sighs that of a sudden
> Are transmuted into laughter!"]

(HCP 480)

The description applies to the *Wintermärchen* as much as it does to *Atta Troll*.

In September 1848, after he had become paralyzed and bedridden, Heine wrote to his brother Maximilian that his capacity for sensual enjoyment had diminished, but not his love of life:

> Wenn ich auch nicht gleich sterbe, so ist doch das Leben für mich auf immer verloren und ich liebe doch das Leben mit so inbrünstiger

Leidenschaft. Für mich gibt es keine schöne Berggipfel mehr, die ich erklimme, keine Frauenlippe, die ich küsse, nicht mal mehr ein guter Rinderbraten in Gesellschaft lauter schmausender Gäste; meine Lippen sind gelähmt wie meine Füße, auch die Eßwerkzeuge sind gelähmt ebensosehr wie die Absonderungskanäle. Ich kann weder kauen noch kacken, werde wie ein Vogel gefüttert. (HSA 22:294)

[Even if I don't die right away, life is lost for me forever, and yet I love life with such intense passion. For me there is no longer a beautiful mountain top to scale, a woman's lip to kiss, not even a good roast beef to eat in the company of many feasting guests; my lips are paralyzed along with my feet, even my eating apparatus is paralyzed along with my digestive tract. I can neither chew nor shit and am fed like a bird.]

Critics of many persuasions might argue (and some have) that Heine makes up for his deprivation by writing about it. But the culinary allusions are more literary than personal, despite the fact that, as Prawer puts it, Heine "can seldom resist—and this is a weakness in his work—the temptations of autobiography."[92] Heine's culinary allusions occur too early, and in a setting where he is too self-aware, for us to brush them off as a quirk connected to his disease. The examples I have cited show that Heine's references to food do not increase drastically as a result of his illness, but are an identifiable characteristic of his style. Food conveys two sides of the same issue; it effects the famous shifts from one mood to the other; and it ironically connects a past aesthetic of taste with a modern poetics in which clashes replace harmony and in which humor is not separated from serious subjects. Heine's culinary allusions allow him to show off his style, and they provide a trap for readers who confuse a subject and its function.

CHAPTER 5

Goethe and Hugo: The License of Taste

Il y a le goût d'en bas et le goût d'en haut. Le goût selon l'abbé de Bernis, et le goût selon Pindare. L'admirable, c'est que, de professeur de rhétorique en professeur de rhétorique, on est venu à qualifier le goût selon Bernis *bon goût,* et le goût selon Pindare *mauvais goût.*

—Hugo, "Le Goût" (1863)

In Goethe's novel *Wilhelm Meister,* Wilhelm's young son Felix is saved because he indecorously drinks directly from the bottle. The adults are frantic. They assume that Felix has drunk from a glass of poison next to the bed of Augustin, the Harpist; Felix misinterprets the frenzy as a reaction to his having drunk from a bottle, and when at last he admits his "sin," he is astonished to earn caresses instead of censure. Natalie picks him up, thrusts him into the arms of his father, and exclaims that his rudeness has saved him: "Glücklicher Vater! rief sie laut, indem sie das Kind aufhob und es ihm in die Arme warf, da hast du deinen Sohn! er hat aus der Flasche getrunken, seine Unart hat ihn gerettet" ["Happy father!" she cried out as she picked up the child and thrust him into Wilhelm's arms. "Here you have your son back! He drank from the bottle, and his rudeness saved him"]. Goethe's own indecorum was never received with such indulgence. Like Felix, he often felt compelled to hide it, but he was never rewarded when it was revealed. Since Goethe's death, posterity has even more assiduously hidden his *Unarten* for him. And yet one could say that his indecorum likewise "saves" him; indecorum is, as Goethe insisted, the prerogative and sometimes even the sign of genius.

Most portraits of Goethe make it appear as if he never wrote or thought anything improper. And while the impression of propriety has much to do with the conventions of portraiture, it often has been

225

confirmed by scholars. Goethe's reputation is that of the stereotypical German poet, of a poet who is sombre, distinguished, and concerned exclusively with things of the spirit. One can argue that myths and stereotypes are based on ignorance or half-truths and must therefore be discounted; someone who has read Goethe, and surely someone who has studied him, will have a more discriminating opinion. But there persists a tendency, on the part of scholars and a more amorphous but mostly German public, to extend to his writings the image we find in the portraits. There is reason to criticize the fashion of overemphasizing biographical details, usually sexual, of great figures; Richard Ellmann speaks for example of the foolishness that results from associating Ben Jonson and Ernest Hemingway because of a shared "anal erotism": "one thing is sure: the daring innovation in Hemingway's style, its fanatical economy, like the humor and lyricism of Ben Jonson, may be disparaged by offering it in the context of anal erotism."[1] But there is no justification for shielding an author's reputation from works that do not conform to one's own sense of decorum, as has been the case for some of Goethe's early plays, the four suppressed *Roman Elegies,* the *Tagebuch* poem, or the *Paralipomena* to *Faust.* The most sustained argument against this variant of censorship has been made by Hans R. Vaget in *Goethe: Der Mann von 60 Jahren,* where he establishes the text of *Das Tagebuch* and interprets the poem in detail (GT 8).[2]

Posterity has played its tricks on Hugo as well. Not the posterity that, in the voice of Gide, answered "Victor Hugo, hélas" when asked to name the most important French poet, but the posterity that has fixed him in France the way Goethe is fixed in Germany: as the grand old man of letters, hence as the embodiment of decorum. French posterity differs slightly from the German kind; the sombre and spiritual stereotype of the German poet has its counterpart in the image of the politically active and sensually ardent French poet. Hugo's revolutionary works—his "Préface de *Cromwell*" for instance—are de rigueur rather than suspect, and besides, they are tempered by his conservative start in *Le Conservateur littéraire,* the journal that he and his brother Eugène edited as young men. What matters in the present context is that both Goethe and Hugo are perceived as the embodiment and standard of literary greatness in their respective countries and beyond, and that their reputation for greatness has too often been identified with decorum. They are institutions, hence "thermometers of taste," to adapt Byron's phrase. Yet since their works are sui generis, as Proust and Benjamin say of all great works, they often are at variance with the laws of taste. In "Zum Schäkespears-Tag" and "La Préface de *Cromwell*," Goethe and Hugo rebel specifically against *der gute Geschmack* and *le bon goût*. These works admittedly precede their authors' reputation for decorum, but later on as well, Goethe and Hugo continue to resent the restrictions imposed on them in the name of a taste that they find false. What is remarkable is not that both authors embrace an aesthetic that challenges the dictates of good taste rigidly applied—the neoclassical aesthetic whose rejection is the common cause of Romanticism—but that they, too, demonstrate their resistance with references to literal taste. The gustatory allusions in *Götz von Berlichingen* (1773) and *Ruy Blas* (1838) have the same function that gustatory allusions do in works of Byron and Heine.

According to the labels of literary history, Goethe and Hugo do not belong together. Goethe is considered the epitome of *Klassik* in Germany, Hugo the quintessential Romantic poet in France. Chronology does not sanction the connection either, since Goethe is fifty years older than Hugo. But the similarities between them are striking: after a revolutionary beginning manifest in poetry rather than politics, both became allied to the conservative politics of a titled nobility. For Hugo the alliance was short-lived, and he subsequently embraced a liberalism that forced him into exile but that together with the success of *Les Misérables* ultimately earned him one of the most remarkable funeral processions in history. More important than the precise details of their politics, however, is the fact that both men were politically active. What Goethe and Hugo share above all is an extraordinary creative range. They wrote works in every literary genre and style, and they wrote non-literary texts as well. Furthermore, their talent as painters influenced their poetic style; Schiller's famous description of Goethe as an "Augenmensch" [person of the eyes] is echoed in Taine's comment that Hugo had an "imagination des yeux" [imagination of the eyes].[3]

Goethe comments to Eckermann in March of 1830 on the connection between his play *Götz von Berlichingen* and French Romantic theater:

"Der Keim der historischen Stücke, die bei ihnen jetzt etwas Neues sind, findet sich schon seit einem halben Jahrhundert in meinem 'Götz.'" (EGG 2:673)

["The germ for the historical plays, which in their country are something new, has existed for half a century in my 'Götz.'"]

227

In a conversation with Eckermann a week later, again on the subject of French literature, there is likewise an element of self-reflection in Goethe's analysis of "this poetic revolution, still in its infancy" (GCE 288) [diese im Werden begriffene poetische Revolution der Literatur] (EGG 2:675). Goethe speaks of the French "revolutionaries" with the same skepticism he expresses in later years toward his own *Werther* and *Götz*. What disturbs him are the dangers of revolution when worthy ideals degenerate into extremes, whether in politics or literature. In politics the effort to correct injustice can yield to blood and atrocities, and in literature, the legitimate desire to cast off constraining forms can be wrongly transferred to inherited subjects as well:

> "So wollten auch die Franzosen bei ihrer jetzigen literarischen Umwälzung anfänglich nichts weiter als eine freiere Form, aber dabei bleiben sie jetzt nicht stehen, sondern sie verwerfen neben der Form auch den bisherigen Inhalt." (EGG 2:676)

> ["Thus the French, in their present literary revolution, desired nothing at first but a freer form; however, they will not stop there, but will reject the traditional contents with the form."] (GCE 288)

He illustrates his claim with culinary metaphors, which he connects with figurative taste. Beautiful subjects from Greek mythology are replaced by supernatural beings like witches and vampires, because the latter are "spicy" [pikant] and appeal to the public "taste." The connection of literal and figurative taste is nearly predictable:

> "An die Stelle des schönen Inhalts griechischer Mythologie treten Teufel, Hexen und Vampire, und die erhabenen Helden der Vorzeit müssen Gaunern und Gallerensklaven den Platz machen. Dergleichen ist pikant! Das wirkt!—Nachdem aber das Publikum diese stark gepfefferte Speise einmal gekostet und sich daran gewöhnt hat, wird es nur immer nach Mehrerem und Stärkerem begierig. Ein junges Talent, das wirken und anerkannt sein will, und nicht groß genug ist, auf eigenem Wege zu gehen, muß sich dem Geschmack des Tages bequemen, ja es muß seine Vorgänger im Schreck- und Schauerlichen noch zu überbieten suchen." (EGG 2:675)

["Instead of the beautiful subjects from Grecian mythology, there are devils, witches, and vampires, and the lofty heroes of antiquity must give place to jugglers and galley slaves. This is piquant! This is effective! But after the public has once tasted this highly seasoned food and become accustomed to it, it will always long for more and stronger. A young man of talent, who would produce an effect and be acknowledged, and who is not great enough to go his own way, must accommodate himself to the taste of the day—nay, must seek to outdo his predecessors in the horrible and the frightful."] (GCE 288–89)

In response to Eckermann's subsequent question about the uses of literary revolution, Goethe tempers his reservations toward its "deformities" [Auswüchse]. What he envisions is an ideal in which no subject is excluded from poetry:

"zuletzt wird der sehr große Vorteil bleiben, daß man neben einer freieren Form auch einen reicheren verschiedenartigeren Inhalt wird erreicht haben und man keinen Gegenstand der breitesten Welt und des mannigfaltigsten Lebens als unpoetisch mehr wird ausschließen." (EGG 2:676)[4]

["but at last this great advantage will remain—besides a freer form, richer and more diversified subjects will have been attained, and no object of the broadest world and the most manifold life will be any longer excluded as unpoetical."] (GCE 289)

From passages like these, one can understand Goethe's reputation for conservatism. But these passages contradict as well as confirm the reputation. His emphasis on the desirability of free forms and his insistence that subjects are not intrinsically unpoetic underscores what we know from his works: that despite his avowed skepticism, Goethe shared the revolutionary aesthetic precepts of the Romantic age.

An illustration of the currency with which Goethe is erroneously portrayed as a dignified ascetic can be found in a text by Roland Barthes. The example is useful because of Barthes's stature and influence and because the text in question is the introduction to his abridged edition of Brillat-Savarin's *Physiologie du goût,* which for many is the urtext of culinary sensibility. Barthes remarks that Brillat-Savarin was an almost exact contemporary of Goethe, and he seems puzzled, even shocked, by the connection: "Goethe et Brillat-Savarin: ces deux noms, rapprochés, font énigme" [Goethe and Brillat-Savarin: these two names, brought together, are a puzzle].[5] His surprise is understandable, because Barthes draws the anachronistic conclusion that because Goethe (1749–1832) and Brillat-Savarin (1755–1826) had nearly the same life span, *Werther* (1774) and *La Physiologie du goût* (1825) must be contemporaneous as well. Equally misleading is that Barthes speaks of Goethe and Werther as if there were identical.

Goethe's *Die Leiden des jungen Werthers* is a novel that chronicles the emotional life of a bright young man with a sensitive—too sensitive— disposition. Werther's enthusiastic responses to the landscape and people of Wahlheim (a town whose name—"chosen home"—has as much appeal for him as the place itself) are expressed in the letters he writes. Goethe's choice of the epistolary form has enormous significance, because the letters reflect Werther's linguistic talent and his artistic limitations at the same time that they document his emotional decline. The letter is the genre best suited to his naive and ultimately perilous belief that artistic expression should be spontaneous and never polished; furthermore, we are presented only with his side of the correspondence, which reinforces our sense of his self-absorption. In the last quarter of the novel, the epistolary form is modified, because Werther's emotional state and gifts of expression have degenerated to such an extent that he can no longer sustain a correspondence, even one that is self-absorbed. An editor pieces together scraps of his writings and his translations of Ossian, who has supplanted Homer in a shift that mirrors Werther's excessive and dangerous turn inward. The change of genre from letter to translation also documents the change from self-absorption to a loss of self.

Barthes alludes to one of the letters near the beginning of the novel in which Werther writes about the simple pleasure of cooking peas and butter in what he calls "his" Wahlheim. Barthes wittily recalls this scene in order to show how a choice of food is a reflection of character: Werther, he says, would not be interested in the "aphrodisiac virtues of the truffle." This is surely true, but Barthes nevertheless misconstrues the passage in several ways:

Certes, Werther ne dédaignait pas de se faire cuire des petits pois au beurre, dans sa retraite de Wahlheim; mais le voit-on s'intéresser aux vertus aphrodisiaques de la truffe et aux éclairs de désir qui traversent le visage des belles gourmandes?[6]

[To be sure, Werther was not averse to having some peas cooked for him in his Wahlheim retreat; but can one imagine him taking an interest in the aphrodisiac qualities of the truffle or in the flashes of desire that come over the face of beautiful women who enjoy their food?]

In the first place, Werther is the one who cooks the peas with butter. If someone else had done it for him, as Barthes implies (*"se faire cuire* des petits pois au beurre"), Werther would not be able to boast of his culinary self-reliance. The false feeling of self-sufficiency that Werther cultivates in Wahlheim is largely responsible for its charm; he further associates Wahlheim and the cooking of peas with "his" Homer and an idyllic existence reminiscent of Rousseau. In the second place, it is wrong to assume that because one of Goethe's characters might not be interested in the "vertus aphrodisiaques de la truffe," the same must be true for Goethe. It would be out of character for Werther to speak of truffles and aphrodisiacs, given his idealized and literary perception of things, but it does not necessarily follow that Goethe has no interest in such things.

The passage from *Werther* in the letter of June 21 to which Barthes alludes bears quoting in full so that one is fully aware of the distinction between Werther and Goethe that Barthes underplays. That distinction lends an undercurrent of irony to the passage, and the source of that irony lies in Goethe's choice of culinary details. Werther is reading "his" Homer while he picks, strings, and cooks his peas, and he identifies his cooking with the activity of Penelope's suitors when they slaughter, butcher, and roast oxen and pork:

Wenn ich so des Morgens mit Sonnenaufgange hinausgehe nach meinem Wahlheim, und dort im Wirtsgarten mir meine Zuckererbsen selbst pflücke, mich hinsetze, und die abfädme und dazwischen lese in meinem Homer. Wenn ich denn in der kleinen Küche mir einen Topf wähle, mir Butter aussteche, meine Schoten ans Feuer stelle, zudecke und mich dazu setze, sie manchmal umzuschütteln. Da fühl ich so lebhaft, wie die herrlichen übermütigen Freier der Penelope Ochsen und Schweine schlachten, zerlegen und braten. Es ist nichts, das mich so mit einer stillen, wahren Empfindung ausfüllte, als die

Züge patriarchalischen Lebens, die ich, Gott sei Dank, ohne Affekta-
tion in meine Lebensart verweben kann. (GM 217)

[When I go out to Wahlheim at sunrise, and with my own hands
gather in the garden the sugar peas for my own dinner; and when I
sit down to string them as I read my Homer, and then, selecting a
saucepan from the little kitchen, fetch out my own butter, put my
peas on the fire, cover the pot, and sit down to stir it occasionally—I
vividly recall the illustrious suitors of Penelope, killing, dressing, and
roasting their own oxen and swine. Nothing fills me with a more pure
and genuine happiness than those traits of patriarchal life which, thank
God, I can imitate without affectation.] (GSW 20)

There is something touchingly absurd about Werther's association of
peas with oxen and pork and about his identification with Penelope's
suitors; the detail brilliantly reveals Werther's misperception of himself
and his surroundings, reflected here in the way he reads Homer. He
resembles Walter Mitty rather more than the suitors of Penelope, and
we wince, though gently, when he echoes Penelope herself and says that
he can "weave" his reading into his life "without affectation"—"Gott sei
Dank, ohne Affektation."

Part of the reason for Barthes's "misreading" is that he wishes to
uphold the stereotypical contrast between German spiritualism and
French sensualism. Barthes juxtaposes Brillat-Savarin and Goethe (alias
Werther) in order to document what he calls the "historical" or "ideo-
logical" influences that run parallel during the nineteenth century. One
of them (which he associates with Brillat-Savarin and materialism) is char-
acterized by a rehabilitation of sensualism, a "joie de vivre," and the other
(which he associates with Goethe and symbolism) is characterized by a
"mal de vivre." Barthes situates the origins of these conflicting strains
"autour de 1825" [around 1825], the year of the *Physiologie du goût*.[7]
Aside from the anachronism of associating *Werther* with that year and the
mistake of identifying Goethe with his hero, there is the additional irony
that Barthes appears to situate Goethe's reputed lack of sensualism
around 1825, when the *Tagebuch* poem and the *West-östlicher Divan*
were already written. There is an explanation for the mistake, however.
Goethe was still alive when the French Romantics read his early works,
which as Goethe says have so much affinity with theirs; from the French
perspective, therefore, Goethe's works seem to be contemporary with

those of the French Romantics, regardless of when they were written. Nerval's translation of *Faust I* and the use Berlioz makes of it in the *Huits scènes de Faust* date from the 1820s and are associated with a living author. What is less understandable, however, and what can only be attributed to a typically simplified notion of Goethe's decorum, is Barthes's assumption that sensuality is absent from Goethe's works.

Werther does not contain striking examples of ambiguous taste, and that absence supports my emphasis on genre as a deciding factor for understanding the sudden wealth of culinary allusions during the Romantic age. In a novel, culinary allusions do not have the same effect as they do in *Götz von Berlichingen,* which is not called a tragedy (part of Goethe's aim having been to distance himself from the terminology as well as the conventions of drama) but a serious play that ends tragically. In the passage from *Werther* to which Barthes refers, as we have seen, Goethe uses culinary details to reveal Werther's enthusiasms and delusions. Elsewhere in Goethe's novel, the motif of bread has the same idyllic and literary quality as the buttered peas. Futhermore, each allusion to food comes from Werther and therefore says more about him than about literary revolution. Yet there is evidence of an aesthetic program in Werther's "patriarchal" interpretaton of peas, even though it is expressed more faintly than in *Götz von Berlichingen.* Werther's sensibility to the aesthetic questions of his time is stunningly rendered through his writing. Werther's style and opinions testify to his belief in the literary revolution of the Sturm und Drang period, and his aesthetic sympathies are evident from his attention to literary details that would otherwise be dismissed as trivial, here the cooking and eating from Homer. This awareness is related to Werther's observation of worms and insects ("Würmgen" and "Mückgen") in the following fragment from his famous letter of 10 May, which for him represent the great chain of being:

wenn ich das Wimmeln der kleinen Welt zwischen Halmen, die unzähligen, unergründlichen Gestalten, all der Würmgen, der Mückgen, näher an meinem Herzen fühle, und fühle die Gegenwart des Allmächtigen, der uns all nach seinem Bilde schuf, das Wehen des Alliebenden, der uns in ewiger Wonne schwebend trägt und erhält, (GM 199)

[when I hear the humming of the little world among the stalks, and am near the countless indescribable forms of the worms and insects, then I feel the presence of the Almighty Who created us in His own image, and the breath of that universal love which sustains us, as we float in an eternity of bliss;] (GSW 6)

When Werther goes to the kitchen himself, picks out a pan, sits next to his peas and shakes them from time to time as they cook, the act is beneath his social standing, hence indecorous. Furthermore he eats alone, which again sets him apart from society, and his choice of peas seems odd for a breakfast (he says that he has gone out at sunrise). His behavior with respect to eating is related to his disregard for social conventions at court, specifically at the count's, where he is snubbed and insulted. This behavior, in turn, is related to his ideas about art. In either case, his actions and thoughts are predicated on a rejection of the laws of "good taste," and it is in large part because he rejects these laws totally and has nothing to put in their place that he cannot survive. In the letter of 26 May he compares rules in art to those in bourgeois society; they guarantee pleasant but mediocre works or a comfortable but dull existence. An artist or citizen who follows the rules will never be guilty of poor taste ("etwas Abgeschmacktes"), but such an artist will never produce anything "natural" or "truly felt" (he repeats the word *wahr* twice):

Man kann zum Vorteile der Regeln viel sagen, ungefähr was man zum Lobe der bürgerlichen Gesellschaft sagen kann. Ein Mensch, der sich nach ihnen bildet, wird nie etwas Abgeschmacktes und Schlechtes hervorbringen, wie einer, der sich durch Gesetze und Wohlstand modeln läßt, nie ein unerträglicher Nachbar, nie ein merkwürdiger Bösewicht werden kann; dagegen wird aber auch alle Regel, man rede was man wolle, das wahre Gefühl von Natur und den wahren Ausdruck derselben zerstören! (GM 207)

[Much may be alleged in favor of rules; about as much as may be said in favor of middle-class society: an artist modeled after them will never produce anything absolutely bad or in poor taste, just as a man who observes the laws of society and obeys decorum can never be a wholly unwelcome neighbour or a real villain. Yet, say what you will of rules, they destroy the genuine feeling of Nature and its true expression.] (GSW 11)

As a dilettante, Werther understands enough about art to reject arbitrary rules from without, the neoclassical laws of good taste; but he does not possess enough creativity—what Goethe elsewhere calls the natural taste of genius—to invent laws of his own.[8] For the most part, however, the gustatory allusions in *Werther* function as they generally do in novels from this period: as elements of characterization and an evocation of milieu. By watching how Werther eats, we observe his progressive spiritualization, the trait that Barthes finds manifest already in the peas and butter; by the end he has stylized himself as a Christ figure who has a "Last Supper" of bread and wine: "Er ließ sich ein Brot und Wein bringen" [He had bread and wine brought to him] (GM 295).[9]

The Literary Feud in *Götz von Berlichingen*

Götz von Berlichingen is so famous for one indecorous detail that the name of its hero denotes a form of invective. One reason for the fame of the "Götz-Zitat" ("Er lecke mich im Arsch" ["He can lick me in the ass"]) is that it contrasts with Goethe's reputation. The association of *Götz* with indecorum aptly reflects the play's reception by Goethe's contemporaries. But as with the case of taste, there are those who welcomed and those who condemned Goethe's indecorum. In his commentary to *Götz*, Dieter Borchmeyer documents the negative response by quoting a scene from Tieck's novel *Der junge Tischlermeister* (1836). Some aristocratic amateurs prepare to perform Goethe's play, and there is a furious outburst against the work's indecorum. One character protests that "Das Dekorum und der Anstand sind doch nicht im allermindesten beobachtet" [Decorum and propriety are not respected in the least], and the work is also referred to as "ein ganz geschmackloses Ungeheuer" [a completely tasteless monstrosity] (GF 785). The negative response, which comes from aristocrats, is expressed in the vocabulary of decorum and taste. Admirers of *Götz*, like admirers of Shakespeare (whom Goethe cites as his model), reject the laws of decorum and taste, whereas critics cite the same laws in support of their censure.[10] Tieck's characters sound like Frederick the Great, who condemns *Götz von Berlichingen* and compares it to Shakespeare when he criticizes German literature. According to Frederick the Great, Shakespeare's mistakes are excusable, because "the birth of the arts is never their point of maturity"; Goethe's imitation, on the other hand, is "disgusting." Taste is the criterion, and although Frederick cites the dictum that one should not argue about tastes ("il ne faut point disputer des goûts"), he quickly reigns in his tolerance by invoking a hierarchy of taste where Racine stands alone at the top and Goethe is at the bottom along with circus artists and marionettes:

> voilà encore un Goetz de Berlichingen qui paraît sur la scène, imitation détestable de ces mauvaises pièces anglaises, et le Parterre applaudit et demande avec enthousiasme la répétition de ces dégoûtantes plati-tudes. Je sais qu'il ne faut point disputer des goûts; cependant permet-tez moi de vous dire que ceux qui trouvent autant de plaisir aux Danseurs de corde, aux marionettes, qu'aux Tragédies de Racine, ne veulent que tuer le temps.[11]

> [and onto the stage comes a Goetz of Berlichingen as well, a detest-able imitation of those bad English plays, and the audience claps and enthusiastically requests a repetition of these disgusting platitudes. I know that there is no arguing about tastes; allow me nevertheless to tell you that those who derive as much pleasure from tightrope walk-ers, from marionettes, as from the tragedies of Racine, want only to kill time.]

Justus Möser answers critics like Frederick the Great by transforming the emphasis on figurative taste into literal taste. His image mirrors the use of ambiguous taste in *Götz*, where it is based on a distinction between the artificial life at court and the natural life of Götz and his followers. To many people, Möser says, Goethe's play has "tasted good" ("hat recht vielen geschmeckt"). By contrast, Frederick the Great's reaction to *Götz* is called a "fruit that tasted sour to him" [eine Frucht (. . .), die ihm den Gaumen zusammengezogen habe], an image that Möser turns into an indictment of aristocratic privilege: if *Götz* tastes "sour" to the king, then it is because his palate is accustomed to pineapple. In "our fatherland" Möser finds such palates thankfully rare:

> Der Zungen, welche an Ananas gewöhnt sind, wird hoffentlich in unserm Vaterlande eine geringe Zahl sein; und wenn von einem Volksstücke die Rede ist, so muß man Geschmack der Hofleute bei Seite setzen.[12]

[Let us hope that in our fatherland only a small number of tongues are accustomed to pineapple; besides, when one is speaks of a drama of the people, the taste of courtiers is irrelevant.]

In the final paragraph of "Zum Schäkespears-Tag," Goethe concludes his manifesto by linking Shakespeare and literary revolution with the rejection of good taste, as I mentioned briefly in chapter 1. He vividly depicts the realm of "so-called good taste" as a sleepy, shadowy, boring place that lacks the body and vitality of his own robust style:

Auf meine Herren! trompeten Sie mir alle edle Seelen, aus dem Elysium, des sogenannten guten Geschmacks, wo sie schlaftrunken, in langweiliger Dämmerung halb sind, halb nicht sind, Leidenschaften im Herzen und kein Mark in den Knochen haben; und weil sie nicht müde genug zu ruhen, und doch zu faul sind um tätig zu sein, ihr Schatten Leben zwischen Myrten und Lorbeergebüschen verschlendern und vergähnen. (GM 414)

[Onto your feet, Gentlemen! Do me the favor of trumpeting all noble souls out of the Elysium of so-called good taste, where they are half present, half absent, drowsily so in a boring twilight. They have passions in their hearts but no marrow in their bones; and because they are not tired enough to rest and yet too lazy to be active, they amble and yawn their shadow of a life away amid myrtle and laurel bushes.]

Immediately preceding this final paragraph Goethe uses the word *fressen*, which wakes up his listeners even before the trumpets are sounded against good taste. The word *fressen*—which like "to gobble" designates either the eating of animals or the bad table manners of people—is meant to shock those "noble souls" schooled on the good taste that is overtly denounced in the final paragraph:

Er [Shakespeare] führt uns durch die ganze Welt, aber wir verzärtelte unerfahrne Menschen schreien bei jeder fremden Heuschrecke die uns begegnet: Herr, er will uns fressen. (GM 414)

[He guides us through the entire world, but we coddled inexperienced people scream whenever we encounter a strange grasshopper: Lord, it (in German "he") wants to gobble us up.]

The antecedent of the pronoun "er" in the sentence "Herr, er will uns fressen" is ambiguous; it applies equally to the "strange grasshopper" of the preceding clause and to Shakespeare, the subject of the sentence. Likewise, the word *fressen* has a double meaning that shifts depending on the perspective, much as *taste* can connote either praise or censure of Shakespeare and the poetic revolution he represents. On the one hand are critics like Voltaire and Frederick the Great, who are afraid of Shakespeare and think that he will "eat them up." On the other hand are poets who admire Shakespeare and use words like *fressen,* the diction of which is "in bad taste."[13] In the same way that literal taste revives the dead metaphor of taste, the word *fressen* awakens the "noble souls" from their stupor.

Goethe uses the word *fressen* to a similar end in *Götz von Berlichingen,* where its significance is heightened by our awareness both of the association with Shakespeare and the word's presence in the autobiography of the historical Götz. *Götz von Berlichingen* is Goethe's declaration of independence from the neoclassical dramatic model of French drama, from the Racinean model that Frederick the Great admires as the embodiment of good taste. Goethe aims in this play to invent a form suited to the German language and to German history, and he chooses Shakespeare as his model; in his masterful interpretative summary of the play, Nicholas Boyle calls *Götz* "a sprawling work, generously and exhilaratingly so if one compares it with the fussily monothematic plays that predominate in German official literature from Lessing to Hebbel and beyond."[14] The figure of Götz is based on the memoirs of a historical figure from the sixteenth century, a contemporary of Luther; but as is usual in historical plays, Goethe has the problems of his own age in mind. Foremost among them is the problem of freedom, aesthetic as well political. Götz is a Promethean figure who thinks on his own and acts in accordance with what he and the early Goethe think of as nature, not in accordance with the artifices and intrigue at the episcopal court of Bamberg; nature is the quality he emphasizes in Shakespeare's characters as well: "Natur! Natur! Nichts so Natur wie Schäkespears Menschen" [Nature! Nature! Nothing so much nature as Shakespeare's figures] he says in "Zum Schäkespears-Tag." Götz is an imperial knight who exerts his independence from princes and bishops while asserting his loyalty to the emperor who stands above them. The clash between the "natural" world of Götz at Jaxthausen and the "artificial" world at the Bamberg court is complicated by the figure of Adalbert von Weislingen, Götz's childhood companion and the lover of Götz's sister; Weislingen is attracted to each world and ultimately betrays them both.

Many of the scenes in *Götz von Berlichingen* take place at table. In the climactic scene at the end of act 3, for example, when Jaxthausen is under siege, everyone is gathered around Götz to eat the food prepared by Elisabeth, his loyal and practical wife, who cooks indefatigably and cheerfully throughout the play (Madame de Staël rightly describes her as a figure from a Dutch painting). Boyle refers to the setting as "probably an unprecedented locale in serious drama,"[15] and Goethe makes sure that we notice it by having Götz encourage his knights to eat and drink:

So bringt uns die Gefahr zusammen. Laßts euch schmecken meine Freunde! Vergeßt das Trinken nicht. (GF 352)

[So we are brought together by danger. Eat heartily, my friends! Don't forget drinking!] (GB 54)

Götz rallies his men with two toasts, the first a somewhat restrained one to the emperor, which they echo with "Es lebe" ["Long live"] and the second a more thrilling one to freedom. "Es lebe die Freiheit" ["Long live freedom"] is repeated three times with increasing intensity, first by the young knight Georg, who always is at the side of Götz, then by Götz himself, and finally by everyone present. Götz tells his men that these must be their dying words and that if freedom outlives them, they can "die in peace"—"können wir ruhig sterben." The greatest good, he says, is to serve freely. In this scene the cries mount into a frenzy that turns the abstract quality of freedom into something nearly tangible.

Given that freedom—aesthetic and political freedom—is the central theme of the play, Goethe's setting of this moment is a matter of enormous consequence. By staging the cry "Es lebe die Freiheit" at table, Goethe demonstrates his artistic freedom. It is in scenes like these that Goethe transfers Götz's "feud" [Fehde] in the play to his own feud with the laws of French neoclassical drama, acting in Borchmeyer's felicitous phrase like a "dramaturgic Götz" who "smashes dramatic conventions with his iron hand" (GF 794). In this scene as in many others, the "dramaturgic Götz" draws attention to the literal taste that he would not be free to use if he followed the rules of figurative good taste. On the one hand, the bottle of wine reveals Götz's nature just as Werther's choice of foods reveals his: this is the last bottle in his besieged castle, and Elisabeth has put it aside for him alone, but Götz wants instead to share it with his men, who need nourishment more than he does: "Gib sie heraus. Sie brauchen Stärkung, nicht ich" (GF 352) [Bring it out! They need the strength, not me] (GB 54). Here as elsewhere we observe the generous nature of Götz, who does not abuse his power over those who serve him (Sauder considers this scene analogous to the Last Supper of Christ).[16] But at the same time, the deliberate association that Götz makes between the bottle of wine and freedom, between his gestures and his ideal, has a conscious application to Goethe's own aesthetic undertaking when he writes the action of pouring wine into his play and identifies wine with lifeblood:

> GÖTZ: *schenkt ein* Es geht just noch einmal herum. Und wenn unser Blut anfängt auf die Neige zu gehen, wie der Wein in dieser Flasche erst schwach, dann tropfenweise rinnt. *Er tröpfelt das letzte in sein Glas.* W as soll unser letztes Wort sein?
> GEORG: Es lebe die Freiheit!
> GÖTZ: Es lebe die Freiheit!
> ALLE: Es lebe die Freiheit! (GF 352)

> [GÖTZ: *(He pours.)* There's just enough for one more round. And when our blood begins to dwindle like the wine in this bottle, first flowing weakly, then drop by drop *(he pours the last drops into his glass)*, what should our last word be?
> GEORG: Long live freedom!
> GÖTZ: Long live freedom!
> ALL: Long live freedom!]

(GB 54)

In the remainder of this scene, in his answers to Georg's questions about the future, Götz consistently illustrates his hopes with gustatory examples. His willingness to talk about eating and drinking reflects his character and vitality while demonstrating the character and vitality of the artist who portrays him in this manner. Götz and Goethe do not try to hide what is natural in deference to the good taste associated with courtly behavior and courtly politics. When Georg doubts the existence of princes who are unaffected and prize freedom over servility, Götz describes some of the princes he has known. He pictures them at table, where they like to be surrounded by equals rather than fawning courtiers:

Gute Menschen, [. . .] [d]enen das Herz aufging, wenn sie viel ihres Gleichen bei sich zu Tisch sahen, und nicht erst die Ritter zu Hofschranzen umzuschaffen brauchten um mit ihnen zu leben. (GF 352)

[Good men (. . .) whose hearts rejoiced when they could view a number of their equals as guests at table, and did not need to transform knights into court toadies in order to live with them.] (GB 55)

After Götz imagines a peaceful utopia with more princes of this sort, there follows a comic (but painfully authentic) moment in which Georg worries that peace would mean the end of his career as a knight: "Würden wir hernach auch reiten?" (GF 353) [And would we still go on riding? (GB 55)]. Götz consoles him with a gustatory image that sounds like *Schlaraffenland* turned ordinary, the image of hunting for food to feed farmers and of sharing meals with them:

Wir wollten die Gebürge von Wölfen säubern, wollten unserm ruhig ackernden Nachbar einen Braten aus dem Wald holen, und dafür die Suppe mit ihm essen. (GF 353)

[We could clear the mountains of wolves, could bring a roast from the forest to our neighbor who plows the soil in peace, and in return we would share his supper with him.] (GB 55)

Götz equates eating with action, and in the last scene of act 4, when he is under house arrest, his frustration is conveyed with a gustatory metaphor. Idleness does not "taste good" to him: "Der Müßiggang will mir gar nicht schmecken" (GF 367) [This idleness is distasteful to me] (GB 65). When he repeats the word *Müßiggang* (idleness) a few lines later, it again calls forth a negative gustatory association. Writing strikes him as an empty form of occupational therapy, something that "sours" him: "Schreiben ist geschäftiger Müßiggang, es kommt mir sauer an" (GF 367) [Writing is a busy form of idleness; it does not bring pleasure] (GB 65). In the penultimate scene of the play, when Elisabeth asks Götz whether he wants something to eat ("Willst du nicht was essen?"), we know that he has lost his vitality and his purpose, because he absently answers no and speaks instead of the sun outside: "Nichts meine Frau.

241

Sieh wie die Sonne draußen scheint" (GF 386) [Nothing, dear wife. Look how the sun is shining outside] (GB 81). In the final scene of the play, when Götz dies with the word freedom on his lips ("Freiheit! Freiheit!") and a glass of water rather than wine, it is a sign that the exhilaration we witnessed in act 3 has turned to desperation. The nearly tangible quality of freedom in the earlier scene has faded, and the wine in that scene has been replaced by water. After Götz cries out "Freiheit! Freiheit!" and dies, Elisabeth answers that there is no freedom except in heaven and that earth is a prison: "Nur droben bei dir. Die Welt ist ein Gefängnis" (GF 388) [Only on high, on high with you. The world is a prison] (GB 82).

Goethe's use of ambiguous taste to express political freedom for Götz and aesthetic freedom for himself is already present in the first scene, though less directly than at the end of act 3 or the end of the play. We know instantly that we are in a tavern, because the play opens when someone orders a brandy and the innkeeper answers that his customer is a glutton—"der Nimmersatt":

> SIEVERS: Hänsel, noch ein Glas Branntewein, und meß christlich.
> WIRT: Du bist der Nimmersatt.
>
> (GF 281)

> [SIEVERS: Hänsel, another glass of brandy, and give us a good Christian measure.
> INNKEEPER: With you it's never enough.]
>
> (GB 2)

With these lines Goethe puts the audience instantly in mind of the aesthetic struggle he is staging. This is not the kind of dialogue his audience would associate with a serious play, for already in the first line, he has stormed the "temple of so-called good taste" and declared his allegiance to Shakespeare. Any but a Shakespearean tragedy would eliminate references to something as commonplace as drinking brandy in a tavern, which is the point he wants to make.[17]

Having touched on ambiguous taste in the first scene, Goethe becomes more insistent in the second, where he connects the theme of freedom to drinking and anticipates the climactic scene in act 3. Götz talks of freedom in his opening monologue, and his accompanying gesture is to pour out wine. Given the cult of action during the Sturm und

242

Drang, gestures are significant, and this one is matched by the significance of Götz's diction, which is colloquial and, as so often in colloquial speech, includes a gustatory idiom. Here as at the end of the play he says: "es wird einem sauer gemacht" (something is "made sour" or becomes difficult), which is the equivalent to saying that something is "distasteful." The connection of food and revolution becomes evident when we learn that what is "made sour" is his "bit of life and freedom." There is likewise significance to the fact that Götz's frustration has a connection to the figure of Weislingen; but we do not know yet that Weislingen is a courtier who used to be Götz's comrade or that his present companion is the boy Georg, who will become Götz's knight. The wine he drinks restores him spritually as well as physically, and he reflects on the process:

> Es wird einem sauer gemacht, das bißchen Leben und Freiheit. Dafür, wenn ich dich habe Weislingen, will ich mirs wohl sein lassen. *Schenkt ein.* Wieder leer! Georg! So langs daran nicht mangelt, und an frischem Mut, lach ich der Fürsten Herrschsucht und Ränke. (GF 283)

> [They make you pay for it, this bit of life and freedom. For that, when I've caught you, Weislingen, I'll have satisfaction. *(Pours a drink.)* Empty again! Georg! As long as I don't lack for a drink and bold courage, I'll laugh at the powerplays and the intrigues of princes.] (GB 4)

Structurally this is the counterpart to the penultimate scene of the play, when Götz refuses to eat. Together the two scenes flank the central scene at table in Jaxthausen.[18]

In the second scene of act 1, drinking occasions the discussion between Götz and Brother Martin on the nature of human existence and the unnaturalness of monastic life. When Brother Martin speaks of the different effects of food and wine, he, too, equates the gustatory with life and liberation: "Essen und trinken mein ich, ist des Menschen leben" [Food and drink, so I believe, are the life of man] (GB 5) he says, to which Götz responds with a "Wohl" [True] that indicates his agreement and is one half of the drinking formula "Zum Wohl"—"To your health" (GF 285). When Brother Martin compares the restorative effect of eating and drinking on Götz and his followers to its soporific effect on monks, we are reminded of the sleepy good taste in "Zum Schäkespears-Tag." Of Götz and his men Martin says that when they have eaten and drunk, they acquire strength, courage, and skill that make them better fit for their work:

> Wenn Ihr gessen und trunken habt, seid Ihr wie neu geboren. Seid stärker, mutiger, geschickter zu Eurem Geschäft. (GF 285)

> [When you have eaten and drunk, you are as if newborn; you're stronger, bolder, more capable of action.] (GB 5)

He contends that food and drink have the opposite effect on monks, who are weakened by them in body and spirit:

> Aber wir, wenn gessen und trunken haben, sind wir grad das Gegenteil von dem, was wir sein sollen. Unsere schläfrige Verdauung stimmt den Kopf nach dem Magen, und in der Schwäche einer überfüllten Ruhe erzeugen sich Begierden, die ihrer Mutter leicht über den Kopf wachsen. (GF 286)

> [But we, when we eat and drink, are just the reverse of what we ought to be. Our sleepy digestion attunes our heads to our bellies, and in the weakness of a gluttonous repose desires are conceived which quickly overwhelm their progenitor.] (GB 5–6)

The assumption that Brother Martin is modeled after Martin Luther is confirmed by his language. Goethe's character uses concrete images to convey philosophical questions, and he associates liberation with sensuality.[19] He attacks the wretchednesses ("Jämmerlichkeiten") of a condition that suppresses and condemns man's sensuality. We readily extend the criticism to literary decorum, which is equally unnatural; Martin's gustatory criticism of monastic life repeats and varies Goethe's criticism of neoclassical good taste.

For Martin, knightly armor represents natural life and liberation. When Götz remarks of his armor that it is both heavy and burdensome ("schwer und beschwerlich," which plays on the meanings of heavy and difficult in the word "schwer"), Martin replies that all things on earth are burdensome ("beschwerlich"), but nothing more so than the suppression of human nature: "Was ist nicht beschwerlich auf dieser Welt, und mir kommt nichts beschwerlicher vor, als nicht Mensch sein dürfen" (GF 287) [What is not tiring in this world? And nothing seems more tiring to me than not to be allowed to be a man] (GB 6). He plays on literal and figurative meanings to illustrate that the Church is unnatural when it requires the separation of body and spirit. The vows of poverty, chastity, and obedience have "condemned" [verdammt] the "best drives" [die besten Triebe] of his entire station because of a mistaken figurative desire [Begierde]—the desire to get closer to God:

> MARTIN: O Herr! was sind die Mühseligkeiten Eures Lebens, gegen die Jämmerlichkeiten eines Stands, der die besten Triebe, durch die wir werden, wachsen und gedeihen, aus mißverstandener Begierde Gott näher zu rücken, verdammt. (GF 287)

> [MARTIN: O Lord! what are the difficulties of your life compared to the wretchedness of a state that condemns the best impulses through which we are made, grow, and mature, all out of a misguided desire to be nearer to God.] (GB 6)

What Martin questions is not the closeness to God, but the artificial means of obtaining it; Goethe analogously does not question the aim of literary decorum, which is excellence in poetry, but the false assumption that decorum alone assures such excellence.

Goethe makes sustained use of gustatory metaphors in this passage: when Martin and Götz use the words *schmecken* (to taste), *Vorschmack* (foretaste), and *fressen,* the metaphors are dead; but Martin revives them, just as he makes the literal act of drinking the basis for his critique of Catholicism. When he raises his glass to Götz, the gesture underscores his comparison of a monastic existence to the worldly life of a man like Götz; Martin contrasts his "Käfig" [cage] with the walls of Götz's castle, which represent independence rather than confinement, and he speaks of the sleep that "tastes" good to Götz because it strengthens rather than weakens him. Such sleep is a "foretaste" of Heaven:

> MARTIN: Wenn Ihr wiederkehrt Herr, in Eure Mauern, mit dem Bewußtsein Eurer Tapferkeit und Stärke, der keine Müdigkeit etwas anhaben kann, Euch zum erstenmal nach langer Zeit, sicher für feindlichen Überfall, entwaffnet auf Euer Bette streckt, und Euch nach dem Schlaf streckt, der Euch besser schmeckt, als mir der Trunk, nach langem Durst; da könnt Ihr von Glück sagen!
> GÖTZ: Davor kommts auch selten.

245

MARTIN: *feuriger:* Und ist wenns kommt, ein Vorschmack des Himmels.

(GF 287)

[MARTIN: When you return, Sir, within your walls, with the knowledge of your bravery and strength, immune to all fatigue, secure for the first time in a long while from enemy raids, you stretch out unarmed upon your bed and reach for sleep, which tastes better to you than a drink does to me after long thirsting; then you can speak of happiness.

GÖTZ: For all that it comes but seldom.

MARTIN: *(more heated)* And when it does happen, it's a taste of Heaven.]

(GB 6–7)

He drinks to the health of Götz's wife, again connecting drinking with sensuality. Götz expresses his sympathy for Martin in an aside and remarks that his station "eats away at his heart": "Er dauert mich! Das Gefühl seines Standes frißt ihm das Herz" (GF 288) [I'm sorry for him! His sense of his station in life consumes his heart] (GB 7) .

The use of the word *fressen* here is figurative and dead. It conveys strong sentiments but would not necessarily call attention to itself in another context. In this play, however, it is very much a "Götzian" word, more so, I would contend, than the notorious "Götz-Zitat" mentioned earlier or the infrequent references to *Scheißkerle* (an invective on the order of "sons of bitches" or today even "fucking bastards"). All of these words have a related function. They are as startling in a serious play with a tragic end as Bruder Martin's exclamation that women are "die Krone der Schöpfung" [the crowning glory of creation] is startling for a monk. In a grander sense they are equally "natural." The "Götz- Zitat" is exemplary rather than isolated, and its function is less far-reaching than Goethe's use of the word *fressen* and his talk of eating and drinking, which have both a thematic and a self-reflexive aesthetic function in the play.

When Götz uses the word "abfressen" in act 2, the metaphor is again a dead one, identical to his usage when he speaks of something "eating away at his heart": "Es hätte mir das Herz abgefressen, wenn ich's ihnen hätte lang schuldig bleiben sollen" (GF 315) [It would have destroyed me if I had failed to repay them for very long] (GB 17). But again, context revives it, because Götz responds here to praise from Selbitz for having initiated his feud ("Fehd") against Nürnberg: the political *Fehd* of Götz against Nuremberg is echoed linguistically in the use of the word *fressen*. In another passage *fressen* imitates the diction and biblical imagery of the historical Götz in his memoirs while altering the context. Goethe's Götz plays on the term *vogelfrei* (literally "free as a bird," but meaning outlawed, because a person can be shot at like a bird) when he speaks of the emperor's writ of execution against him. He interprets *vogelfrei* to mean that he will be converted into food for birds in the sky and animals on the fields: "Der Kaiser hat Exekution gegen mich verordnet, die mein Fleisch den Vögeln unter dem Himmel, und den Tieren auf dem Felde zu fressen vorschneiden soll" [The emperor has put out a writ of execution against me so that my flesh will be cut up as food for the birds under the heavens and beasts in the fields].[20]

The other examples of the word *fressen* in the play, taken together with the word's significance in "Zum Schäkespears-Tag," reiterate the connection to a Götzian mentality. Mostly it is used by the knights of Götz, as for example in the first scene of the play, where one of them says "das ist ein gefunden Fressen" (GF 283) ["That is handing it to him on a plate"—which Hamlin translates as "What a stroke of good luck!" (GB 3)]; here the word exemplifies the colloquial diction and rhythms that are a hallmark of Goethe's revolutionary style. Lerse also uses the word when he is melting lead from the windows of Jaxthausen so that they can be reused as ammunition. His comments on unpredictability vary the image from Goethe's historical source, except that here worms as well as birds do the eating: "da mich mein Vater machte, dachte er nicht welcher Vogel unter dem Himmel, welcher Wurm auf der Erde mich fressen mögte" (GF 350) [When my father begot me, he wasn't thinking what bird in the sky, what worm in the earth might feed on me] (GB 53). And Sickingen uses the word *fressen* when he curses Weislingen and says that his conscience and shame should "devour him to death" (GB 63): "Gewissen und Schande sollen ihn zu tod fressen" (GF 363).

Given the Götzian aura of the word, it at first seems odd to hear Weislingen say "fressen" three times near the end of the play in what appears to be an unremarkable way. But the choice of this word in particular expresses Weislingen's lost affinity to Götz: Boyle for example considers Götz and Weislingen to be a dual figure who projects two sides of Goethe's self. For Weislingen the metaphor is truly dead, a vestige of his kinship to Götz but a sign of his betrayal. In the first example, Weislingen's choice of *fressen* mirrors Sickingen's curse, and their different usage mirrors their philosophical differences. *Fressen* is applied passively to Weislingen—he is "eaten up"—and actively to Sickigen, whose growing reputation is compared to a stream that has "eaten up" a few brooks: "Sein Ansehn nimmt zu wie ein Strom, der nur einmal ein Paar Bäche gefressen hat" (GF 364) [His prestige swells like a surging river] (GB 63). In the second example, Weislingen uses the idiomatic phrase that Götz used before, and the identical phrase heightens the contrast between them: to Adelheid Weislingen says that his jealousy of the future emperor Carl is "eating away at his heart": "Es frißt mich am Herzen der fürchterliche Gedanke!" (GF 365) [It gnaws at my heart, the very thought is terrible] (GB 64). The third example occurs in Weislingen's monologue, which he delivers just after he has been poisoned by Franz and just before he sees Götz's sister Marie, the woman he has abandoned. His position in between the two worlds is reflected here in his vocabulary. He says that he is weak and empty, that his bones are hollow, and that a fever has "devoured" his marrow: "Ich bin so krank, so schwach. Alle meine Gebeine sind hohl. Ein elendes Fieber hat das Mark ausgefressen" (GF 381) [I feel so sick, so weak. All my limbs are hollow. A wretched fever has devoured the marrow] (GB 77). We are reminded that the bond between Weislingen and Götz has been betrayed not because Weislingen is evil, but because he is weak: in German the lack of "marrow" is the equivalent to a lack of backbone in English.

It would be impossible for anyone at court besides Weislingen to use *fressen,* even in the figurative sense it has in "am Herzen fressen" or in its literal application to animals. Whereas everyone at Jaxthausen speaks of the food and wine in front of them, the people at the court of Bamberg eat but do not mention it. Just as Brother Martin uses culinary examples to criticize the unnaturalness of life in a monastery, Goethe uses them (and their absence) to emphasize the unnaturalness of life at court. The first scene in Bamberg is set in the dining room at the bishop's palace, and we know from the stage directions that dessert is being served: "der Nachtisch und die große Pokale werden aufgetragen" (GF 300) [Dessert and large drinking chalices are are brought in] (GB 16). The choice of dessert is a sociological detail that reflects the ostentation of courtly life and its distance from the simplicity and generosity of life at Jaxthausen; sweets are a luxury available mostly to the aristocracy.[21] More important still is that the people in Bamberg, unlike those at Jaxthausen, do not reflect on what they do. The only "Gerichte" [dishes] mentioned there are judicial (in German *Gerichte* also means "courts of law"), and in their toasts, the people at court never refer to the act of drinking. Even the stage directions for the Bamberg scenes are different from those set in Jaxthausen (what Boyle calls the "second drama"). We read that the people drink ("sie trinken"), but we never read that they pour what they drink, as we do in the case of Götz; the people here are served by others. Only Liebetraut makes a reference that can be construed as gustatory, and that suits his role as a kind of court jester. Furthermore, his comment is prompted by a reproach from Olearius that he is too quick to speak out ("Es scheint Ihr seid dazu bestellt Wahrheiten zu sagen") (GF 303) [It would seem that you are employed for speaking the blunt truth] (GB 18), to which he responds that when he has the "heart" for something (meaning the courage or the interest), then it appears on his mouth. He uses the word *Maul* for mouth, which also refers to the jaws of animals and is therefore the linguistic equivalent to *fressen* for eating, even though the word was less indecorous in the eighteenth century than it is today: "Weil ich's Herz dazu habe, so fehlt mirs nicht am Maul" (GF 303) [Since I have the head for it, I don't lack the tongue] (GB 19). Olearius is by contrast a man of pretense who proudly explains that his name is a Latin translation of Öhlmann, clearly a "talking" name. When he refers to dinner, Olearius again hides behind Latin: "Post coenam stabis seu passus mille meabis" (GF 305). In the context of this play, such details are meant to reveal the hypocrisy at court, where people eat and drink but act as if they did not, in contrast to Götz and his followers.

As we saw from "Zum Schäkespears-Tag," Goethe associates Shakespeare with a new kind of taste that in *Götz von Berlichingen* is represented by literal taste. Even the wordplay on which the connection is based doubtless owes something to Shakespeare's punning; the wordplays in *Götz* (in the scene with Brother Martin, for example) have a Shakespearean association that is as strong as the disregard for the three unities. During the period of *Götz* and *Werther*, Goethe is more concerned with inventing a new taste than he is with rejecting the old one: those who populate the "Elysium" of good taste are portrayed as doddering and impotent, but Goethe (unlike Werther) does not feel threatened by them. Only later did Goethe become hostile toward the figurative taste of a tyrannical public, and it is an irony of literary history (albeit an understandable one) that he most resented the dictates of institutional taste after he had himself become an influential figure at the court of Carl August in Weimar.

Ambiguous Taste in Goethe's Translation of
Le Neveu de Rameau

In the 1790s and early 1800s—the time of his correspondence with Schiller, whose transformation from rebellion to decorum parallels Goethe's own—the blatant indecorum in *Götz* was replaced by more indirect but nevertheless unmistakable expressions of literary freedom. Goethe seemed to find taste more inhibiting then than he had before, and sometimes during this period he even begins to sound like Werther. What remained constant was the assurance that "so-called" good taste is antithetical to genius. All along he defended the poetry of indecorum and the poet's privilege to treat any subject in any setting. The comments to Eckermann quoted earlier show that he was preoccupied with decorum throughout his life, and one need only think of his works and their chronology (the "Römische Elegien," including the suppressed ones, *Wilhelm Meister,* "Das Tagebuch," and especially *Faust*) to realize that despite the changes in his public demeanor, his aesthetic principles evolved but did not change radically after the Sturm und Drang period. His feelings about decorum were mixed, and in *Torquato Tasso* he juxtaposes the standards of decorum for society with those for poetry. But it is the princess rather than Tasso who says that permission depends on propriety: "Erlaubt ist, was sich ziemt." T. J. Reed emphasizes Goethe's ability to join freedom with genre, and he neatly defines Goethe's classicism as "a personal and individual—if we want to push the paradox to the extreme, a Romantic—Classicism."[22]

Goethe's translation of Diderot's *Le Neveu de Rameau* and the notes that he wrote to accompany it offer an important document of Goethe's aesthetic, in particular of the conflict between the freedom poets need and the restrictions a public imposes on them in the name of taste. Surely it is not coincidental that while he was translating Diderot, Goethe was also reworking and directing a performance of *Götz* in Weimar. Diderot's dialogue between his stylized self ("Moi") and the brilliant and iconoclastic Rameau ("Lui")—both of them projections of Diderot—is a revolutionary and indecorous text; in it Diderot treats an array of philosophical and ethical issues, principal among them the nature of genius and its battle with mediocrity. What further attracted Goethe to *Le Neveu de Rameau* was Diderot's ability to give structure to a work that on the surface seems chaotic. Ambiguous taste is central to this structural tour de force: each of the many allusions to eating raises aesthetic, ethical, philosophical, and social questions, thus illustrating Rameau's theory that all human activity, great and small, is related to chewing—the theory of "mastication universelle." The impression of structural chaos is dispelled by a regular return to the dinner table, which is the fixed point of Rameau's universe and consequently becomes the fixed point of Diderot's work.

Goethe undertook the translation of Diderot's dialogue at the urging of Schiller, who probably realized how salutary is would be for Goethe to reproduce this particular work.[23] Goethe's spirits were increasingly low during the winter of 1804–5. It is common to speak of a *Schaffenskrise* for that period—a crisis in his ability to create—that was aggravated by an awareness of the mediocrity and pettiness around him. Schiller and Goethe seem to have thought of translation as a kind of therapy, and Schiller was working on a translation of Racine's *Phèdre* during the same winter. On 14 January 1805, Schiller wrote to Goethe about the benefits of translation, which allows a person to be active, and subliminally creative, during times of crisis:

Ich bin jetzt froh, daß ich den Entschluß gefaßt und ausgeführt habe, mich mit einer Übersetzung zu beschäftigen. So ist doch aus diesen Tagen des Elends wenigstens etwas entsprungen, und ich habe indessen doch gelebt und gehandelt. (GS 2:1038)

[I am glad now that I made and carried out the decision to work on a translation. As a result, at least something has taken shape during these days of misery, when I was still able to live and act.]

In his preface to Diderot's *Essai sur la Peinture,* part of which he translated in 1798, Goethe likewise mentions the creative benefits of translation. He calls his preface the "Geständnisse des Übersetzers" (Confessions of The Translator), and his confessions concern the act of creation rather than the derivative act of translation. What he confesses in the first paragraph is his familiarity with creative impotence, the reluctance to begin writing: "man nimmt die Feder in die Hand, und noch zaudert

man, anzufangen." But in the next paragraph he uses the image of con-
versation, with Diderot as his interlocutor, to show how the hindrances
are overcome: "Schnell sind alle Stockungen gehoben, wir lassen uns
lebhaft ein, wir vernehmen, wir erwidern" [All hesitations are rapidly
overcome, we become animatedly engaged, we listen, we answer].[24]
Goethe's notes to *Le Neveu de Rameau* are the fruits of another of his
"conversations" with an author he has translated.

In *Le Neveu de Rameau* Diderot evokes a milieu whose credo in
aesthetic matters is the stultifying and mindless doctrine of good taste;
he presents a microcosm of this society at the table of Bertin, a wealthy
financier, which is the locus both of Rameau's culinary pleasures and of
his ultimate disgrace. In one scene Bertin and his guests chew while
discoursing on figurative taste. They have just finished sketching the plan
for a play by Palissot (an enemy of Diderot, who in this work embodies
meanness and mediocrity). That subject leads them to the topic of taste,
which Bertin proposes to define. As Bertin raises his hand so that every-
one will listen to him, "Lui" interrupts his narration and consequently
Bertin to say that he cannot remember what the definition was:

> Et puis, nous voilà embarqués dans une dissertation sur le goût. Alors
> le patron fait signe de main qu'on l'écoute; car c'est surtout de goût
> qu'il se pique. Le goût, dit-il, . . . le goût est une chose . . . ma foi, je
> ne sais quelle chose il disait que c'était; ni lui, non plus. (NdR 58)

> [Then we're off onto a discussion of taste, and the boss makes a sign
> with his hand that he wants to be heard, because taste is what he
> prides himself on having. "Taste," says he, "taste is a thing which—"
> I've forgotten what he said it was, and so has he.] (DRN 49)

Bertin considers himself an expert on figurative taste, but it is clear
from this scene that his expertise extends only as far as literal taste: Ber-
tin's attraction for the second-rate intellectuals and artists at his table is
exclusively culinary. These people flatter Bertin's self-importance in return
for dinner, and Rameau describes Bertin's entourage as a "ménagerie," a
sad group of parasites of whom he is the leader: "un tas de pauvres
honteux, plats parasites desquels j'ai l'honneur d'être, brave chef d'une
troupe timide" (NdR 57) [a mob of shamefuls, of poor dull parasites at
whose head I have the honor to be, myself the brave leader of a timorous
band] (DRN 48). The work of these guests is to dissemble; they are

ravenous and out of sorts even though they appear to be merry, and their taste is manifest only literally at the dinner table:

Nous paraissons gais; mais au fond nous avons tous de l'humeur et grand appétit. Des loups ne sont pas plus affamés; des tigres ne sont pas plus cruels. (NdR 57)[25]

[We seem to be jolly, but actually we are all grumpy and fiercely hungry. Wolves are not more voracious nor tigers more cruel.] (DRN 48)

Diderot's emphasis on appetite reflects Rameau's theory of *mastication universelle*, as I said earlier, and the connection to figurative taste reflects the larger issues in the work.

Goethe was clearly alert to Diderot's association of literal and figurative taste. Not only does it resemble his own in *Götz*, but he also cites and translates the passage about *mastication universelle* from Mercier in an appendix to his translation and notes, "Nachträgliches zu 'Rameaus Neffe'":

er lebte in den Kaffees und führte alle Wunder der Tapferkeit, alle Wirkungen des Genies, alle Opfer des Heldentums, genug alles was nur Großes in der Welt geschehen mochte, auf ein kräftiges Kauen zurück. Ihn zu hören, hatte jenes alles keinen andern Zweck, keinen andern Erfolg als etwas unter die Zähne zu bringen. (RN 282)[26]

[he lived in coffee houses and attributed all miracles of bravery, all effects of genius, all sacrifices of heroism, in short all great things that have ever occurred across the universe, to a powerful chewing. To hear him, all such things had no other aim, no other outcome but to put something under a person's teeth.]

In his translation, Goethe underscores the connection at one point by changing the word *sot* ("fool") to *abgeschmackt* ("tasteless"), and he opens his note on taste by quoting Bertin's aborted dictum on taste:

Der Geschmack, sagt er . . . der Geschmack ist ein Ding . . . bei Gott, ich weiß nicht, zu was für einem Ding er den Geschmack machte, wußte er es doch selbst nicht. (RN 245)

Goethe then interprets the significance of this passage and illustrates it with another play on literal and figurative taste. He says that Diderot ridicules his countrymen for having the word taste constantly "on their lips" (the German phrase is "in their mouths") and for using the term indiscriminately to censure works of art:

> In dieser Stelle will Diderot seine Landsleute lächerlich darstellen, die, mit und ohne Begriff, das Wort Geschmack immer im Munde führen und manche bedeutende Produktion, indem sie ihr den Mangel an Geschmack vorwerfen, heruntersetzen. (RN 245)

> [In this passage, Diderot wants to ridicule those of his compatriots who, with or without any understanding of the term, have the word taste perpetually on their lips and deride significant works for their lack of taste.]

The note on "Taste" (which is not so much a note as a quieter version of "Zum Schäkespears-Tag") contains an attack on the equation of greatness with decorum. Goethe denounces the belief that taste, not genius, fosters creativity, and he differentiates between two kinds of figurative taste—one negative and the other positive. One is the inhibiting kind imposed on artists of genius by mediocre minds; the other is an innate sense of taste that every genius possesses: "Der Geschmack ist dem Genie angeboren" [Taste is innate to genius] (RN 248). The distinction is crucial, because it explains why Goethe himself continues to use figurative taste as a measure of artistic merit. What Goethe rejects is the division of texts according to their content and without an awareness of form or style. He further criticizes the French for transferring society's divisions to poetry and for judging a work of art on the basis of propriety ("Convenancen") and a "particular behavior" [ein besonderes Betragen] (RN 247). He holds the court of Louis XIV responsible for the false notion of taste, thereby merging literary and political categories in a revolutionary undercurrent familiar from the Romantic age.

Goethe expects us to extend what he says of the French to his own countrymen; what he attacks here is a mentality that in the voice of Frederick the Great condemned *Götz* and was later responsible for the suppression of four *Roman Elegies*.[27] Goethe does not deny the usefulness of genre or of decorum, but he uses the examples of Shakespeare and Calderón to show that one must judge works on their intrinsic merits, not by applying fixed rules. He insists that poets alone can judge whether divisions are appropriate: "nur der Künstler darf und kann die Scheidung unternehmen, die er auch unternimmt; denn er ist meist glücklich genug zu fühlen, was in diesen oder jenen Kreis gehört" [only the artist may and can make the division that he does then make; because he usually has felicity enough to sense what does or does not belong in this or that circle] (RN 248). The taste of those who do not create has a constraining effect that saps the strength from those who do:

Doch leider ist der Geschmack der nicht hervorbringenden Naturen verneinend, beengend, ausschließend und nimmt zuletzt der hervorbringenden Klasse Kraft und Leben. (RN 248)

[But alas, the taste of those who do not create is negative, confining, and exclusive; ultimately it depletes strength and vitality from those who do create.]

In the note on Palissot, Goethe again emphasizes that a genius must be free from prescriptions. He varies the image of sleeping and waking that he used in "Zum Schäkespears-Tag" and compares the genius to a sleepwalker who walks over mountain peaks without faltering. A mediocre person tumbles down ("herunterplumpt"), even a waking state:

Dem Genie ist nichts vorzuschreiben, es läuft glücklich wie ein Nachtwandler über die scharfen Gipfelrücken weg, von denen die wache Mittelmäßigkeit beim ersten Versuche herunterplumpt. (RN 258)

[One can't give instructions to a genius, who like a somnambulist walks serenely and without faltering over steep mountain peaks, whereas the mediocre, even in a waking state, tumble down on the first try.]

Goethe's translation of *Le Neveu de Rameau* and the notes that accompany it bear the same relation to each other as the dialogue between "Lui" and "Moi." Goethe's annotations (which make for good reading in their own right, as Schiller remarked) are a model of critical insight and a fitting tribute to *Le Neveu de Rameau*.[28] But when they are read together with the translation, they change our understanding of Goethe's cuts, which he claims to have made out of respect for the taste of his public. Goethe made a few changes and omissions, one of which appears at first glance to have been prompted by his own sense of decorum. In the annotations, however, he repudiates his emendations, which he blames on the intolerance of a conservative readership that lacks the competency to judge works of art: "Das Publikum, im ganzen genommen, ist nicht fähig, irgendein Talent zu beurteilen" (RN 275). He stresses the care with which Diderot composed his works, even when he was indecorous, and hopes that this "classical" work will soon be published in full and in the French original so that readers have access to the passages where he was not "permitted" to "follow" Diderot to the "peaks of his impertinence." The word *peaks* ("Gipfel") echoes the image of the genius who sleepwalks without faltering:

> das Werk ist so glücklich aus- und durchgedacht als erfunden. Ja selbst die äußersten Gipfel der Frechheit, wohin wir ihm nicht folgen durften, erreicht es mit zweckmäßigem Bewußtsein. Möge dem Besitzer des französischen Originals gefallen, dem Publikum auch dieses baldigst mitzuteilen; als das klassische Werk eines abgeschiedenen bedeutenden Mannes mag alsdann sein Ganzes in völliger unberührter Gestalt hervortreten. (RN 273)

> [the work is as felicitously thought out and completed as conceived. He reaches even the highest peaks of impudence—where we were not permitted to follow him—with a sureness of purpose. May it please the owner of the French original to share the text with the public as soon as possible; then it may appear whole and untouched, as the classical work of a departed and distinguished figure.]

But Goethe's rendition is more complete than he claims. His translation is not that much more proper than Diderot's original, and certainly not as different as his commentary suggests. The tension he implies between his conviction and his practice is a fiction and a ruse that allows him to make fun of and to subvert the constraints of negative good taste. His fiction reflects the satirical method of *Le Neveu de Rameau* and allows him to express aesthetic convictions that "deconstruct" his pretense of decorum. By emphasizing his irritation at the need to suppress certain passages, Goethe toys with the expectations of his readers, who imagine an original more indecorous than it is. He does this on a small and on a large scale. On the small scale, he adopts the practice still current today of writing out the first and last letters of improper words; the practice is absurd, because the omission calls more rather than less attention to the offending word. On a larger scale, Goethe draws attention to a passage that he calls too indecent to translate. By committing the same improprieties as Diderot in most cases, but without comment, and drawing attention to an isolated example of impropriety in another, he plays with the reader's imagination; what he omits is actually no more likely to shock than what he leaves in. Goethe adopts the convention of deletion in order to undermine it.

Goethe leaves "Lui's" scatological comments unchanged and avoids some but not all of the sexual ones. Rameau's remarks about the importance of digestion and the chamber pot's function as the great equalizer are translated in full. They are accompanied, in Goethe's text as they are in Diderot's, by his praise of "precious dung," the exclamation "O stercus pretiosum!" which is not more decorous because it is in Latin. Goethe's translation is indistinguishable in tone from Diderot's original:

Le point important c'est	Der Hauptpunkt im Leben
d'aller aisément, librement,	ist doch nur frei, leicht, angenehm,
agréablement, copieusement	häufig alle Abende auf den
tous les soirs à la garderobe:	Nachtstuhl zu gehen.
O stercus pretiosum! Voilà	O stercus pretiosum! das ist
le grand résultat de la vie dans	das große Resultat des Lebens
tous les états. (NdR 25)	in allen Ständen. (RN 34)[29]

Or again, in the central scene of the dialogue, the passage in which "Lui" finally tells why and how he was banned from the house of his benefactors, Goethe retains the scatological Italian wordplay with which Rameau insults the abbé (who responds by laughing at it) and Bertin (who responds by throwing him out). Rameau tells the abbé, a newcomer in the parasitical household, that at every meal he will move down one seat at table until he comes to rest next to Rameau himself, a rascal (Barzun translates "a poor bugger") just like him: "bis Ihr endlich stationär werdet neben mir armem plattem Schuft Euresgleichen, *che siedo sempre come un maestoso c[azzo] fra duoi c[oglion]i*" [who sit like a majestic cock between two testicles, where the words *cazzo* and *coglioni* also mean fool] (RN 90). Goethe leaves out all but the first and last letters of the offend-

ing words, but surely this passage represents the "Gipfel der Frechheit"—
the "apex of impertinence"—both linguistically and structurally, thus dis-
proving Goethe's pretended claim that he was not "permitted" to follow
Diderot that far.[30]

The first of two passages Goethe leaves out is a relatively harmless one
in which Rameau enumerates the immoral actions of Palissot, among
them the rumor that he has slept with the publisher David's wife. This
omission is remarkable only in contrast to the second one. It lacks the
structural importance of the breaches of decorum Goethe retains and
probably was deleted for a simple practical reason: that Palissot was still
alive, as Goethe mentions in his letter to Schiller of 21 December 1804.
Furthermore, Goethe probably felt an obligation to Palissot, whose liter-
ary history, *Mémoires pour servir à l'histoire de notre littérature depuis
François 1er jusqu'à nos jours,* was a major source for his notes, a fact
that Schlösser discovered with considerable amusement.[31] The second
passage that Goethe omits is a short but graphic description of the com-
motion caused in Bertin's house early one morning. Bertin cries out for
help, and the reason for his distress is described in detail: he is suffocating
under the considerable weight of his mistress, the mediocre actress Made-
moiselle Hus (whose name Rameau combines with that of Bertin to
compose a satirical mock-Latin form, Bertinhus). In the translation, the
passage is replaced by a sentence expressing Goethe's shock at Diderot's
impropriety; he calls Rameau's story "scandalous," "ridiculous," and
"scurrilous," and says that the slander here "reaches its peak" (a phrase
that Goethe has taught us to interpret):

Hier erzählt Rameau von seinen Wohltätern ein skandalöses Märchen,
das zugleich lächerlich und infamierend ist, und seine Mißreden er-
reichen ihren Gipfel. (RN 143)

[At this point Rameau relates a scandalous tale about his benefactors
that is both ridiculous and scurrilous, and his defamation reaches its
peak.]

The words *scandalös* and *infamierend* must be read exactly as we are told
to interpret Rameau's applause for the dramatic performances of Made-
moiselle Hus: "à contresens," as the opposite. Rameau claps as a conces-

sion to his patrons, not out of conviction, and his applause demonstrates his theory of *mastication universelle*. But he wants to make sure that his true feelings are clear, and he accompanies his solitary clapping with a few ironic words: "Ma ressource était de jeter quelques mots ironiques qui sauvassent du ridicule mon applaudissement solitaire, qu'on interprétait à contresens" (NdR 66–67) [All I could do to avoid the ridicule incurred by my isolated applause was to throw in a few ironic words which gave it a contrary interpretation.] (DRN 55). In similar fashion, Goethe suppresses the passage as a concession to figurative taste; but he lets us know his true feelings by using the word *Gipfel*, the word he associated with genius in the note on taste. Perhaps Goethe also wanted to imply that he would never defame his own benefactors in this way. Or perhaps there is a linguistic reason for not rendering this passage, which contains an obscene wordplay on "parties casuelles." The phrase refers both to Bertin's function as "Trésorier des Parties Casuelles" and to the lower part of his body, and the ambiguity has no equivalent in German. More important than the omission, however, is that Goethe draws attention to it, both here and in the notes. He makes his readers think that he respects their sense of decorum, but instead he tricks them into imagining an original more indecorous than it really is.

A principal attraction of *Le Neveu de Rameau* for Goethe, as I have said, was its form. In the note entitled "Rameaus Neffe," Goethe corrects the popular misconception that Diderot could not give structure to his ideas; he argues instead that Diderot combines heterogeneous elements taken from reality into an "ideal whole": "gegenwärtige Schrift gibt ein Zeugnis, wie glücklich er die heterogensten Elemente der Wirklichkeit in ein ideales Ganze zu vereinigen wußte" (RN 272). Diderot's aesthetic principle of structuring by contrast and of binding what seems to be heterogeneous is characteristic of Romanticism; that he consistently thwarted the expectations and offended the taste of his contemporaries helps to explain why he did not publish *Le Neveu de Rameau* during his lifetime and why it was so well received by the authors of a later generation. Goethe's annotations reflect something of Diderot's method; despite the apparent arbitrariness of their alphabetical sequence, they reveal a form resembling that of the work they explicate. Goethe's translation is remarkably faithful, and his changes have more to do with subversion than decorum.

Taste and *Das Tagebuch*

For Goethe, who completed *Die Wahlverwandtschaften* in 1809, the therapy of translating worked, if not instantly. Traces of the strength and inspiration that came from assuming Diderot's voice are especially evident in *Das Tagebuch* (1810), which Vaget has associated with the *Schaffenskrise* of 1805, the same year as the translation of *Le Neveu de Rameau*. To support his claim, Vaget cites the dearth of entries in Goethe's journal.[32] The act of translating great works resembles the regular activity of keeping a journal. Neither is in itself a particularly creative act, but both help cure the creative impotence that, according to Vaget's reading, is represented in *Das Tagebuch* as sexual impotence. Diderot's dialogue and Goethe's poem, both of which address questions of creativity (and neither of which was published during its author's lifetime), defy literary decorum and invent a style that poeticizes taboos. In *Das Tagebuch* as in *Le Neveu de Rameau,* heresy becomes the norm without becoming predictable.

Das Tagebuch is a narrative poem of twenty-four stanzas, written in the ottava rima stanza that Byron later chose for *Don Juan*. The narrator is a traveler on a business trip, a projection of the poet whom one envisions as an elder Wilhelm Meister; he is on his way home after a lengthy absence, eager to return to his wife, when his carriage breaks down. Because it is late at night, he must stop at an inn. The young woman who greats him there is as much a beacon as the lamp she holds, and while he waits for dinner in his room—and while everyone else is sleeping—he settles down to write letters and then to record the details of the day in his diary. The diary substitutes for his wife's presence while he is away from her, and he keeps it for their mutual pleasure when they are together again (the equation of loving and writing is made already at this stage). But on this particular night, the diary gives him trouble. He finds himself unable to formulate with his usual facility and precision, and he is distracted both by the nearly tangible presence of his wife, whom he had thought to rejoin that night, and by the real presence of the young woman, who has brought his supper and begun to serve him. Just as she is carving the chicken, and in a moment of burlesque that Goethe renders admirably in the final couplet of the sixth octave, he jumps up and grabs her with such eagerness and haste that he knocks over a chair. She gently rebukes him, but says that she will be back later when her guardian (naturally an "old dragon") is asleep. She comes to him as promised and explains that despite appearances he is her first lover, but that she was attracted to him instantly: "Ich sah, ich liebte, schwur dich zu genießen." Her confession flusters him, however, and he feels more like a novice than she. For what he insists is the first time in his life, he is impotent. She falls asleep, and he broods; he remembers the first time he made love to his wife, and he remembers his erection on their wedding day as they stood at the altar in front of a crucifix. His memories rekindle his ardor, and he begins to awaken the girl but thinks better of it, recalling the source of his potency. Instead, he gets up and writes in his journal, now without effort, and the stanza that reproduces what he has written, the twenty-second, has the sound of a love poem. We see from this octave why the traveler calls the journal an act of love and of pleasure; in it we witness the connection between loving and writing.

Aside from illustrating the connection between loving and writing, the twenty-second stanza contains a line in which Goethe condenses another major idea of the poem, the notion that health is proven or tested by illness (the emphasis is his): "*Die Krankheit erst bewähret den Gesunden.*" In *Le Neveu de Rameau*, "Lui" expresses a related thought when he says that there would be nothing excellent if everything were excellent: "Si tout ici bas était excellent, il n'y aurait rien d'excellent" (NdR 14). Goethe introduces the idea in the epigrammatic final couplet of the first octave, where he says that virtue is strengthened through its battle with temptation:

> Denn zeigt sich auch ein Dämon, uns versuchend,
> So waltet was, gerettet ist die Tugend.
>
> (GT 1)

> [Why fret? For when by some wild imp we're tempted
> Another force prevails, and sin's preempted.]
>
> (GD 101)

Goethe illustrates the principle throughout the poem by confronting institutions with something that calls them into question. The institution of marriage is confronted with adultery, for example, and the institution of religion is confronted with blasphemy. Most important of all, poetic institutions—what Vaget calls the "established canon of poetic forms" and what one could also designate simply as taste—are confronted with indecorous subjects. In each case the institution reaffirms its strength, its

261

"health" (which is why Goethe's aesthetic resembles Hugo's more than that of Byron or Heine), but the reaffirmation likewise entails a liberation: the bonds of marriage are strengthened for the traveler by what Vaget calls the "redefinition of marriage in which Eros is viewed as a moral force"; exclusive spirituality, represented by a crucified Christ, is displaced by the fusion of sensuality and spirituality, embodied by the God Priapus; and the laws of so-called good taste, mechanically upheld by an ignorant public, are replaced by the poet's intrinsic sense of taste, which for Goethe, as we have seen, is innate to genius.

In *Das Tagebuch,* given the association between creative and sexual impotence, Goethe demands the license to speak of erotic subjects. But something more is at stake. At issue is the poet's liberty to write about any subject in any chosen form—the liberty to exercise the taste innate to genius. That for Goethe erotic poetry exemplifies larger poetical issues is suggested by several factors. For one thing, there is the choice of the ottava rima stanza, a form that Goethe uses for profound poetic and philosophical concerns (see GT 46–47 and GD 20–21). For another, there is Goethe's testimony in the conversation with Eckermann of 25 February 1824 about the *Tagebuch,* the *Roman Elegies,* and Byron's *Don Juan.* Goethe speaks about poetic freedom in general, not just about the freedom to depict erotic subjects, and what he calls hindrances to that freedom can be designated as the two forms of figurative taste, both of them negative: the demands of a prudish readership and the tyrannical dictates of fashion. He says that poets could be more direct if they could count on the intellectual qualities and the education of their readership; as it is, however, he must be cautious and consider the "mixed world" that receives his works:

"[Der Dichter] hat zu bedenken, daß seine Werke in die Hände einer gemischten Welt kommen, und er hat daher Ursache, sich in acht zu nehmen, daß er der Mehrzahl guter Menschen durch eine zu große Offenheit kein Ärgernis gebe." (EGG I:81)

["(The poet) must remember that his works will fall into the hands of a mixed society, and must therefore take care lest by over-great openness he may give offense to the majority of good men."] (GCE 34)

Furthermore, time—which here is a synonym for taste—is tyrannical, strange, and moody:

"Und dann ist die Zeit ein wunderlich Ding. Sie ist ein Tyrann, der seine Launen hat und der zu dem, was einer sagt und tut, in jedem Jahrhundert ein ander Gesicht macht." (EGG I: 81–82)

["Then, Time is a whimsical tyrant, which in every century has a different face for all that one says and does." (GCE 34)]

In this conversation, Goethe restates one of the themes from *Götz* and *Rameaus Neffe*—the theme that a poet's creativity is restricted by the dictates of negative taste. In the imagery of *Das Tagebuch*, they can render the poet impotent.

Once one has noticed the connection between the concerns of this poem and the note on "Geschmack," the introduction of gustatory details in the fifth and sixth stanzas of *Das Tagebuch* appears in the light of a code. In particular, the connection helps to explain a curious line in the sixth stanza, "Und was das tolle Zeug in uns befiedert." These are the stanzas in which Goethe introduces the connection between writing (or of not being able to write) and loving, and he does so with an irony evident in rhyme (*fasse/lasse*) and gesture (his knocking over of a chair).[33] Writing, loving, and irony are all related to Goethe's ambiguous understanding of figurative taste, and the reference to literal taste binds the three by demonstrating how the stifling of negative taste can be undone and replaced by creative taste:

> Nun setzt ich mich zu meiner Tasch und Briefen
> Und meines Tagebuchs Genauigkeiten,
> Um so wie sonst, wenn alle Menschen schliefen,
> Mir und der Trauten Freude zu bereiten;
> Doch weiß ich nicht, die Tintenworte liefen
> Nicht so wie sonst in alle Kleinigkeiten:
> Das Mädchen kam, des Abendessens Bürde
> Verteilte sie gewandt mit Gruß und Würde.
>
> Sie geht und kommt; ich spreche, sie erwidert.
> Mit jedem Wort erscheint sie mir geschmückter.
> Und wie sie leicht mir nun das Huhn zergliedert,
> Bewegend Hand und Arm, geschickt, geschickter—
> Was auch das tolle Zeug in uns befiedert,
> Genug, ich bin verworrner, bin verrückter,

263

Den Stuhl umwerfend spring ich auf und fasse
Das schöne Kind; sie lispelt: Lasse, lasse!

(GT 36–37)

[So I sat down to my portfolio,
My letters, and my diary's exact
Reports: nocturnal words, which I would show
As always to my dearest. Yet they lacked
Somehow tonight their usual easy flow;
The ink ran sluggish round each trifling fact.
The girl brought up my supper, greeted me
And laid it out with skill and dignity.

She comes and goes, and as we talk I'm stricken
With growing admiration for her charm.
I watch how cleverly she carves my chicken
With quick, deft movements of her hand and arm:
How my mad feathers sprout, my pulses quicken!
In short, my head's confused, my heart is warm,
And up I jump, knock the chair over, seize
The pretty creature—but she whispers: "Please."]

(GD 103–5)

Goethe's introduction of the young woman together with "des Abend-essens Bürde" is a detail, a banal one. One could pass it off, along with the other details about the traveler's journey and his arrival at the inn, as a conventional element of travel literature, augmented here by the nearly axiomatic association of food and eros. But since it is not conventional to write travel literature or to write about food in ottava rima, and since there is a self-consciousness in this passage that allows the persona to ironize his actions, such explanations are unsatisfactory. The placement of the two lines is important, since the final couplet of the ottava rima stanza is traditionally reserved for emphasis. Goethe must have a reason for putting this couplet, introduced by a colon, at the end of a stanza in which we are told that insignificant details ("Kleinigkeiten") are impor-tant to the traveler's writing and that he is frustrated when the Kleinigkeiten do not come to mind. In a real sense Kleinigkeiten may be banal, but in writing that status changes. In writing, no detail is unimpor-tant, and by extension, no subject is too low to be worthy of depiction.

264

As Goethe says in the conversation with Eckermann quoted earlier, no subject can be said to be unpoetic if it is properly treated by the poet: "im Grunde bleibt *kein* realer Gegenstand unpoetisch, sobald der Dichter ihn gehörig zu gebrauchen weiß" (EGG 1:236) [at bottom *no* real object is unpoetical if the poet knows how to use it properly] (GCE 171).

In the sixth stanza, the traveler's writing is forgotten in favor of small talk with the young woman who is carving the chicken for his supper. The persona's desire, which is expressed with exaggeration and self-irony when he overturns his chair, likewise makes him forget his earlier frustration. Vaget comments that it is the girl's dexterity that first arouses the traveler, a dexterity that underscores unforced sensuality in the scene. He also reads the line "Was auch das tolle Zeug in uns befiedert" (which he calls "a strange line") in this light. This is surely true, but I believe that there is something else besides. If eros in this poem is symbolic of creativity, and if eros is identified with the references to food, then there must also be a connection between food and creativity. The progression is not merely syllogistic; it derives from the inner logic of the poem and from the resemblance of culinary details in *Das Tagebuch* to their function in the rest of Goethe's works. The connection between eros and food and of both to writing is confirmed in the line "Was auch das tolle Zeug in uns befiedert." Vaget defines the word "befiedert" as "beschleunigen, in Bewegung bringen" and interprets it as a euphemism for sensuality and libido, a connection that is confirmed when we recall Goethe's use of the same word in the third of the *Roman Elegies,* where he applies it to the feathers on Cupid's arrows. But the word also has a connection to the chicken the young woman is carving, a connection retained by David Luke, who translates the line as "How my mad feathers sprout." Along with the meaning of "to bring into motion" that Vaget suggests, the word can be understood as "to inspire." In a literal and grammatical sense, the phrase "das tolle Zeug" [the crazy stuff] refers to the young woman and her chicken, which "inspire" the traveler's desires; why the carved chicken inspires him as well as the girl—and why the two together are called "das tolle Zeug"—seems either incomprehensible or silly until we understand how literal taste is connected both to eros and to poetry. Food can "inspire" as well as eros can, not only by displacement, as in some examples from *Tom Jones,* but also in the sense that any subject, the trivial and the taboo as well as the elevated, can be a source of poetry. Read in this manner, the graphic depiction of the woman laden with supper and dexterously cutting chicken contains a playful allusion to figurative taste—to the fact that the subject of food is excluded by what for Goethe is negative taste, but that it can inspire the innate taste of a poetic genius.

For Goethe, as we have seen, figurative taste is itself ambiguous, and at this point in the poem, when the traveler is unable to write out "alle Kleinigkeiten," figurative taste appears to designate the external kind of taste that inhibits creativity, the kind that leads to impotence as it is represented a few stanzas later in the poem. Later on, however, the meaning shifts. In the twentieth stanza, at precisely the same distance from the end of the poem that the stanzas about food stand from the beginning, the persona regains his potency. What actually restores his sexual potency and, a few stanzas later, his ability to write, is the blasphemy in the infamous seventeenth octave. It is both an affront to the empty decorum of inhibiting taste and an affirmation of the poet's innate taste. In retrospect we realize that the poet was not in danger of losing his creative or sensual powers; the indecorous attention to details ("alle Kleinigkeiten"), represented early on in the allusions to literal taste, is a signal that a crisis must be overcome before it can be depicted, as Vaget says. By writing about literal taste, which as I have been arguing is the emblematic taboo, Goethe writes against the negative, inhibiting kind of figurative taste.

Goethe and Hugo through Heine's Eyes: "Ein antithetischer Leckerbissen"

One would expect to find more of a kinship between Heine and Hugo than between Hugo and Goethe. Heine's aesthetics of contrast would seem to put him into the company of Hugo, whose collection of poems "Les Rayons et les Ombres" is commonly said to exemplify his poetics. But the affinity holds only in part, since Hugo's contrasts, rather than clashing, either complement each other or are resolved. Hugo insists on an ultimate harmony of what he calls the sublime and the grotesque, which puts him closer to Goethe than to Heine (though a *lack* of resolution puts Goethe and Heine closer to each other). Hans Robert Jauss touches on the difference between Heine and Hugo in his essay "Das Ende der Kunstperiode—Aspekte der literarischen Revolution bei Heine, Hugo und Stendhal," but he skirts the connection between Hugo and Goethe.[34] Jauss's initial emphasis on the links between Hugo and Heine subsequently makes him uneasy, as it must, because of Hugo's inability to free himself entirely from the rules of French *classicisme* and because of Hugo's Christian philosophy, according to which opposites are harmonized:

> Aber wo für Hugo die Antithese des Idealen und des "Positiven" auf die christlich verbürgte Harmonie der ganzen Schöpfung verweist, bleiben das Pathetische und das "Komische" für Heine am Ende widerspenstig nebeneinander bestehen.

> [But whereas for Hugo the antithesis between the ideal and the "positive" reflects a Christian belief in the harmony of the entire universe, for Heine pathos and the "comic" ultimately remain stubbornly simultaneous.]

A sense of cosmic harmony is what ultimately brings Hugo closer to Goethe than to Heine, but the issue is not so much one of separating Heine and Hugo as of bringing Goethe into the circle of literary revolution.

The affinities and differences among Heine, Hugo, and Goethe begin to make sense when we consider literary revolution from a perspective that is wide enough to include Goethe. Jauss does not do so, because for him, as his title indicates, *Kunstperiode* is at odds with the "literary revolution" of Heine, Hugo, and Stendhal. *Kunstperiode* is Heine's designation (via Hegel) for a period dominated by Goethe's aesthetic, and it is meant to contrast with a later period in which literature is touched by political engagement. But one should not forget that Heine stresses the distance of his works from Goethe's in order to distract from his affinity to Goethe, and that he suffers in part from an "anxiety of influence."[35] Furthermore, the opposition between *Kunstperiode* and literary revolution that Jauss makes in his title posits an identity or at least a causality between literary revolution and politics; used in opposition to *Kunstperiode,* the phrase *literary revolution* seems to have lost its metaphorical dimension and to have a direct relation to politics. The opposition is flawed from both sides: with respect to Goethe, the aestheticism attributed to the *Kunstperiode* is a falsification, and with respect to literary revolution, the emphasis belongs on the word *literary.*

Heine draws attention to the affinity between Hugo and Goethe, partly in order to put the same distance between himself and Hugo that he puts between himself and Goethe. In *Über die französische Bühne* (1837), Heine praises Hugo for his "Sinn für das Plastische" [sense of plastic form], exactly the quality he attributed to Goethe and Romantic aesthetics twenty years earlier in the short piece "Die Romantik" (1820):

> Dazu kommt eine flache Kritik, welche das Beste, was wir an ihm loben müssen, sein Talent der sinnlichen Gestaltung, für einen Fehler erklärt, und sie sagen: es mangle seinen Schöpfungen die innerliche Poesie, *la poésie intime,* Umriß und Farbe seien ihm die Hauptsache, er gebe äußerlich faßbare Poesie, er sei materiell, kurz sie tadeln an ihm eben die löblichste Eigenschaft, seinen Sinn für das Plastische. (DHA 12:1.259)

> [In addition, there is a false criticism which declares his finest and most laudable characteristic, his talent for the artistic portrayal of what is perceptible to the senses, to be a defect, and they say that his creations lack heartfelt poetry, *la poësie intime;* that outline and color are for him the main thing; that he provides literature that is easy to understand because of external qualities; that he is inclined toward the material; in short, they criticize in him the very most commendable quality, his feeling for vividness.] (SW 110)

There is a note of self-commentary in this passage, one that becomes more pronounced when Heine defends Hugo against the charge that he is an "egoist" who lacks ideals—the charge that he is not "politically correct." He mounts a similar defense of Goethe earlier in *Die romantische Schule* (DHA 8:1.148–64, especially 151–52), but in *Über die französische Bühne* Heine speaks not merely in defense of Hugo and Goethe, but for himself as well:

> ich bin für die Autonomie der Kunst; weder der Religion, noch der Politik soll sie als Magd dienen, sie ist sich selber letzter Zweck, wie die Welt selbst. (DHA 12:1.259)

> [I am in favor of the autonomy of art. It should serve neither religion nor politics as maid servant; like the world itself, it is its own ultimate purpose.] (SW 109–10)

This does not mean that there is no political content to poetry; it means that the poet does not equate political content with a political program. From passages like these it is clear that an opposition between "Kunstperiode" and "literary revolution" is facile and untenable.

Partly because of Hugo's personality, partly because of his politics, partly because of certain antipathies of long standing toward French poetry, and partly in order to safeguard his own originality, Heine did not continue to profess admiration for Hugo. What in *Über die französische Bühne* was judged favorably later forms the basis for Heine's attacks. His defense of Hugo's "egoism" becomes the source of a derisive pun on Hugo's name, for example: "er ist ein Egoist, und damit ich noch Schlimmeres sage, er ist ein Hugoist" [he is an egoist, and to make it even worse, he is a Hugoist] (DHA 13:1.44).[36] In *Über die französische Bühne*, embedded in his praise of Hugo, Heine had humorously depicted Hugo's muse as a "clumsy" one with German and English traits and "two left hands." But the satirical note was softened by the context, which included references to Goethe and Shakespeare. Later on, however, the tolerance for Hugo's "geschmacklose Auswüchse" [tasteless deformities] becomes an almost obsessive insistence on Hugo's "deformity" and his "lack of taste."

Heine's shift is less sudden than it seems. Already in the last chapter of *Die romantische Schule,* Heine had begun to formulate his attack on Hugo by emphasizing the question of taste. In book 3, chapter 6, Heine criticizes the French craze for medieval themes and contrasts it with the related fad among German Romantics. We know from the manuscript that Heine originally planned to cite Hugo's *Notre Dame de Paris* (1831) as exemplary of the trend. But he omitted a direct reference to Hugo and replaced it instead with an allusive wordplay on Hugo's name that easily can be overlooked.[37] Heine inverts the syllables of Hugo's name, pronounced in the German way, and speaks of a "gothischer Haut-gout." The word *Haut-gout* is the German designation for a gamey smell, which repeats Heine's olfactory image at the beginning of the chapter in connection with the excavation of Charlemagne's grave and the popular *Deutsche Legende* of the brothers Grimm. In other words, the current "taste" for medieval themes is one that "smells" or has an *Haut-gout,* and Hugo is most at fault. The decision not to name Hugo specifically is in keeping with Heine's tendency, when he speaks of Hugo, to extend his

criticism to French literature generally; besides, the specificity of ad homi-
nem polemic would be out of place in a concluding chapter.

Even when Heine turns against Hugo, he makes an association to
Goethe, but less with respect to substance than technique. In the
"Spätere Notiz" to article 5 of *Lutezia*, Heine composes his caricature
of Hugo by equating his physical appearance with his literary style. In *Die
Romantische Schule*, Heine depicted Goethe in the same way:

> [Goethes] äußere Erscheinung war eben so bedeutsam wie das Wort,
> das in seinen Schriften lebte; auch seine Gestalt war harmonisch, klar,
> freudig, edel gemessen, und man konnte griechische Kunst an ihm
> studieren wie an einer Antique. (DHA 8:12.162)

> [(Goethe's) outward appearance was just as distinctive as the words
> that lived in his writings; even his figure was harmonious, clear, joyous,
> nobly proportioned, and you could study Greek art in him just as in
> a classical statue.] (SW 179)

Goethe's "Greek" body and style is opposed to "Christian" categories
like "worm-humility" [Wurmdemut]. Goethe's eyes, for example, are as
steady as those of a Greek god, not "sinningly shy" and "shifting" like
those of a Christian:

> Dieser würdevolle Leib war nie gekrümmt von christlicher Wurmde-
> mut, die Züge dieses Antlitzes waren nicht verzerrt von christlicher
> Zerknirschung, diese Augen waren nicht christlich sünderhaft scheu,
> nicht andächtelnd und himmelnd, nicht flimmernd bewegt:—nein,
> seine Augen waren ruhig wie die eines Gottes. (DHA 8:1.162)

> [This majestic form was never contorted by groveling Christian humil-
> ity; the features of this countenance were not disfigured by Christian
> contrition; these eyes were not downcast with a Christian sense of sin,
> not over-pious and canting, not swimming with emotion:—no, his
> eyes were as calm as a god's.] (SW 179)

Part of Heine's technique consists of matching his own style to his sub-
ject. The present participles are meant to recall the Voss translation of
Homer as well as Heine's echoes of that translation in some of his own

Nordsee poems ("nicht andächtelnd und himmelnd, nicht flimmernd bewegt"). Heine's caricature of Hugo follows the same pattern. He attributes to Hugo the deformity of one of his characters, Quasimodo, and equates the physical deformity with an aesthetic one; Heine's own puns and grotesque images here—often culinary, because of the emphasis on taste—are chosen to mirror his subject.

The recurring motif in Heine's Hugo criticism is the phrase "bad taste." The half-affectionate reference to Hugo's "geschmacklose Auswüchse" in *Über die französische Bühne* evolves into the malicious theory that Hugo's originality consists entirely of poor taste. Since good taste is the predominant characteristic of French authors—so the theory goes—Hugo's lack of it sets him apart from other French authors:

Sonderbar! Die Eigenschaft, die ihm so viel fehlt, ist eben diejenige, die bei den Franzosen am meisten gilt, und zu ihren schönsten Eigentümlichkeiten gehört. Es ist dieses der Geschmack. Da sie den Geschmack bei allen französischen Schriftstellern antrafen, mochte der gänzliche Mangel desselben bei Victor Hugo ihnen vielleicht eben als eine Originalität erscheinen. (DHA 13:1.44)

[Strange! The quality he so lacks is the very quality the French value most and that is one of their handsomest traits. It is taste. Since they find taste in the works of all French authors, perhaps it is the total lack of it that strikes them as original in Victor Hugo.]

Heine's criticism extends beyond Hugo, as was the case at the end of *Die romantische Schule*. He implies that French literature is uniformly dull because of the neoclassical dominance of taste, but he insists that an absence of taste does not guarantee good literature. Heine's principal criticism of Hugo is that his lack of taste is insincere, that it is motivated by the urge to be different rather than aesthetic conviction. Heine criticizes Hugo for being unnatural, for lacking honesty and coherence, and he twice uses a form of the word *lügen* (to lie)—"verlogen" and "belügen"—to characterize Hugo's writing: "Was wir bei ihm am unleidlichsten vermissen, ist das, was wir Deutsche Natur nennen: er ist gemacht, verlogen, und oft im selben Verse sucht die eine Hälfte die andre zu belügen" [What we find most deplorably absent from his works is what we Germans call nature: he is contrived, insincere, and often, within the same line, one half belies the other] (DHA 13:1.44). Goethe makes essentially the same argument when he speaks to Eckermann about the poetic revolution of the French Romantics.

The bad taste Heine has in mind when he criticizes Hugo is a variant of ambiguous taste, since its motive is the negation of neoclassical taste. This is particularly clear in article 55 of *Lutezia,* where Heine dismisses the play *Les Burgraves* as an "Abhub unserer romantischen Küche, versifiziertes Sauerkraut" [the scum of our Romantic cookery, versified sauerkraut] (DHA 14:1.44) and compares what he calls Hugo's false and contradictory tone to roasted ice cream, an "antithetical delicacy" served by the Chinese:

> Diese kalte Passion, die uns in so flammenden Redensarten aufgetischt wird, erinnert mich immer an das gebratene Eis, das die Chinesen so künstlich zu bereiten wissen, indem sie kleine Stückchen Gefrorenes, eingewickelt in einen dünnen Teig, einige Minuten übers Feuer halten: ein antithetischer Leckerbissen, den man schnell verschlucken muß, und wobei man Lippe und Zunge an der heißen Rinde verbrennt, den Magen aber erkältet. (DHA 14:1.45)

> [This cold passion, which is served up to us in flaming phrases, always reminds me of the roasted ice cream that the Chinese know how to prepare so artfully by holding over the flame tiny pieces of ice cream wrapped in a thin pastry: an antithetical delicacy that one must swallow quickly and that burns the lips and the tongue while chilling the stomach.]

Such culinary examples must be read with a consciousness of the neoclassical taste or French *classicisme* that the Romantics rejected. For Hugo as for Heine, culinary referents are the paradigmatic taboo, as we have seen; they exemplify what Heine calls Hugo's "bad taste" and are used to replace the restrictive good taste of neoclassicism.[38] But something else is also at work here: as he does in the case of Goethe, Heine tries to distract from his own similarities to Hugo, specifically from the fact that the motive for Hugo's "bad taste" is much the same as his own. Heine chooses culinary images here that are literally not to his taste so that he can demonstrate his own lack of taste for Hugo and for French *classicisme,* but he also includes a note of self-parody in his culinary polemics, evident for instance in the reference to "our Romantic cookery."

Hugo's Poetics and Don César's Pâté in *Ruy Blas*

Heine's criticism of Hugo in *Lutezia* could serve as a critique, albeit exaggerated, of *Ruy Blas,* which he seems to have seen either in rehearsal or in performance.[39] The phrase "antithetical tidbit" [antithetisches Leckerbissen] in article 55 of *Lutezia* admirably characterizes the work, not least because of the role Hugo assigns to ambiguous taste in the play. In *Ruy Blas* there is the same parallel between aesthetic and thematic questions that was evident in *Götz:* Hugo uses gustatory allusions as an aesthetic shock that underscores the shock of his main theme, the love between a queen and a lackey. The queen's love for Ruy Blas, a man of the people, is mirrored aesthetically by the revolutionary implications of eating in a tragedy (Hugo insists polemically on the term *drame,* but like *Götz* this is a serious play with a tragic end). In *Ruy Blas,* Hugo presents a Romantic hero, one who combines poetry and politics, and a Romantic aesthetic, one that combines the sublime and the ridiculous.

Ruy Blas is a young man whose nobility comes from his talents, not from his birth; he is a "génie," a dreamer and lover who is also a brilliant prime minister. Hunger has forced him to give up his poetical and political ambitions and to become the lackey of Don Salluste, who is the devil incarnate (in Hugo's aesthetic theory a manifestation of the "grotesque"); when the play opens, Don Salluste has just been exiled by the queen for refusing to marry a servant of hers, whom he has seduced and who has borne his child. Don Salluste's revenge will be to set things up so that the queen falls in love with his own servant, Ruy Blas; he will then expose and disgrace her. In the course of the first act Don Salluste lays his plan, which is based on a Faustian bargain with his dissolute cousin Don César, a highbrow bandit who composes verses while his gang carries out robberies of his invention. Don César is a Byronic figure who lacks melancholy (just as Don Salluste is a Goethean Mephistopholes who lacks charm and wit), and like Don Salluste he is another manifestation of the "grotesque." Four years earlier Don César was the companion of Ruy Blas, who knew him only as Zafari, and the two were so much alike that people took them for brothers. Don Salluste's plan takes shape quickly, because he has noticed the similarity between Ruy Blas and Don César and has overheard Ruy Blas confess to Don César that he is in love with the queen. Within six months (and by act 3), Ruy Blas has risen to prime minister and declared his love to the queen, who loves him in return. But Don Salluste does not get his revenge. Ruy Blas kills him just before he can expose the queen; and before Ruy Blas dies of poison, the queen calls him by his real name and tells him that she loves him. Hugo upsets the categories of society and of drama by giving aristocratic manners to a man in livery and the "soul of a servant" to a nobleman; in the penultimate scene of the play, after Ruy Blas's true identity has been revealed to the queen and he has proudly acknowledged it, he says to Don Salluste, "J'ai l'habit d'un laquais, et vous en avez l'âme!" [I have the clothes of a lackey, and you have the soul of one] (RB 2154).

Ten years before *Ruy Blas,* Hugo used literal taste as the representative taboo in the "Préface de *Cromwell*" of 1827, a literary manifesto that bears the same relation to *Ruy Blas* as "Zum Schäkespears-Tag" to *Götz.* The "Préface de *Cromwell,*" which has outlived the play to which is was originally attached, documents the struggle of the Romantic age wittily and with erudition. Hugo refers specifically to the rules of classical French theater, which he considers representative of all aesthetic restrictions and which come under the heading of "good taste." Goethe's attempt to rouse those who slumber in the "Elysium of good taste" has its counterpart in Hugo's contemptuous dismissal of "old false taste" near the end of his preface: "Mais ce qu'il faut détruire avant tout, c'est le vieux faux goût" [But what we must destroy above all is the old, false taste]. The remark follows Hugo's memorable analogy between an ancien régime in literature and one in politics, both of which must be deposed. Like Goethe, however, Hugo distinguishes between the taste imposed by narrow-minded critics and the taste native to genius; he concludes the "Préface de *Cromwell*" with an aphoristic sentence that reiterates the distinction: "Le goût, c'est la raison du génie" [Taste is the reason of genius] (HC 451). Like Goethe some sixty years earlier, Hugo considers Shakespeare the embodiment of genius and natural taste.

Near the end of his preface, in what amounts to a peroration, Hugo uses a gustatory image to summarize his ideas about Romantic theater. The passage is typical in style as well as substance because of the rhetorical use of questions, anaphora, and asyndeton to challenge and convince. Hugo compares his theories of the "drame romantique" with the practice of classical drama. He begins with the image of pleasure in general and speaks of "jouissances," doubtless because of its erotic connotations; he then moves indirectly to the culinary by saying that the "pleasures" of the audience are "sliced" [tranchées] into tragic and comic, sublime and grotesque, whereas they should be "ground and mixed":

Que fait-on en effet maintenant? On divise les jouissances du spectateur en deux parts bien tranchées. On lui donne d'abord deux heures de plaisir sérieux, puis une heure de plaisir folâtre; avec l'heure d'entr'actes que nous ne comptons pas dans le plaisir, en tout quatre heures. Que ferait le drame romantique? Il broierait et mêlerait artistement ces deux espèces de plaisir. Il ferait passer à chaque instant l'auditoire du sérieux au rire, des excitations bouffonnes aux émotions déchirantes, du grave au doux, du plaisant au sévère. (HC 450)

[What is the present practice? The delights of spectators are sliced into two distinct parts. First they are given two hours of serious pleasure, then an hour of jolly pleasure; including the hour of intermissions that we do not count as a part of the pleasure, that makes four hours in all. What would Romantic drama do? It would grind and mix these two kinds of pleasure artistically. At every instant it would make the audience pass from something serious to laughter, from farcical excitement to wrenching emotion, from something grave to something gentle, from something agreeable to something severe.]

Hugo illustrates the different kinds of drama with gustatory images. "Romantic drama" is described as culinary and positive, whereas "classical drama" is negative and medicinal:

La scène romantique ferait un mets piquant, varié, savoureux, de ce qui sur le théâtre classique est une médecine divisée en deux pilules. (HC 450)

[The Romantic stage would concoct a spicy, varied, tasty dish from what on the classical stage is a medicine divided into two pills.]

The connection of literal and figurative taste is repeated a page later, where Hugo condemns the doctrine of good taste and its bad influence on literature of the eighteenth century; this is the passage in which he speaks of the need to destroy the "old false taste." Yet in the "Préface de *Cromwell*," as later in *Ruy Blas*, Hugo betrays a lingering respect for decorum in spite of his aggressive contempt for *classicisme*. He makes apologetic asides about the "triviality" of an image or the "vulgarity" of his diction, and he quickly follows a reference to wine with a request for the "permission" to mention yet another triviality of this kind: "Le vin, qu'on nous permette une trivialité de plus, cesse-t-il d'être du vin pour être dans une bouteille?" [Wine—if I may be allowed yet another triviality—does it cease being wine because it is in a bottle?] (HC 440). One could argue—as I did earlier in discussing Goethe's notes for *Rameaus Neffe*—that this sort of remark is meant ironically. But Hugo's practice in *Ruy Blas* leads me to believe instead that Hugo, in spite of the revolutionary diction of the "Préface de *Cromwell*," is restrained by a neoclassical tradition that is particularly evident in *Ruy Blas*. Hugo speaks of contrasts that are separate rather than simultaneous.

Ruy Blas exemplifies the coexistence yet separation of "sublime" and "grotesque," because the two are distributed according to act and hardly intermingle. Much of act 4 shows Don César at table. He comments on what he eats, and he even offers wine to an astonished servant. This act of the play was the most controversial, as one would expect; critics objected on moral, political, and aesthetic grounds, and Hugo was reproached for his "abuse of antitheses and its corollary, a taste for base and vulgar things."[40] Don César is not the only character who mentions food, however. So does Ruy Blas. But Ruy Blas differs as much from Don César in his gustatory references as he does in his behavior after acquiring the name of Don César. Ruy Blas opens his lengthy speech to the ministers in act 3 with the phrase "Bon appétit," which is doubly indecorous here because of the allusion to food and to money. The phrase is an ironic reference to the image of nobles "eating up" the treasury of Spain, and it shows how Ruy Blas, who as I have said is at times a projection of the poet, possesses a linguistic awareness that is calculated to demonstrate his poetic genius. To the audience, the image echoes that of the comte de Camporéal, who has just described the earlier Don César (whom he naturally assumes to be the man who is actually Ruy Blas) as a profligate capable of "eating up all of Peru in a year" (RB 1011). The image of "eating" money is also used by Don César in act 1 to describe his own profligacy. Eating, whether in a financial or real sense, is attached to Don César like a leitmotif, and from the start it is the sign of his indecorum. When he "introduces" himself by recounting his past, Don César connects his name with eating:

Je m'appelle César, comte de Garofa;
Mais le sort de folie en naissant me coiffa.

J'étais riche, j'avais des palais, des domaines,
Je pouvais largement renter les Célimènes.
Bah! mes vingt ans n'étaient pas encor révolus
Que j'avais mangé tout! il ne me restait plus
De mes prospérités, ou réelles, ou fausses,
Qu'un tas de créanciers hurlant après mes chausses.

(RB 143–50; my emphasis)

[My name is César, count of Garofa; but at birth, destiny bestowed me with folly. I was rich, I had palaces, domains, I could support many a Célimène. Bah! *I hadn't even reached the age of twenty when I had already eaten everything up!* The only thing that remained of my real or imagined prosperity were a heap of creditors on my tracks.]

In his speech to the ministers from act 3, however, Ruy Blas extends the gustatory image to the ministers themselves. He portrays them with a cannibalistic image that recalls Delacroix's *Raft of the Medusa* and its literary successor in canto 2 of *Don Juan:*

Tous voulant dévorer leur voisin éperdu,
Morsures d'affamés sur un vaisseau perdu!

(RB 1103–4)

[All of them wanting to devour their frantic neighbor, the bites of famished people on a lost vessel.]

Further on, Ruy Blas compares the ministers to vermin devouring a lion, the lion being his image for the Spanish people:

Ce grand peuple espagnol aux membres énervés,
Qui s'est couché dans l'ombre et sur qui vous vivez,
 Expire dans cet antre où son sort se termine,
Triste comme un lion mangé par la vermine.

(RB 1135–38)

[This great Spanish people with jittery limbs that has laid itself down in the shadow and off of which you live; it is expiring in the lair where its fate is coming to an end, sad like a lion eaten up by vermin.]

277

When Hugo has his characters use such imagery, he revives the dead metaphor of good taste and actively rejects the neoclassical injunction to suppress references to the body. But if we look more closely, we find that he has merely transposed the requirements of a neoclassicist aesthetic. Even though Ruy Blas chooses an audacious vehicle for his metaphor, he remains metaphorical; his manner of speaking thus remains in harmony with his status as a "sublime" character. In act 1, Ruy Blas speaks not of food but of hunger, which he loathes because he considers it responsible for his loss of liberty; he explicitly identifies hunger with liberty, which in poetical terms is the liberty to speak about food or any subject. When he speaks of "picking up bread where he found it on the street," Ruy Blas speaks figuratively, bread having become identified with the necessity of choosing servitude over starvation.

> Si bien qu'un jour, mourant de faim sur le pavé,
> J'ai ramassé du pain, frère, où j'en ai trouvé:
> Dans la fainéantise et dans l'ignominie.
>
> (RB 311–13)

> [So that one day, dying of hunger on the street, brother, I picked up some bread where I found it: in sloth and ignominy.]

His ideals have been sacrificed to material need, and he associates food with the opulence and corruption that anticipate his sarcasm in act 3, when he greets the ministers by wishing them "Bon appétit." Ruy Blas says that when he was twenty, he had faith in his "genius." He assumed that he could save the world ("Je croyais, pauvre esprit, qu'au monde je manquais") until he succumbed to hunger and became a lackey (Hugo rhymes "laquais" with "manquais"):

> Oh! quand j'avais vingt ans, crédule à mon génie,
> Je me perdais, marchant pieds nus dans les chemins,
> En méditations sur le sort des humains;
> J'avais bâti des plans sur tout,—une montagne
> De projets;—je plaignais le malheur de l'Espagne;
> Je croyais, pauvre esprit, qu'au monde je manquais...—
> Ami, le résultat, tu le vois:—un laquais!
>
> (RB 311–20)

[Oh! When I was twenty, believing in my genius, I would lose myself in meditations about the fate of mankind, walking barefoot on the roads; I had invented plans for everything—a mountain of projects; I pitied the misfortune of Spain; I thought, pour soul, that I was what the world lacked . . . —Friend, you see the result: a lackey!]

Don César responds with a less cynical version of the theory of *mastication universelle* that Rameau champions in *Le Neveu de Rameau*. Even for Don César, however, food and greatness are incompatible. He says that when a great man has to pass through the low "door of hunger," he must bend down further than anyone else:

Oui, je le sais, la faim est une porte basse:
Et, par nécessité, lorsqu'il faut qu'il y passe,
Le plus grand est celui qui se courbe le plus.

(RB 321–23)

[Yes, I know, hunger is a low door, and the greatest man, when by necessity he must pass through it, is the one who has to bend down furthest.]

For the figure of Ruy Blas, food provides an image rather than sustenance.

In the fourth act, Don César's literal references to food are grotesque in the same way that Ruy Blas's metaphorical language is sublime. Don César's actions, like those of Ruy Blas, are partially motivated by hunger, but they are the actions of the present. We watch him eat instead of hearing about his earlier hunger, and at one point—at a moment that acquires great dramatic significance—he puts off seeking revenge from Don Salluste until after he has eaten:

Mais je vais me venger de vous, cousin damné,
Epouvantablement quand j'aurai déjeuné.

(RB 1599–1600)

[But I will get revenge from you, cursed cousin, dreadfully so, after I have dined.]

It is in character for Don César to eat the meal that was actually prepared for Ruy Blas, thus allowing Ruy Blas to remain sublime. Ruy Blas and Don César share a name, but only for a while, and neither is aware of the other's identity. Yet we lose all trace of the common past that Ruy Blas described with such enthusiasm in act 1 (RB 287–88). Even the shared name is discarded by Ruy Blas at the end of the play when he proudly resumes his own. Only in one sense do the two characters combine traits that are both sublime and grotesque: both have lived on different and incompatible social levels, Ruy Blas having assumed a false aristocratic title and Don César having pretended to be a man of the people. But even then, no mixture takes place; their motives separate them, and the idealism and love of Ruy Blas contrast with the sensualism and bohemianism of Don César. In an aesthetic sense one can consider each figure to be a mixture of sublime and grotesque, because Ruy Blas, though not an aristocrat, is a tragic figure, and Don César, although he is an aristocrat, is a comic figure. But for Ruy Blas especially, there is a separation rather than a mixture of opposites; his only grotesque trait comes from artificial social hierarchies, not from his character or his actions. Don César's comic traits, on the other hand, have a sublime side and a tragic outcome. He is consequently the more interesting figure of the two, at least from the point of view of poetic revolution. Don César's willingness to discard the title and life of an aristocrat mirrors Hugo's inclusion of common themes in the aristocratic frame of the drama. This is more striking than the reverse, Ruy Blas's elevation to the aristocracy, which is short-lived and remains an illusion that is destroyed in the end. For the queen to be in love with a lackey shocks more than the lackey's love for the queen, just as it is more shocking for Don César to act the part of a nonaristocrat; the reaction of Hugo's contemporaries makes that abundantly clear.

From the earliest drafts of *Ruy Blas* we can deduce that Hugo identified Don César with questions that are both aesthetic and thematic; Don César, not Ruy Blas, is associated with the genesis of the work.[41] Perhaps it is more appropriate to call Hugo a dramaturgic Don César than a dramaturgic Ruy Blas, because from the start Don César is associated with poetry. When Don Salluste accuses his cousin of having headed a gang of bandits, Don César answers that he was there, but only to advise. When there was violence, he wrote verses:

J'ai toujours dédaigné de battre un argousin.
J'étais là. Rien de plus. Pendant les estocades,
Je marchais en faisant des vers sous les arcades.

(RB 84–86)

[I always refused to fight a cop. I was there. Nothing more. When there were murderous attacks, I walked under the arcades composing poetry.]

This sublimation through poetry recurs when Don César speaks in the same scene of countering his hunger with love letters. He associates writing with food (and love with food) when he speaks of replacing one with the other. He reads love letters while smelling something from a kitchen, and the phrase "cuisine au soupirail ardent," though literally it refers to the hot odors coming from a small basement kitchen, also evokes the "burning sighs" of a lover:

Souvent, pauvre, amoureux, n'ayant rien sous la dent,
J'avise une cuisine au soupirail ardent
D'où la vapeur des mets aux narines me monte;
Je m'assieds là, j'y lis les billets doux du comte,
Et, trompant l'estomac et le cœur tour à tour,
J'ai l'odeur du festin et l'ombre de l'amour!

(RB 138–40)

[Often, when I am poor and in love and have nothing to eat, I espy a kitchen with a glowing basement window from which the vapor of foods rises to my nostrils; I sit down there and read the love letters of the count, and alternately deceiving my stomach and my heart, I have the smell of a banquet and the shadow of love!]

A similarly conscious combination of poetry and food recurs in the fourth act. Again it is Don César who associates eating and drinking with poetry. But instead of making the gustatory a figure for something grand, as Ruy Blas does, he turns poetry, nature, and the king into figures for his gustatory pleasures. What he takes for a bookshelf turns out to be a pantry, and he "reads" the wine "written" by that famous poet, the sun, punning on the word *spiritueux* to show that his gustatory comments have a literary application:

> *Il va chercher dans un coin la petite table ronde, l'apporte sur le devant du théâtre et la charge joyeusement de tout ce que contient le garde-manger, bouteilles, plats, etc., il ajoute un verre, une assiette, une four-chette, etc.—Puis il prend une des bouteilles.*
>
> Lisons d'abord ceci.
>> *Il emplit le verre, et boit d'un trait.*
>>> C'est une oeuvre admirable
>>> De ce fameux poète appelé le soleil!
>>> Xérès-des-Chevaliers n'a rien de plus vermeil.
>> *Il s'assied, se verse un second verre et boit.*
>> Quel livre vaut cela? Trouvez-moi quelque chose
>> De plus spiritueux!
>>
>> (RB 1:1622–26)

> [[*He fetches the little round table from a corner, brings it to the front of the stage and joyfully ladens it with everything in the pantry—bottles, platters, etc., adding a glass, a plate, a fork, etc. Then he takes one of the bottles.*)
>
> First let's read this.
>> (*He fills the glass and drinks it down in one gulp.*)
>> This is an admirable work by the famous poet called the sun. Xérès-des-Chevaliers doesn't have anything redder.
>> (*He sits down, pours himself a second glass, and drinks.*)
>> What book is worth this? Find me something with more spirit!]

He then eats heartily and praises the pâté in front of him as the "king of pâtés":

>> *Il boit.*
>>> Ah. Dieu, cela repose!
>> Mangeons.
>>> *Il entame le pâté.*
>>>> Chiens d'alguazils! je les ai déroutés.
>>> Ils ont perdu ma trace.
>>> *Il mange.*

Oh! le roi des pâtés!
Quant au maître du lieu, s'il survient... —
    Il va au buffet et en rapporte un verre et un couvert qu'il
pose sur la table.
                    Je l'invite.
—Pourvu qu'il n'aille pas me chasser! Mangeons vite.
    Il met les morceaux doubles.
Mon dîner fait, j'irai visiter la maison.
                                (RB 1626–31)

[(*He drinks.*)
Ah, Lord, that is soothing! Let's eat.
    (*He cuts into the pâté.*)
Lousy cops! I put them off the scent. They've lost my trail.
    (*He eats.*)
Oh! The king of pâtés! As for the master of this place, if he
appears...
    (*He goes to the buffet and brings back a glass and some*
silverware, which he lays on the table.)
I'll invite him to join me—assuming that he doesn't go and
chase me! Let's eat quickly.
    (*He eats pieces twice the normal size.*)
Once my dinner is done, I'll take a tour of the house.]

To the reader of the play, the radical poetics of this scene are even more evident than they are to an audience, because Hugo manipulates alexandrines so that they resemble prose (like Byron when he uses the ottava rima stanza) and because he undercuts his dextrous and prosaic alexandrines with explicit stage directions. Hugo's use of ambiguous taste in this scene anticipates the scandalized comments of his public, which were made, predictably, on the grounds of taste. Two typical comments are that Hugo has never taunted "the good sense and the taste of his audience" so much as he does in the fourth act, or the fuming of another critic that in this act Hugo "outrages good taste and language for more than 200 lines" (RB 1:114). Heine's insistence on Hugo's "bad taste" mimics the critical response to the play.

Despite the aesthetic implications of Don César's gustatory performance, however, he is mainly a buffoon. If it were not for the tragic outcome that he unwittingly impels (and that makes us want to cry out as if we were at a Punch and Judy show, as Warning cleverly observes[42]), he would resemble a figure from Molière. This, it could be argued, is precisely Hugo's aim: for a buffoon—an aristocratic one—to be the source of harm not just in a novel (where the phenomenon is common enough), but in a serious drama as well. Yet we tend to forget that Don César is an aristocrat and a poet, just as we tend to forget that Ruy Blas is a man of the people; the line between sublime and grotesque remains clearly drawn. Some critics argue that Ruy Blas and Don César are doubles; they share a name, though unwittingly, and they used to be taken for brothers.[43] The argument holds only in the sense that the two are present within the same play. As characters they remain separate, and Ruy Blas's sublime status, as I have said, remains intact, just as Don César's grotesque status dominates. Since they are themselves not aware of anything that would connect them, not even of their shared name, and since their past companionship seems contrived, it is hard to consider them two parts of one self; only in the abstract, as representatives of Hugo's dramatic theory, can one call them doubles. A comparison to Heine's doubles or to "Lui" and "Moi" in *Le Neveu de Rameau* makes that abundantly clear.

The only character who seems to overcome the separation between the sublime and the grotesque is the queen, and once more the gustatory referents serve as a gauge. No doubt exists about her sublime traits, both as the beautiful woman loved by Ruy Blas and, more literally, as a person of royalty. But she also appears in a comic scene where Hugo has her express on a humorous level the important distinction between her feelings as a woman and her function as a queen. In the second act, which is entitled "The Queen of Spain" (La Reine d'Espagne), the queen tries vainly to relieve her boredom. Every time she suggests an activity, the duchess of Albuquerque—who as *camerera major* is the embodiment or rather the caricature of decorum—stands up, curtseys, and announces that the suggested activity would be improper. Both the repetition and the laws themselves are comic; in this context, the absurd rigidity recalls that of neoclassical drama, where everything is similarly ordered according to the dictates of good taste. Hugo makes the connection with the expedient of ambiguous taste; the rules of decorum clash most strongly with the queen's final request, which is that she be served something to eat:

LA REINE
Qu'on me serve à goûter!

284

CASILDA

Oui, c'est très amusant.

LA REINE

Casilda je t'invite.

CASILDA, *à part, regardant la camerera*

Oh! respectable aïeule!

LA DUCHESSE, *avec une révérence*

Quand le roi n'est pas là, la reine mange seule.

Elle se rassied.

(RB 660–62)

[THE QUEEN

Let me be served something to eat!

CASILDA

Yes, that is most amusing.

THE QUEEN

Casilda, you are my guest.

CASILDA, (*aside, looking at the camerera*)

Oh! Distinguished ancestor!

THE DUCHESS, (*with a curtsey*)

When the king is not here, the queen eats alone.]

The queen is beside herself ("poussée à bout"), and the list of forbidden things reaches its climax when she says that she cannot even eat as she pleases since she has become queen:

LA REINE, *poussée à bout*

Ne pouvoir—O mon Dieu! qu'est-ce que je ferai?—
Ni sortir, ni jouer, ni manger à mon gré!
Vraiment, je meurs depuis un an que je suis reine.

(RB 663–65)

[THE QUEEN, (*beside herself*)

Not to be able—O, my lord! What will I do?—Not to be able to go out, to play, or to eat as I please! Really, I have been dying during the year that I have been queen.]

Hugo presents the queen as a human being, not as the embodiment of decorum. Nevertheless, the laws of decorum prevail, for Hugo as well as

285

the queen, and we never see her eat. Like Ruy Blas, she remains sublime. When he has his characters speak of ordinary things, Hugo demonstrates what he calls "superior taste," the taste innate to artists of genius, who may choose and who implicitly purify even the most banal subject. Hugo speaks of this "superior taste" in a short essay of 1863 called "Le Goût." The essay was written while Hugo was exiled in Guernsey and is contemporary with his lengthy consideration of genius in *William Shakespeare* (1864). Both "Le Goût" and *William Shakespeare,* which repeat many of the ideas and even echo some of the phrases from the "Préface de *Cromwell,*" are necessarily related to the discussion of *Ruy Blas* and more generally to the phenomenon of ambiguous taste. In "Le Goût," Hugo uses the rather startling image of immaculate conception to describe what in *Ruy Blas* would be the "superior taste" of the queen and Ruy Blas, who remain "immaculate" even when they speak of literal taste. Figures like these—and the poets who create them—are capable of embracing what is material or low and remaining "virginal." This is the "law of genius"—the "règle du génie":

> Ce goût supérieur, que nous venons, non de définir, mais de caractériser, c'est la règle du génie, inaccessible à tout ce qui n'est pas lui, hauteur qui embrasse tout et reste vierge, Yungfrau [*sic*]. (HC 571)

> [This superior taste that we have just characterized, not defined, is the law of genius, inaccessible to all others, a loftiness that embraces everything yet remains virginal, Jungfrau.]

This kind of taste, which he also calls the "taste from above" ("grand goût, le goût d'en haut"), is capable of transfiguring material and recognizable things into something idealized. The *grand goût* is another name for the symbolist method that Goethe and Heine also practice and describe, an aesthetic in which real and common things are made recognizable before they are poeticized. It is the same quality that Heine praises as "plasticity" in Goethe's and Hugo's works.

In the commentary to *Lutezia* from the Düsseldorf edition, Volkmar Hansen explains Heine's criticism of Hugo as evidence of an allegiance to a neoclassical aesthetic. What Heine objects to in Hugo, according to Hansen, is an absence of harmony and the failure to aestheticize ugliness. Hansen bases his argument on the passage I interpreted earlier in which

Hugo is said to lack taste (DHA 13:1.891), and he claims that Heine is offended by Hugo's "naturalism," which lacks the filter of aesthetic distance. To my mind the opposite is the case, as I have meant to illustrate in this discussion of Goethe and Hugo. Hugo's mixture of sublime and ridiculous in *Ruy Blas,* though it takes place within the same work, keeps them separate, much in accordance with the rules of neoclassicism; Heine's own practice is very different, and his criticism of Hugo is related to his rejection of French *classicisme.* Furthermore, it is not true that naturalism fails to "aestheticize" ugliness, as Hansen argues; Hugo's works—if one thinks of them as prenaturalist—demonstrate the contrary, as one sees in *Ruy Blas.* The process of aestheticisation is more dramatic still in *L'Assommoir,* an acknowledged work of naturalism, where Zola poeticizes ugliness and argot and where meals are assigned a symbolic function. Warning and Jauss remark, correctly in my view, that Hugo seems uncomfortable with the literary revolution he proclaims. But if Hugo is in some ways closer to the inherited classicism he repudiates than he is to the naturalists in his own century, that is largely because of his fate as an intermediary between them. What Heine notices and criticizes in Hugo is not the "naturalism" of his ugliness but the absence of what he and Goethe call "Natur" when they speak of Shakespeare's indecorum and a new kind of taste. Heine criticizes what he finds "mendacious" [verlogen] in Hugo, but the charge can be turned against him, at least in the critique of Hugo. As I have argued, Heine attempts to put a greater distance than actually exists between Hugo's works, Goethe's, and his own. What the three authors share—along with the other authors in this study—is a common revolutionary impulse, one that calls into question the opposition between a *Kunstperiode* without revolution and a literary revolution dominated by political rather than aesthetic questions.

In *Die romantische Schule,* as a part of his stylized portrait of Goethe, Heine relates his pilgrimage to Weimar. He tells of wanting to address Goethe in Greek and of saying instead, in German, that the plums on the road between Jena and Weimar taste very good. With winsome self-irony Heine comments on this descent from the sublime speeches he had imagined beforehand to the banality of his actual conversation:

> Ich war nahe dran ihn griechisch anzureden; da ich aber merkte, daß er deutsch verstand, so erzählte ich ihm auf deutsch: daß die Plaumen auf dem Wege zwischen Jena und Weimar sehr gut schmeckten. Ich

hatte in so manchen langen Winternächten darüber nachgedacht, wie
viel Erhabenes und Tiefsinniges ich dem Goethe sagen würde, wenn
ich ihn mal sähe. Und als ich ihn endlich sah, sagte ich ihm, daß die
sächsischen Pflaumen sehr gut schmeckten. (DHA 8:1.163)

[I was about to address him in Greek, but noticing that he understood
German, I told him in German that the plums along the road between
Jena and Weimar tasted very good. During so many long winter nights
I had thought about how many lofty and profound things I would say
to Goethe if I ever saw him. And when at last I saw him, I told him
that Saxon plums tasted very good.] (SW 180)

Goethe's only response is to smile his Olympian smile: "Und Goethe
lächelte" [And Goethe smiled]. But the smile is conspiratorial as well as
Olympian. Here as in the poet's conversation with his mother in *Deutsch-
land. Ein Wintermärchen,* the culinary details have more than an evasive
or flippant purpose: given the skill with which Heine reveals the things
he pretends to hide, among them his affinity to Goethe, one can construe
the smile as a sign of Goethe's complicitous understanding of Heine's
culinary allusions. The proximity of Goethe's mysterious smile to Heine's
impertinent culinary commentary is a reminder that, despite their differ-
ences, they have in common a rebellion against poetic laws and a determi-
nation to create new forms. Although Heine speaks of Goethe in this
passage, his own style is unmistakable. He uses the distinctive technique
that Prawer calls his "verbal caricature,"[44] edging his way into the portrait
with a subdued and comic version of his characteristic *Stimmungsbre-
chung.*

Posterity's version of Goethe and Hugo is largely falsified. Goethe is
less conservative than his reputation allows, and Hugo is more so. Both
authors are poetic revolutionaries who reject the thoughtless application
of neoclassical rules in the name of good taste and who use ambiguous
taste to do so; but they continue to use the exclusively figurative sense
of taste as an aesthetic measure. As important to them as the discrepancy
between literal and figurative taste is a change in the meaning of figurative
taste. For them figurative taste is an inborn particularity of genius, and
when they choose a subject like eating—or any subject that is common
or coarse—they are guided by their innate sense of taste, which Hugo
says can "sublimate" anything and make "ugliness grand and evil beauti-
ful":

L'art a, comme la flamme, une puissance de sublimation. Jetez dans l'art, comme dans la flamme, les poisons, les ordures, les rouilles, les oxydes, l'arsenic, le vert-de-gris, faites passer ces incandescences à travers le prisme ou à travers la poésie, vous aurez des spectres splendides, et le laid deviendra le grand, et le mal deviendra le beau. (HC 577)

[Art has a power of sublimation, like a flame. Throw into art, as into a flame, poisons, garbage, rust, oxides, arsenic, verdigris, make these incandescences pass through a prism or through poetry, and you will have a splendid spectrum. The ugly will become great, and the bad will become beautiful.]

Taste is the guiding principle of this transfiguration and the sign—or the license—of genius. Hugo equates taste with genius and inspiration, both of which are connected to godliness, a connection underscored by the Biblical rhythms in these passages:

Dans le goût, comme dans le génie, il y a de l'infini. Le goût, ce pourquoi mystérieux, cette raison de chaque mot employé, cette préférence obscure et souveraine qui, au fond du cerveau, rend des lois propres à chaque esprit, cette seconde conscience donnée aux seuls poëtes, et aussi lumineuse que l'autre, cette intuition impérieuse de la limite invisible, fait partie, comme l'inspiration même, de la redoutable puissance inconnue. (HC 577–78)

[In taste, as in genius, there is something of infinity. Taste, that mysterious wherefore, that motive for every word chosen, that obscure and sovereign preference which, at the back of the brain, produces the laws appropriate to each mind, that second conscience granted to poets alone and as luminous as the other, that imperious intuition of an invisible boundary—taste belongs, like inspiration itself, to the redoubtable unknown power.]

The loftiness, even bombast, of Hugo's language distinguishes him from Goethe, but the sentiment is shared by both poets. For them, unlike Byron and Heine, ugliness yields to harmony or beauty; for them, genius is the license of taste.

The Effects of Poetic Revolution: From Ambiguous to Symbolist Taste

Il y a des auteurs originaux dont la moindre hardiesse révolte parce qu'ils n'ont pas d'abord flatté les goûts du public et ne lui ont pas servi les lieux communs auxquels il est habitué; c'est de la même manière que Swann indignait M. Verdurin. Pour Swann comme pour eux, c'était la nouveauté de son langage qui faisait croire à la noirceur de ses intentions.

—Proust, *Un Amour de Swann*

Food has always been an accepted, almost a conventional element of comedy, from Aristophanes to Molière to Chaplin (for example in *The Gold Rush* or *The Great Dictator*). In novels, too, the culinary has always played a part, from Rabelais to Fielding to Günter Grass. Nor is there any reluctance to represent eating in a hybrid genre like opera, which began to flourish, logically enough, in the climate of aesthetic revolution. Food is present in operas regardless of whether the outcome is tragic: Mozart's *Don Giovanni* ends with a lavish dinner of allegorical significance, and Verdi's *La Traviata* opens with a ball and a banquet. In Strauss and Hofmannsthal's *Der Rosenkavalier,* the Marschallin breakfasts in the first act, while Baron Ochs tries to seduce Mariandl/Octavian over dinner in the last; and in their opera *Ariadne,* ambiguous taste is used to express the aesthetic issues at the center of the work: different styles of opera are described with culinary images, and the performance in the second act follows a meal (much to the dismay of the earnest young composer). Hofmannsthal uses the culinary weapon of poetic revolutionaries to tell the story of that revolution and to demonstrate its successful outcome.

Until the Romantic age, however, eating does not figure in lyric poetry or serious drama. One can therefore measure the progress of poetic revolution during the nineteenth century by noting the prevalence of culinary allusions in works of all genres. They are present not only in the novels of George Eliot, Flaubert, or Fontane, and not only in the comedies of Nestroy, but also in the poems of Rimbaud and the dramas of Gerhart Hauptmann. Genre and subjects no longer have the same meaning at the end of the nineteenth century that they did at the beginning, and culinary allusions provide incontrovertible proof of that fact. Critics like Alois Wierlacher and James Brown have posited a connection between the literary depiction of food in the nineteenth century and the realist novel, the rise of which they link to the rise of the middle class. There is a logic to this theory: since eating has always been depicted in novels, there will be more eating scenes if there are more novels. But if the prevalence of novels were alone responsible for an increase in culinary allusions, how then would one explain the increased presence of food in drama and lyric poetry? Besides, the function of culinary allusions is not uniform, even in the novel. As in *Tom Jones*, they can still evoke a milieu, as they do in Balzac's description of the Pension Vauquer from *Le Père Goriot*; eating habits still convey character in *Bleak House*, where Dickens satirizes the evangelical minister Chadband by applying the biblical word "vessel" to his gluttonous behavior at teatime. But by the end of the nineteenth century, food, like prose—and like all banal subjects—can also transcend its prosaic associations; it need no longer cause an automatic shift from the sublime to the ridiculous, as it sometimes did in Byron's *Don Juan* or Heine's poems. Poetic revolution has toppled the hierarchies of subject, style, and genre. Any subject—as Goethe and Hugo emphasize when they discuss figurative taste—can be sublimated or transfigured, and the novel itself has changed from a form that permits indecorum to one in which indecorum is poeticized.[1]

Assumptions about the subject of food or the form of the novel that were still common in the eighteenth and the first part of the nineteenth centuries do not apply to the works of Thomas Mann and Proust. In their works, references to food lack the emblematic function of what I have called ambiguous taste; they reflect instead a symbolist aesthetic in which meaning is assigned to any subject, even the coarsest, and where a mimetic depiction becomes the basis for the poet's subjective, sometimes arcane, interpretation of the world. Food is only one subject among many that can acquire this symbolic function; consequently, culinary allusions no longer have a special status or draw attention to themselves as they did in the works of Romantic authors, where they exemplified both the rejection of an earlier aesthetic and the creation of a new one.

292

This change is apparent in Mann's first novel, *Buddenbrooks,* which was published exactly at the turn of the century, in 1901. The culinary details in *Buddenbrooks,* of which there are many (as there are in all of Mann's novels), represent milieu and character, but they represent something besides; like many details in the novel, the culinary allusions are related to and reflect the theme of physical decline and spiritual refinement. In part 1, the Buddenbrooks celebrate their move to the new house in the Mengstrasse, and the exact description of their dinner is the mimetic basis for a similar gathering on Christmas Eve in part 8, chapter 8. The two passages are related in the same way as the subject and significance of a symbolist poem by Baudelaire or a *Dinggedicht* by Rilke. These two passages bear the same kind of relationship to each other that a musical theme in an opera of Wagner bears to its subsequent use as a leitmotif.[2] This technique of connecting objects and ideas that intrinsically are not analogous is a realization of what Baudelaire calls *correspondances* in the poem of that name from *Les Fleurs du mal* and *traduction* (translation) when he writes about the meaning and structure of Wagner's *Tannhäuser.*

Once we are alert to such connections, we recognize a correlation between the enormous quantities of heavy food and the physical and financial well-being of the characters at the opening of *Buddenbrooks;* analogously, the scarce attention to food at the dinner near the end of the novel mirrors the gradual spiritualization of the family and its physical and financial disintegration. Thomas has by this time turned ascetic and barely touches or tolerates a feast like the lavish one with which the novel opens. The "symbolist" function of culinary details is apparent in other passages as well. Thirty-three years after the celebration in the Mengstrasse, for example, when Thomas hosts a celebration for the one hundredth anniversary of the Buddenbrook firm, there is only a brief mention of food. Food has lost its material significance and is perceived only as a necessary but tedious part of the commemorative ritual in the Fischergrube, where Thomas has built his new house (8, 5). We learn that something has been prepared for the guests to eat, but not what; that the family will dine without Thomas at noon; and that Thomas himself dreads the dinner with his business associates in the Ratskeller. Only one culinary detail is related with any precision for the day of the celebration: while the members of his family take their leave, Thomas has a late breakfast. He irritably gulps down tea and an egg, and he concludes his meal on the stairs with a few hasty puffs at one of the Russian cigarettes that for him have taken the place of more substantial food. This chapter is framed by a brief reference to Thomas's solitary supper three chapters before (8, 2), and by the dinner on Christmas Eve in the Mengstrasse three chapters later. Toward the end of the novel, Thomas will complain of "Appetitlosigkeit," a lack of appetite that accompanies his insomnia and several other physical ailments (10, 5).

The flash of culinary indulgence near the end of the novel, when the family gathers for Christmas Eve, proves indigestible. Mann anticipates the change when he presents the first meal, but naturally we are not yet in a position to understand how, because we cannot grasp the significance of a symbol on first sight or of a leitmotif until it has been repeated. At the opening celebration in the Mengstrasse, Christian, who is seven, over-eats and feels miserable as a consequence; he gets consolation from Ida Jungmann and from repeating a swear word—he is "damned miserable" [verdammt elend] (1, 7). His weak constitution is associated with the power of words for him, even (or perhaps especially) the power of pro-fanities, and with his vivid imagination, which is illustrated a few chapters later when he fantasizes about swallowing a peach pit (2, 3). These traits prefigure in comic form the musical talent and physical fragility of Hanno: Christian's talent as a mimic and his delicate constitution harbor the spiritual refinement and physical decline that reach their peak in the figure of Hanno. At the dinner in the Mengstrasse near the end of the novel, Hanno eats an enormous amount of sweets. Like Christian some thirty years earlier, Hanno suffers indigestion and is consoled both by Ida Jung-mann and a more spiritualized version of Christian's profanity: by thoughts of his theater, his harmonium, his book on mythology, and of the choir (8, 8).

In the opening book of *Buddenbrooks*, Mann describes in loving detail the new house in the Mengstraße and the meal being served there. In every sense this book is the "exposition" of the novel: characters first acquire a phrase that is associated with them for the rest of the novel, and places are likewise introduced. As yet we have no exact idea of the novel's theme, no sense of how the realistic description can acquire nonliteral meaning; the only hint of thematic significance at this stage comes from the novel's subtitle, *Verfall einer Familie* (disintegration of a family), but even then we do not know how the disintegration will manifest itself. Some thirty years later, when the family is gathered together on the same spot for an equally festive meal, the same or similar details have been transfigured and we have been taught to interpret them. The robust bourgeois mentality and materialist, even sensualist enjoyment at the opening of the novel—to which Christian's indigestion offers a comic contrast—has yielded its place to things of the spirit. Christian's weakness has moved from the periphery to the center. Sensuality has been replaced by the religious fervor of the *Konsulin* and the artistic enthusiasm of Hanno, who eats absentmindedly rather than with hunger or attention. Hanno is so absorbed in his book on mythology that he eats only "mechanically" and because it is a part of the ritual ("[er] aß mechanisch und weil es zur Sache gehörte"); he scarcely notices the discomfort caused by an overfilled stomach, which he identifies instead with the excitement and "melancholic bliss" [wehmütige Glückseligkeit] of the evening. Hanno does not lack interest in terrestrial pleasures, but the food he enjoys is mostly sweet, just as his father enjoys his Russian cigarettes more than substantial food; like his father, he must be reminded to eat, and when he finally sits at the table on Christmas Eve, Hanno eats barely anything until his appetite is aroused by dessert. There is indeed something "wehmütig" or "melancholy" about the meal, because the physical resemblance between the meal at the housewarming and the meal on Christmas Eve brings the differences between them into relief. We now connect culinary details with various forms of physical decline: with the account of James Möllendorpf's death in 7, 3, for example, where we learn that the diabetic elder senator, alone in a rented room, ate himself to death by indulging his passion for cake, or with the decline of Thomas and Hanno. The material quality of culinary details has been superseded by a series of associations that have little to do with food, and the culinary details in the novel have undergone the same transformation from material to spiritual that we observe among the members of the Buddenbrooks family.

Proust's *A la recherche du temps perdu* offers more evidence of the change from ambiguous to symbolist taste. In Proust's work, the revolution of genre and subject has been fully realized; recognizable literary boundaries no longer exist. I refer not to the theme of time and its suspension through the artist's control, but to the fusion of poetry and prose, essay and fiction, tragedy and comedy, and to the universal reach of Proust's subjects. The step in Napoleon's phrase between the sublime and the ridiculous, which was an appropriate motto for the Romantic age, has been closed. The simultaneity between sublime and ridiculous is apparent in the way the narrator manipulates us, for instance in details like the good-night kiss and the unexpected tolerance of the narrator's father, or in Swann's surprise when he raps on the wrong shutters; on the grander scale it is evident in the narrator's technique of reversal (his use of "personnages préparés") and in the revelations and metamorphoses at the end of the novel. But it is his use of metaphors that best marks the changed aesthetic. The poetry of the novel lies in the narrator's vision of connections like Baudelaire's *correspondances;* the narrator finds poetry in all things, just as he senses humor in all situations, and a division between prose and verse has been replaced by the poeticization of all subjects that Goethe, Heine, Byron, and Hugo proclaimed a century earlier. The democratization of subjects, if one retains the link to Napoleon, is revealed in the narrator's ability to describe his poetic process by using culinary images, which he does with self-irony but without affectation. When Proust compares art and cooking, we do not perceive the connection as ludicrous, the way we do in Molière's *Les Femmes savantes.* He compares his pleasure in reading Bergotte to the pleasure of a cook, and he compares the color of the hawthorns to strawberries mashed in cream, thereby reversing the traditional, and traditionally comic, relationship between tenor and vehicle.

When he likens Françoise's culinary art to the art of Michelangelo in *A l'ombre des jeunes filles en fleur,* the narrator describes his own craft as well. The gentle irony in this passage is directed by the narrator at himself as much as toward Françoise, and the undertone of seriousness later rises to the surface when he asks himself whether he should not compose his novel in the same manner as Françoise when she composes her "bœuf à la gelée." The irony here is not an expression of the narrator's contempt toward his own creation, but of the distance and humor that he considers integral to it:

> [Françoise] vivait dans l'effervescence de la création; comme elle attachait une importance extrême à la qualité intrinsèque des matériaux qui devaient entrer dans la fabrication de son oeuvre, elle allait elle-même aux Halles se faire donner les plus beaux carrés de romsteck, de jarret de boeuf, de pied de veau, comme Michel-Ange passant huit mois dans les montagnes de Carrare à choisir les blocs de marbre les plus parfaits pour le monument de Jules II. (PR 1:437)

> [(Françoise) had been living in the effervescence of creation; since she attached the utmost importance to the intrinsic quality of the materials which were to enter into the fabric of her work, she had gone herself

to the Halles to procure the best cuts of rump-steak, shin of beef, calves'-feet, just as Michelangelo spent eight months in the mountains of Carrara choosing the most perfect blocks of marble for the monument of Julius II.] (PK 1:480)

This comparison is embedded in the long passage about the narrator's visit to see the actress Berma in *Phèdre* and his discussion of the performance and of literature with M. de Norpois, whose visit has occasioned the creative ardor of Françoise. It is in the middle of the conversation with M. de Norpois that Françoise presents her creation; she has become the "Michel-Ange de notre cuisine," and the beef and carrots rest on enormous blocks of aspic that have been metamorphosed into a sculptor's materials. Passages like these, which one finds throughout the work, are representative of the novel's style and texture. They are marked by a natural lyricism that mingles with irony and humor.[3]

In a parallel passage from *Combray*, Françoise's chocolate cream has the attributes of a musical composition. The dish, which Françoise prepares specially for the narrator's father, provides the climax of one of her copious dinners; it betokens both her "inspiration" and her vanity. Anyone who turns it down is put in the same category as the Philistine who notes only the superficial or material qualities of a work presented to him by the artist. If her "audience" does not eat everything up, Françoise reacts like a composer who sees someone leave the concert hall before his piece has ended:

Celui qui eût refusé d'en goûter en disant: "J'ai fini, je n'ai plus faim," se serait immédiatement ravalé au rang de ces goujats qui, même dans le présent qu'un artiste leur fait d'une de ses œuvres, regardent au poids et à la matière alors que n'y valent que l'intention et la signature. Même en laisser une seule goutte dans le plat eût témoigné de la même impolitesse que se lever avant la fin du morceau au nez du compositeur. (PR 1:71)

[Anyone who refused to partake of it, saying: "No, thank you, I've finished; I'm not hungry any more," would at once have been relegated to the level of those Philistines who, even when an artist makes them a present of one of his works, examine its weight and material, whereas what is of value is the creator's intention and his signature. To have left even the tiniest morsel in the dish would have shown as much discourtesy as to rise and leave a concert hall before the end of a piece under the composer's very eyes.] (PK 1:77)

Françoise's attitude differs little from that of the composer Vinteuil in his struggle between pride and modesty.

There is a similar parallel between the asparagus painted by Elstir and the repeated presence of real asparagus in Françoise's kitchen during one of the narrator's summers in Combray. Again Proust makes the analogy between Françoise's and the artist's creation and between the character and the works of an artist: the sweetness of her cooking clashes with the intermittent brutality of her character. In this passage, Proust varies the connection by envisioning Françoise as a fairy or a giant who has been transformed into a cook. The passage from *Combray* in which the author begins the aesthetic transfiguration of asparagus that Elstir completes in his paintings exemplifies the fusion of exact depiction and figurative meaning, terrestrial and sublime, poetry and playfulness that is a trademark of Proust. The narrator imagines the asparagus to be "delicious" creatures who, like Françoise, have undergone a metamorphosis, and he thinks, too, of the metamorphosis they will perform during the night on the smell of his urine:

> [M]on ravissement était devant les asperges, trempées d'outremer et de rose et dont l'épi, finement pignoché de mauve et d'azur, se dégrade insensiblement jusqu'au pied—encore souillé pourtant du sol de leur plant—par des irisations qui ne sont pas de la terre. Il me semblait que ces nuances célestes trahissaient les délicieuses créatures qui s'étaient amusées à se métamorphoser en légumes et qui, à travers le déguisement de leur chair comestible et ferme, laissaient apercevoir en ces couleurs naissantes d'aurore, en ces ébauches d'arc-en-ciel, en cette extinction de soirs bleus, cette essence précieuse que je reconnaissais encore quand, toute la nuit qui suivait un dîner où j'en avais mangé, elles jouaient, dans leurs farces poétiques et grossières comme une féerie de Shakespeare, à changer mon pot de chambre en un vase de parfum. (PR 1:119)

> [But what most enraptured me were the asparagus tinged with ultramarine and pink which shaded off from their heads, finely stippled in mauve and azure, through a series of imperceptible gradations to their white feel—still stained a little by the soil of their garden-bed—with

an irridescence that was not of this world. I felt that these celestial hues indicated the presence of exquisite creatures who had been pleased to assume vegetable form and who, through the disguise of their firm, comestible flesh, allowed me to discern in this radiance of earliest dawn, these hinted rainbows, these blue evening shades, that precious quality I should recognise again when, all night long after a dinner at which I had partaken of them, they played (lyrical and coarse in their jesting as the fairies in Shakespeare's Dream) at transforming my chamber pot into a vase of aromatic perfume.] (PK 1:131)

This is not the same chamber pot as the one in Heine's *Deutschland. Ein Wintermärchen*. Proust fuses the poetic and the coarse—which like the Romantics he associates with Shakespeare—when he describes the tricks played by these personified vegetables; he fuses abstraction and sensuality when he combines his memory of their beauty with the scent they will produce in his chamber pot.

In *A la recherche du temps perdu*, the sensuality of eating helps the narrator to reconstruct the past, since Proust's central thematic and structural principle of involuntary memory is introduced through the taste of a madeleine dipped in linden tea (probably the most famous of all literary allusions to food). For Proust, food is further associated with the theme of habit, and it is one of the subjects through which the narrator can poeticize the banality of real existence, as is evident from the asparagus, first in Françoise's kitchen and then in Elstir's paintings. But food is only one of a number of subjects that possess such power. By Proust's time, it is anachronistic to speak of the "ambiguity of taste," just as it was anachronistic to justify the indecorum of Byron or Heine by citing the satirical models of classical authors. Proust's novel demonstrates not the disappearance of categories such as high and low, but their mixture in a form that dissolves generic boundaries. When Walter Benjamin evokes figs or an omelette in two short texts from the 1930s that resemble prose poems, he renders layers of time and experience in the same manner as Proust with the madeleine. The same is true for M. F. K. Fisher, who for example in *The Gastronomical Me* (1943) uses descriptions of food to summon places to her readers' minds or as a starting point for her narration of historical or emotional moments. To call Fisher a "food writer," as an astute writer put it in one of the "Topics of the Times" (28 February 1991), is "like calling Mozart a tunesmith."

By the twentieth century, good taste has lost its prescriptive power in literature. Ambiguous taste has therefore lost its ambiguity, which in turn means that food has lost its emblematic revolutionary function. One can say of culinary references what M. H. Abrams says of sexual ones: that it is "as much a literary convention to be outspoken on sexual matters as it was to be reticent in the age of Dickens."[4] When Proust juxtaposes literal and figurative taste in the passage about Françoise's dinner and M. de Norpois's visit, he recalls the neoclassical aesthetic as something that has been outgrown. M. de Norpois's insistence on "good taste" among actors immediately precedes his praise of Françoise's cooking. The irony in this passage is based on the contrast between the narrator's response as an adolescent, when he is intimidated by the reactionary aesthetic precepts of M. de Norpois, and the wisdom of the author as an adult, an artist sure of his vocation; that irony is underscored when Proust reverses the historical status of literal and figurative taste by setting literal taste, in the form of Françoise's boeuf à la gelée, above the figurative taste championed by M. de Norpois, a man who judges but cannot create.

A similar reversal in the status of literal and figurative taste is more recently apparent in Günter Grass's novel *Der Butt* (*The Flounder*) of 1979 and Vikram Seth's novel in verse of 1988, *The Golden Gate*. Grass structures his novel on a culinary motif and equates cooking with literary creation and procreation; the narrative is divided into nine chapters for each of nine cooks that the first-person narrator "carries inside of me" and each of which represents a month in his wife's pregnancy. In the second section of the novel, Grass summons the specter of good taste in the first of the poems he mixes among his chapters in the style of Romantic authors. He calls the poem "Worüber ich schreibe" (What I am writing about) and emphasizes both the metaphorical nature of his references to food and his distance from an aesthetic determined by the laws of good taste. When he says that he is writing "about the nausea of facing a full plate" and "about good taste" ("Über den Ekel vor vollem Teller, / über den guten Geschmack"), he has reversed the status of literal and figurative taste, like Proust in the case of M. de Norpois. More pointedly and provocatively than Proust, Grass evokes ambiguous taste as one of the stations of literary history presented in his novel. Grass provokes his readers' expectations more aggressively than Proust: when he speaks of good taste in this first poem, his irony comes from the distance between the narrator and the reader, not from a difference in perspective between the author as an adolescent and as an adult who has become an artist.

The Golden Gate by Vikram Seth is a spellbinding evocation of life in contemporary California, where one of the main preoccupations is eating. Seth writes using a fourteen-line stanza for which the model is Johnston's translation of *Eugene Onegin,* as he tells us in the opening of the fifth chapter (5.1–5.5). Like Pushkin in the case of *Eugene Onegin* (another work that confirms the argument about ambiguous taste, as I mentioned earlier), Seth calls his work a novel. But whereas Pushkin chose the designation of novel partly so that he could appease contemporary taste and defend his indecorum with genre, Seth's narrator is confronted with the opposite dilemma: his editor responds enthusiastically to the news that he is writing a novel, until he learns that it is written in verse. Others are said to share the editor's skepticism of verse:

> Professor, publisher, and critic
> Each voiced his doubts. I felt misplaced.
> A writer is a mere arthritic
> Among these muscular Gods of Taste.
> As for that sad blancmange, a poet—
> The world is hard; he ought to know it. (5.2)

Poetry is again connected to figurative and literal taste, here in the move from "Gods of Taste" to "that sad blancmange, a poet," and the passage seems to revert to the prescriptions of the late eighteenth and early nineteenth centuries. But the impression is deceptive. Like Proust and Grass, Seth's allusion to ambiguous taste is historical: the "sad blancmange, a poet" contains a specific allusion to Pushkin's poem (5.32) and therefore becomes a shorthand or code for recalling the function of ambiguous taste in *Eugene Onegin.*

Seth varies the use of ambiguous taste in Pushkin and applies it to the only restriction that survives in the name of taste: the prejudices of his readers. His defense of verse, however, which he makes with culinary images, is an hommage to Pushkin, not an example of rebellious indecorum:

> How can I (careless of time) use
> The dusty bread molds of Onegin
> In the brave bakery of Reagan?
> The loaves will surely fail to rise
> Or else go stale before my eyes. (5.3)

301

The effects of poetic revolution are palpable in this passage. Decorum is no longer a determinant of form or imagery. Goethe was accurate when he said that as a result of poetic revolution, "besides a freer form, richer and more diversified subjects will have been attained, and no object of the broadest world and the most manifold life will be any longer excluded as unpoetical" (GCE 289). The neoclassical doctrine of good taste has no power or even meaning today, and genre is not what influences an author's choice to include or exclude references to literal taste and the other "lower" senses. There are "Gods of Taste" who still have power, however, mostly commercial power. Works like those of Mann, Proust, Grass, and Seth proclaim the victories of poetic revolution under the motto "Good taste is dead," but they also complete the slogan, like Proust's asparagus in metamorphosed form: "Long live taste."

Notes

Introduction

1. Erich Auerbach (*Mimesis: The Representation of Reality in Western Literature,* trans. Willard R. Trask [Princeton: Princeton University Press, 1953]) points out that even Shakespeare, though famous for his mixture of styles and of tragic with the comic, never allows commoners to assume a tragic role, except, perhaps, in the case of Shylock.
2. Mikhail Bakhtin, *Rabelais and His World,* trans. Helene Iswolsky (Cambridge, Mass: MIT Press, 1968; rpt. Bloomington: Indiana University Press, 1984), 154.
3. See James W. Brown, *Fictional Meals and Their Function in the French Novel, 1789–1848* (Toronto: University of Toronto Press, 1984); and Alois Wierlacher, *Vom Essen in der deutschen Literatur: Mahlzeiten in Erzähltexten von Goethe bis Grass* (Stuttgart: Kohlhammer, 1987).
4. Among the earliest are the books by Karin Kiwus and Henning Grunwald, eds. *Vom Essen und Trinken* (Frankfurt am Main: Insel, 1978); or Herbert Heckmann, *Die Freuden des Essens: Ein kulturgeschichtliches Lesebuch vom Genuß der Speisen aber auch vom Leid des Hungers* (Munich: Hanser, 1979). In recent years, such books have begun to acquire the status of a vogue likewise evident in the novel of culinary and poetic collage by Jacqueline Deval, *Reckless Appetites. A Culinary Romance* (Hopewell, N.J.: Ecco Press, 1993).
5. Louis Marin, *La Parole mangée et autres essais théologico-politiques* (Paris: Méridiens Klincksieck, 1986). See especially the chapter "La Parole mangée ou le corps divin saisi par les signes."
6. Gerhard Neumann makes the apple of knowledge in the Old Testament and the doctrine of transubstantiation in the New Testament the focus for his convincing analysis in "Das Essen und die Literatur," *Literarwissenschaftliches Jahrbuch im Auftrage der Görres-Gesellschaft* 23 (1982): 173–90.
7. Meyer Schapiro, "The Apples of Cézanne: An Essay on the Meaning of Still-life" (1968) in *Modern Art: Nineteenth and Twentieth Centuries: Selected Papers* (New York: George Braziller, 1978), 1–38, here 21.
8. M. H. Abrams, *A Glossary of Literary Terms,* 5th ed. (New York: Holt, Rinehart and Winston, 1988), 184.

9. This self-conscious phenomenon is one that James W. Brown (*Fictional Meals*) attributes to changes in the actual preparation of food for this period. Brown's emphasis is the inverse of my own, for he speaks here of a poeticization of food in actuality, not in poetry. But his findings support the thesis presented here.

10. Quoted by Georges May in the first chapter of *Quatre visages de Denis Diderot*, "Diderot gastronome" (Paris: Boivin, 1951), 13–33, an essay of historical as well as intrinsic interest, being a prescient example of scholarly attention to the conjunction of culinary and literary questions.

11. Auerbach, *Mimesis*, 430–31.

12. René Wellek, *A History of Modern Criticism, 1750–1950, vol. 2, The Romantic Age* (New Haven: Yale University Press, 1955), 2.—I understand the term *neoclassic* to refer to the conservative aesthetic doctrine of the seventeenth and eighteenth centuries, the premises and ideals of which are to be found in the *Ars poetica* of Horace and Boileau's equally influential imitation, the *Art poétique* (1674). The term is customarily applied to English literature between 1660 and either 1789 or 1798 (when Wordsworth and Coleridge published their *Lyrical Ballads*); the term *neoclassicism* is useful, because it separates between the classicism of antiquity and that of later periods and because it is distinct from the term *Klassik* in Germany.

13. Walter Jackson Bate, *From Classic to Romantic: Premises of Taste in Eighteenth-Century England* (Cambridge, Mass.: Harvard University Press, 1946), i.

14. See for example the "Brief über den Roman" in Schlegel's *Gespräch über die Poesie;* I discuss Schlegel's notion of romantic irony and the distinction between a literary spirit and a literary period more fully in "'Die Puppenspiele meines Humors': Heine and Romantic Irony," *Studies in Romanticism* 26 (1987): 399–419. See, too, M. H. Abrams, *The Mirror and the Lamp: Romantic Theory and the Critical Tradition* (Oxford: Oxford University Press, 1953; rpt. New York: Norton, 1958), especially 70, 237, and 242. On the frustrations of designating trends and periods, specifically what is "modern," see Hans Robert Jauss, *Literaturgeschichte als Provokation* (Frankfurt am Main: Suhrkamp, 1970).

15. From Nabakov's copiously annotated translation of *Eugene Onegin* it is clear that for Pushkin, too, ambiguous taste is emblematic of poetic revolution. My attention to metaphor, wordplay, and ambiguity requires that works be treated in the original; otherwise Pushkin would have figured as another of my main examples.

16. Walter Benjamin, "Zum Bilde Prousts," in *Gesammelte Schriften*, vol. 2, book 1, ed. Tillman Rexroth (Frankfurt am Main: Suhrkamp, 1977), 2:1, 310–24.

17. Marcel Proust, *Correspondance*, ed. Philip Kolb (Paris: Plon, 1991), 19:642–44.

Chapter 1

1. Jonathan Bate, *Shakespeare and the English Romantic Imagination*, 2d ed. (Oxford: Clarendon Press, 1989), 6. Bate cites Blake's original remark a few pages earlier (3): "To Generalize is to be an Idiot. To Particularize is the Alone Distinction of Merit." Bate's book complements mine and offers background for the argument advanced here.

2. Johann Christoph Gottsched, *Ausgewählte Werke*, vol. 6, book 1, *Versuch einer critischen Dichtkunst, erster allgemeiner Theil*, ed. Joachim Birke and Brigitte Birke (Berlin and New York: Walter de Gruyter, 1973), 176. See, too, the discussion of decorum and neoclassicism in the chapter "Neoclassicism and the New Trends of the Time" in Wellek, *History of Modern Criticism*, vol. 1, *The Later Eighteenth Century*, 12–30, as well as W. Jackson Bate, *The Burden of the Past and the English Poet* (Cambridge, Mass: Harvard University Press, 1970), 18–21.

3. For a discussion of the English "School of Taste," see Bate, *From Classic to Romantic*, especially part 4 of chapter 2.

4. Norbert Elias, *Über den Prozeß der Zivilisation: Soziogenetische und psychogenetische Untersuchungen*, vol. 1, *Wandlungen des Verhaltens in den weltlichen Oberschichten des Abendlandes*, 2d ed. (Bern: Francke, 1969; rpt. Frankfurt am Main: Suhrkamp, 1981).

5. Friedrich Schlegel also uses the adjective *sogenannt* to disparage the phrase *good taste*, but without alluding to literal taste. In the chapter "Epochen der Dichtkunst" from the *Gespräch über die Poesie*, Schlegel speaks dismissively of "this wan mental illness of so-called good taste" [diese schwächliche Geisteskrankheit des sogenannten guten Geschmacks], *Kritische Friedrich-Schlegel-Ausgabe*, ed. Ernst Behler, Jean-Jacques Anstett, and Hans Eichner, vol. 2 (Munich: Schöningh, 1958), 302.

6. Bate, *Shakespeare and Romantic Imagination*, 9.

7. See Caroline Spurgeon, *Shakespeare's Imagery and What It Tells Us* (Cambridge: Cambridge University Press, 1935). In all fairness—and to give further evidence of the dangers of generalizing—it should be noted that the phrase Hugo quotes in the "Préface de *Cromwell*" and that is particularly appropriate here comes from Voltaire: "A la mort, et allons dîner." See Hans Robert Jauss, "Das Ende der Kunstperiode—Aspekte der literarischen Revolution bei Heine, Hugo und Stendhal," in *Literaturgeschichte als Provokation*, 123.

8. Quoted by Wellek, *History of Modern Criticism*, 1:33—34. The remark is from Voltaire's *Letters concerning the English Nation* (1733), which were first published in English.

9. Friedrich der Grosse, *De la littérature allemande*, ed. Christoph Gutknecht and Peter Kerner (Hamburg: Helmut Buske, 1969), 60–61. See, too, the first chapter of Elias, *Prozeß der Zivilisation*, vol. 1, especially 10–17, where Elias writes of the contradiction between Frederick the Great's opinions about art and his ideas about politics; also in this passage, Elias analyzes the dominance of a rationally determined doctrine of taste in the eighteenth century.

10. Bakhtin, *Rabelais and His World*, 117. In the essay "Epic and Novel: Toward a Methodology for the Study of the Novel," Bakhtin speaks, too, of the revolutionary power of laughter, which "destroys the epic, and in general destroys any hierarchical (distancing and valorized) distance" (*The Dialogic Imagination: Four Essays*, ed. Michael Holquist, trans. Caryl Emerson and Michael Holquist [Austin: University of Texas Press, 1981], 23).

11. See Walter Redfern, *Puns* (Oxford: Basil Blackwell, 1984), who quotes the abbé Deville (53). Redfern's title itself attacks scholarly hierarchies, since he could more decorously have chosen the term *wordplay*. The subversive qualities of the pun (which Redfern at one point calls an "agent of disorder" [14] and at another describes as "anti-decorum" [17]), have increasingly made it

a favorite tool of literary critics, some of whom are witty and some of whom are simply trendy.

12. See Molly Mahood, *Shakespeare's Wordplay* (London: Methuen, 1957). Mahood points out that Samuel Johnson, despite his objections to Shakespeare's puns, observed them readily and was one of their ablest commentators. On Shakespeare and puns, see also Redfern, *Puns*, 47–49.

13. This is related to but not precisely the same as the "figura" that Auerbach discusses in *Mimesis* and that he traces back to the doctrine of Christianity; on the connection of Romantic sensibility and the symbolist method, see Hugo Friedrich's famous study, *Die Struktur der modernen Lyrik*, 2d ed. (Hamburg: Rowohlt, 1956); and, more recently, the book by Brigitte Peucker, *Lyric Descent in the Romantic Tradition* (New Haven: Yale University Press, 1987).

14. Paul Fry, "Literature and Our Discontents," *Yale Review* 73 (1984): 603–16.

15. See, for example, Irmgard Bitsch et al., eds., *Essen und Trinken in Mittelalter und Neuzeit* (Sigmaringen: Thorbecke, 1987); a collection of essays on Proust and taste, *Marcel Proust: Geschmack und Neigung*, ed. Volker Knapp (Tübingen: Stauffenberg, 1989); and *Modern Language Notes* 106, no. 4 (September 1991), special issue, Cultural Representations of Food. One exception that shows how the subject is becoming institutionalized is the issue of *Mosaic* edited by Evelyn J. Hinz, Diet and Discourse: Eating, Drinking, and Literature (summer–fall 1991). See especially the contribution by Norman Kiell, "Food in Literature: A Selective Bibliography," 211–63.

16. Susan J. Leonardi, "Recipes for Reading: Summer Pasta, Lobster à la Riseholme, and Key Lime Pie," *PMLA* 104 (1989): 340–49.

17. Brillat-Savarin, *Physiologie du goût*, ed. Roland Barthes (Paris: Hermann, 1975), in the preface entitled "Lecture de Brillat-Savarin," 7–33, here 27.

18. See my review of Wierlacher's book in *German Quarterly* 62 (1989): 101–3, and of Hardt's in *German Quarterly* 63 (1990): 572–74. Some welcome exceptions to these extremes, one older and the other recent, are the first chapter of May's *Denis Diderot*, "Diderot gastronome"; and the essay by Neumann, "Essen und Literatur." Ronald W. Tobin has edited a series of essays written with flair, *Littérature et gastronomie* (Paris, Seattle: Papers on French Seventeeth-Century Literature, 1985), and has recently published a book on Molière and gastronomy: *Tarte à la crème: Comedy and Gastronomy in Molière's Theater* (Columbus: Ohio State University Press, 1990).

19. The "lower" sense of smell has likewise been excluded from works of the high style, and for identical reasons. Its role has been even more rigorously bracketed by literary scholars than the sense of taste, which makes still more dramatic the appearance of Hans J. Rindisbacher's study, *The Smell of Books: A Cultural and Historical Study of Olfactory Perception in Literature* (Ann Arbor: University of Michigan Press, 1992).

20. Freud, *Der Witz und seine Beziehung zum Unbewußten* (1905), where the theory is predicated on the very literary belief that nothing is accidental and that all mental processes are related. See, too, Freud's short piece "Der Humor" (1927), in *Studienausgabe*, ed. Alexander Mitscherlich et al. (Frankfurt am Main: Fischer, 1982), 4:275–82.

21. Roland Barthes, "Pour une psycho-sociologie de l'alimentation contemporaine," English translation by Elborg Forster in *Selections from the Annales: Économies, Sociétés, Civilisations,* vol. 5, *Food and Drink in History,* ed. Robert Forster and Orest Ranum (Baltimore: Johns Hopkins University Press, 1979), 155–73, here 168 and 169.
22. Jean-François Revel, *Un Festin en paroles: Histoire littéraire de la sensibilité gastronomique de l'Antiquité à nos jours* (Paris: Pauvert, 1979), 17.
23. Quoted by Wierlacher, *Essen,* 43.
24. For an analysis of the culinary details in *Madame Bovary,* see Lilian R. Furst, "The Role of Food in *Madame Bovary,*" *Orbis litterarum* 34 (1979): 53–65; and James W. Brown, "Aesthetic and Ideological Coalescence in the Alimentary Sign: *Madame Bovary,*" in *Fictional Meals,* 131–69.

Chapter 2

1. Bakhtin, *Rabelais and His World,* 34.
2. See Tobin, *Tarte à la crème,* in particular chap. 9, "Sixth Service: *Les Femmes savantes,* or Consuming Passions," 123–44. Tobin (whose study had not appeared when I wrote the present chapter) emphasizes the sexual innuendo rather than the aesthetic consequences of the double meanings in this play; but his reading of *Les Femmes savantes* supports my own, especially in connection with the interpretation of the *Critique de l'Ecole des femmes* in chapter 3.
3. On the revelatory nature of double entendre in the play, see J. H. Périvier, "Equivoques moliéresques: Le sonnet de Trissotin," *Revue des Sciences Humaines* 38 (1973): 543–54.
4. Tobin, *Tarte à la crème,* 124–28, esp. 125. See, too, the preface to *Les Femmes savantes* by Georges Couton in the Pléiade edition, MFS 975–84, where he discusses Molière's models for Trissotin.
5. See Harry Levin, *Playboys and Killjoys: An Essay on the Theory and Practice of Comedy* (New York: Oxford University Press, 1987), specifically in the chapter "Metacomedy," 123–32.
6. For an excellent account of Fielding's own eating habits and their relation to his character, see Martin C. Battestin, with Ruthe R. Battestin, *Henry Fielding: A Life* (London: Routledge, 1989), 149–50.
7. In his discussion of the film, Martin C. Battestin considers the adaptation of this scene to be "the most impressive single instance of Osborne's and Richardson's genius in translating Fielding's style, attitudes, and intentions into their own medium" ("Osborne's *Tom Jones:* Adapting a Classic," *Virginia Quarterly Review* 42 (1966): 378–93, here 388). Battestin's unequivocal approval is related to what I consider a mischaracterization of the author's reference to heroes and their hungers; Battestin says of the authorial comments that they are a "reluctant admission that even the most accomplished of heroes have more of the mortal than the divine about them: even Ulysses must eat" (389). To my mind (as will become more clear in what follows) Fielding's comment is not a "reluctant admission," but rather one of many wise reminders to the reader not to flatten human nature by idealizing it.
8. William Empson, "*Tom Jones,*" in *Twentieth-Century Interpretations of "Tom Jones,*" ed. Martin C. Battestin (Englewood Cliffs, N.J.: Prentice-Hall, 1968), 33–55.

9. On the necessity of reading the novel twice in order to "judge" properly, see Martin C. Battestin, *The Providence of Wit: Aspects of Form in Augustan Literature and the Arts* (Oxford: Clarendon Press, 1974), especially the chapter "Fielding: The Definition of Wisdom"; and Patrick Reilly, *"Tom Jones": Adventure and Providence* (Boston: Twayne, 1991), who in the chapter "Judging the Jurors" calls it a "cliché of criticism" (94) that the novel must be read twice. Reilly gives a good account of why this is so.

10. Battestin, *The Providence of Wit*, 172 and 176.

11. It may be that by naming the turtle and the alderman, Fielding is alluding here to the etymology of satire as *satura lanx* or "full plate."

12. In his gloss of the landlady's comments, Battestin refers to an article written by Fielding in *Covent-Garden Journal*, 3 March 1752, where he uses the exchange of perry for champagne "as the basis for an elaborate metaphor contrasting false wit and true" (TJ, 533, n. 1).

13. See Michael Bliss, "Fielding's Bill of Fare in *Tom Jones*," *English Literary History* 30 (1963): 236–43, who says that Fielding's opening metaphor contains an "ethical as well as esthetic theory" (239–40).

14. Elke Liebs discusses gustatory myths of creation in the chapter "Schöpfungsmythen" from *Das Köstlichste von allem: Von der Lust am Essen und dem Hunger nach Liebe* (Zurich: Kreuz, 1988), 14–31. The ironic equation of creator and cook is one that recurs frequently in Heine's works, as will become evident later on.

15. Battestin, *The Providence of Wit* , 142–3. Michael Bliss argues that in his image of the cook, Fielding expresses a theory that "locates both ethical good and artistic value in gratuitous ornament" and later calls this Fielding's "straw position" ("Fielding's Bill of Fare," 238, 239). I find no evidence for this claim, especially given the lines from Pope that Fielding quotes by way of illustration. I believe that Bliss misconstrues the distinction that Fielding draws between a subject—which may ostensibly be the same for a number of authors—and the skill with which that subject is depicted; when he calls himself a cook, the narrator is playful in his imagery but serious in evoking his craft. Fielding will return, in varied form, to the same distinction in the last of the prefatory chapters, where he defends himself against the accusation that he is scurrilous.

16. Andrew Wright, *Mask and Feast* (Berkeley and Los Angeles: University of California Press, 1965), 31–32. Like most critics, Wright does not deal with the comparison of the author and a cook, only with the image of the author as the master of an ordinary.

17. Battestin, *The Providence of Wit*, 185.

18. Simon Vary, *Henry Fielding* (Cambridge: Cambridge University Press, 1986), 94.

19. On the prefatory chapters and the asides, see Irvin Ehrenpreis, *Tom Jones* (London: Edward Arnold, 1964), especially in chapter 1, "Author."

20. Reilly, *Tom Jones*, 66.

21. Wright, *Mask and Feast*, particularly in the chapter "Tom Jones: Life as Art," 31–44 (reprinted in Battestin, *Twentieth-Century Interpretations*, 56–67), here 37.

22. For a compelling account of order and disorder from the anthropological and sociological point of view, see Margaret Visser, *The Rituals of Dinner: The*

Origins, Evolution, Eccentricities, and Meaning of Table Manners (New York: Grove Weidenfeld, 1991).

Chapter 3

1. Paul West, *Byron and the Spoiler's Art* (New York: St. Martin's, 1960), 14. E. D. Hirsch speaks of "reversals in taste" as a shift "that tells us, probably, more about ourselves than about Byron, and has blinded us on occasion to essential qualities in the very poems we like best" ("Byron and the Terrestrial Paradise," in *From Sensibility to Romanticism*, ed. Frederick W. Hilles and Harold Bloom [New York: Oxford University Press, 1965], 467–68). Hirsch makes some useful comments about "mobility" and about the transition from drunkenness to sobriety as an image of Byron's stance in the poem. Frederick W. Shilstone takes up Hirsch's comments in his article "The Dissipated Muse: Wine, Women, and Byronic Song," *Colby Library Quarterly* 20 (1984): 36–46.
2. Andrew Rutherford, *Byron: A Critical Study* (Palo Alto, Calif.: Stanford University Press, 1969), 179.
3. Michael G. Cooke, *The Blind Man Traces the Circle* (Princeton: Princeton University Press, 1969), 199. Cooke remarks that "The problem of his indecorum, especially at the culmination of the Siege of Ismail, comes in for unindignant and overdue reassessment" (xi), and he is echoed by Jerome J. McGann in *Don Juan in Context* (Chicago: University of Chicago Press, 1976). M. K. Joseph, on the other hand, calls the rape passage "the only lapse in human understanding in the whole poem" (*Byron the Poet* [London: Gollancz, 1964], 280), and Rutherford speaks of "a blemish, a breach of decorum" (*Byron*, 172) in the mockery of Catholic burial from the shipwreck passage in 2.55.
4. George M. Ridenour, *The Style of "Don Juan"* (New Haven: Yale University Press, 1960), 19.
5. Cooke opens *Blind Man* with a reference to Wordsworth's comment in his "Essay Supplementary to the Preface" (1815) that "as far as he is great and at the same time *original*, [the English poet] has had the task of *creating* the taste by which it is to be enjoyed: so has it been, so will it continue to be" (quoted in Cooke, 3). Cooke speaks further of the tension between the audience and a poet of satire as being "uneasy and problematical" when it "stands out in lyrical or philosophical poetry." He considers such tension, for Byron as for Wordsworth, under the sign of Romantic revolution. See chapter 1, "Byron and the Romantic Lyric."
6. Mark Storey, *Byron and the Eye of Appetite* (New York: St. Martin's, 1986), 184.
7. Clearly the disparity between the surface and the substance is related to the argument in Lovell's famous essay about the theme of "appearance vs. reality" in *Don Juan* (Ernest J. Lovell, "Irony and Image in *Don Juan*," in *The Major Romantic Poets: A Symposium in Reappraisal*, ed. Clarence D. Thorpe, Carlos Baker, and Bennett Weaver [Carbondale: Southern Illinois University Press, 1957], 129-48). Cooke takes issue with the idea of "appearance and reality" on the grounds that it is hard to know what "reality" is, given Byron's "doctrine of uncertainty." This seems to me rather a semantic than a substantive question (Cooke himself entitles his final chapter in *Blind Man*, "The

Limits of Skepticism: The Byronic Affirmation"); masking and unmasking, like the raising and thwarting of expectations, reach into every part of the poem.

8. For a discussion of the variability of taste, which is the domain of reception theory, see the pioneering study of Levin L. Schücking, *Soziologie der literarischen Geschmacksbildung* (1931), 3d ed. (Bern: Francke, 1961).

9. For a discussion of how this image is associated with the French Revolution and, through Goya, becomes a statement of aesthetic as well as political revolution, see Ronald Paulson, *Representations of Revolution (1789 - 1820)* (New Haven: Yale University Press, 1983), 24ff. and 367ff. See, too, Storey, *Eye of Appetite,* chap. 1.

10. Since this chapter was written, an analysis of *Don Juan* has appeared that reaches many of the conclusions that I do about the function of taste in the poem; see Carol Shiner Wilson, "Stuffing the Verdant Goose: Culinary Esthetics in *Don Juan,*" *Mosaic* 24 (1991): 33–52.

11. Elizabeth Boyd, *Byron's "Don Juan." A Critical Study* (New Brunswick, N.J.: Rutgers University Press, 1945), 46.

12. See Wilma Paterson, "Was Byron Anorexic?," *World Medicine,* 15 May 1982, 35–38, where the argument is carelessly and simplistically constructed, however.

13. Joseph, *Byron the Poet* , 228.

14. Peter Graham, *"Don Juan" and Regency England* (Charlottesville: University Press of Virginia, 1990), 174.

15. Roland Barthes, "L'écrivain en vacances," in *Mythologies* (Paris: Editions du Seuil, 1957), 30–31. [To endow the writer publicly with a good fleshly body, to reveal that he likes dry white wine and underdone steak, is to make even more miraculous for me, and of a more divine essence, the products of his art.] *Mythologies,* trans. Annette Lavers (New York: Hill and Wang, 1972), 31.

16. See Arthur C. Danto, *The Transfiguration of the Commonplace: A Philosophy of Art* (Cambridge, Mass.: Harvard University Press, 1981).

17. "What a dreadful thing life is, don't you agree? It is a soup with a lot of hair on top, but which must be eaten nevertheless" (Flaubert, *Correspondance,* ed. Jean Bruneau [Paris: Gallimard, 1973], vol. 2, letter of 24 February 1852 to Henriette Collier). In an article written a few years later, "Pour une psycho-sociologie de l'alimentation contemporaine," Barthes distances himself from the attitudes in *Mythologies* and derides scholars for their association of gastronomy with triviality. As I mentioned in chapter 1 with reference to this article, Barthes has historians in mind, not literary critics.

18. Andrew Rutherford, ed. *Byron: The Critical Heritage* (New York: Barnes and Noble, 1970), 179; hereafter cited as *The Critical Heritage.* For a discussion of Byron and Southey, specifically with respect to *Don Juan,* see the chapter "Southey's *Letters from England: By Manuel Alvarez Espriella, Translated from the Spanish* (1807)" in Graham, *Don Juan.*

19. Rutherford, *The Critical Heritage,* 197.

20. Rutherford, *The Critical Heritage,* 186.

21. Bate, *Shakespeare and Romantic Imagination,* 233.

22. Thomas Bourke, who in other respects is a good reader of *Don Juan,* insists that there are "at most" three or four puns in the whole poem (*Stilbruch als Stilmittel: Studien zur Literatur der Spät- und Nachromantik* [Frankfurt am Main: Peter Lang, 1980], 214). Ridenour, on the other hand, argues: "There is little point in merely listing examples of Byron's word-play, but one might

be permitted a mild protest against the condescension with which it seems often to be dismissed. The examples already cited might suggest that Byron usually knew what he was doing" (*Style,* 137). Ridenour speaks more hesitantly than he probably would now. Cooke is also slightly hesitant about acknowledging the importance of the pun; in a footnote, he asks whether it is "sheer mischief" to notice Byron's plays on words (*Blind Man,* 139). In discussing Byron's play with Russian names in the war cantos, Cooke remarks—again in a footnote—that "The penetration and complexity of [Byron's] response to 'names' is commendable on philosophical as well as satirical grounds" (188). It is Cooke who most articulately states the reasons for the pun's significance, though he is referring specifically to Byron's use of rhymes and wit: "In having recourse to wit, to wicked rhymes and 'fastbreak' stanza patterns, Byron is not gratuitously, or even mainly out to scuttle standard values, which in the long run his kind of examination may stimulate one to prune, prop, and furnish with constant, conscious nurture. Rather he impugns, by demonstration, the overwhelming power of one source of standard values, namely language. Byron takes care to remind us that such values frequently have a linguistic base, and being skeptical of the extent to which 'words make rules' (XVII.iii), he brings language itself under the poem's panoramic machinery of examination" (155–56).

23. In *"Don Juan" in Context,* McGann calls Byron's decision to name the divisions in his poem "cantos" "the most important event in Byron's literary career" (60).

24. In *"Don Juan" in Context,* Jerome McGann comments that Byron "set out to save both past and present" (73) and that the Horatian rules of decorum and style "were the exact opposite of dead prescriptions" (76). Like Ridenour before him, McGann uses his remarkable erudition to show Byron's awareness and understanding of a classical tradition, but it seems to me that McGann pays too little attention to the evolution of that tradition by the time Byron was writing. For Byron to know and show that rules attributed to Horace are removed from their source does not erase the conditioning engendered by their misapplication. Levin Schücking's analogy to fashion when he discusses the sociology of literary taste is most pertinent: fashions that seemed normal once will after a while seem strange. Etymology exemplifies the process, and it is therefore surprising, given the attention McGann pays in his edition of *Don Juan* to wordplay and etymology, that he should succumb for the sake of argument to anachronistic thinking. It is also inconsistent with his otherwise admirable emphasis, indicated as early as the title, on "the importance of context upon ideas and actions" (*"Don Juan" in Context,* 106).

On the use of tradition in order to set oneself apart from it, see Peucker's chapter on Trakl in *Lyric Descent;* and J. Hillis Miller, "The Critic as Host," in *Deconstruction and Criticism,* ed. Harold Bloom et al. (New York: Continuum, 1979), 217–53.

25. Ridenour, *Style,* xi; M. K. Joseph, "The Artist and the Mirror: The Narrator in *Don Juan,"* in *Twentieth-Century Interpretations of "Don Juan,"* ed. Edward E. Bostetter (Englewood Cliffs, N.J.: Prentice-Hall, 1969), 36. *Don Juan* has inspired more good commentary than one might assume from reading Cecil Y. Lang's article "Narcissus Jilted: Byron, *Don Juan,* and the Biographical Imperative," in *Historical Studies and Literary Criticism,* ed. Jerome J. McGann (Madison: University of Wisconsin Press, 1985), 143–79. Lang's

article contains much that is ingenious and much that should be taken seriously; but it seems to me neither as radical nor as "biographical" as he implies and consequently makes me wonder what all the fuss is about. Why does he fail to cite Peter Manning, *Byron and His Fictions* (Detroit: Wayne State University Press, 1978), which steals some of his thunder? For an excellent and extensive discussion of *Don Juan* criticism into the early 1980s, see the Byron chapter by John Clubbe in *English Romantic Poets*, ed. Frank Jordan, 4th ed. (New York: Modern Language Association, 1985).

26. Wilson, "Stuffing the Verdant Goose," considers Byron's mention of olla podrida to be a self-reflexive designation for the genre of his poem.

27. See Graham, *Don Juan* on this stanza. I quote at length because of the evidence Graham provides for the poetological importance I attribute to wordplay in general and to ambiguous taste in particular: "Along with lining portmanteaus, wrapping pastries was a fate for which literary works gone aground were destined in Byron's day—so the cooks are not only themselves 'oblivious' to the merits of *Don Juan,* they also act to promote its oblivion in the wider world. There is considerable delight in seeing Byron's skill at fusing Parnassus, the inland mountain of Apollo and the Muses, with the rocky coast of Cornwall, so deadly to ships, then blending the Cornish pillagers of shipwrecks with the metropolitan purveyors of Cornish pasties and other baked goods. The hybrid phrase 'Castilian tea' adds further refinements. The idea of brewing tea for salon frequenters from the waters of the Parnassian spring Castilia suggests, as does 'Cornish plunderers of Parnassian wrecks,' a distinctively English debasement of something sacred—a sacrilege both literally and symbolically appropriate to the circumstances" (148).

28. Ridenour comments that "if *Don Juan* has any one serious defect as a work of art it is that in spite of its insistent casualness it makes its point with such single-minded perseverance" (*Style,* ix). Such concessions—as if it were necessary to defend one's interest in the poem—are themselves a tribute to taste, to the taste that for a long time refused to acknowledge the qualities of *Don Juan.* There is a progressive diminution in defensiveness from Ridenour to Cooke, however. Cooke's preface opens with the following sentence: "There have been times, in the peculiar evolution of Byron studies, when critics have made it appear somehow unseeemly to praise Byron as a poet unless such praise came parceled up with some pointed strictures" (*Blind Man,* vii). In his edition, McGann relaxes the emphasis on the poem's "flaws" that he sometimes placed in *"Don Juan" in Context.*

29. Joseph, *Byron the Poet,* 228. Ridenour has some good pages on the banquet in canto 15. The article by W. Paul Elledge, "Byron's Hungry Sinner: The Quest Motif in *Don Juan,*" *JEGP* 69 (1970): 1–13, has some interesting comments; Elledge considers eating representative of "tragic lessons of human paradox" and gives his interpretation a Freudian slant.

30. Alvin Kernan, *The Plot of Satire* (New Haven: Yale University Press, 1965), 171–221, here 182.

31. William Makepeace Thackeray, "Memorials of Gormandising: In a Letter to Oliver Yorke, Esq., by M. A. Titmarsh," *Fraser's Magazine for Town and Country* 138 (1841): 710–25, here 712–13.

32. Ridenour's analysis of the dedication is essential reading; it seems to me, however, that he stresses Byron's adherence to tradition so much that he slights his deviance from it. Yet tradition is valuable as a gauge of innovation,

just as biographical details make an author's poetic transformation more clear. Byron's ability to appropriate and innovate is evident in his combination of the pun on blackbirds in a pie, which was the well-known joke of a contemporary (cf. DJ/P 565), and of images from *Hints from Horace*, where flight is connected with a fish and with gustatory as well as sexual metaphors:

One falls while following elegance too fast,
Another soars, inflated with bombast;
Too low a third crawls on, afraid to fly,
He spins his subject to satiety;
Absurdly wavering, he at last engraves
Fish in the woods, and boars beneath the waves!

(BPW 1:291)

33. Rutherford, *Byron*, 56.
34. The association of Milton is reiterated later in the poem, for example in the lines "Since Eve ate apples, much depends on dinner" (13.99). In *Byron and Joyce through Homer: "Don Juan" and "Ulysses"* (New York: Columbia University Press, 1981), Hermione de Almeida makes some persuasive comments about this line and other culinary details in the poem, for instance on 70 and 201. In chapter 1 she discusses Byron's use of and independence from Homer and remarks, for example, that "if Homer is touchstone he is also punching-bag, if he is point of direction he is also point of diversion" (20). Her emphasis on the differences rather than the similarities between Byron and his predecessors is clearly drawn and useful.
35. Over the past twenty-five years, the references to this play on words are themselves revealing of changes in scholarly decorum: from Ridenour (1960) to Cooke (1969) to the Penguin edition (1979) to McGann in the Oxford edition (1986). Byron comments on the indecorum of nicknames elsewhere in the poem, for example in canto 8:

Up came John Johnson (I will not say Jack,
   For that were vulgar, cold and commonplace
On great occasions, such as an attack
On cities, as hath been the present case).

(DJ/0 8.97)

36. *Criticism: The Major Texts,* ed. W. J. Bate, enlarged ed. (New York: Harcourt Brace Javanovich, 1970), 367 (I am grateful to Paul Fry for drawing my attention to this connection). In his notes to the Oxford edition, McGann ascribes considerable importance to the role of Coleridge's *Biographia Literaria* in the genesis of Byron's poem (DJ/O 668).
37. Cooke quotes these passages from Wordsworth in the first chapter of *Blind Man*, 5–6. What Cooke says about the meaning of truth for Byron needs to be kept in mind along with a sense of Byron's playfulness: "as in his repeated demands for a poetry of truth, a poetry that was profitable to society, logical, and moral, [Byron] seems typically to have made over the terms he undeniably borrowed from the Enlightenment. Truth for him carries little of the idea of tradition and authority, of standard and systematic values which are available and beneficial to the individual; it means candor and pervasive dis-

tinction" (13). Cooke also discusses the meaning of truth in the poem "I Would I Were a Careless Child" (23-25), where the following lines are particularly appropriate:

Once I beheld a splendid dream,
A visionary scene of bliss:
Truth!—wherefore did thy hated beam
Awake me to a world like this?

In *Don Juan,* the "hated beam" has evolved into an acceptance characterized by humor, resignation, and control. On Byron's attitude toward the poetry of Wordsworth and Coleridge and Keats, and on his "use" of it in *Don Juan,* see McGann, *"Don Juan" in Context.*

38. The connection of Southey to ambiguous taste is repeated, too, in the comment that a poet who wants to eat must do what the audience wants: "An eastern antijacobin at last / He turn'd, preferring pudding to *no* praise" (3.79). Southey is not identical to Haidée's poet, however; as Graham remarks in *Don Juan:* "because the singer of 'The Isles of Greece' is not purely Southey, or Byron, or Crashaw, or Horace, he can be pure poet" (191).

39. Bostetter, *Twentieth-Century Interpretations,* xxiii.

40. W. H. Auden, "A That-There Poet," in Bostetter, *Twentieth-Century Intepretations,* 16. Ridenour considers the meaning of the motto to be a changeable one within the poem: "Whatever the Horation *Difficile* meant at the beginning of *Don Juan,* it has now come to refer to the commonplace humanity set before the prospective epic poet of the early 19th century" (*Style,* 108). On Byron's manipulation of language and its connection to the Horatian motto, see, too, the essay by Peter J. Manning, "*Don Juan* and Byron's Imperceptiveness to the English Word," *Studies in Romanticism* 18 (1979): 207–33, recently reprinted in Robert F. Gleckner, *Critical Essays on Byron* (New York: G. K. Hall, 1991), 109–33.

41. McGann adds another layer to the function and meaning of "true" when he remarks that the rhyme of Juan with "true one" contains "an oblique reference to the biblical 'true Messiah,' a notion which Byron has been playing with throughout his poem's Preface and Dedication" (DJ/O 673).

42. Byron's transformations of the Don Juan myth have often been noted; see Boyd, *Byron's "Don Juan";* and, on the inversion of expectations as exemplifications of irony, Lilian Furst, *Fictions of Romantic Irony* (Cambridge, Mass.: Harvard University Press, 1984).

43. Graham, *Don Juan,* 8.

44. Ridenour, *Style,* 141.

45. See Furst, *Fictions of Romantic Irony,* 115. The image is similar to Ridenour's, but more vivid.

46. On the subject of art and nature in the poem, it is important to keep in mind the distinction made by Ridenour: "the overt contrast between art and nature is in some ways less significant in the world of *Don Juan* than is the contrast between the two aspects of either nature or art taken in themselves" (*Style,* 49–50). Ridenour takes up Byron's association of art and nature is his discussion of the banquet at Norman Abbey, and he connects the octave on *goût* and the gout to the theme of the Fall, which he associates with the gout.

47. Cooke, *Blind Man,* 141; McGann, *"Don Juan" in Context,* 107. McGann's comment about "multiple meanings" is anticipated by Joseph, who speaks of a "technique of organised multiplicity" (*Byron the Poet,* 259).

48. Others who emphasize the simultaneous opposites in the poem are Cooke, who says that any "apparent confusion in his work results from an extraordinary accuracy in rendering the simultaneity of plural states," which he calls "a keynote of Byron's style" (*Blind Man,* 119); or Anne K. Mellor, *English Romantic Irony* (Cambridge, Mass.: Harvard University Press, 1980), who calls *Don Juan* "that *locus classicus* of English romantic irony" (31) and says that the "achievement of *Don Juan* is to balance the antithetical impulses without reconciling or synthesizing them" (58); or de Almeida, *Byron and Joyce,* who comments on the simultaneity of high and low, 126–30.

49. The connection of bad art with disease is present as early as the dedication; Ridenour comments that "[Southey] embodies a disease that has become epidemic of late, especially among poets ('a common case'), and it is the satirist's function to diagnose the 'case' and expose the real nature of the infection" (*Style,* 1).

50. See Wilson's interpretation of the wordplay on *goût* and gout in "Stuffing the Verdant Goose," 46–47.

51. According to McGann, the acute accent was added later, which confirms my claim about its purpose.

52. Lovell, "Irony and Image," 26. Graham remarks of the banquet: "All the world is ransacked for the aristocratic table, then the French dictionary is pillaged to name the exotic dishes" (*Don Juan,* 47).

53. Brecht, *Gesammelte Werke in 20 Bänden,* vol. 9, *Gedichte 2* (Frankfurt am Main: Suhrkamp, 1967), 633.

54. Ridenour, *Style,* 35–41.

55. Ridenour, *Style,* 39.

56. The passage offers an excellent illustration of what de Almeida shows in chapter 1 of *Byron and Joyce.*

57. The network of allusions becomes even more complex if we add the possible connection between Cleopatra's pearls and digestion mentioned in DJ/P 741; the reference to Cleopatra's melted pearls follows a reference to the poet's Muse and "squeamish people" (64), and the whole passage is full of double entendre.

58. See, too, James Hogg, "Byron's Vascillating Attitude towards Napoleon," in *Byron: Poetry and Politics,* ed. James Hogg and Erwin A. Stürzl (Salzburg: Salzburg Studies in English Literature, 1975).

59. Revel, *Un Festin en paroles,* 216.

60. Lang's pronouncement that "this multilayered passage is the richest lode in all *Don Juan*" ("Narcissus Jilted," 168) is a dubious exaggeration for a poem so rich. Nevertheless, his comments about Lord Henry provide an example of intelligent and useful biographical criticism.

61. Cooke's dismissive comment that Byron's reference to Molière in 13.94 "is more pedantic than significant" (*Blind Man,* 133) seems to me debatable, especially given its placement after the description of Norman Abbey and in the midst of a series of gustatory references. I suspect that as much could be uncovered in the reference to Molière as Cooke uncovers concerning Congreve. I am thinking for example of the scene in the second act of Molière's own *Don Juan,* the one in which he makes love to two women simulta-

neously: the virtuosic use of double entendre is a comic exposition of Don Juan's double-dealings and hypocrisy in Molière's play, but it is also related to the questions of simultaneous opposites that I have been discussing here. Furthermore, both authors share a religious skepticism, a contempt for "cant," and a mistrust of decorum for decorum's sake.

62. Ridenour says that "the turbot (*rhombus*) is an almost indispensable part of the equipment of the satirist who is treating of social decay in terms of diet. Pope mentions it twice in his 'imitation' of Horace's *Serm.* ii.ii. It is almost as conventional as Pope's and Byron's mechanical references to the appetite of aldermen" (*Style*, 35-36). The turbot is one of the items on the "bill of fare" at the Amundeville banquet in canto 15.

63. See Cooke, who says that Byron "has contrived or conspired to keep enough of the cultural sense of the Fall to elicit a distinct emotional reaction to the evidence of man's imperfection, much as Milton makes poetic capital of a mythological currency he is thematically devaluating (Hesperian fables true, if true, here only). For Byron effectively collapses the religious and moral propositions founded on that evidence" (*Blind Man*, 130–31).

64. There may be an allusion here to Coleridge's poem "The Rime of the Ancient Mariner," of which McGann finds other echoes in the shipwreck passage. See the discussion of the cannibalism by Philip W. Martin, *Byron, a Poet before His Public* (Cambridge: Cambridge University Press, 1982), 208-18, who argues that Byron alludes to the shipwreck of the *Medusa* but pretends, coyly and decorously, not to mention it.

65. See Robert F. Gleckner, *Byron and the Ruins of Paradise* (Baltimore: Johns Hopkins University Press, 1967), 343-44, who emphasizes the connection of violence and Christ in another of Byron's literal interpretations of the Bible: Lambro is called a "fisher of men," and the phrase is repeated later to "describe the more civilized piracy, slavery, and slaughter of love amid society in exactly the same phrase, 'Fishers for men' (XII, 59)."

66. McGann, DJ/O 676. On this passage, see, too, Storey, *Eye of Appetite*, 188.

67. Cooke quotes from this letter in a note to *Blind Man* and has some pertinent remarks on the relation between the sensual and the ideal, especially 154–55.

68. Cooke, *Blind Man*, 201.

69. BLJ 1:190, letter of 25 January 1809 to Robert Charles Dallas. Fielding advances the same argument about the naming of genres in his preface to *Joseph Andrews* and some of the prefatory chapters from *Tom Jones*.

70. See the article by Hans Jürgen Diller, "The Function of Verse in Byron's *Don Juan*," in *The Constance Byron Symposium, 1977*, ed. James Hogg (Salzburg: Salzburg Studies in English Literature, 1978), 5–20, where he discusses the question of verse from the perspective of Russian formalism.

71. de Almeida, *Byron and Joyce*, 119.

72. *Kritische Friedrich-Schlegel-Ausgabe* 2:173.

73. Philip Martin argues that one of the most distinctive qualities about this poem is Byron's "aristocratic independence" and his refusal to consider the taste of his mostly middle-class readership (*Poet before His Public*, 184, 191); he also speaks of the tone in parts as the "table talk of elitist minority." I am not entirely comfortable with this thesis, but if one accepts it, it adds another irony to the literary rejection of "aristocratic" genres.

Chapter 4

1. See Barker Fairley, "Heine and the Festive Board," *University of Toronto Quarterly* 36 (1967): 209–19, here 209; Werner Vordtriede, *Heine-Kommentar* (Munich: Winkler, 1970), 28–33; Bernd Wetzel, "Das Motiv des Essens und seine Bedeutung für das Werk Heinrich Heines" (diss. University of Munich, 1972). Wetzel is also struck by the implications of Fairley's admission that he did not notice the culinary references until Hofrichter pointed them out to him. See my discussion of Wetzel in "Wine, Women, and Song: Sensory Referents in the Works of Heinrich Heine" (Ph.D. diss., Yale University 1979).
2. Fairley, "Festive Board," 214.
3. T. J. Reed, "Heines Appetit," in *Heine-Jahrbuch* 22 (1983): 9–29; here 17 and 18. See, too, Albrecht Betz, *Ästhetik und Politik: Heinrich Heines Prosa* (Munich: Hanser, 1971).
4. Peter Rühmkorf, "Suppentopf und Guillotine: Zu Heines Frauengestalten," *Heine-Jahrbuch* 24 (1985): 255–78.
5. One exception is Rolf Hosfeld, *Die Welt als Füllhorn: Heine* (Berlin: Oberbaum, 1984), whose Bakhtinian reading acknowledges the function of this chapter. See, too, Dierk Möller's "Nachwort" to his Reclam edition of *Ideen. Das Buch Le Grand* (Stuttgart, 1972), where he mentions the importance of chapter 14, but without elaboration. Two other critics who consistently note the structural importance of culinary allusions in Heine's works are Slobodan Grubačić, *Heines Erzählprosa: Ein Versuch* (Stuttgart: Kohlhammer, 1975); and Gerhard Höhn, *Heine-Handbuch: Zeit, Person, Werk* (Stuttgart: Metzler, 1987).
6. Jeffrey L. Sammons, *The Elusive Poet* (New Haven: Yale University Press, 1969), 298–99.
7. Betz considers *Schnabelewopski* from a political point of view in *Ästhetik und Politik,* and the interpretation contains many pertinent observations. Betz focuses too much on one class of society, however, and distorts a major theme of *Schnabelewopski,* which is that materialism is not limited to one class, one country, or one gender, but is instead a human trait. It is not accurate to equate the term *Philister,* which designates a mentality, and the word *Bourgeois,* which designates a class, as Betz does (93); such oversimplification in the midst of much subtlety is the flaw in Betz's reading of the Simson chapter as well, which he calls a "Schluß-Allegorie" in which Simson is identical to Börne.
8. Immermann's awareness that food has a paradigmatic and innovative function for Heine is evident from the *Xenien* he wrote at Heine's request for *Die Bäder von Lucca;* Wetzel notes the similarity in "Motiv des Essens," 69.
9. Höhn, *Heine-Handbuch,* passim.
10. See Wolfgang Preisendanz, who quotes a sampling of contemporary responses to Heine's revolutionary style in the chapter "Der Funktionsübergang von Dichtung und Publizistik" from *Heinrich Heine. Werkstrukturen und Epochenbezüge,* 2d ed. (Munich: Fink, 1983), 21–23.
11. Luciano Zagari and Paolo Chiarini, eds. *Zu Heinrich Heine* (Stuttgart: Ernst Klett, 1981), 5–21, here 6. The authors stress that such scrutiny is not to be

confused with an *Ehrenrettung,* the kind of defensive apology or vindication that frequently are present in discussions of Heine.

12. How Heine makes details reflect the whole, in particular in *Die Bäder von Lucca,* is a subject I have examined in another context. See "Heine as Freud's Double in *Der Witz und seine Beziehung zum Unbewußten,*" *Heine-Jahrbuch* 31 (1992): 137–62.

13. See Stefan Bodo Würffel, who makes the point eloquently in *Der produktive Widerspruch: Heinrich Heines negative Dialektik* (Bern: Francke, 1986), 87.

14. Michael Perraudin (*Heinrich Heine: Poetry in Context.* [London: Berg, 1989]) examines Heine's use of models like the *Volkslied* or Goethe to create his own, original style. The fact that Perraudin does not deal with "Sie saßen und tranken am Teetisch" implies that the poem is not one in which Heine cites another poet; that would confirm my argument that in this poem Heine demonstrates a new style.

15. See Wulf Wülfing, "Skandalöser 'Witz': Untersuchungen zu Heines Rhetorik," in *Artistik und Engagement,* ed. Wolfgang Kuttenkeuler (Stuttgart: Metzler, 1977), 43–65, who is right to question Preisendanz's charge that Heine's is merely sophomoric. See Grappin in DHA 1:2.837, who considers Heine's comic tone to be an innovation; he speaks of a "Lustspielszene." Peter Christian Giese gives a good reading of this poem in "Das Symposion am Teetisch. Heinrich Heine: 'Lyrisches Intermezzo,' Nr. 50," *Heine-Jahrbuch* 26 (1987): 208–18. The relationship Giese perceives (210) between the watered-down conversation at table, literally represented by what he assumes to be weak tea, and stimulating conversation, resembles the contrast between a watered-down neoclassical aesthetic and Heine's more robust style. Giese's closing argument is that this poem is an ironic variation on Plato's *Symposium* (213).

16. Giese, "Das Symposion am Teetisch," 209; Giese likewise stresses the function of contrasts in the poem (see especially 210).

17. Höhn, *Heine-Handbuch,* 51.

18. Benno von Wiese discusses this changing quality of language in *Signaturen: Zu Heinrich Heine und seinem Werk* (Berlin: Erich Schmidt, 1976), albeit from another perspective. See, too, Kurt Weinberg, *Henri Heine, Romantique défroqué* (New Haven: Yale University Press, 1954), who was the first to make a serious study of Heine's relation to French symbolist poetry. There is no mention of Heine in *Struktur der modernen Lyrik,* Hugo Friedrich's study of German "symbolism" as a model for the French.

19. Louis Marin, "La Parole mangée ou le corps divin saisi par les signes," in *La Parole mangée,* 11–35. See, too, Neumann, "Essen und Literatur," whose intelligent treatment of food and literature includes a discussion of the literal representation of transubstantiation in Kleist and Kafka.

20. S. S. Prawer, *The Tragic Satirist* (Cambridge: Cambridge University Press, 1961), 146–47. Heine's treatment of the Eucharist in "Vitzliputzli" contrasts with his depiction of Spanish foods in part 1, where it is associated with the Spanish homeland (ironically designated as "die traute Christenheimat") (DHA 3:1.62).

21. For other ways in which Heine's practice accords with Schlegel's theories, see Kolb, "'Die Puppenspiele meines Humors.'"

22. Claudia Albert underscores this flaw in an otherwise laudatory review of the book in *Arbitrium* 3 (1990): 338–40.

23. A related prejudice of Adorno's with respect to Heine's position as a Jew was discussed by Peter Uwe Hohendahl in "Ambiguous Celebration: Adorno as Reader of Heine" (paper presented at the annual meeting of the Modern Language Association, Washington, D.C., 28 December 1989). On Adorno's reading of Heine, see Hosfeld in the chapter "Hinter den Kulissen des lyrischen Ich," *Die Welt als Füllhorn*, 66–68; and Paul Peters, *Heinrich Heine "Dichterjude": Die Geschichte einer Schmähung* (Frankfurt am Main: Hain, 1990).

24. [Heine's own innovation exists on a formal level, but it is a level of form that itself sustains meaning.] Hosfeld, *Die Welt als Füllhorn*, 151.

25. See Prawer, *The Tragic Satirist*, and *Heine's Jewish Comedy. A Study of His Portraits of Jews and Judaism* (Oxford: Clarendon Press, 1983): "It has of late become clear that Heine's work is all of a piece, that the procedures of his poetry are not abandoned in his prose *Pictures of Travel*, his attempts at narrative fiction, and his journalistic reports" (27).

26. Heine says this in the first of the "Bruchstücke" of *Die Götter im Exil*, called "Stil-Anathema," DHA 9:294. See, too, Wülfing's comments on "Stil und Zensur" in "Skandalöser 'Witz.'"

27. Ritchie Robertson, *Heine* (New York: Grove Press, 1988), viii. Robertson also remarks (like Sengle in the Heine chapter of *Biedermeierzeit*) that "Some of [Heine's] admirers, one feels, cannot quite admit that someone who is so much fun to read can be a great writer" (viii).

28. See the discussion of the shift as it progresses through the nineteenth and into the twentieth centuries in Peucker, *Lyric Descent*. See, too, Dieter Lamping, *Das lyrische Gedicht: Definitionen zu Theorie und Geschichte der Gattung* (Göttingen: Vandenhoeck and Ruprecht, 1989).

29. The way prose and poetry are mixed to establish a new style is intelligently treated by Alfred Opitz in his edition of *Reisebilder II* (DHA 7). See, too, Thomas Bourke, *Stilbruch als Stilmittel*, esp. chaps. 1 and 5, where Bourke discusses the expectations raised merely by seeing verse.

30. *Der produktive Widerspruch*, 8; Würffel quotes Briegleb's explanation for his ordering of texts, which is that Heine is not the kind of "Klassiker" or "classical author" who maintains the purity of genre.

31. Prawer says that the "Doppelgänger" poem "may fairly be called the key-poem of the whole *Buch der Lieder* and a key-figure of Heine's poetry as a whole" (*The Tragic Satirist*, 2). See Perraudin's interpretation of the "Doppelgänger" poem in *Heinrich Heine*, 72–80.

32. For examples of the criticism that Heine's poems contain too much "truth," see Erich Mayser, *Heinrich Heines "Buch der Lieder" im 19. Jahrhundert* (Stuttgart: Akademischer Verlag Hans-Dieter Heinz, 1978). Much contemporary criticism of Heine also revolved around the terms *poetisch* and *prosaisch*, which is further reflected in the passage from Heine's preface.

33. See my discussion of this connection, for Freud as well as Heine, in "Heine as Freud's Double."

34. Perraudin, *Heinrich Heine*, 175–76.

35. Sammons, *The Elusive Poet*, 132 and 149. Although I differ with Sammons about some of the culinary allusions in *Buch Le Grand*, my reading does not diverge from his (which remains useful and fresh twenty-five years after it was written).

319

36. In his interpretation of this work (*Heines Erzählprosa,* 41–58), Grubačić speaks of the paradigmatic quality of Heine's "Dauerdissonanzen" [perpetual dissonances], of a "Kontrastharmonie" [harmony of contrast], and of the simultaneity of Heine's opposites (47, 55, and 57).

37. Sammons, *The Elusive Poet,* 122; and Grubačić, *Heines Erzählprosa,* 45.

38. Sammons, *The Elusive Poet,* 125.

39. Heine, *Buch Le Grand,* ed. Möller, 77.

40. Möller's omission is surprising in light of his emphasis on the importance of eating and drinking as a metaphor in the work (90). In *Signaturen,* Benno von Wiese considers these details to be autobiographical childhood memories and nothing more (32). Sammons, on the other hand, interprets each item in the list, which he summarizes as "a catalogue of elements that make up the present persona"; he does not omit the soup, but associates it with sensual enjoyment (*This Elusive Poet,* 136).

41. See the interpretation of the wordplay on *Schürzen* in Sammons, *The Elusive Poet,* 136; the pun does not translate.

42. Sterne, *A Sentimental Journey,* ed. Garner D. Stout Jr. (Berkeley and Los Angeles: University of California Press, 1967), 210.

43. Washington Irving, *Tales of a Traveller,* ed. Andrew B. Myers (New York: American Library, 1991), 384 and 385.

44. Preisendanz, "Glückslandschaften als Gegenwelt: Modalitäten des Idyllischen bei Heine," in *Heinrich Heine* 158–74, here 171.

45. Preisendanz, *Heinrich Heine,* 122–23.

46. Sammons, *The Elusive Poet,* 138.

47. Sammons, *The Elusive Poet,* 127.

48. Sammons says of the recovery that "pride in poetic genius inspires an ultimately invincible love of life. In the center resides the irony that allows a substantially healthy self-awareness" (*The Elusive Poet,* 129).

49. Perraudin, *Heinrich Heine,* chap. 4, "From 'Die Weihe' to 'Im Hafen': 'Beginning and End of My Lyrical Youth,'" 119–42, 120, 132, and 121 respectively.

50. Perraudin, *Heinrich Heine,* 140.

51. The word *ménagerie* is the one Diderot uses in *Le Neveu de Rameau* when he has "Lui" describe the table at Bertin's, where the writers and artists are also called "parasites." In the critical edition to Diderot's dialogue, Jean Fabre glosses the word *ménagerie* as having been introduced in the eighteenth century to designate literary societies that are sustained by powerful patrons. On the function of Diderot's banquet and its connection to Trimalchio's banquet in the *Satyricon* of Petronius (which is a model for Heine as well), see Beatrice C. Fink, "The Banquet as Phenomenon or Structure in Selected Eighteenth-century French Novels," *Studies on Voltaire and the Eighteenth Century* 152 (1976): 729–40.

52. It has rightly been observed (for example by Hosfeld, *Die Welt als Füllhorn,* 126) that the figure of Napoleon is himself representative of ambiguity; for this reason, too, he is an appropriate projection of the poet's attitutes and aesthetic. See Höhn's summary of the role Napoleon plays in *Buch Le Grand* (*Heine-Handbuch,* 178–80).

53. Many critics have commented perceptively about Heine and Sterne, among them Grubačić, *Heines Erzählprosa,* 54; Nigel Reeves, *Heinrich Heine: Poetry and Politics* (Oxford: Oxford University Press, 1974), 113–16, who calls *Buch*

Le Grand "a miniature *Tristram Shandy*"; Jürgen Jacobs, "Zu Heines *Ideen. Das Buch Le Grand*," *Heine-Jahrbuch* 7 (1968): 3–11; Jost Hermand in his commentary to the work (DHA 6:830); and especially Hosfeld throughout his interpretation of *Buch Le Grand* in *Die Welt als Füllhorn*, 95–132.

54. The French lesson offers another stylization of the two strands that the poet is working into his aesthetic: the students are reading both the *Art poétique* of Horace and an "Histoire allemande."

55. Jost Hermand, *Der frühe Heine: Ein Kommentar zu den "Reisebildern"* (Munich: Winkler, 1976), especially 107–9. Hermand speaks of the title as "ein wesentlich weiter gefaßtes gesellschaftspolitisches und geschichtsphilosophisches Programm" [a much more broadly conceived programmatic statement about social politics and the history of philosophy] (107). Sammons speaks of the passage as "a concentrated attack of the poetic sensibility upon the more trivial products of the rational mind, a satire upon thoughtless rigor by means of the poetic technique of verbal association" (*The Elusive Poet*, 144); Grubačić calls the passage a parody of philosophical idealism (*Heines Erzählprosa*, 45); and Hosfeld connects the "Ideen" to "Ideen-Assoziationen" as a principal of structure in the literary and philosophical tradition of Sterne, Locke, and Hegel ("Le Grands Trommel," in *Die Welt als Füllhorn*, 95–132).

56. Irving's phrase here, "to imbibe their principles of taste," has little bearing on the present discussion, except as more evidence that "taste" is invariably mentioned in connection with literary tradition.

57. Hosfeld, *Die Welt als Füllhorn*, argues that this passage is written in the style of Menippean satire, but it is equally important to note Heine's personalized version of the tradition.

58. Laura Hofrichter, *Heinrich Heine*, trans. Barker Fairley (Oxford: Clarendon Press, 1963), 50–51.

59. Fairley, "Festive Board," 210; Sammons, *The Elusive Poet*, 321.

60. Sammons, *The Elusive Poet*, 301, and *Heinrich Heine: A Modern Biography* (Princeton: Princeton University Press, 1979), 186.

61. Manfred Windfuhr, "Heines Fragment eines Schelmenromans: *Aus den Memoiren des Herren von Schnabelewopski*," in *Heinrich Heine*, ed. Helmut Koopmann (Darmstadt: Wissenschaftliche Buchgesellschaft, 1975), 232–56, here 232. See the convincing rebuttal of Windfuhr's argument about the picaresque by Gerhard Kluge, "Heinrich Heines Fragment *Aus den Memoiren des Herren von Schnabelewopski* und das Problem des Schelmischen," in *Amsterdamer Beiträge zur neueren Germanistik* 20 (1985–86): 41–52. Kluge concludes that the work stands outside of fixed categories and that if one must speak of a typology, it can only be that of the "Zerrissenen" that "begins during Romanticism and reaches well into the Modern period" (51).

62. Grubačić, *Heines Erzählprosa*, 79–96.

63. Grubačić, *Heines Erzählprosa*, 82.

64. Höhn takes up a phrase from Grubačić, "komisches Erzählen" [narrative of comedy] to characterize the work, and he, too, speaks of how certain elements—among them the culinary and the erotic—acquire a structural function in the work (*Heine-Handbuch*, 278). Another recent article uses *Schnabelewopski* as its focus for a discussion of self-censorship; see Michael G. Levine, "Heines Ghost Writer: Zum Problem der Selbstzensur im *Schnabelewopski*" *Heine-Jahrbuch* 26 (1987): 9–28.

65. See the notes of the Briegleb edition; Sammons, *Heine: A Modern Biography,* 185; and Sammons, *Heinrich Heine* (Stuttgart: Metzler, 1991), 74–75.
66. Barry G. Thomas, "The van der Pissen Scene in Heinrich Heine's *Schnabelewopski:* A suggestion," *German Quarterly* 51 (1978): 39–46, here 41. Grubačić explains this scene as an enactment of carnivalistic symbols (*Heines Erzählprosa,* 92–94); I find his argument less persuasive than that of Thomas, because Grubačić does not take into account the way rituals have become removed from their source.
67. Thomas, "Van der Pissen Scene," 41.
68. See Kluge, who considers the punning expressive of the narrator's "complex dualistic perception of reality" rather than simply a characteristic of the picaro's effort to provoke ("Heines Fragment," 44).
69. On the figure of Amor, see Grubačić, *Heines Erzählprosa,* 85.
70. On the relationship of food, love, and money, see Betz, *Ästhetik und Politik,* 85–86.
71. Grubačić goes so far as to speak of a "nihilism" in matters of form and to extend that nihilism to Heine's view of the world (*Heines Erzählprosa,* 92). This seems to me extreme, and I believe that the problem for Heine (as for Byron) is rooted in his frustration at the practical application of laws, poetic or otherwise, not in their spirit.
72. I do not agree with Sammons that the Jan Steen passage is "a kind of wistful programmatic description of an aesthetic purpose that is implied but not really achieved in *Schnabelewopski*" (*The Elusive Poet,* 323).
73. See Grubačić, *Heines Erzählprosa,* 90.
74. On the function of the dreams in this work, see Betz, *Ästhetik und Politik,* 97–101; and Grubačić, *Heines Erzählprosa,* 84–85.
75. On the work's structure, see Grubačić, *Heines Erzählprosa,* 81; and Levine. "Heines Ghost Writer," 14.
76. See Grubačić on the use of models here (*Heines Erzählprosa,* 83). Levine concentrates on this passage in his interpretation of self-censorship in *Schnabelewopski;* but he seems to me to misconstrue this passage, because Heine actually reveals everything he pretends to conceal ("Heine's Ghost Writer," 17–19).
77. There is possibly another allusion to Byron in *Schnabelewopski,* to the poem "The Dream," in which Byron says of dreams that "they do divide our being." See Perraudin, *Heinrich Heine,* 90–92 and 95, who discusses this poem with respect to *Buch der Lieder.* The allusion to *Don Juan* in this passage of *Schnabelewopski* should lay to rest the misconception that Heine did not know Byron's poem; already in the early twenties, when he wrote the *Briefe aus Berlin,* he must at least have known *about* the poem, because he otherwise could not have quoted Southey's condemnation of the "Satanic school," which is a reaction to *Don Juan.* See Hofrichter, *Heinrich Heine,* 47, who says that "We wonder whether [Heine] would have said this if he had read the late Byron, *Don Juan,* for example"; or Bourke, *Stilbruch als Stilmittel,* 227–29, who wishes to preserve Heine's "originality" and appears to be more anxious about influence than Heine was (though I agree with Bourke's main argument, which is that there is an affinity between the two poets that cannot be reduced to a simple question of influence). As so often, S. S. Prawer is the exception. When he speaks of Byron, he has the whole Byron in mind, not just the Byron of the early poems or of *Childe Harold,* and in *Frankenstein's*

Island: England and the English in the Writings of Heinrich Heine, he notes the allusion to *Don Juan* in *Schnabelewopski* (Cambridge: Cambridge University Press, 1987), 160–61.

78. Stefan Bodo Würffel analyzes the Barbarossa passage and its anachronistic, critical nature; he shows for example how the refrain "Sonne, du klagende Flamme" demonstrates the poet's distance from the tradition represented by Barbarossa, since "Sonne" is for Heine a metaphor for freedom and the refrain itself is taken from a French song current during the French Revolution. See *Der produktive Widerspruch,* 220–32. See, too, Jürgen Brummack's rehabilitation of the Hamburg section of the poem and his emphasis on the Aristophanic model in *Satirische Dichtungen* (Munich: Fink, 1979), 181ff.

79. See Woesler, DHA 4:920. For a detailed discussion of Heine and Aristophanes, see Robert Holub, *Heinrich Heine's Reception of German Grecophilia: The Function and Application of the Hellenic Tradition in the First Half of the Nineteenth Century* (Heidelberg: Carl Winter, 1981).

80. Jürgen Walter, *Heinrich Heine. Epoche-Werk-Wirkung,* ed. Jürgen Brummack (Munich: C. H. Beck, 1980), 246.

81. Here I am at odds with critics like Würffel and Holub, who stress Heine's utopian vision. Würffel does, however, reject the idea of a utopian vision for *Deutschland. Ein Wintermärchen.* In the essay "Heine and Utopia" (*Heine-Jahrbuch* 27 [1988]: 86–112), Robert Holub redefines utopia so that it is more compatible with reality and therefore with Heine; see, too, his essay "Heine and the New World" in *Colloquia Germanica* 22 (1989): 101–13.

82. Walter, *Heinrich Heine,* 250.

83. See Reed's article "Heines Appetit," which treats this passage and takes its title from it. Both Walter (*Heinrich Heine,* esp. 242–44) and Höhn (*Heine-Handbuch,* esp. 100–101) list a series of examples illustrative of Heine's style in this and similar passages.

84. Sammons, *The Elusive Poet,* 292.

85. See the explication of this caput by W. Bellmann, "'Cacatum non est pictum'—ein Zitat in Heines *Wintermärchen,*" *Wirkendes Wort* 33 (1983): 213–15. Bellmann finds models for Heine's indecency in Lenz and Brentano and demonstrates how carefully Heine chooses the figures in this caput so that it becomes a "Berlin-Kapitel" in which Berlin is made to stand for all of Germany.

86. S. S. Prawer, "Heines satirische Versdichtung," in *Der Berliner Germanistentagung 1968, Vorträge und Berichte,* ed. Karl Heinz Borck and Rudolf Henss (Heidelberg: Carl Winter, 1970), 179–95, here 189. Prawer explains but disapproves of the indecorum here: "Doch gilt wohl auch von Heine, was Dryden einst über Horaz schrieb: 'He can have no fine palate who feeds so heartily on garbage'" (189).

87. Perraudin, *Heinrich Heine,* 171.

88. Sammons persuasively argues that the two poems must be treated together ("Hunting Bears and Trapping Wolves: *Atta Troll* and *Deutschland,*" in *The Elusive Poet,* 274–300) See, too, the article by Joachim Bark, "Heine im Vormärz: Radikalisierung oder Verweigerung? Eine Untersuchung der Versepen," *Der Deutschunterricht* 31, no. 22 (1979): 47–60.

89. See Fairley's chapter on images of the dance in *Heinrich Heine: An Interpretation* (Oxford: Clarendon Press, 1954) and Benno von Wiese's more exten-

sive interpretation of the dance from *Signaturen* ("Das tanzende Universum," 67–133, esp. 88–103).

90. The equation of smells and modernity is one that Rindisbacher rightly posits in his book, *Smell of Books*. The equation is evident in Heine's use of olfactory referents, although Rindisbacher does not mention him, wanting rather to make "modernity" begin later than Heine wrote.

91. See Prawer's discussion of Heine's technique here in *The Tragic Satirist,* 73–77.

92. Prawer, *The Tragic Satirist,* 66.

Chapter 5

1. Richard Ellmann, "Freud and Literary Biography," *American Scholar* 53 (1984): 465–78, here 476. With respect to Goethe, Rudolf Augstein makes a similar argument in a lengthy review of Kurt Eissler's psychoanalytic study of Goethe, *Der Spiegel,* 30 April 1984, 212–28.

2. See, too, H. G. Haile, "Prudery in the Publication History of Goethe's *Roman Elegies,*" *German Quarterly* 49 (1976): 287–94, and Albrecht Schöne's discussion of Goethe's "Selbstzensur" in the *Paralipomena* to *Faust* ("Satanskult: *Walpurgisnacht*" in *Götterzeichen, Liebeszauber, Satanskult: Neue Einblicke in alte Goethetexte* [Munich: C. H. Beck, 1982], 107–216).

3. For a detailed study of Hugo and German literature, see Charles Dédeyan, *Victor Hugo et l'Allemagne* (Paris: Minard, 1964–65).

4. Goethe repeats this sentiment in the conversation with Eckermann of 5 July 1827 that I quote in chapter 1.

5. Brillat-Savarin, *Physiologie du goût,* 32.

6. Brillat-Savarin, *Physiologie du goût,* 32–33.

7. Brillat-Savarin, *Physiologie du goût,* 33.

8. For a discussion of Goethe as a dilettante, see the chapter on *Die Leiden des jungen Werthers* by Hans R. Vaget in *Goethes Erzählkunst,* ed. Paul Michael Lützeler and James E. McLeod (Stuttgart: Reclam, 1985), 37–72.

9. Wierlacher briefly discusses the gustatory allusions in *Werther* as a reflection of his "illness" (*Essen,* 27). That sounds logical at first, because a loss of appetite often is a symptom of illness, Bärlach's culinary excesses at the end of Dürrenmatt's *Der Richter und sein Henker* being a notable exception. However, the correlation in *Werther* is less explicit than Wierlacher implies. Werther speaks in one letter of not being hungry (30 November 1771; GM 269), but later on, in the final narrated segment of the work, on 21 December, there is no mention of his failing to eat the meal he has brought to his room: "Er ließ sich das Essen auf die Stube bringen, und nach Tische ritt er hinaus zum Amtmanne" (GM 281). His final biblical meal of bread and wine further contradicts Wierlacher's conclusion. Another weakness in Wierlacher's argument is that he supports it with a passage taken out of context: when Lotte says, "Werther, Sie sind sehr krank, Ihre Lieblingsgerichte widerstehen Ihnen" (GM 273; 4 December 1771), she speaks figuratively. She refers here to his favorite *tunes,* not to his favorite dishes, which she has just played for him and which he was unable to enjoy.

Since this chapter was written, Gerhard Kurz has published a study of the poetological significance of culinary allusions in *Faust:* "Das Drama als Ragout: Zur Metaphorik des Essens und Trinkens in Goethes *Faust,*" in *Inter-*

preting Goethe's "Faust" Today, ed. Jane K. Brown, Meredith Lee, and Thomas P. Saine (Columbia, S.C.: Camden House, 1994): 174–86.

10. See the commentary in the Munich and Frankfurt editions of Goethe's works, the "Dokumente zur Wirkungsgeschichte" in GM 958–74, and the segment "Wirkung" of GF 780–90. On the influence of Shakespeare, see the remarks of Nicholas Boyle in *Goethe: The Poet and the Age,* vol. *1, The Poetry of Desire (1749–1790)* (Oxford: Clarendon Press, 1991), 114–16.

11. Friedrich der Grosse, "De la littérature allemande," 60–61.

12. Möser's entire text is published in the edition of Frederick the Great's essay, 121–41. Möser also uses the vocabulary of taste to compare Shakespeare's and Voltaire's portrayal of the death of Caesar: "Man sieht die Verschiedenheit der Wege, worauf diese Nationen zum Tempel des Geschmacks gegangen sind, nicht deutlicher, als wenn man den Tod *Cäsars,* so wie ihn *Shakespeare* und *Voltaire* uns gegeben haben, nebeneinander stellt" [One cannot observe more distinctly the different paths these nations have taken to reach the temple of taste than by comparing the death of Caesar portrayed by Shakespeare and Voltaire] (129). Möser mimics Voltaire's title, *Le Temple du goût,* but he does not object to the notion of taste, only to the rigid application of taste that Voltaire and Frederick the Great require.

13. See Borchmeyer on contemporary judgments of *Götz* according to a Shakespearean or a neoclassical model (GF 794).

14. Boyle, *The Poetry of Desire,* 116; the entire passage (114–25) is well worth reading.

15. Boyle, *The Poetry of Desire,* 119. Boyle speaks of the "'documentary' method" that Goethe uses when he has his characters perform "secondary physical action" such as pouring wine while they are speaking about something else.

16. See GM 920.

17. Some critics consider the allusion to Shakespeare to be more specific yet. See Gerhard Sauder's commentary to *Götz* (GM 976), where he cites Hannah Fischer-Lamberg's edition of *Der junge Goethe* (Berlin and New York: De Gruyter, 1963–73), 2:333 and 3:458.

18. These three scenes are also pivotal as evidence of Goethe's Shakespearean disregard for the unities of time and place. We move from the tavern to Jaxthausen to the prison; furthermore, we gauge from the presence of Georg in these three scenes how much time has elapsed: he is a boy in the first (a "Bub") and peripheral to the action; in act 3 he is Götz's principal interlocuter; and in the last of the three scenes the news of Georg's death makes Götz lose all hope and want to die himself.

19. See Borchmeyer, GF 801. The identification of Luther with sensuality and liberation is one that Heine likewise makes in memorable passages from *Zur Geschichte der Religion und Philosophie in Deutschland* and *Die romantische Schule.*

20. The original that Goethe cites is quoted by Borchmeyer: "und in etlich Städten schossen die Pfaffen und München auf der Canzel mit Lichtern zu mir, und erlaubten mich den Vögeln in Lüfften, sie solten mich fressen" (GF 810).

21. What Revel says about the culinary details in Boccaccio's *Decameron* applies here (*Un Festin en paroles,* 146). He notes that the lords and ladies eat only sweets, which are considered "distinguished" [nourritures distinguées]; to

show them eating cold meats (*charcuterie*) or something unappetizing (a "galimafré") would be to "depoeticize" the food (and clearly the setting).

22. T. J. Reed, *Goethe* (Oxford: Oxford University Press, 1984), 54. See, too, Reed's discussion of the connection between freedom and classicism, which he links to the Enlightenment in the essay "Goethe and Enlightenment," in *Enlightenment Essays in Memory of Robert Shackleton* (Oxford: Voltaire Foundation at the Taylor Institution, 1988), 257–70. On the relationship between Goethe's classicism and the Enlightenment, see, too, the articles by Gottfried Willems: "Goethe—ein 'Überwinder der Aufklärung'? Thesen zur Revision des Klassik-Bildes," *Germanisch-Romanische Monatsschrift* 40 (1990): 22–40, and "Aneignung statt Begegnung: Über die Stilisierung Goethes zum 'klassischen Nationalautor' der Deutschen," *Begegnung mit dem 'Fremden'. Grenzen-Traditionen-Vergleiche, Akten des VIII. Internationalen Germanisten-Kongresses, Tokyo 1990,* ed. Eijiro Iwasaki and Yoshinori Shichiji (Munich: iudicium, 1992): 7:70–80.

23. For a more extensive account of the circumstances surrounding the discovery of Diderot's text and Goethe's decision to translate it, see Rudolf Schlösser, *Rameaus Neffe: Studien und Untersuchungen zur Einführung in Goethes Übersetzung des Diderotschen Dialogs* (Berlin: Alexander Duncker, 1900); Roland Mortier, *Diderot en Allemagne, 1750–1850* (Paris: Presses Universitaires de France, 1954); and the introduction to the critical edition of *Le Neveu de Rameau* by Jean Fabre (NdR).

24. Quoted from the Weimar edition of Goethe's works, ed. Rudolf Schlösser (Weimar: Böhlau, 1900), 45:247–8. Herbert Dieckmann discusses the translation in "Diderot und Goethe," *Deutsche Vierteljahrsschrift* 10 (1932): 478–503; rpt. in Dieckmann, *Diderot und die Aufklärung: Aufsätze zur europäischen Literatur des 18. Jahrhunderts* (Stuttgart: Metzler, 1972), 196–218.

25. See the interpretations of this scene by Jean Starobinski, "Le Dîner chez Bertin" in *Das Komische,* ed. Wolfgang Preisendanz and Rainer Warning (Munich: Fink, 1976, 191–204), and Walter E. Rex, "Two Scenes from *Le Neveu de Rameau,*" *Diderot Studies* 20 (1981): 245–66.

26. The French original is printed as an appendix to Fabre's edition, NdR 252–54.

27. On the suppression of the *Roman Elegies,* see Haile, "Prudery."

28. In his letter to Goethe of 24 April 1805, Schiller says of these notes: "Ich habe 15 Artikel darin gefunden, die für sich selbst interessieren, und schon die Hälfte dieser Zahl würde die Anmerkungen gerechtfertigt haben" [I have found fifteen articles that would be of interest in and of themselves, and even half that number would justify the annotations] (GS 2:1050).

29. "The important thing is to keep the bowels moving freely, agreeably, copiously, every night. *O stercus pretiosum!* That is the great end of life in all social conditions" (DRN 24)

30. See the interpretation of this passage by Starobinski, who emphasizes the symbolic nature of the table and of the seating order. Starobinski speaks, too, of the use of Italian here as a means of both suppressing and communicating something improper. Rameau, he says, provokes even further by seeming to hide something when actually he is an "exhibitionist" to whom is attributed a "derisive phallic majesty" that is grotesque ("Le Dîner chez Bertin," 193).

31. See Schlösser, *Rameaus Neffe*, 188ff.
32. Vaget, GT 117. I am indebted to Vaget's argumentation here and in his introduction to the bilingual edition of the *Roman Elegies* and of *The Diary*.
33. See Vaget, GT 55–57.
34. Jauss, *Literaturgeschichte als Provokation*, 125–26.
35. That Heine's works possess an aesthetic affinity to Goethe's has recently been shown in detail by George Peters and Michael Perraudin. See George F. Peters, *Heine and Goethe: Der große Heide Nr. 2* (Frankfurt am Main: Peter Lang, 1989); and Perraudin, *Heinrich Heine*.
36. On Heine's reception of Hugo, see Michel Espagne, "La Bosse de Victor Hugo: Manuscrits de H. Heine et histoire littéraire de la France," *Romanistische Zeitschrift für Literaturgeschichte: Cahiers d'histoire des littératures romanes* 19 (1982): 322–37. Less accurate, but nonetheless interesting, is the article by Abraham Avni, "Heine and Hugo: The Biblical Connection," *Neophilologus* 68 (1984): 405–20. See, too, Höhn, *Heine-Handbuch* 75, 137, and esp. 322–23.
37. See the variants for this passage, DHA 8:2.1282.
38. The importance of genre is evident if one compares Hugo's treatment of food in a novel like *Les Misérables* (1862) to the culinary referents in a drama like *Ruy Blas*. On *Les Misérables*, see James W. Brown, "An Alimentary Portrait of the Ghetto: The Meal as a Signal for Reform," in *Fictional Meals*, 91–130.
39. Hugo scribbled Heine's name on a list of people who were either present or invited to attend one or the other, as we know from the notes he took while he was working on the performance. See RB 2:60.
40. See Ubersfeld's discussion of the critical response to this act in RB 1:115.
41. See the discussion of the work's genesis by Ubersfeld in RB 1:32, and her interpretation of the figure of Don César, RB 1:31–37 and 70–72.
42. Rainer Warning, "Hugo, *Ruy Blas*," in *Das Französische Theater. Vom Barock bis zur Gegenwart*, ed. Jürgen von Stackelberg (Düsseldorf: Bagel, 1968), 139–64, here 148.
43. See, for example, Ubersfeld's comments: "Ce qui s'impose c'est cette double image de la fracture du moi, celle de Ruy Blas, celle de Don César, c'est la lutte vaine et sans espoir, pour cette réconciliation de soi qui serait le salut, contre les forces incompréhensibles et imbrisables de la fatalité de l'histoire" (RB 1:70).
44. See S. S. Prawer, *Coal-Smoke and Englishmen: A Study of Verbal Caricature in the Writings of Heinrich Heine* (London: Institute of Germanic Studies, University of London, 1984). See, too, his longer studies, *Heine's Jewish Comedy* (1983) and *Frankenstein's Island* (1986).

Conclusion

1. How much this is so is likewise evident from the literary treatment of smells, as Rindisbacher demonstrates in *The Smell of Books* when he analyzes the symbolist function of olfactory referents in literature from the middle of the nineteenth century to the present.
2. I discuss Thomas Mann's "symbolist" method in *Buddenbrooks* and its connection to Wagner in "Thomas Mann's Translation of Wagner into *Buddenbrooks*," *Germanic Review* 61 (1986): 146–53. On the function of the leitmotif in Mann's novel, see Hans R. Vaget, "Mann und Wagner: Zur Funktion

des Leitmotivs in *Der Ring des Nibelungen* und *Buddenbrooks*" in *Literatur und Musik: Ein Handbuch zur Theorie und Praxis eines komparatistischen Grenzgebietes,* ed. Steven Scher (Berlin: Erich Schmidt, 1984), 326–46.

3. See Ulrich Schulz-Buschhaus, "Françoise oder die Poetik eines 'bon dîner'," in Knapp, *Marcel Proust,* 143–59. Schulz-Buschhaus reads the culinary details against Boileau's satires and a culinary parody of the *Art poétique* from the beginning of the nineteenth century. He makes a useful distinction between the "repas ridicule" in Boileau's satire and the "repas sublime" of Proust (148–49), although it seems to me that the merging rather than the juxtaposition of sublime and ridiculous is more crucial to Proust's aesthetic. See, too, Anne Borel, Alain Senderens, and Jean-Bernard Naudin, *Proust, la cuisine retrouvée* (Paris: Société Nouvelle des Éditions du Chêne, 1991). Proust's association of Françoise's cooking with artistic creation resembles Isak Dinesen's use of the same analogy in the story "Babette's Feast."

4. Abrams, *Glossary of Literary Terms,* under the definition for "Conventions."

Bibliography

Abrams, M. H. *A Glossary of Literary Terms*. 5th ed. New York: Holt, Rinehart and Winston, 1988.

Abrams, M. H. *The Mirror and the Lamp: Romantic Theory and the Critical Tradition*. London: Oxford University Press, 1953. Reprint New York: Norton, 1958.

Abrams, M. H. *Natural Supernaturalism: Tradition and Revolution in Romantic Literature*. New York: Norton, 1971.

Auerbach, Erich. *Literary Language and Its Public in Latin Antiquity and in the Middle Ages*. Trans. Ralph Mannheim. New York: Pantheon Books, 1965.

Auerbach, Erich. *Mimesis. The Representation of Reality in Western Literature*. Trans. Willard R. Trask. Princeton: Princeton University Press, 1953.

Avni, Abraham. "Heine and Hugo: The Biblical Connection." *Neophilologus* 68 (1984): 405–20.

Bakhtin, Mikhail. *The Dialogic Imagination: Four Essays*. Ed. Michael Holquist, trans. Caryl Emerson and Michael Holquist. Austin: University of Texas Press, 1981.

Bakhtin, Mikhail. *Rabelais and His World*. Trans. Helene Iswolsky. Cambridge, Mass.: MIT Press, 1968. Reprint Bloomington: Indiana University Press, 1984.

Bark, Joachim. "Heine im Vormärz: Radikalisierung oder Verweigerung? Eine Untersuchung der Versepen." *Der Deutschunterricht* 31, no. 2 (1979): 47–60.

Barthes, Roland. *Mythologies*. Paris: Editions du Seuil, 1957.

Bate, Jonathan. *Shakespeare and the English Romantic Imagination*. 2d ed. Oxford: Clarendon Press, 1989.

Bate, Walter Jackson. *The Burden of the Past and the English Poet*. Cambridge, Mass.: Harvard University Press, 1970.

Bate, Walter Jackson. *From Classic to Romantic: Premises of Taste in Eighteenth-Century England*. Cambridge, Mass.: Harvard University Press, 1946.

Battestin, Martin C. "Osborne's *Tom Jones*: Adapting a Classic." *Virginia Quarterly Review* 42 (1966): 378–93.

Battestin, Martin. C. *The Providence of Wit: Aspects of Form in Augustan Literature and the Arts.* Oxford: Clarendon Press, 1974.

Battestin, Martin C., with Ruthe R. Battestin. *Henry Fielding: A Life.* London: Routledge, 1989.

Bauer, George. "Eating Out: With Barthes." In *Literary Gastronomy,* ed. David Bevan, 39–48. Amsterdam: Rodopi, 1988.

Beaty, Frederick L. *Byron the Satirist.* Dekalb: Northern Illinois University Press, 1985.

Bellmann, W. "'Cacatum non est pictum'—ein Zitat in Heines *Wintermärchen.*" *Wirkendes Wort* 33 (1983): 213–15.

Benjamin, Walter. *Gesammelte Schriften.* Ed. Tillman Rexroth. Vol. 4, book 1, *Denkbilder: Essen.* Frankfurt am Main: Suhrkamp, 1972.

Betz, Albrecht. *Ästhetik und Politik: Heinrich Heines Prosa.* Munich: Hanser, 1971.

Bitsch, Irmgard, et al., eds. *Essen und Trinken in Mittelalter und Neuzeit.* Sigmaringen: Thorbecke, 1987.

Bliss, Michael. "Fielding's Bill of Fare in *Tom Jones.*" *English Literary History* 30 (1963): 236–43.

Borel, Anne, Alain Senderens, and Jean-Bernard Naudin. *Proust, la cuisine retrouvée.* Paris: Société Nouvelle des Éditions du Chêne, 1991.

Bostetter, Edward E., ed. *Twentieth-Century Interpretations of "Don Juan."* Englewood Cliffs, N.J.: Prentice-Hall, 1969.

Bourke, Thomas. *Stilbruch als Stilmittel: Studien zur Literatur der Spät- und Nachromantik.* Frankfurt am Main: Peter Lang, 1980.

Boyd, Elizabeth F. *Byron's "Don Juan": A Critical Study.* New Brunswick, N.J.: Rutgers University Press, 1945.

Boyle, Nicholas. *Goethe: The Poet and the Age.* Vol. 1, *The Poetry of Desire.* Oxford: Clarendon Press, 1991.

Brillat-Savarin. *Physiologie du goût.* Ed. Roland Barthes. Paris: Hermann, 1975.

Brown, James W. *Fictional Meals and Their Function in the French Novel, 1789–1848.* Toronto: University of Toronto Press, 1984.

Brummack, Jürgen. *Satirische Dichtungen.* Munich: Fink, 1979.

Brummack, Jürgen, ed. *Heinrich Heine: Epoche, Werk, Wirkung.* Munich: C. H. Beck, 1980.

Burke, Edmund. *A Philosophical Enquiry into the Origin of our Ideas of the Sublime and Beautiful.* 1759.

Butler, Marilyn. *Romantics, Rebels, and Reactionaries: English Literature and Its Background, 1760–1830.* Oxford: Oxford University Press, 1981.

Clubbe, John. "George Gordon, Lord Byron." In *The English Romantic Poets,* ed. Frank Jordan, 465–592. New York: The Modern Language Association, 1985.

Cooke, Michael. *The Blind Man Traces the Circle.* Princeton: Princeton University Press, 1969.

Cooke, Michael. "Byron's Don Juan: The Obsession and Self-Discipline of Spontaneity." *Studies in Romanticism* 14 (1975): 285–302.

Corbin, Alain. *Le Miasme et la jonquille: L'odorat et l'imaginaire social 18e–19e siècle.* Paris: Aubier Montaigne, 1982.

Danto, Arthur C. *The Transfiguration of the Commonplace: A Philosophy of Art.* Cambridge, Mass.: Harvard University Press, 1981.

de Almeida, Hermione. *Byron and Joyce through Homer: "Don Juan" and "Ulysses."* New York: Columbia University Press, 1981.

Dédeyan, Charles. *Victor Hugo et l'Allemagne.* Paris: Minard, 1964–65.

Deval, Jacqueline. *Reckless Appetites. A Culinary Romance.* Hopewell, N.J.: Ecco Press, 1993.

Dieckmann, Herbert. "Diderot und Goethe." In *Diderot und die Aufklärung. Aufsätze zur europäischen Literatur des 18. Jahrhunderts,* 196–218. Stuttgart: Metzler, 1972.

Diller, Hans Jürgen. "The Function of Verse in Byron's 'Don Juan.'" In *The Constance Byron Symposium,* ed. James Hogg, 5–20. Salzburg: Salzburg Studies in English Literature, 1977.

Ehrenpreis, Irvin. *Tom Jones.* London: Edward Arnold, 1964.

Elias, Norbert. *Über den Prozeß der Zivilisation: Soziogenetische und psychogenetische Untersuchungen.* 2d ed. Bern: Francke, 1969. Reprint Frankfurt am Main: Suhrkamp, 1981.

Elledge, W. Paul. "Byron's Hungry Sinner: The Quest Motif in Don Juan." *JEGP* 69 (1970): 1–13.

Ellmann, Richard. "Freud and Literary Biography." *American Scholar* 53 (1984): 465–78.

Empson, William. *Tom Jones.* In *Twentieth-Century Interpretations of "Tom Jones,"* ed. Martin C. Battestin, 33–55, Englewood Cliffs, N.J.: Prentice-Hall, 1968.

Espagne, Michel. "La Bosse de Victor Hugo: Manuscrits de H. Heine et histoire littéraire de la France." *Romanische Zeitschrift für Literaturgeschichte: Cahiers d'histoire des littératures romanes* 19 (1982): 322–37.

Fairley, Barker. *Heinrich Heine: An Interpretation.* Oxford: Clarendon Press, 1954.

Fairley, Barker. "Heine and the Festive Board." *University of Toronto Quarterly* 36 (1967): 209–19.

Fink, Beatrice C. "The Banquet as Phenomenon or Structure in Selected Eighteenth-century French Novels." *Studies on Voltaire and the Eighteenth Century* 152 (1976): 729–40.

Flaubert, Gustave. *Correspondance.* Ed. Jean Bruneau. 2 vols. Paris: Gallimard, 1973.

Forster, Robert, and Orest Ranum, eds. *Selections from the Annales,* vol. 5: *Food and Drink in History.* Baltimore: Johns Hopkins University Press, 1979.

Friedrich der Große. *De la littérature allemande.* Ed. Christoph Gutknecht and Peter Kerner. Hamburg: Helmut Buske: 1969.

Friedrich, Hugo. *Die Struktur der modernen Lyrik.* 2d ed. Hamburg: Rowohlt, 1956.

Fry, Paul. "Literature and Our Discontents." *Yale Review* 73 (1984): 603–16.

Furst, Lilian R. *Fictions of Romantic Irony.* Cambridge, Mass.: Harvard University Press, 1984.

Furst, Lilian R. "The Role of Food in *Madame Bovary.*" *Orbis litterarum* 34 (1979): 53–65.

Garber, Frederick. *Self, Text, and Romantic Irony: The Example of Byron.* Princeton: Princeton University Press, 1988.

Giese, Peter Christian. "Das Symposion am Teetisch: Heinrich Heine: 'Lyrisches Intermezzo,' Nr. 50." *Heine-Jahrbuch* 26 (1987): 208–18.

Gleckner, Robert F. *Byron and the Ruins of Paradise.* Baltimore: Johns Hopkins University Press, 1967.

Gleckner, Robert F., ed. *Critical Essays on Byron.* New York: G. K. Hall, 1991.

Graham, Peter W. *"Don Juan" and Regency England.* Charlottesville: University Press of Virginia, 1990.

Grubačić, Slobodan. *Heines Erzählprosa: Ein Versuch.* Stuttgart: Kohlhammer, 1975.

Haile, H. G. "Prudery in the Publication History of Goethe's *Roman Elegies.*" *German Quarterly* 49 (1976): 287–94.

Heckmann, Herbert. *Die Freude des Essens: Ein kulturgeschichtliches Lesebuch vom Genuß der Speisen aber auch vom Leid des Hungers.* Munich: Hanser, 1979.

Hermand, Jost. *Der frühe Heine: Ein Kommentar zu den "Reisebildern."* Munich: Winkler, 1976.

Hinz, Evelyn J., ed. "Diet and Discourse: Eating, Drinking, and Literature." *Mosaic* 23 (1991).

Hirsch, E. D. "Byron and the Terrestrial Paradise." In *From Sensibility to Romanticism,* eds. Frederick W. Hilles and Harold Bloom, 467–86. New York: Oxford University Press, 1965.

Hoffmeister, Gerhart. *Byron und der europäische Byronismus.* Darmstadt: Wissenschaftliche Buchgesellschaft, 1983.

Hofrichter, Laura. *Heinrich Heine.* Trans. Barker Fairley. Oxford: Clarendon Press, 1963.

Hogg, James. "Byron's Vascillating Attitude Towards Napoleon." In *Byron: Poetry and Politics,* ed. James Hogg and Erwin A. Stürzl. Salzburg: Salzburg Studies in English Literature, 1975.

Höhn, Gerhard. *Heine-Handbuch: Zeit, Person, Werk.* Stuttgart: Metzler, 1987.

Holub, Robert. "Heine and the New World." *Colloquia Germanica* 22 (1989): 101–13.

Holub, Robert. "Heine and Utopia." *Heine-Jahrbuch* 27 (1988): 86–112.

Holub, Robert. *Heinrich Heine's Reception of German Grecophilia: The Function and Application of the Hellenic Tradition in the First Half of the Nineteenth Century.* Heidelberg: Carl Winter, 1981.

Hosfeld, Rolf. *Die Welt als Füllhorn: Heine.* Berlin: Oberbaum, 1984.

Jack, Ian. *The Poet and His Audience.* New York: Cambridge University Press, 1984.

Jacobs, Jürgen. "Zu Heines *Ideen. Das Buch Le Grand.*" *Heine-Jahrbuch* 7 (1968): 3–11.

Jauss, Hans Robert. *Literaturgeschichte als Provokation.* Frankfurt am Main: Suhrkamp, 1970.

Joseph, M. K. *Byron the Poet.* London: Gollancz, 1964.

Kelsall, Malcolm. *Byron's Politics.* Sussex: Harvester Press, 1987.

Kernan, Alvin. *The Plot of Satire.* New Haven: Yale University Press, 1965.

Kiwus, Karin, and Henning Grunwald, eds. *Vom Essen und Trinken.* Frankfurt am Main: Insel, 1978.

Kleinspehn, Thomas. *Warum sind wir so unersättlich? Über den Bedeutungswandel des Essens.* Frankfurt am Main: Suhrkamp, 1987.

Kluge, Gerhard. "Heinrich Heines Fragment *Aus den Memoiren des Herren von Schnabelewopski* und das Problem des Schelmischen." *Amsterdamer Beiträge zur neueren Germanistik* 20 (1985–86): 41–52.

Knapp, Volker, ed. *Marcel Proust: Geschmack und Neigung.* Tübingen: Stauffenberg, 1989.

Kolb, Jocelyne. "Heine as Freud's Double in *Der Witz und seine Beziehung zum Unbewußten.*" *Heine-Jahrbuch* 31 (1992): 137–62.

Kolb, Jocelyne. "'Die Puppenspiele meines Humors': Heine and Romantic Irony." *Studies in Romanticism* 26 (1987): 399–419.

Kolb, Jocelyne. "Thomas Mann's Translation of Wagner into *Buddenbrooks.*" *Germanic Review* 61 (1986): 146–53.

Koopmann, Helmut, ed. *Heinrich Heine.* Darmstadt: Wissenschaftliche Buchgesellschaft, 1975.

Kroeber, Karl. *Romantic Narrative Art.* Madison: University of Wisconsin Press, 1960.

Lamping, Dieter. *Das lyrische Gedicht: Definitionen zu Theorie und Geschichte der Gattung.* Göttingen: Vandenhoeck and Ruprecht, 1989.

Lang, Cecil Y. "Narcissus Jilted: Byron, *Don Juan,*' and the Biographical Imperative." In *Historical Studies and Literary Criticism,* ed. Jerome J. McGann, 143–79. Madison: University of Wisconsin Press, 1985.

Levin, Harry. *Playboys and Killjoys: An Essay on the Theory and Practice of Comedy.* New York: Oxford University Press, 1987.

Levine, Michael G. "Heines Ghost Writer: Zum Problem der Selbstzensur im *Schnabelewopski.*" *Heine-Jahrbuch* 26 (1987): 9–28.

Liebs, Elke. *Das Köstlichste von allem: Von der Lust am Essen und dem Hunger nach Liebe.* Zurich: Kreuz, 1988.

Lovell, Ernest J. "Irony and Image in *Don Juan.*" In *The Major Romantic Poets: A Symposium in Reappraisal,* eds. Carlos Baker, Clarence D. Thorpe, and Bennett Weaver, 129–48. Carbondale: Southern Illinois University Press, 1957.

Lovell, Ernest J., ed. *Lady Blessington's Conversations of Lord Byron.* Princeton: Princeton University Press, 1969.

Lovell, Ernest J., ed. *Medwin's Conversations of Lord Byron.* Princeton: Princeton University Press, 1966.

Luke, E. J. "The Publishing of Byron's *Don Juan.*" *PMLA* 70 (1965): 199–209.

Mahood, Molly. *Shakespeare's Wordplay.* London: Methuen, 1957.

Manning, Peter J. *Byron and His Fictions.* Detroit: Wayne State University Press, 1978.

Manning, Peter J. "*Don Juan* and Byron's Imperceptiveness to the English Word." *Studies in Romanticism* 18 (1979): 207–33.

Marchand, Leslie. *Byron: A Portrait.* New York: Knopf, 1970.

Marcuse, Ludwig. *Obszön: Geschichte einer Entrüstung.* Munich: Paul List, 1962.

Marin, Louis. *La Parole mangée et autres essais théologico-politiques.* Paris: Méridiens Klincksieck, 1986.

Martin, Philip W. *Byron, a Poet before His Public.* Cambridge: Cambridge University Press, 1982.

Mattenklott, Gerd. *Der übersichtliche Leib.* Reinbek bei Hamburg: Rowohlt, 1982.

Matzneff, Gabriel. *La Diétique de Lord Byron.* Paris: La Table Ronde, 1984.

Maurer, Karl. "Entgrenzung und Auflösung des Gesamtgefüges in der europäischen Romantik und Vorromantik." In *Die nicht mehr schönen Künste,* ed. Hans Robert Jauss, 319–41. Munich: Fink, 1968.

May, Georges. *Quatre Visages de Denis Diderot.* Paris: Boivin, 1951.

Mayser, Erich. *Heinrich Heines "Buch der Lieder" im 19. Jahrhundert.* Stuttgart: Akademischer Verlag Hans-Dieter Heinz, 1978.

McGann, Jerome J. *"Don Juan" in Context.* Chicago: University of Chicago Press, 1976.

Mellor, Anne K. *English Romantic Irony.* Cambridge, Mass.: Harvard University Press, 1980.

Miller, J. Hillis. "The Critic as Host." In *Deconstruction and Criticism,* ed. Harold Bloom et al., 217–53. New York: Continuum, 1979.

Mortier, Roland. *Diderot en Allemagne, 1750–1850.* Paris: Presses Universitaires de France, 1954.

Neumann, Gerhard. "Das Essen und die Literatur." *Literaturwissenschaftliches Wörterbuch im Auftrag der Görres-Gesellschaft.* N.S. 23 (1982): 173–90.

Österle, Günter. "Entwurf einer Monographie des ästhetisch Häßlichen. Die Geschichte einer ästhetischen Kategorie von Friedrich Schlegels Studium-Aufsatz bis zu Karl Rosenkranz' Ästhetik des Häßlichen als Suche nach dem Ursprung der Moderne." In *Zur Modernität der Romantik,* ed. Dieter Bänsch, 217–97. Stuttgart: Metzler, 1977.

Paterson, Wilma. "Was Byron Anorexic?" *World Medicine,* 15 May 1982, 35–38.

Paulson, Ronald. *Representations of Revolutions, 1789–1820.* New Haven: Yale University Press, 1983.

Périvier, J. H. "Equivoques molièresques: Le sonnet de Trissotin." *Revue des Sciences Humaines* 38 (1973): 543–54.

Perraudin, Michael. *Heinrich Heine: Poetry in Context. A Study of Buch der Lieder.* London: Berg, 1989.

Peters, George F. *Heine and Goethe: Der große Heide Nr. 2.* Frankfurt am Main: Peter Lang, 1989.

Peters, Paul. *Heinrich Heine "Dichterjude": Die Geschichte einer Schmähung.* Frankfurt am Main: Hain, 1990.

Peucker, Brigitte. *Lyric Descent in the Romantic Tradition.* New Haven: Yale University Press, 1987.

Posner, Roland. "Kulinarische Semiotik." *Zeitschrift für Semiotik* 4 (1982): 319–428.

Prawer, S. S. *Heine's Shakespeare: A Study in Contexts.* Oxford: Clarendon Press, 1970.

Prawer, S. S. "Heines satirische Versdichtung." In *Der Berliner Germanistentag 1968: Vorträge und Berichte,* eds. Karl Heinz Borck und Rudolf Henss, 179–95. Heidelberg: Carl Winter, 1970.

Prawer, S. S. *Coal-Smoke and Englishmen. A Study of Verbal Caricature in the Writings of Heinrich Heine.* London: Institute of Germanic Studies, University of London, 1984.

Prawer, S. S. *Frankenstein's Island: England and the English in the Writings of Heinrich Heine.* Cambridge: Cambridge University Press, 1987.

Prawer, S. S. *Heine's Jewish Comedy: A Study of His Portraits of Jews and Judaism.* Oxford: Clarendon Press, 1983.

Prawer, S. S. *The Tragic Satirist.* Cambridge: Cambridge University Press, 1961.

Preisendanz, Wolfgang. *Heinrich Heine: Werkstrukturen und Epochenbezüge.* 2d ed. Munich: Fink, 1983.

Redfern, Walter. *Puns.* Oxford: Basil Blackwell, 1984.

Reed, T. J. *The Classical Centre: Goethe and Weimar 1775–1832.* London: Croom Helm; New York: Barnes and Noble, 1980.

Reed, T. J. *Goethe.* Oxford: Oxford University Press, 1984.

Reed, T. J. "Goethe and Enlightenment." In *Enlightenment Essays in Memory of Robert Shackleton.* Oxford: The Voltaire Foundation at the Taylor Institution, 1988. 257–70.

Reed, T. J. "Heines Appetit." *Heine-Jahrbuch* 22 (1983): 9–29.

Reeves, Nigel. *Heinrich Heine: Poetry and Politics.* Oxford: Oxford University Press, 1974.

Reilly, Patrick. *"Tom Jones": Adventure and Providence.* Boston: Twayne, 1991.

Revel, Jean-François. *Un Festin en paroles: Histoire littéraire de la sensibilité gastronomique de l'Antiquité à nos jours.* Paris: Pauvert, 1979.

Rex, Walter E. "Two Scenes from *Le Neveu de Rameau*." *Diderot Studies* 20 (1981): 245–66.

Ridenour, George M. *The Style of "Don Juan."* New Haven: Yale University Press, 1960.

Rindisbacher, Hans J. *The Smell of Books: A Cultural-Historical Study of Olfactory Perception in Literature*. Ann Arbor: University of Michigan Press, 1992.

Robertson, Ritchie. *Heine*. New York: Grove Press, 1988.

Rühmkorf, Peter. "Suppentopf und Guillotine: Zu Heines Frauengestalten." *Heine-Jahrbuch* 24 (1985): 255–78.

Rutherford, Andrew. *Byron: A Critical Study*. Palo Alto, Calif.: Stanford University Press, 1969.

Rutherford, Andrew, ed. *Byron: The Critical Heritage*. New York: Barnes and Noble, 1970.

Sammons, Jeffrey L. *Heinrich Heine: The Elusive Poet*. New Haven: Yale University Press, 1969.

Sammons, Jeffrey L. *Heinrich Heine: A Modern Biography*. Princeton: Princeton University Press, 1979.

Sammons, Jeffrey L. *Heinrich Heine*. Stuttgart: Metzler, 1991.

Schapiro, Meyer. "The Apples of Cézanne: An Essay on the Meaning of Still-life." *Modern Art. 19th and 20th Centuries*. New York: George Braziller, 1978. 1-38.

Schivelbusch, Wolfgang. *Das Paradies, der Geschmack und die Vernunft*. Frankfurt am Main: Ullstein, 1983.

Schlegel, Friedrich. *Kritische Friedrich-Schlegel-Ausgabe*, eds. Ernst Behler, Jean-Jacques Anstett, and Hans Eichner. Vol. 2. Munich: Schöningh, 1958.

Schlösser, Rudolf. *"Rameaus Neffe": Studien und Untersuchungen zur Einführung in Goethes Übersetzung des Diderotschen Dialogs*. Berlin: Alexander Duncker, 1900.

Schön, Erich. *Der Verlust der Sinnlichkeit oder Die Verwandlungen des Lesers. Mentalitätswandel um 1800*. Stuttgart: Klett-Cotta, 1987.

Schöne, Albrecht. *Götterzeichen, Liebeszauber, Satanskult: Neue Einblicke in alte Goethetexte*. Munich: C. H. Beck, 1982.

Schücking, Levin L. *Soziologie der literarischen Geschmacksbildung*. 3d ed. Bern: Francke, 1961.

Schulz-Buschhaus, Ulrich. "Françoise oder die Poetik eines 'bon dîner.'" In *Marcel Proust: Geschmack und Neigung*, ed. Volker Knapp, 143–59. Tübingen: Stauffenberg, 1989.

Sengle, Friedrich. *Biedermeierzeit: Deutsche Literatur im Spannungsfeld zwischen Restauration und Revolution 1815–1848*. Vol. 3, *Die Dichter*. Stuttgart: Metzler, 1980.

Shilstone, Frederick W. "The Dissipated Muse: Wine, Women, and Byronic Song." *Colby Literary Quarterly* 20 (1984): 36–46.

Spitzer, Leo. *Die Umschreibungen des Begriffes "Hunger" im Italienischen: Stilistisch-onomasiologische Studie auf Grund von unveröffentlichtem Zensurmaterial*. Halle: Beihefte zur Zeitschrift für Romanische Philologie, 1920.

Spurgeon, Caroline. *Shakespeare's Imagery and What It Tells Us*. Cambridge: Cambridge University Press, 1935.

Starobinski, Jean. "Le Dîner chez Bertin." In *Das Komische,* eds. Wolfgang Preisendanz und Rainer Warning, 191–204. Munich: Fink, 1976.

Steinwachs, Ginka. "An-Sätze zu einer gastronomischen Maientik." In *Aufmerksamkeit: Klaus Heinrich zum 50. Geburtstag,* 541–63. Frankfurt am Main: Roter Stern, 1979.

Sterne, Lawrence. *A Sentimental Journey,* ed. Garner D. Stout Jr. Berkeley and Los Angeles: University of California Press, 1967.

Storey, Mark. *Byron and the Eye of Appetite.* New York: St. Martin's, 1986.

Thackeray, William Makepeace. "Memorials of Gourmandising: In a Letter to Oliver York Esq., by M. A. Titmarsh." In *Fraser's Magazine for Town and Country* 138 (1841): 710–25.

Thomas, Barry G. "The van der Pissen Scene in Heinrich Heine's *Schnabelewopski:* A suggestion." *German Quarterly* 51 (1978): 39–46.

Thomsen, Christian W. *Menschenfresser in der Kunst und Literatur, in fernen Ländern, Mythen, Märchen und Satiren, in Dramen, Liedern, Epen und Romanen: Eine kannibalische Text-Bild-Dokumentation.* Vienna: Christian Brandstätter, 1983.

Tobin, Ronald W., ed. *Littérature et gastronomie.* Paris, Seattle: Papers on French Seventeenth-Century Literature, 1985.

Tobin, Ronald W. *Tarte à la crème: Comedy and Gastronomy in Molière's Theater.* Columbus: Ohio State University Press, 1990.

Toussaint-Samat, Maguelonne. *Histoire naturelle et morale de la nourriture.* Paris: Bordas, 1987.

Trueblood, Paul Graham. *Lord Byron.* New York: Twayne, 1969.

Vaget, Hans R. *Goethe: Der Mann von 60 Jahren.* Königstein/Ts.: Athenäum, 1982.

Vaget, Hans R. *"Die Leiden des jungen Werthers."* In *Goethes Erzählkunst,* eds. Paul Michael Lützeler und James E. McLeod. Stuttgart: Reclam, 1985. 37–72.

Vaget, Hans R. "Mann und Wagner: Zur Funktion des Leitmotivs in *Der Ring des Nibelungen* und *Buddenbrooks."* In *Literatur und Musik: Ein Handbuch zur Theorie und Praxis eines komparatistischen Grenzgebietes,* ed. Steven P. Scher, 326–46. Berlin: Erich Schmidt, 1984.

Varey, Simon. *Henry Fielding.* Cambridge: Cambridge University Press, 1986.

Visser, Margaret. *Much Depends on Dinner: The Extraordinary History, Mythology, Allure and Obsessions, Perils and Taboos of an Ordinary Meal.* New York: Grove Press, 1987.

Visser, Margaret. *The Rituals of Dinner: The Origins, Evolution, Eccentricities, and Meaning of Table Manners.* New York: Grove Weidenfeld, 1991.

Vordtriede, Werner. *Heine-Kommentar.* Munich: Winkler, 1970.

Warning, Rainer. "Hugo, *Ruy Blas."* In *Das Französische Theater: Vom Barock bis zur Gegenwart,* ed. Jürgen von Stackelberg, 139–64. Düsseldorf: Bagel, 1968.

Weinberg, Kurt. *Henri Heine, Romantique défroqué.* New Haven: Yale University Press, 1954.

Wellek, René. *A History of Modern Criticism, 1750–1950*. New Haven: Yale University Press, 1955–91.

West, Paul. *Byron and the Spoiler's Art*. New York: St. Martin's, 1960.

West, Paul, ed. *Byron: A Collection of Critical Essays*. Englewood Cliffs, N.J.: Prentice-Hall, 1963.

Wetzel, Bernd. "Das Motiv des Essens und seine Bedeutung für das Werk Heinrich Heines." Diss., University of Munich, 1972.

Wierlacher, Alois. *Vom Essen in der deutschen Literatur: Mahlzeiten in Erzähltexten von Goethe bis Grass*. Stuttgart: Kohlhammer, 1987.

Wiese, Benno von. *Signaturen: Zu Heinrich Heine und seinem Werk*. Berlin: Erich Schmidt, 1976.

Willems, Gottfried. "Aneignung statt Begegnung: Über die Stilisierung Goethes zum 'klassischen Nationalautor' der Deutschen." In *Begegnung mit dem 'Fremden': Grenzen, Traditionen, Vergleiche, Akten des VIII. Internationalen Germanisten-Kongresses, Tokyo 1990,* eds. Eijiro Iwasaki and Yoshinori Shichiji, 7:70–80. Munich: iudicium, 1992.

Willems, Gottfried. "Goethe—ein 'Überwinder der Aufklärung'? Thesen zur Revision des Klassik-Bildes." *Germanisch-Romanische Monatsschrift* 40 (1990): 22–40.

Wilson, Carol Shiner. "Stuffing the Verdant Goose: Culinary Esthetics in *Don Juan*." *Mosaic* 24 (1991): 33–52.

Windfuhr, Manfred. "Heines Fragment eines Schelmenromans. *Aus den Memoiren des Herren von Schnabelewopski*." In *Heinrich Heine*, ed. Helmut Koopmann, 232–56. Darmstadt: Wissenschaftliche Buchgesellschaft, 1985.

Wright, Andrew. *Mask and Feast*. Berkeley and Los Angeles: University of California Press, 1965.

Wülfing, Wulf. "Skandalöser 'Witz': Untersuchungen zu Heines Rhetorik." In *Artistik und Engagement,* ed. Wolfgang Kuttenkeuler, 43-65. Stuttgart: Metzler, 1977.

Würffel, Stefan Bodo. *Der produktive Widerspruch: Heinrich Heines negative Dialektik*. Bern: Francke, 1986.

Zagari, Luciano, and Paolo Chiarini, eds. *Zu Heinrich Heine*. Stuttgart: Ernst Klett, 1981.

Index